JUST

OUTSIDE

THE

SPOTLIGHT

Just Outside the Spotlight:

GROWING UP WITH EILEEN HECKART

LUKE YANKEE

FOREWORD BY MARY TYLER MOORE

BACK STAGE BOOKS
NEW YORK

Senior Editor: Mark Glubke
Project Editor: Gary Sunshine
Cover Design: Mark Von Bronkhorst
Interior Design: Areta Buk
Production Manager: Ellen Greene

Front cover photos by Marcus Blechman (early 1940s headshot); Martha Swope (*Butterflies are Free*);
Corbis/UPI (Academy Awards); early headshot (Mohammad Ozier/The New York Times). Other cover
photos from author's personal collection.

First published in 2006 by Back Stage Books,
an imprint of Watson-Guptill Publications,
a division of VNU Business Media, Inc.
770 Broadway, New York, NY 10003
www.wgpub.com.com

Library of Congress Control Number: 2006921113

ISBN: 0-8230-7888-4

Manufactured in the United States of America

First printing 2006

1 2 3 4 5 6 7 8 9 / 11 10 09 08 07 06

FOR MY LIFE PARTNER, DON HILL—

WHO TAKES THE JOURNEY WITH ME AND ENRICHES MY LIFE

IN MORE WAYS THAN I COULD EVER IMAGINE POSSIBLE.

Contents

Foreword

When I first saw the script "Mary's Aunt" that was to become an episode of *The Mary Tyler Moore Show*, it was with particular interest that I read the description and dialog of the character 'Aunt Flo.' The first actress who came to mind was Eileen Heckart who I had seen many times on film and in the theater. Having no idea whether or not she would undertake a television role, I nevertheless set my mind on her alone.

I'm grateful to Jim Brooks and Alan Burns, the producers of our show, not only for the talent and heart they put into the writing, but for their determination and foresight to independently suggest Miss Heckart to me. She played the hell out of that character as well as several subsequent appearances in the series (which won her two Emmy nominations). At first, she terrified me a little because she was such a great, multilayered actress and also because she was so like my own Aunt Berte, who was one of the first women to rise to executive level in television. You didn't get there without will and determination. I loved Aunt Berte dearly and embraced Eileen as 'Aunt Flo,' but the two kept merging in my mind. And so, because I had practically grown up with Aunt Berte, I was now facing the personification of her as a bit of a dictator. Eileen, over the few days of rehearsal, before our filming, allowed me to get to know her. Because of that I saw the softer side of my dear aunt. It was a bit of an eye-opener, if not a true revelation.

Everybody loved Eileen's performances and when our filming was over for each night, the audiences who had come to see the shows gave her standing ovations as she took her bows.

I confessed to her one day that my husband and I had just built a country home in upstate New York and I was intimidated by the professional kitchen I was presented with. I don't cook. She gave me counsel and the next time she came on the show presented me with a needlepoint sampler she had made that said in old English script, "Screw Gourmet Cooking." I miss her humor and devilment.

—*Mary Tyler Moore*

Curtain Up!

MY FAVORITE PHOTO WITH MAMA. THIS IS THE WAY I ALWAYS WANT TO REMEMBER US.

AS YOU APPROACHED our house at 135 Comstock Hill Road on a weekend night, particularly during the summer, you were bound to hear laughter and the tinkling of ice cubes in highball glasses. These were the times my parents entertained the most. In the living room of our Colonial manor house, Daddy would be tending bar while my mother held court. When Mama was telling stories, time as I knew it stood still. When I was little, her stories were better than Bugs Bunny, Soupy Sales, or even Nanny's warm chocolate-chip cookies. As I got older, they were more important than the Arts & Leisure section of the Sunday *New York Times*, learning a new monologue for acting class, or listening to Ethel Merman sing "Some People" from *Gypsy* for the nine thousandth time on the hi-fi. If I was in another part of the house and I heard that booming, whisky tenor voice come wafting out of the living room, I ran downstairs for the evening's performance.

Maybe there'd be a new anecdote or a forgotten detail brought to light, a remembered story that she'd never told before. I took my place in the orange velvet wingback chair and leaned forward so I wouldn't miss a word. Even though I could recite most of the stories from memory by the time I was ten, I absorbed each one as if for the first time. When Mama was "on" it was the greatest drug in the world. She could be talking about doing a film with Marilyn Monroe, being cut to ribbons by Bette Davis, having lunch at the White House with Lyndon Johnson, or going to last week's PTA meeting. The stories were always funny, brash, outrageous, and made me burst with pride to be her son.

Mama was Anna Eileen Heckart Yankee, known on Broadway and in Hollywood as Eileen Heckart. One of the hardest-working character actresses for more than fifty years, she acted with everyone from Lillian Gish to Ellen Degeneres. She received an Oscar, a Tony, two Emmys, a Golden Globe, four honorary doctorates, and was inducted into the Theatre Hall of Fame. She had a longer career than many because she was most often the "second banana," the one just outside the spotlight.

In the summer, the stories got even better. Guests enjoyed Vivian Vance's gazpacho by the pool, then lounged around the living room in silk robes, caftans, and beach towels over bathing suits, while they sipped vodka martinis before going down to dinner.

On this particular evening, it was just the regulars: Morton D'Acosta, director of *The Music Man* and *Auntie Mame*; Jan Miner, the actress best known as Madge the Manicurist of Palmolive Dishwashing Liquid fame; Teresa Wright, the co-star of *The Pride of the Yankees*, Hitchcock's *Shadow of a Doubt* and *Mrs. Miniver*; and her husband, Robert Anderson, the Pulitzer Prize-winning playwright of *Tea and Sympathy* and *I Never Sang for My Father*. The jokes and stories seemed to go on forever. Other people's stories made Mama's even better. Maybe she was competitive that way; maybe it was simply that the audience was already warmed up. Whatever the reason, the stories seemed more exciting tonight, as if I'd never heard any of them before.

Reaching into the engraved, silver cigarette box on the table, Mama took the floor. "So there I am," she said, securing the unlit cigarette in her heavily lipsticked mouth, "I'm walking to the set across a sea of extras when Bette Davis shouted, "Heckart, you and I are the only two here who know this isn't acting, it's stunt work!"

The room howled with laughter.

Bob Anderson told a story about working on *Tea and Sympathy* in London with Ingrid Bergman, with whom he was rumored to have had an affair. Jan Miner had just finished doing the film *Lenny* and told endless stories about Dustin Hoffman and Bobby Fosse. Morton D'Acosta (known to this crowd as "Tec") told tales of Roz Russell in *Auntie Mame*.

Mama sat on the brown and white sectional sofa with the swirling paisley pattern. In front of her was a cocktail table with a turquoise star embedded in the center. Since the table was marble, she had dispensed with coasters long ago. There were wet rings from where she had put down her French provincial jelly-jar glass filled with half-melted ice and Dewar's Scotch, heavily diluted with water. The weaker the drinks were, the longer the evening lasted.

On the cocktail table at all times was a pewter apple about the size of a softball. When you flipped it over, it concealed a cigarette lighter. The other object on the table was a sky-blue cake plate. Probably Victorian, it had an intricate pattern around its border of roses and lace with holes where a ribbon once might have been wound through it. At all times, the plate overflowed with ashes and True Blue cigarette butts.

As Mama turned her head to light another cigarette with the pewter apple, Teresa Wright admired her single earring. It was a large, pounded silver hoop. The earring was so big, it looked like it belonged on a window curtain rather than a human ear. Mama spoke in a husky, authoritative voice, made richer by years of True Blue filter tips.

"I was at a PTA meeting at Philip's school last week. His geometry teacher came up to me—some round little pouter pigeon of a lady in sensible shoes. She said, 'Oh, what a shame, you've lost your other earring.' I just looked at her and said, 'Honey, it takes a lotta class to just wear one!'"

As her audience once again erupted in laughter, she took a sip of her watery scotch and caressed the blonde curls of the seven-year-old boy sitting next to her. Her antique gold bracelets clanked against one another as she touched his angelic face. Even though this was clearly a grown-up conversation, he was a fixture, a part of the club.

I was that little boy.

Sometimes, I even helped out as she told a story. If Mama forgot her lines, I was right there to pitch in as a prompter.

"Luke, who directed that film?" she asked me.

"George Cukor," I replied, without missing a beat.

"Exactly!" she'd say, and off she'd go into another little bit of Heaven. I loved watching the way my mother commanded a room, holding everyone captive with her words. She could make them laugh, cry, or fill them with a sense of wonder. To me, this was magic. My only fear was being told it was time for bed.

During the course of my lifetime, I heard my mother and her celebrated guests tell one incredible story after another. From the age of twelve I used to say to her, "Mama, you need to put all these stories down on paper. You should write a book."

"Darling," she'd say with a throaty laugh. "No one would want to read a book about me. It's all as forgettable as last winter's snow."

Considered one of the greatest character actresses of the last generation, Eileen Heckart was far from a household name, but she worked all the time. She was respected in Hollywood and revered on Broadway.

Renowned British theater critic Kenneth Tynan once called her, "The greatest *thin* actress in America."

Marlene Dietrich once said of her, "If she were acting in Europe, she'd be Queen of the Boards."

I once said of her, "She throws the best birthday parties of any mom in Fairfield County."

This book is a memoir, a tribute to a gifted actress and a bygone era. It is also the story of a loving mother, a tender wife, a classy diva, and a one hell of a broad—as seen through the eyes of her youngest son. In the course of a career spanning more than half a century on Broadway and in Hollywood, "Heckie," as she was known to her friends (a nickname she never liked, but grew to love), worked with or came to know some of the most important stars of all time. Through it all, she sustained a marriage for fifty-three years to my father, Jack Yankee, and raised three sons. She was funny, warm, outrageous, and exasperating. She was a puddle of emotion one minute and tough as nails the next. She was beef jerky on the outside and Jell-o pudding on the inside. She was my mama.

After she died on New Year's Eve, 2001, my older brother Mark and I commenced going through Mama and Daddy's house and deciding what to keep, what to sell, and what to pitch.

As we came across yellowed photographs, tattered programs, and dusty videotapes, Mark said, "Hey Luke, do you know what this picture is from?"

"Oh sure," I replied. "I love that one. That's from the awards ceremony with Cary Grant."

Mark paused from tossing a broken pencil sharpener into the trash and stared at the photograph. "What awards ceremony with Cary Grant?"

"Oh, you remember," I said. "When Mama won the Straw Hat Award for *Remember Me*, that mystery she did in summer stock with Robert Stack? You know that great story she used to tell about how Cary Grant presented the award to her and then offered to fly her home in his private plane?"

"No," Mark said. "I don't remember that story."

"Of course you do," I said. "Mama used to tell it all the time."

Then it occurred to me. He wasn't in the living room as often as I was. He'd probably heard it once, maybe twice, but he hadn't committed it to memory. As this happened time and again, I realized I was the only one of the three boys who knew all of these stories. It made sense that I would have listened more attentively, since I wanted to be in show business from the time I could talk. Each story was emblazoned in my mind. All those times being exposed to the show business greats—having white wine and brie with Paul Newman and Joanne Woodward, huddled around the kitchen table eating cream cheese and olives with Vivian Vance, lounging around the dining room over coffee and chocolate mousse with Julie Harris, or sitting on a chaise by the pool downing Kool-Aid and Cheez Doodles with Doris Roberts. And I was the designated storyteller.

⊗⊗⊗

Some of Mama's best stories were about her friendship with Marlene Dietrich. I was reminded of this as I became friendly with Dietrich's only daughter, Maria Riva, who lived near my weekend home in Palm Springs, California. Maria's daughter-in-law, Marilee Warner, had produced a reading of a play I'd co-written. Mama had always spoken of Maria with such warmth and said, "She's so goddamn elegant. Just like her mother."

I'd always wanted to meet Maria and as we got friendly, I relished every opportunity to speak with her. Maria is a refined European lady, who calls herself, "a poor man's Dietrich." Personally, I wouldn't call her a poor man's *anything*.

One night, when Maria and I were swapping stories about our mothers, my playwriting partner, Jim Bontempo, said, "You should put together an evening and call it *Diva Dish!*"

A flashing neon sign went off in my head.

Maria was working on plenty of her own projects and had no interest in developing it. Besides, she'd already written a book about her mother. I took the idea and ran with it.

A few weeks later, I put together a presentation in my living room for five or six showbiz savvy friends. I projected a few photos on the wall, told a few stories, and ran a few video clips. After I finished, I turned to the assembled group, notepad in hand.

"Well?" I asked, "Do I have something here?"

"Luke," they all said, "You're sitting on a gold mine."

My friends were right. The gold mine was the legacy I had inherited. These weren't just "dishy" showbiz stories. Mama was so much more than that. They became life lessons about how to enter a room as if you belonged there, how to treat people with respect, to stand up for what you believe in, and how to hone your craft, whatever it may be. They were lessons about what defines greatness and the art and culture that shaped our world for the past fifty years. These stories were insights into another time, the Golden Age of Broadway and Hollywood. Best of all, they were Mama. Telling them kept her alive and made me not miss her so much. At the same time, it made the loss even more palpable. It put me back in the living room of my childhood, just outside the spotlight.

As I write this, I have spent the past three years touring with my one-man show, *Diva Dish!* I tell what it was like growing up with this larger-than-life presence and all her famous friends. From the first performance onward, audience members said to me, "Luke, where's the book? I want to hear more!" The show has evolved from me sitting on a stool and talking to a more complete solo performance. It is a portrait of a life in and out of the public eye and always lived to the fullest. Part autobiography, part memoir, and part tribute, the show and this book are my way of passing on some of the show-business lore I grew up with and paying homage to the person who shaped my life the most.

These are my recollections of the stories as she told them and as I remember them. If it brings you half as much pleasure to read this as it has given me to write it, we'll have a wonderful time together.

A Diva Begins

ANNA EILEEN IN HER BATHING SUIT—AGE 7

HER BIRTH NAME was Anna Eileen Stark. She thought her mother, Esther Stark, was one of the prettiest young women in Columbus, Ohio. Esther was a wild, uncontrollable girl with a penchant for rumble seats, bootleg liquor, and fast boys. There are so many different accounts from various relatives of my mother's dubious lineage, it's difficult to piece them all together. Since Esther was very attractive, men were always coming onto her. Esther's mother was a strict disciplinarian, so she longed to break free. As a result, she often went with these men and, for the price of a day at the racetrack, a night at the speakeasy, or a few shots of bathtub gin, she was what they called "a good sport." At not much more than eighteen, Esther got pregnant. Her mother was furious. Her first husband, Mr. Stark, was a poor man who had been killed in France in World War I. She had recently remarried into Columbus society. Her new husband, J.W. Heckart, was a very rich man. In fact, he was one of the leading building contractors in the booming, Midwestern metropolis.

Now that the new Mrs. Heckart had gained the status and greater respectability that came with marrying a man of means, she was damned if she was going to let the birth of a little bastard destroy everything. She had to find a suitable husband for Esther and fast. What about that nice boy who delivered the groceries, Leo Herbert? Leo had always had a crush on Esther and he came from a good family. He'd do as well as anyone. But Leo wasn't comfortable about calling this child his own. Neither was Esther, for that matter. She certainly didn't want to be a mother and she didn't want to be tied down to a boring, conventional boy like Leo. But her mother had decided. Esther would marry Leo and J.W. Heckart would legally adopt the child. Dear, sweet Leo never knew what hit him. No doubt there was some sort of financial arrangement between Leo's family and J.W., but one didn't discuss such things.

On March 29, 1919, Anna Eileen Herbert was born, and her surname was quickly changed to Heckart. She always hated the name "Anna Eileen." Very few people ever called her that outside of the immediate family. "Isn't that the dumbest name you ever heard?" she often said. "I mean, Ann Eileen or even Eileen Ann is sort of pretty. And I like the name Anna. But to put it in front of Eileen and have all those clunky vowels together? Anna Eileen? It's just plain stupid."

For the most part, Anna Eileen's childhood was difficult and painful. As Esther got a little older, saddled with a child she didn't want and a loveless marriage, she returned to the wild behavior of her single days. She was married five times before Anna Eileen was in high school. This was scandalous in the 1920s and 30s. Most of the time, Anna Eileen lived with her mother, but some of these husbands didn't like having a kid around. Periodically, she would be shipped off for long stretches of time to live with her grandmother. Now that Mrs. Heckart was a woman of means, she lorded her wealth over Esther, but insisted she make her own way in the world. Except when it came to the child. For all of her stern, Irish coldness, Mrs. Heckart made sure her newly adopted daughter was well cared for and looked the part of a child from the "right part of town." At the same time, her grand-mother was a woman who couldn't stand any type of a scene or public outburst. As a girl, Anna Eileen learned very early on how to use this to her advantage. If she wanted another hot-fudge sundae in the lunchroom at Woolworth's, all she had to do was scrape the bottom of her dish a few times. The sound attracted attention, which drove her grandmother crazy.

"Stop that!" she said. "I'll get you another!"

Mrs. Heckart demanded respect and she got it. Anna Eileen never referred to her with any term of endearment—it was always Grandmother, with a capital G. The two had a fierce understanding of one another from an early age.

Since all of Esther's husbands were poor, Grandmother also took it upon herself to outfit Anna Eileen for school. "I'll not have my granddaughter in hand-me-downs from the Salvation Army!" Mrs. Heckart proclaimed. Each year, in spring and fall, grandmother and granddaughter made their semiannual pilgrimage to F&R Lazarus department store in downtown Columbus. One of my favorite stories about Mama's childhood (and one of the few she told with any regularity) centers on one of these shopping expeditions. Anna Eileen was twelve and getting her spring and summer wardrobe. As they walked through the ladies' department at F&R Lazarus, Anna Eileen spotted a forest green fedora with a long pheasant feather stretching from front to back and attached in the front with a rhinestone pin. The young girl stopped in her tracks and stared. Anna Eileen approached the hat on the wire stand, caressing it before putting it on. As she looked at her reflection in the mirror, she was transfixed.

MY GRANDMOTHER, ESTHER STARK

"Grandmother," she said, "I'd like to get this hat, please?"

Mrs. Heckart glanced across the showroom at the hat and kept on walking, shaking her head, "It's too old for you," the woman said.

"What do you mean?" Anna Eileen whined. "I really want it, Grandmother!"

Mrs. Heckart grabbed her granddaughter's arm, speaking in firm, hushed tones. "You are too young to wear a hat like that! The answer is no!"

They bought a few more blouses, a new bathing suit, even a pair of alligator shoes. Still, Anna Eileen had one thing on her mind. As they headed to the check-out counter, she picked up the hat and placed it in their shopping basket. Once at the counter, her grandmother removed the hat and tossed it onto an empty counter. Anna Eileen retrieved the hat and placed it on her head. Grandmother snatched it off and placed it on a mannequin nearby. The two of them stared at each other for a moment.

Finally, Anna Eileen screamed at the top of her lungs, "Are you going to buy me that hat or not?!"

Grandmother was outraged. She forced the child into an alcove by the fitting rooms so no one could see them. She held Anna Eileen's face in her claw-like hand as she spoke in a fierce whisper. "You may not have that hat and I will NOT hear another word about it!"

Grandmother released her grip. Without saying a word, they returned to the counter where the sales lady was completing the order.

In an instant, Anna Eileen threw herself down on the ground in the middle of the department store and started kicking and screaming with all her might. She was twelve years old and behaving like she was six.

"I want that hat!" the child screamed. "I want it and I'm not leaving here until I get it!"

Mrs. Heckart was mortified. She turned to the dumbfounded saleslady and said through clenched teeth, "Wrap . . . up . . . the . . . hat . . . NOW!"

Anna Eileen's outburst stopped as abruptly as it had started. She picked herself up, dusted herself off and followed Grandmother to the parking garage. Neither of them said a word. Anna Eileen was penitent. She knew she was going to have to pay for her hat, but she didn't know how. Once in the garage, Mrs. Heckart handed the valet the claim check for the Packard. As the attendant walked away, the two were alone for the first time. In one, lightning-quick gesture, Grandmother made a tight fist with her kid-gloved hand and punched her granddaughter in the jaw, knocking a few teeth loose in the process. Anna Eileen went sprawling onto the pavement, hitting her head on a parking stanchion. As she lay there in a daze, the girl thought to herself, "Well, at least I have my hat!"

⊗⊗⊗

Anna Eileen had a group of chums from childhood she always referred to as "The Girls." The Girls were all from wealthy families in Upper Arlington, one of the rich suburbs of Columbus. Anna Eileen never really felt like she belonged in this group, but the Girls embraced her, partially because she was funny and made them laugh and probably in part because of her grandparents' wealth, which made her socially acceptable in the eyes of their parents.

The Girls would take turns having bridge parties once a month at one another's homes. As the time approached when Anna Eileen knew she couldn't go any longer without reciprocating, she became increasingly nervous. By now, Esther was getting drunk practically every afternoon. As a result, Anna Eileen was never comfortable bringing friends home after school. The teenager was never sure what state of inebriation her mother would be in, so she didn't risk it. She was terrified that Esther would make a drunken scene and embarrass her. Unlike the other girls who could afford snacks and Cokes easily, Anna Eileen saved her meager allowance for a month and a half to be able to afford to host the event.

As luck would have it, that afternoon Esther was passed out drunk upstairs and never came near the parlor where the girls were playing cards. Even so, Anna Eileen was a nervous wreck the entire time. Her eyes were darting around the room to the point where she was trumping aces and playing a very bad game of bridge. She jumped at the squeak of a door or a car passing by on South Cassingham Road. Hard as Anna Eileen tried to make this a nice afternoon, her skittishness made it a difficult time for everyone.

The next day in school, Bobbie Moore, a soft and gentle young woman, said, "You know, Anna Eileen, it's awfully far for us to come on the trolley all the way out to your house. By the time we get there, it doesn't leave us much time to play bridge. Thank you for hosting, but you really don't have to do it anymore."

Anna Eileen looked at her friend with tears of relief and gratitude. No one said another word about it, but it was understood between them. The Girls may not have known the specific reason, but it was clear that Anna Eileen was ashamed of her home and her family. For the rest of her childhood, she never invited anyone to her home again.

Esther had a son by Leo Herbert, named Bob, and two daughters by another husband, Ann and Marilyn, who were Anna Eileen's half-sisters. She had very little in common with Bob, Ann and Marilyn, other than growing up under the same roof. After Bob's birth, when Esther regained her figure, she started sleeping around again. Finally, sweet, young Leo couldn't take it anymore and he left.

All in all, Anna Eileen had a fairly loveless childhood. She told me once that she thought the sound of a horn honking was the saddest sound in the world. I think there were many times in her youth when a dashing young man pulled up in his car, honked the horn and Esther disappeared into it, leaving Anna Eileen behind.

Esther's fifth husband finally stuck. His name was Van Purcell and he ran a successful dry cleaning business in Bexley, a suburb of Columbus. Van was a large, clumsy man with crass manners and a fondness for White Castle Sliders, Miller's High Life, and bathroom humor. Anna Eileen didn't care for Van that much, but she tolerated him because he seemed to make Esther happy, which made her drink less—at least for a while. They got married when Anna Eileen was thirteen. He called her "Leener," a nickname she hated.

Every night when Van came home from a long day at the dry cleaners, he would walk into the house, remove his coat and hang it on a hook by the door—only there was no hook. As his coat would slide to the floor, Van would chortle with laughter as Anna Eileen ran to pick it up. This went on for years and became a ritual the young girl hated as much as she did ironing, which she did three times a week for the entire family of five. As the eldest, she had to do most of the chores, and often cooked dinner and cared for her brother and sisters if Esther was too drunk. As Anna Eileen stood hunched for hours over the stove or the ironing board in the tiny, airless house, often burning her fingers and sweating, she vowed that when she grew up and got married, she would provide a loving home for her children where they would be proud to bring their friends.

The young girl couldn't wait to get out of this life. Her only escape was at the movies. She saved her allowance and would take a streetcar downtown to see two or three features in a day for a quarter. She longed to drag a mink stole like Joan Crawford or smoke like Bette Davis. When she returned home, Anna Eileen would act out the entire film for Esther. If she was sober enough to listen, she applauded and laughed with joy.

Years later, when the family returned to Columbus while Mama was performing as a guest artist at Ohio State University, we drove past the house on South Cassingham Road.

Looking up at it, she said to me, "There it is. Isn't it a mean, little house?"

Clearly, the house itself wasn't mean, but whatever went on inside it must have been. I often wondered if any of Esther's many husbands tried to abuse my mother, either physically or sexually. She was always uncomfortable when talking about her childhood and couldn't stand any film or story that even remotely suggested child abuse. She never talked about it and she never looked back.

ANNA EILEEN AS A TEENAGE BOBBYSOXER

The toughness of her childhood would serve her well in later years. By the time Anna Eileen got to college at Ohio State University (the only school her family could afford), she had dropped the "Anna" to everyone except Esther and Grandmother and was known simply as Eileen or "Heckie." This was a moniker given to her by one of her Pi Beta Phi sorority sisters that managed to stick for the rest of her life.

A young actor in the cast of a new play asked Miss Heckart, "May I call you 'Heckie'?"

She replied, "Honey, you have to have known me at least twenty-five years to call me that. But you may call me Eileen."

For as much as she never liked this nickname, she also relished its uniqueness. There were a number of Eileens in the entertainment industry—fellow character actress Eileen Brennan, British actress Eileen Atkins, opera singer Eileen Farrell, and classical actress Eileen Herlie, to name a few. But there was only one "Heckie."

There was no drama department at Ohio State, so Eileen was an English major and got involved in every on-and-off campus theatrical group that would cast her. She joined a popular OSU drama group called the Strollers and played many leading roles. There, she met a business major named John Harrison Yankee, Jr. Jack Yankee was a tall, handsome, well-spoken young man with a pleasant demeanor and a lovely singing voice. He had grown up in German Town on the other side of Columbus, raised by his mother and four maiden aunts who doted on him. His father, Jack Yankee, Sr., was a World War I veteran who had been shell-shocked and spent most of his life in a VA hospital. Jack was always told the derivation of the name Yankee was Norwegian. It had originally been spelled "Jenke" (pronounced "Yen-kee") and was Americanized somewhere along the way. (I have had to tell this story many times over the years, as people always think it is a made-up name.) Jack was a good student and he was involved in many honorary organizations at OSU.

It was during one of the Strollers productions where Jack was performing and working as treasurer that he became enamored of Anna Eileen, the tall girl with the raspy voice. Together, they starred in a number of Strollers productions, including Clifford Odets's *Golden Boy* and Noel Coward's *Ways and Means*. Jack had no interest in the unstable lifestyle of a professional actor, but he was aware that his new girlfriend had lofty ambitions to go to New York City and have a career in the theater. He was attracted to her independent spirit, her tender heart and her wisecracking sense of humor. They made each other laugh for the next fifty-three years. He worshipped and adored her. Often, she would see him across the room or out in the yard and say softly, "He's so dear." They were best friends and constant companions.

Jack recognized Eileen's passion for acting and knew that was one of the qualities that made her so vibrant, so alive. At the same time, he hated being away from her.

Over the years, when Eileen would be on the road for long stretches of time, he'd rail, "You're going to give up this effing business!"

But in his heart, he knew she never would. He was the rock who supported us all, quietly working for forty years as an insurance executive and never wanting to make a fuss. Jack never spoke ill of Eileen. He was a tender, loyal husband and a wonderfully caring, supportive father. Jack Yankee was one of kindest men I ever met. He was the type of man anyone would have wanted to have as a best friend. He was confident, generous, laughed easily, and he immediately made you feel like you'd known him all your life. Since he always let my mother be the center of attention, it has taken me most of my life to realize what a gift he was.

As Franklin Roosevelt made his famous Pearl Harbor speech, Eileen cried in Jack's arms. They knew he would have to go off to war. Jack opted for the Navy. One spring evening before he was shipped off to boot camp in Florida, Jack proposed. Eileen replied that she'd have to think about

ANNA EILEEN AND JACK ON THEIR WEDDING DAY

it. For the next two days, she planned her trousseau, told her girlfriends, and called all her relatives.

At the end of the week, Jack called. "Are you going to give me an answer?" he asked.

In all her excitement, she'd forgotten to tell him. "Of course I'll marry you!" she said.

In order to have some quality time together before he shipped out, she rented a room in Jacksonville, Florida where he was doing his basic training. They were married there on June 26, 1942.

Jack wore his Navy dress whites for the ceremony and looked every bit the dashing officer. They had their honeymoon in Vero Beach before he was shipped off to the Aleutian Islands while Eileen went to New York to try and make a go at a career on Broadway.

Learning the Ropes

THE YOUNG EILEEN HECKART. PHOTO BY MARCUS BLECHMAN

"HONEY," my mother used to say to me, "there was no one more naïve about show business than I was when I got off the train from Columbus in my saddle shoes."

When Eileen Heckart first came to New York, the young actress worked every part-time position she could, usually holding down two or three jobs at once. She called time on badminton players at the Carlyle Hotel. She worked in the women's toiletries department at Abraham & Strauss. She told me about a woman who worked alongside her with a heavy Brooklyn accent, who answered the phone, "Hello merdem, this is the terlet-goods depertment!" When I was eight years old, I thought this was the funniest thing in the entire world. I made her repeat it endlessly, until I was rolling on the floor in gales of laugher. For the rest of my life, I would often start one of our daily phone conversations by saying, "Hello merdem!"

Eileen's first job in show business was as a prop girl on the popular radio show, *The Goldbergs*. One of her chief responsibilities was operating the pedal on Molly Goldberg's sewing machine. Even with such a menial task, Eileen was thrilled to be a working professional in radio.

While she was pounding the pavements and taking classes at the American Theatre Wing, she reconnected with Paul Lipson, an actor from OSU who had graduated a year ahead of her. After graduation, Paul had worked at a resort in

AS MRS. COW IN *TINKER'S DAM*—WITH DORT CLARK AS MR. SHEEP

the Catskills doing revue sketches. Eileen was so impressed to have a friend and classmate who had actually gotten paid to act. Paul would remain a friend for the rest of her life. He was in the original Broadway production of *Fiddler on the Roof*, playing Tevye when it became the longest running musical in Broadway history and playing most of the male roles in the show over the course of twenty-two years.

Paul showed the young actress many tricks for living on a budget in Manhattan. There was one Jewish deli on Fourteenth Street that was famous for its vegetable soup. You could get a large bowl, brimming with carrots, onions and celery, for a quarter and all the pumpernickel bread you could eat. They would wait until the restaurant was particularly crowded, so the waiters were preoccupied with other tables. Once their soup had arrived, Paul said under his breath, "Now Heckie, eat the vegetables, but try not to eat any of the broth." When she had done as instructed, Paul called the waiter over. "Look at this!" he said, pointing to their bowls. "There are hardly any vegetables in our soup! You must not have dipped the ladle down very far!" The unsuspecting waiter would return with two fresh bowls brimming with vegetables, giving the hungry actors two bowls of soup for the price of one.

In the fall of 1943, Heckart managed to land several roles for the Blackfriars Guild, a small group which would be equivalent to Off-Off-Broadway today. She had roles in *Moment Musicale* and in a revue called *Tinker's Dam*, where she played a cow draped across a piano à la Helen Morgan singing "Love For Sale."

She was cast as a townsperson in the 1944 New York City Center revival of Thornton Wilder's *Our Town*, starring Martha Scott and Montgomery Clift, reprising the roles they had done in the film version of the famous play about life in a small New Hampshire town. It was produced and directed by Jed Harris, one of the most feared and hated people in show business. Harris was a taskmaster with a vile temper and a poisonous tongue. In fact, Laurence Olivier is said to have based his portrayal of Shakespeare's evil King Richard III on Jed Harris. One of the ways Harris demonstrated his abuse of power in *Our Town* was in the wedding scene where George runs across the rocks in the backyard in the rain to greet his fiancée Emily (Martha Scott). Wilder's play is completely dependent on theatrical magic. There was no rain and no rocks, so everything was being pantomimed by Montgomery Clift.

"Poor Monty Clift," Mama used to say. "I watched that son-of-a-bitch Jed Harris make him run back and forth on those rocks twenty-seven times at a dress rehearsal before he let Monty go on with the scene."

In addition to being one of the guests at the wedding, the young Heckart also played one of the mourners at the graveyard in Act Three. She wore a long, black raincoat. When Harris saw that Martha Scott's cloak was shorter than her wedding dress, betraying the moment when Emily is revealed at the graveside, he demanded that Heckart exchange coats with the leading lady. "Boy," Eileen said under her breath, "that's what it means to be a star!"

After *Our Town* closed, she was cast in a small role on tour in a comedy called *Janie,* which played Detroit, Buffalo, and Toronto. There were two other young women in the cast who would teach Heckart valuable life lessons and become cherished friends. One was an African-American actress named Rosetta Le Noire. "Rosie," as she was affectionately known, was a strong-willed, caring woman. Her race was never an issue for Eileen. Rosie was her friend and that was all that mattered. Heckart quickly learned, however, that the rest of the world didn't view things the same way in 1944. There were many restaurants where Rosie couldn't dine or hotels that wouldn't welcome her. While the rest of the cast went their own way, Mama would say, "Well, if Rosie isn't staying here, neither am I!" The two of them would traipse around Buffalo until they found accommodations for the pair of them. Heckart tried speaking to the company manager about it on several occasions, but with Rosie being the only black member of the cast, it was too troublesome to find that many rooms in a decent hotel that accepted "coloreds." Le Noire never forgot Heckart's kindness. She went on to become a major force in the black theater movement, creating AMAS Repertory Theatre in Manhattan, launching such successful shows as *Bubbling Brown Sugar* and *Eubie!* She also became a mentor and second mother to actors like Sidney Poitier and Gregory Hines. Late in her career, she played the grandmother on the successful sitcom *Family Matters* and achieved some financial security in her golden years.

Rosetta was so close to our family, she would often introduce me to people by saying, "This is my son!" Their eyes would dart from the short, African-American lady to the gangly boy with blonde hair and blue eyes. Bea Arthur once replied, "Rosie, if this is your son, we have to talk."

The other member of the *Janie* company with whom Heckart bonded was a young woman named Grace Carney. Gracie was from a wealthy family and didn't have to work, but she was passionate about the theater. She was a bright little lady whose feet didn't quite touch the ground, reminiscent of Helen Hayes. A devout Catholic, Gracie went to mass every day. While they were on tour in Toronto, Mama found a number of small bottles of Chanel No. 5 that she wanted to take back to the states as Christmas gifts. She was over her quota for customs and asked Gracie to take a few back for her. Gracie happily agreed. The following day, just before the matinee, Gracie came to her as she was packing the last few items into her trunk.

"Heckie," Gracie said, "I just broke the tip off my brand new umbrella in the grate of the radiator at mass. That was God's way of telling me He doesn't want me to take your perfume."

"But Gracie," she said, "The customs man is coming to the theater during the show today. It's too late to ask anyone else."

"I'm sorry, Heckie," she said, handing her the bottles of perfume. "God will show you the way."

Not having time to wait for a message from the Almighty before her matinee, Heckart simply hid the five extra bottles under her blouses and didn't declare them. That afternoon during the performance, pangs of guilt enslaved her. After all, Gracie *was* a daily communicant. Who would have a better hotline to God? Eileen was convinced she would be punished if she didn't declare her extra perfume. At intermission, she ran downstairs to the customs officer in the basement of the theater.

"I lied!" she shrieked, tears flowing down her face. "I have five extra ounces of Chanel Number Five in my trunk!"

"Aw jeez lady," the annoyed customs official said, "I've already sealed the trunks. Don't bother me!"

Grace Carney was such a good friend to Mama, she was asked to become my Godmother. She was one of the most generous people I have ever known. She gave me expensive gifts, stocks and bonds and showed up to every children's theater and high-school production I ever did. I adored her. Part of Gracie's charm was that she went to such extremes in the name of love. In the mid-sixties, she had a Japanese rock garden installed in the front yard of her beautiful estate in Westport, Connecticut. That summer, she signed up for Japanese lessons at the local YMCA so she could talk to her garden and learn the proper terms of endearment in Japanese. Whether it was her gentle spirit or the soothing words in their native tongue, those bonsai trees sure grew rapidly.

One of Eileen's chums in New York was a young actor and director named Morton (Tec) D'Acosta. Tec (pronounced "teak," like the wood) was beginning to get established as a theater director and had been offered a contract as business manager (what would now be called an artistic director) with the Port Players, a summer stock company in Milwaukee, Wisconsin. When she returned from *Janie*, he asked his friend Heckie to be his leading lady for the 1944 summer season. The young actress was thrilled. She would get to play ten major roles in as many weeks. This was fertile training ground where Heckart began to hone her craft. The season included *Decision, My Sister Eileen, One Sunday Afternoon, Three's a Family, Personal Appearance, The Milky Way, Junior Miss,* and *Double Door.* While most of these plays were forgettable summer stock fluff, she received great reviews as Ruth, the wisecracking older sister in *My Sister Eileen* and as Anne, the tough prizefighter's babe in *The Milky Way.* In his review in the *Milwaukee Journal,* theater critic Edward Halline called her a sterling and saucy comedienne and also loved her work in *My Sister Eileen.*

Later that same year, Heckart was cast in a small, supporting role in a USO tour of *Over 21* with Dorothy Gish. This began a lasting friendship with the Gish sisters, icons of the silent era. In addition, doing a USO tour made her feel closer to Jack and not miss him quite so much. She spent the last three months of 1944 touring army bases with Miss Gish and the rest of the cast, then returned to New York.

While Jack was on leave over Christmas, Eileen arranged for the two of them to have dinner with the Gish sisters. He brought them both orchid corsages and escorted each of them home on his arm. They doted on the attention from such a handsome young man in uniform. "Eileen dear," Dorothy said, "you've got quite a catch. Doug Fairbanks has nothing on Jack Yankee and that's a fact!"

In February 1945, Eileen toured the boroughs of New York City playing the female lead in a production of Philip Barry's *Holiday* for the Equity Library Theatre. This was where Heckart was to be "discovered." In the *New York World-Telegram,* theater critic Burton Rascoe said, "The other afternoon, in the basement theater of the George Bruce branch of the New York Public Library at 518 West 125th Street, I sat with John Golden, Elliott Nugent, and Raymond Massey while a group of players, working *gratis* for the Equity Library Theatre Project, gave a presentation of Philp Barry's *Holiday* . . . the presentation was very good . . . As Mr. Golden, Mr. Nugent and I rode uptown in Mr. Golden's car, I overheard them discussing the abilities of the actors in the play . . . I chipped in my penny's worth that Miss Heckart was almost as good as Hope Williams was in the original production. They were casting a couple of plays. They took down the name with the intention of asking her to come in and read some lines of theatrical offerings they were working on. This may mean a job for this very good player."

It did. At that time, Elliott Nugent was starring on Broadway in *The Voice of the Turtle* and they were seeking a new understudy for his leading lady, Audrey Christie. This sweet, three-character comedy also starred Margaret Sullivan. Heckart read for the role and with Nugent's encouragement, she landed it. At last, she was working on Broadway.

Audrey Christie, eight years her senior, was a respected actress at the time. The two women understood one another on a basic, human level and hung out together a lot more than a leading lady and her understudy normally would. Mama would stop by Audrey's dressing room every night at half hour and chat. As an understudy, she memorized every move the star made. If she were to go on, Heckart was prepared to give a carbon copy of Audrey Christie's performance. The producer was an elegant man named Alfred de Liagre. He wore a cape and a monocle, and carried a silver-tipped walking stick. If you called Central Casting and asked them to send you a fancy-looking European Broadway producer, they'd send Alfred de Liagre.

After Heckart had stood by for three-and-a-half months without going on once, Tec D'Acosta called.

"Heckie," he said, "Do you want to come back to Milwaukee this summer? I've got even better roles for you."

"But Tec," she said, "I have a contract standing by for Audrey Christie on Broadway."

"I know," D'Acosta said. "And in the next three months, how many times do you think you'll get to go on? I'm offering you a chance to play ten different leading roles, parts that any actress would kill for."

She went into Alfred de Laigre's office to give him the news.

"Mr. de Liagre," she said, "I've got an offer to be a leading lady in a summer stock company, so I'm giving you my notice."

The gentleman put down his monocle and looked up from the box-office grosses he was studying.

"Well, my dear," he said, "I'm sorry to lose you, but I wish you well."

"Thanks, Mr. de Liagre," she continued. "And since I'm going to be leaving the show, I'd like to go on two weeks from Saturday for the matinee."

In her Midwestern naïveté, the young Eileen Heckart thought an understudy automatically got to play a performance or two. She waited and waited for her costume fitting and when one never materialized, she saved her pennies and went to a sale at Gimbel's and outfitted herself.

"I beg your pardon?" the confused producer said, wiping his monocle on his handkerchief.

"Saturday the ninth, sir. I've bought fourteen tickets for that performance and I've invited my agent and all my friends."

"But, my dear," the stunned producer said, "What about costumes?"

"Oh, I've taken care of that. I have all the outfits."

De Liagre shuffled the papers in front of him. After a moment, he replied, "I'm sorry, but this just isn't a good time."

Eileen's face flushed with dread and embarrassment.

"So . . . you're not going to let me play one performance?"

"I'm sorry," de Liagre repeated. "This isn't a good time."

The young actress left the producer's office and burst into tears. The nice man at the box office took pity on her and said he would refund her the money for the fourteen tickets.

When it was past half hour and she didn't come to see Audrey Christie, the star came looking for her. Audrey found her huddled in the corner of an empty dressing room, her eyes red from crying. Audrey asked her what was the matter and Eileen explained about her meeting with the producer.

The leading lady comforted her understudy, but said little more. After the performance that night, Audrey went into Alfred de Liagre's office.

"Another magnificent performance tonight, my darling," the producer said to his star. "And we're sold out through the weekend."

"That's swell, Delly," she said. "Listen, on Saturday the ninth, I have to have dental surgery. I'm going to have a terrible toothache afterwards, so Heckart is going to have to go on for the matinee."

Seeing right through her plot, the Frenchman rapped his cane on the desk. "But, you cannot do this to me!" he snapped.

"Take me up on Equity charges if you have to," she said. "But on Saturday the ninth, I have a toothache. Heckart plays the matinee."

It was one of the greatest lessons Mama ever had in generosity and theater etiquette. Many actors are afraid of their understudies. I've heard people say, "Good God! What if they go on and they're better than I am?!" That to me is the mark of a very insecure actor. Even if they *are* better, they're still the understudy.

Two weeks later, on Saturday the ninth, it was announced that the role normally played by Audrey Christie would be played by Eileen Heckart. It was her first time on Broadway in a leading role. The young Heckart did everything she could to totally duplicate Audrey Christie's performance. In later years, she told me, "Honey I even drew breath where Audrey Christie did. And I was just terrible!" Mama came off the stage that night in tears once again. She gave a mechanical performance that wasn't honest or true to herself. Heckart had bombed and she knew it. Still, she'd played a lead on Broadway and no one could ever take that away from her.

The fourteen tickets she had purchased paid off. Her agent got her an audition for a tour of a pre-Broadway tryout, of a play called *Windy Hill*, starring Kay Francis. Heckart got the role, which would start rehearsals after her second season in Milwaukee, in the fall of 1945.

Somehow, Walter Winchell got wind of it and said in his column the following week, "Audrey Christie of *The Voice of the Turtle* is 'good people' as they say in the Navy. Outta the goodness of her heart, she let her understudy go on the other Satdee matinee—because the kid never had the chance in all the months of the hit's run. But understudy Eileen Heckart did such a good job (in that one perf), it got her a lead role in a Fall production."

Flash forward eleven years to 1957. Mama is playing Lottie, the eccentric sister in William Inge's *The Dark at the Top of the Stairs* on Broadway. Who was her understudy? Audrey Christie. For no apparent reason, while Heckart's star was on the rise, Christie's had begun to wane. It was one of the harsh realities of show business that Mama never quite understood. Shortly after *Dark* opened to favorable reviews, Mama went to Audrey and said, "So, when do you want to go on?" The wheel had come full circle.

When *Dark* closed, as Mama was packing up her dressing room, Audrey Christie came to her and said, "All right honey, go out and get us our next one."

If a show had more than a limited engagement, Mama always let her understudy play. Maree Cheatham, a dear friend and marvelous actress who starred for thirty years in daytime television, understudied Mama on Broadway in the seventies in a short-lived play, *Ladies at the Alamo*. While they were in previews, Mama said to Maree, "Listen, sweetie, I don't think this thing is going to run more than a couple of weeks, but if it does, you come to me and let me know when you'd like to go on and I'll be sick that night." Maree was flabbergasted. She'd never heard of an actress doing anything like that before and, like her predecessor, she always remembered it.

⊗⊗⊗

Eileen had a wonderful time doing her second season of stock for Tec D'Acosta with the Port Players. She did *The Doughgirls, SNAFU, Suds in Your Eyes, Blithe Spirit* (playing Elvira, the cunning, sexy ghost), *Chicken Every Sunday, Love*

Rides the Rails, *The Little Foxes* (playing Regina, which would become one of her signature roles), *Uncle Harry*, *Kiss and Tell*, *But Not Goodbye*, and *Dark Eyes*. For the last one, she played a Spaniard and dyed her hair jet black using sewing machine oil. It leaked all over her pillowcases at night, but the theater-loving woman at the boarding house where she was staying never said a word.

That Fall, she returned to New York and began rehearsals for the pre-Broadway tour of *Windy Hill*, starring Kay Francis. This rather turgid love story toured for several months, but after a spate of bad reviews on the road, it never made it to Broadway.

In June 1946, my mother did another season of stock, but higher up the ladder this time. She was hired for the Cambridge Summer Theatre in Boston, a company that jobbed in Broadway stars for the leading roles. That season, she performed in Agatha Christie's *Ten Little Indians* with Michael Whalen, *Sailor Beware* with an up-and-coming actor named Karl Malden, Saroyan's classic *The Time of Your Life* with James Dunn, and as the long-suffering wife of a vaudeville comic in *Burlesque* opposite Bert Lahr.

One piece of acting advice Mama shared with me repeatedly was something she had gleaned from Bert Lahr during the run of *Burlesque*. Lahr (who was famous for playing the Cowardly Lion in *The Wizard of Oz*) "phoned in" a particular matinee performance. Heckart thought he may have been hung over, but whatever the reason, his acting was monosyllabic and disconnected. He was simply going through the motions. To compensate, the young Heckart pushed and made her performance twice as big.

By the time the matinee curtain came down, she'd given herself a headache. As they were walking offstage after the curtain call, Bert Lahr turned to her and said, "You know Heckart, ya can't act for two!"

"You're right, Bert," she said. "I'll never do that again."

Mama loved to tell me that story. When I started acting in my teens, anytime she felt my performance was forced or rushed, she reminded me of Bert Lahr.

That summer in Cambridge, Eileen also played the gun moll in *Blind Alley* with Zachary Scott as the lead. Scott was a dashing movie star, having played the stylish roué opposite Joan Crawford in *Mildred Pierce* and a tough gunslinger in Westerns like *The Southerner* and *Stallion Road*. He took a liking to the young ingénue and introduced her to the finer things in life. He took her to nightclubs, taught her how to drink champagne, and eat lobster. He made the education of the Columbus girl his own pet project. Scott loved being her Pygmalion and knew from whence he spoke. He was a Texas boy who'd been rough around the edges until he "made good" himself.

One day, he took her to meet Stark Young. In addition to being the well-known drama critic for the *New Republic*, Young was a painter, a sculptor, a poet and one of the most sophisticated, cosmopolitan men about town of the age. Young had the two of them to lunch at his Fifth Avenue penthouse for a grand and luxurious afternoon. Heckart's self-consciousness resulted in a bad case of the jitters, but

MAMA WITH ZACHARY SCOTT AT THE STORK CLUB—CIRCA 1950

Zack Scott's charm and ease (not to mention a strong Bloody Mary) gave her the courage to seize the day.

Afterwards, Eileen said to her friend, "Now what do you send someone as rich and elegant as that for a 'thank you' gift?"

"Send him a casaba melon," Scott replied.

"What?" she asked.

"A casaba melon," he repeated.

Eileen had to hunt all over Manhattan to find a casaba in February, but she finally did. At six dollars, she thought it an obscene price for a piece of fruit, but she sent it with a sweet, simple note.

Stark Young telephoned her immediately. "Casaba melons are my favorite!" he exclaimed. "Where on earth did you find one in the dead of winter? You are one classy lady, Miss Heckart!"

She was learning—and the matinee idol proved to be a wonderful teacher.

⊗⊗⊗

The young Heckart's next foray into understudying was in 1949 in a Broadway revival of Sidney Howard's *They Knew What They Wanted* starring Paul Muni. She understudied leading lady Carol Stone, who had enjoyed great success in *Dark of the Moon*. Paul Muni was a great film and stage actor and Mama was intimidated by him. She became friendly with Bella, Muni's wife of many years. The two of them sat in rehearsals and watched Muni's shenanigans. At fifty-four, he was a little long in the tooth for the role of the Italian immigrant landowner in Napa Valley who receives a mail-order bride. Muni had no respect for the director, Robert Perry. The star was having difficulty with his hearing, or so it seemed, whenever he didn't like the direction.

As he sat there and repeatedly said, "Hmm?" to the director, Heckart and Bella sat quietly in the back of the theater.

At one point, Bella leaned over to Mama and whispered, "I wish Muni wouldn't rehearse in those awful carpet slippers."

From the stage, Muni bellowed back, "What did you say, Bella?"

He couldn't hear the director in the second row, but he could sure as hell hear his wife in the twenty-fourth.

One day, Carol Stone was delayed at a costume fitting when they were about to have a run-through. Muni turned to Heckart and said, "What about the kid here? She's the understudy."

The young actress froze.

"I'm sorry, Mr. Muni, but I don't know the part well enough," she said.

Muni shrugged, and shuffled away in his carpet slippers and ratty cardigan. The stage manager held a script instead.

Of course, this was a bald-faced lie. Heckart had all the lines down perfectly, but she was terrified to be playing opposite the great Paul Muni, even without an audience.

⊗⊗⊗

In 1949, on the strength of her stage work, Eileen Heckart started to get work in that new medium, television. Over the next four years, she played in dozens of dramatic roles on such shows as *Suspense*, *Philco Television Playhouse*, *Studio One*, *Kraft Television Theater*, and *Goodyear Television Playhouse*. Good stage actors were in great demand for these teleplays, many of them theater pieces that were simply adapted for the camera. She was getting the opportunity to hone her craft in front of an audience from coast to coast and work with some great directors who went on to become movers and shakers in Hollywood, including Martin Ritt (who directed *Norma Rae*), Mark Rydell (*The Rose* and *On Golden Pond*), and Delbert Mann (*Marty*). Between theater and television, Eileen Heckart was now working constantly and developing a reputation as a solid character actress.

In 1952, my mother did a play on Broadway called *In Any Language*. She knew this romantic comedy didn't have a very strong script, but she admired the leading

MAMA AND UTA HAGEN IN *IN ANY LANGUAGE*. © EILEEN DARBY IMAGES—REPRINTED WITH PERMISSION

lady, Uta Hagen, and she wanted to have an opportunity to work with the legendary director, George Abbott. One of the male leads was an up-and-coming young actor named Walter Matthau. During the out of town tryout in Boston, there were constant rewrites, but the playwright just couldn't seem to get the play to work.

One Saturday night after a preview in Boston, Mr. Abbott assembled the company onstage for notes. Once he had finished, he asked his two leading ladies to stay for a while.

As Heckart and Hagen sprawled on the couch, totally spent, Mr. Abbott said, "I'd like to thank the two of you for all your hard work this week. Now, if we could just get the end of the second act to work. The last scene doesn't feel right yet and I'd like to run through it once or twice."

"Now?" Uta Hagen asked.

"Yes, if you wouldn't mind," Mr. Abbot replied.

Mama sighed a little and started to take her position. Uta didn't budge.

"No, George!" Uta Hagen said. "Eileen and I are exhausted. We've had constant rewrites and rehearsals every day this week, we played two shows today, and I am *not* rehearsing another thing tonight. The answer is NO!"

As Mama recounted this story to me, she told me how glad she was that Uta had the moxie to stand up to George Abbott. She would have been too afraid of losing her job.

The bleary-eyed stage manager hovered in the wings, wondering if he was going to get more than four hours of sleep that night. Mr. Abbott immediately backed off.

"You're right, Uta, and I apologize," the director said. "You have both been wonderful this week—above and beyond the call of duty. To make it up to you, if you aren't too tired, I'd like to take you across the common to the Ritz for a drink."

They accepted his penitent offer.

One of the qualities that made George Abbott such a respected director as well as a strong producer is that he was very tight with a buck. He knew how to turn one costume into four with different accessories and he never wasted anything. He carried this penury into his personal life, so for him to be offering to pick up the check for cocktails—at The Ritz, no less—did not go unnoticed.

When the waiter came by, Mr. Abbott, an avowed tea-totaller said, "I'll have a ginger ale. And you, ladies?"

As Mama started to say, "I'll have a scotch and . . ." Uta grabbed her arm.

Hagen turned to the waiter. "My friend and I will have a bottle of your best Dom Perignom!"

Mr. Abbott turned white. He sat there for the next hour nursing his Canada Dry Ginger Ale while his two leading ladies got drunk as lords on very expensive champagne. Mr. Abbott learned a painful lesson about overworking his stars in the future.

The New York critics lambasted the weak script of *In Any Language* and it closed after five weeks. After they had posted the closing notice, Walter Matthau couldn't wait for the run to end. He was bored and ready to move on, so he started goofing onstage and playing practical jokes on his fellow actors. My mother never approved of this sort of unprofessional behavior, regardless of the circumstances. She said to me, "They paid the same price as the opening-night audience and they deserve the same performance."

During a scene where she was leaning over to straighten the sofa cushions, Matthau came up behind and goosed her. She felt her cheeks flush with embarrassment as the audience tittered, but she did nothing until the scene was over. Once they were backstage, Heckart slapped him hard across the face.

"You son of a bitch!" she said. "Don't you ever do anything like that again!"

He never did.

MAMA WITH BABY MARK

The young actress was so focused on her career, she put off having a child for fear it would get in the way. After awhile, Eileen felt that she was being unfair to Jack, who longed for a family. When the couple started consciously trying to have a baby, Eileen went to auditions with a new sense of freedom. She didn't have that air of desperation she'd had when she was starting out. There was a sense of something greater and far more important in her life. Ironically, this was when she started getting roles. Adopting a more relaxed attitude in her career worked entirely to her advantage. Her shift in energy gave her the confidence she needed to win the part time and time again.

In the spring of 1951, Eileen was thrilled to learn that she was pregnant. Michael, their first son, was born with the umbilical cord wrapped around his neck. He lived less than an hour. Eileen and Jack were devastated. For days afterward, she couldn't stop crying. They vowed to have another child as soon as it was safe for her to do so. Less than a year later, she was pregnant again. Mark Kelly Yankee was born on June 16, 1952, happy and healthy. Mama said, "He looked like a cherub painted by Peter Paul Rubens, with thick, black curls on top of a tiny head and large, expressive eyes."

She took a career hiatus of a few months and then started auditioning again. Little did she know the next stage role she was offered would change her life.

Life's a "Picnic"

MAMA ENTERING THE STAGE DOOR OF THE MUSIC BOX THEATRE DURING THE RUN OF
PICNIC—1954

WILLIAM INGE'S *Picnic* is the play that put my mother on the map. It launched
a number of other successful careers and she used to tell a lot of wonderful stories
about it. But first, I'll let her tell you in her own words how she got the part.

*Eileen Heckart's Acceptance Speech for the Lucille Lortel Lifetime Achievement
in Theatre Award—October 2000 (Presented to her by Mary Tyler Moore)*

*There have been times in my life when I think someone will stop me on the street
and say,"Ah,* The Bad Seed *or Mary Tyler Moore's Aunt Flo." And after a while,
you think, "Those are the only two things they ever saw?" Well, Mary just talked
about the whole ball of wax. But first, you have to get the part in order to show*

that you can do it. So, it doesn't have to do with a body of work really, but one remarkable moment when I read a play called Picnic. *In those days, I was with Maynard Morris at MCA and we were handled by different agents for different things. He just handled me for theater, and you couldn't read the whole play, they just gave you sides. So, I read the sides. You know those moments when you say, "That's mine, I know that's mine."*

The day of the readings came and I guess they had them for two or three days. The place was jammed and Maynard said, "You're due at three o'clock." So, I went there in my suit and brogues (I mean, she's a schoolteacher, after all), and I waited and I waited and at five o'clock, Maynard came up to me and he said, "Josh Logan has just cast Jesse Royce Landis." This was a very famous character woman who was about fifteen years older than I. Now, I'm that lace-curtain, shanty Irish and when I get angry, the cords stand out in my throat. I can't speak, they just turn very red and large. Then Maynard said, "But he's going to finish seeing people."

I went in and I just stood there and Josh Logan was dancing around me and talked and talked, keeping things bright. Finally, he looked at me and said, "You haven't said a word. Are you right for this or not?" I said, "Mr. Logan, I have never been more right in my life." And he said, "Well, I think you better read."

So, I read and they said, "Thank you." I put down the script and left. Two weeks later, Marshall Jameson, who was Josh's right-hand man, called and said, "Mr. Logan would like to see you." I said, "I am not *understudying. I did it twice—no more." He said, "I don't think that's what it's about." So, I went in and I read for Mr. Logan. And then, a third time, I read for Mr. Logan. And a fourth time. Meanwhile, we had just bought a house and Jack lost his job and had gone to the bank to ask, "How can I refinance this?" They asked, "What collateral do you have?" He said, "A pregnant wife." You know, that bank carried us for thirty-five dollars a month for five years. It was quite wonderful.*

Mark, at this point, our oldest son, was six months old. When the fourth call came, Jack was moonlighting in a jewelry store and they didn't like him to get calls. So, I knew I'd have to take the baby in with me because we couldn't afford a sitter. I brought him on the train and had all the paraphernalia, and I took him to the office of Bill McCaffrey, who was my television agent at that time. Art Carney babysat him that first half hour, then June Lockhart took over when it was time to change the diapers. I finished the audition and I came back in about an hour. As Art Carney handed the baby back to me, he said, "How do you feel about him having coffee and donuts?" I just looked at him and said, "At six months, not at all!" And Art said, "Well, too bad—he's already had three cups of coffee and four donuts!" I packed Mark up and we went to Grand Central Station. He slept until we got off the train and then all hell broke loose. Oh God, was he fussy! I put him in the car seat, we got home, and the telephone's ringing. Mark was still screaming. How he could scream so long, I don't know. I put him down on the doormat, I couldn't find the damn keys and we had a big, tri-color collie named Mr. Pushkin who's barking because he's lonely and he has to pee and he's hungry, too.

I got the door open. I got Mark in, I got him on the couch and I picked up the telephone and Maynard Morris says, "The part is yours." I said, "Thank you." I put down the phone and I fed Mark and I bathed Mark and I put Mark to bed and I walked the dog and fed the dog. I sat by myself about eight o'clock and went, "It's mine! It's really mine!" *I thought I needed to celebrate, but we didn't even have any cooking sherry. I knew Jack didn't want me to use the phone because we were so broke. I had to tell somebody, so I called Jean Carson collect. She didn't have any money either, so I said, "I'll pay you back, I really will!"*

But, the wonderful thing was, after all that, after we were rehearsing for a couple of weeks, Alan Anderson, who was Maxwell Anderson's son, was our stage manager. He said to me, "It's quite marvelous how you got the part" and I said, "Well yes, thank you." He said, "No, Josh hadn't made up his mind. I went over to the Playwright's Office and that's where Maxwell Anderson and Elmer Rice and Robert Sherwood and all these other people were. Elia Kazan is doing Tea *and* Sympathy *and I looked at the casting sheet and your name was penciled in as the schoolteacher at the top of the play." I said, "Yeah?" He said, "Well I went right back and told Josh, "Elia Kazan wants her," and Josh said, "Well, Kazan can't have her. I've got her."*

Thank you.

⊗⊗⊗

Picnic was a very important play for most of the people involved. In addition to being the show that brought Eileen Heckart and Kim Stanley to prominence in the American theater, it's also the show where Kim's understudy, a young woman named Joanne Woodward, met her future husband, Paul Newman. Paul was playing the small, supporting role of the rich boy-next-door. The prestigious Theatre Guild producers didn't think he was sexy enough to play the leading man.

Picnic is a real slice of Americana. The playwright, William Inge, was a Kansas native who wrote about his sad, lonely, small-town childhood with great sensitivity and compassion. It is the story of a charismatic young drifter named Hal who wanders into a small town in Kansas looking for work. He does odd jobs for one of the local women, a widow with two daughters. Hal winds up falling in love with Madge, one of the young daughters, and running off with her.

While *Picnic* seems tame by today's standards, in 1953, it was considered risqué, practically immoral. The sexuality between Madge and Hal as they danced in the backyard was sensual, passionate, and incredibly titillating for postwar audiences who were used to wholesome couples like Spencer Tracy and Katherine Hepburn. Prior to this, sex was merely suggested onstage. In *Picnic,* Hal and Madge were red hot, and so was the audience's reaction to them.

The majority of the play takes place before the Labor Day picnic, the big event of the summer in this small, Kansas town. Eileen Heckart played a spinster school-teacher named Rosemary who is desperate to get married and leave the other old maids behind. After having too much to drink at the picnic, Rosemary lets her lackluster boyfriend, Howard (played by Arthur O'Connell) make love to her and then insists that he marry her. In her climactic scene, Rosemary gets down on her knees to her embarrassed suitor and sobs, "You gotta marry me Howard! You gotta! Please!"

Over the years, this scene has become one of the more poignant, heartbreaking moments of modern American drama. Part of this is due to Inge's strong script, but I am certain that part of it also has to do with my mother's moving perform- ance in the original production. Because of her own sad and often lonely upbringing with Esther, she was able to capture the quiet desperation of this sort of character beautifully. Eileen Heckart was best known for playing the type of woman who would have you in stitches one minute and break your heart the next. This became her trademark.

Brooks Atkinson in the *New York Times* said, "Eileen Heckart as a school teacher with a hunger for life and a knack for getting it helps to bring to life all the cross-currents of Mr. Inge's sensitive writing."

The *New York Post* called her work "excellent" and the *New York Journal American* said she was "superlative."

William Inge was deeply moved by my mother's work and they became quite close, as close as one could get to this shy, reclusive individual. Inge was a closeted gay man who grew up in the Heartland, where homosexuality was *verboten*, causing him to withdraw even further. While he and Mama did several projects together and maintained contact for the rest of his life, I don't know that she ever felt like she really knew him. When she learned that he had committed suicide at the age of sixty, I know Mama was sad, but not terribly surprised.

Occasionally, he would call her when he was drunk, in a deep depression, or both. While she liked the man and respected his talent, this was painful for her. As a little boy, I remember her telling me about her conversations with Inge. I didn't understand what depression was, but when Mama spoke of this man she had to hold back her tears of empathy.

Mama also loved working with the director of *Picnic*, Joshua Logan. Having directed such Broadway blockbusters as *Annie Get Your Gun*, *Mister Roberts*, and *South Pacific*, Logan could have his pick of Broadway projects. Whether it was a hit or a flop, anything he did garnered attention and *Picnic* was no exception. Mama also appreciated his outgoing, gregarious nature.

She said, "Honey, Josh could do any part in the play better than we could. He loved it when you didn't understand one of his notes, because then he could get up and perform the whole scene for you. Josh was a wonderful actor!"

Heckart thought Paul Newman was a talented, young actor and a charming, down-to-earth guy. Everyone in the company was delighted when Paul started dating Joanne Woodward (the understudy to Janice Rule and Kim Stanley), because the cast sincerely liked them both.

Mama worked with Paul and Joanne several times over the years and stayed friendly with them her entire life. A few years later, she played Paul's mother in

Robert Wise's *Somebody Up There Likes Me*, the biopic about prize-fighter Rocky Graziano. Heckart was only six years older, but in typical Hollywood style, when they dressed her down, they made it work.

Even though the Newmans settled in nearby Westport, they were the type of friends who didn't see one another very often, but whenever they did, they were able to pick up right where they left off. My brothers and I really enjoyed them both and we always had fun when they came to the house. To the rest of the world, they may have been one of the most famous show-business couples in America. To the Yankees, they were basic, unpretentious people who loved their kids as much as one another.

Years later, one summer afternoon while we were sitting by the pool, Paul told a wonderful story which demonstrates his kindness and total lack of pretense. In the late sixties, Newman was at the height of his popularity as an international movie star. He was shooting a film one summer in a small, New England college town. There was a local woman who was a huge Paul Newman fan and she was at a fever pitch that he was going to be working for a few weeks in her little hamlet. She fantasized day and night about running into him and wondered how she would react when the big moment finally arrived.

It was a hot, July day at the local ice-cream parlor and the line was out the door. As the woman stood in the queue, she realized that Mr. Newman was in line directly behind her.

She took her compact out of her large purse and every few minutes she would look in the mirror to gaze at her favorite matinee idol, whom she was close enough to touch. With quivering hands, she got up to the counter, ordered her ice-cream cone, paid for it, and left. When the woman got outside, she looked down and realized her hands were empty. Her purse was slung over her shoulder, but in her nervousness and excitement, she figured she must have left her ice-cream cone in the store.

Just then, Paul Newman came out of the ice cream parlor. He saw the woman looking around frantically, retracing her steps in her mind. Paul came up behind her and tapped her on the shoulder.

"Pardon me, ma'am,' he said. "You put it in your handbag."

The shocked matron opened her purse and there was a dripping, strawberry ice-cream cone in the middle of her purse, melting all over. In the heat of the moment, she'd flung it in there with her wallet.

She looked up at Paul and said, "Thank you." He tipped his baseball cap, smiled and walked away.

⊗⊗⊗

In *Picnic*, Ralph Meeker played the leading role of Hal, the drifter. Meeker was a handsome and talented young man who was very nervous about playing a macho stud because he was gay. Although he got wonderful reviews, he never felt adequate in the role. To make him feel more secure, at the suggestion of Logan, Meeker was having padded jockstraps flown in from Paris to enhance his manhood.

One night, Mama felt he was overacting in his big scene in Act Two. As they were walking offstage, she said, "A little big tonight, weren't we, Ralph?"

He looked at her and said, "Gee, do you think it's too much?"

"Well, don't you think it was a little over the top?" she replied.

Meeker turned his back, dropped his jeans, and removed half of the sock-like padding from his crotch. He zipped up, turned back around and said, "Is that better, Heckie?"

"What are you doing?" she gasped. "I was talking about your performance in the second act!"

Kim Stanley played Millie, the younger sister and tomboy. She was a product of the Actors Studio and an avid disciple of Lee Strasberg and "The Method," made popular by Marlon Brando. She loved the experimentation process in rehearsals and relished the opportunity to explore, to try different choices with her character. She hated having to "set" her performance once the show opened and often got bored during a long run. Heckart, on the other hand, couldn't wait for rehearsals to end. She felt she learned how a role really worked by getting feedback from a live audience. While she respected most of her directors, she loved making a role totally her own and discovering the rhythm by playing eight shows a week.

Aside from this major difference in their work habits, Kim and Eileen were cut from the same cloth. They were both outspoken dames who called 'em as they saw 'em. While they both enjoyed their roles and were happy to be a part of such a successful Broadway production, neither of them thought it was a particularly good script. When audiences came to the previews and talked about it rapturously, they gave each other blank strares.

Kim said, "Heckart, are they seeing the same play? I don't get it, do you?"

"No, Kim, I really don't."

When the New York critics lauded *Picnic* as one of the great new American dramas, the two young actresses were even more confused. In fact, Mama was so sure that *Picnic* was going to have a short run, she accepted a job doing a live television drama a few weeks after the play opened.

As the play went on to win the Outer Critics Circle Award and the Pulitzer Prize, Kim Stanley was beside herself. One night, as she arrived at the dressing room they shared, Stanley shut the door and spoke in hushed tones.

"Okay, Heckart," she said. "I have a plan. I've bought a ticket for next Tuesday night's performance. I'm going tell the stage manager I have the flu and I can't go on. I'm going to sit in the tenth row in a raincoat and a pair of sunglasses and a big, floppy hat, and I'm going to find out what the hell this turkey is all about! You mustn't tell a soul! Now, after the performance, you meet me at Downey's on Eighth Avenue and I'll give you a full report!"

Mama was thrilled with Kim's plot and couldn't wait to hear her reaction. The following Tuesday night, before the curtain was raised, the stage manager announced that the role of Millie, normally played by Kim Stanley, would be played by Miss Joanne Woodward. After the performance, Mama changed as quickly as she could and went around the corner to Downey's. As she entered the bar, she saw Kim Stanley sitting at the counter with six shots of whiskey lined up, three for each of them. As Heckart approached, she saw that Kim Stanley was doubled over with laughter.

Kim turned to her and said, "Oh, my God! It is so much WORSE than we thought!"

Regardless of her opinion of the play, for her performance as Rosemary, Mama received the Outer Critics Circle Award and the Theatre World Award as Best Newcomer.

Before the opening night performance of *Picnic*, Josh Logan made his rounds to congratulate everyone and wish them well. When he got to Miss Heckart's dressing room, he said, "This role is going to change your life."

"I don't see how," she replied.

Logan kissed her on the forehead. As he walked away, he looked over his shoulder and said, "You'll see."

Nanny

NANNY AND ME AT MAMA AND DADDY'S 25TH WEDDING ANNIVERSARY CELEBRATION—
1968

SHORTLY AFTER Mark's first birthday, one of the greatest gifts our family ever received arrived in a most unusual package. While young Miss Heckart was enjoying her first major Broadway success in *Picnic*, Jack was establishing himself in the insurance business and taking a night job doing bookkeeping for the Elgin Watch Company to make extra money. The Yankees also had a baby boy who needed constant care. They had been through a variety of babysitters. The good ones didn't last and the bad ones couldn't leave soon enough. There was one night when my father came home and found the babysitter passed out drunk on the sofa. My brother Mark was crawling around on the fieldstone patio right on the edge of a twenty-foot drop. If Jack had come home a few minutes later, the baby would have gone right over the edge.

My parents contacted an employment agency and started interviewing trained nannies. None of the candidates the agency sent over satisfied Eileen. They were too strict, too lax, or wouldn't handle a baby so young. My parents weren't sure what to do.

Meanwhile, there was a forty-year-old woman from Glasgow who needed a miracle. Agnes Johnston Stewart, known to her friends as Nan, had been a baby nurse in the pediatrics ward at Columbia Presbyterian Hospital in Manhattan. Two years prior, she had suffered a brain aneurysm that had left her partially paralyzed. Her right leg had practically no feeling and she dragged it around like a dead weight. The limb was practically useless. Her doctors said she would never walk again, but they underestimated this stoic Scotswoman's determination. Nan taught herself to speak again, and, although she walked with a noticeable limp, she was far more mobile than anyone anticipated. She went on several interviews to be a nurse or a personal assistant, but when prospective employers saw her twisted right leg, she was rejected immediately. Nan was living in Norwalk, Connecticut with a girlhood friend named Dorothy Coagie from her days as a camp counselor at Lake Louise in Banff, Canada. The last thing Nan wanted to do was to return to the poverty of her life in Glasgow, but she was running out of money fast.

The woman at the employment agency said, "Don't despair, dear. God has a place for you."

Two days later, she had an interview scheduled with a Mrs. Yankee. When Dorothy dropped Nan off at the old fieldstone house, Nan insisted on leaving her cane in the car, refusing to appear handicapped. The house had no railing and she had to get down on her hands and knees to climb up the cobblestone steps in her best tartan skirt.

As Eileen greeted Nan at the door, she was struck by her presence. Unlike the other women she'd been interviewing, this one was sweet and gentle, with a light behind her eyes. The two women felt as if they had always known one another.

Even so, as Eileen watched Nan limp across the floor, she wondered how this physically challenged woman could possibly take care of an infant. She tried very hard not to look at the woman's paralyzed appendage as they spoke. Nan talked about the pediatrics ward where she had worked and the other children she had cared for as a private nanny before her illness. Eileen listened as the woman recited her resume. When she was finished, they stared at each other in silence. Eileen didn't have to say anything. It was clear what she was thinking.

With steely determination, Nan spoke. "Yes," she said, "I have an affliction. But I know that if God will give me a baby to take care of, I'll be all right."

Eileen reached over and clasped the woman's hand. "I have a matinee tomorrow. Would that be too soon to start?"

Nan looked confused. "But . . . don't you want to check my references?" she asked.

"Honey, you just gave 'em."

Nan Stewart, lovingly referred to as Nanny, was with our family for thirty-five years. She cooked, cleaned, helped raise the boys, bathed us in the kitchen sink, and referred to herself as "Yer mummy's understudy."

When she was too old and sick to take care of us, we took care of her. After I was born and the family moved to the big, Colonial house with all the gardens on Comstock Hill Road, the former gardener's quarters across the driveway became Nanny's cottage. Mama always said she couldn't have had a career without an exceptional husband and an exceptional nurse.

Nanny was the closest thing I ever knew to unconditional love. She fed me as a baby, dressed me for school every day, fixed my meals during the week, and was a constant source of comfort. The sound of her clomping up the stairs on her one good leg to wake me every morning was a kind of music to me. Whenever Mama was away doing a film or a television show, Nanny was always there with a kind word, a freshly baked chocolate chip cookie and a hug smelling of Jergen's Lotion. Most of the time, she had a threaded needle in her lapel just in case anything needed to be mended.

If anyone had a reason to be angry or bitter due to the hand God dealt her, it was Nan Stewart, but she never showed a trace of negativity. She was the eternal optimist. Whenever Mama would say, "I have an audition tomorrow," Nanny would say, "When do you start rehearsals?"

"But I haven't got the part yet, Nan."

"No, but you will."

Many times, when I wanted a change of pace, I'd pack an overnight bag and trot across the driveway to Nanny's in my Winnie the Pooh pajamas. She was always there with a cup of tea and a bag of honey-dipped pears from the local health-food store. She loved to laugh, adored animals, and she was the queen of corny jokes. When I would say, "Hi, Nanny! What's up?" she would reply in a thick Scottish burr, "My head's up. My hair's a wee bit higher."

I have never known a more kind, gentle and loving spirit.

⊗⊗⊗

One of my favorite stories about Nanny was one that showed her Scottish practicality. I was about a year old and she kept me on a blanket with my toys in the middle of the kitchen floor while she did her morning chores. While her back was turned, I got into the pantry and managed to dump a five-pound can of coffee all over the kitchen floor. I was using the coffee scoop as a shovel, spooning coffee everywhere and having a grand time with the sandpile I had created. About twenty minutes later, Mama stumbled downstairs for her morning coffee as Nanny was stringing beans for the evening dinner. Mama was never at her best before her first cup of java and as she saw me sitting there digging in my pile of coffee, she stopped in her tracks.

"Nan," she said in her gravelly morning voice, "Are you just going to let him play in that?"

"Och well," Nanny said, "He's already made the mess. He might as well have a good time!"

Mama realized she was absolutely right. "If it had been me," she said later, "I'd have swept up the coffee right away and everybody would have been miserable. This way, Luke got to have his fun and the coffee got cleaned up at noon instead of ten. It wasn't any more of a mess and everybody was happy."

⊗⊗⊗

Over the years, Mama and Daddy financed several trips for Nanny to return to Glasgow to see her relatives. When I was seven, she talked about her upcoming trip. Half joking and off the cuff, she said, "I'll bring you back a kilt and teach you to do the Highland Fling!"

"Will you *really*, Nanny?" I asked with wide eyes.

"Well, I suppose I could, if you want," she said.

She was stuck now. It was all I could talk about for weeks. I told all my friends that I was getting a real kilt all the way from Scotland in the Dress Stewart tartan, which was Nanny's clan.

As Nan made final preparations for her trip, carefully taking my measurements, Mama said, "Nan, this is very thoughtful of you, but you don't have to do this. After all, it *is* your vacation."

"No, I want to do it," she replied.

The poor lady had no idea what she'd gotten herself into. She spent a good part of her vacation traipsing around Glasgow trying to find a kilt and all the accoutrements for a seven-year-old boy. After a week of shopping, she had tracked down the kilt, the tie, the sporran, the hat, the knee socks—everything but the gold buckled shoes. She enrolled all her friends and relatives.

"We simply *must* find shoes for Luke!" her brother Bill said.

Finally, her cousin Agnes located some in a store in Dundee. They could be shipped to Glasgow just in time for her departure.

As soon as Nanny stepped off the plane at JFK, I squealed, "Did you get it? Did you, Nanny?"

"I did!" she nodded.

It was all I could do to contain myself until she got home and unpacked. Both Nan and Daddy helped me figure out all the buckles and clasps. The only part I couldn't manage myself was tying the necktie. I wore my kilt everywhere. Anytime we had company that summer, or if an event could be construed as a special occasion, I disappeared to my room and came back in my kilt. I wore it to school for Show & Tell, I wore it when my parents had dinner guests. One spring afternoon, Mama was picking up Mark at junior-high school and she asked if I wanted to come along.

"How long until we leave?" I asked.

"Ten minutes," she replied.

That was just enough time to run upstairs and get dressed in my tartans.

While we waited for Mark to come out of school, I stood there outside Mama's cream-colored Buick Skylark. I greeted all of Mark's junior-high-school friends.

"Hi!" I said. "I'm wearing a kilt all the way from Scotland!"

Some of the junior high school boys laughed at this funny-looking kid in a skirt. The teenage girls thought I was adorable. When Mark came out of the building and saw me standing there chatting up all his amused buddies, he turned crimson.

"Oh, here's my brother!" I shouted and pointed. "Hi Mark!"

He wanted to crawl into a hole and die. Through clenched teeth, he growled at my mother, "For Chrissake Ma, get him in the car!"

ME IN MY KILT—POPPING THE KNEE

He'd spent the whole year building up a reputation of coolness, of being "hip" and "with it." Now, his little brother had destroyed it all in a matter of minutes.

As we drove off, I waved to my adoring public. "Bye!" I shouted. "Hope to see you again soon!"

Mark slinked down as low as he possibly could in the front seat, contemplating how he could graduate without ever having to go back to Saxe Junior High again.

That summer, there was a photo session in the backyard with my father's Polaroid camera. Although he was a little suspect at how much his youngest son seemed to enjoy playing dress-up, Mama insisted he get some pictures.

"Before he grows out of the damn thing, Jack."

"That can't happen soon enough for me!" he replied.

No matter how Daddy posed me, I insisted on bending one knee. He tried everything to make me look butch, standing me on the front steps of the house, straddling the patio furniture. Regardless of my father's attempt at a macho stance, I always popped my knee at the last second. Finally, when I saw how exasperated he was getting, as we were running out of film I let him take one with my fists on my hips and both feet planted on the ground.

"That's wonderful!" he said as he snapped the photo.

But for all the others, the knee was bent. I just thought it looked better. If he hadn't been turning a blind eye to the fact that I was a homosexual in the making, this would have been a clue.

That year for Halloween, Dad borrowed a kilt from a family friend and the two of us went trick-or-treating as a pair of Scotsmen. It was way too cold to wear it through the winter and by the following spring, I'd outgrown it and it was passed down to Nanny's grand-niece. Secretly, I think my father was thrilled. I know Nanny was pleased I'd gotten such use out of her gift.

I had always wanted to document the story of Nanny's first interview with Mama. In the summer of 1994, I took a film production workshop at the University of Southern California. Our final assignment was to make a short film, telling a story visually, with a minimal use of sound. I found someone with a long, winding flight of steps in front of her Spanish house in the Silverlake area of Los Angeles and I asked a friend, a wonderful character actress named Lois De Banzie, to play Nan. Lois had been nominated for a Tony for the recent Broadway revival of *Morning's at Seven* and was a friend of the family. She was from Scotland and had actually met Nanny at several of the family Christmas parties, which made her the perfect choice.

The day the class ended, after we had viewed our completed short films, I was on my way to see an ailing Nanny in a nursing home in Connecticut. I had to find a way show her my little film. I was told USC was very strict about the release and ownership of these student projects, because they didn't want the next Spielberg or Lucas walking off with a project the school had commissioned and financed. I asked other students about getting permission to make a dub of my completed film.

My classmate Jennifer said, "Luke, forget about it. There's no way you can make it happen. You have to speak to the assistant dean and this time of year, it's impossible to even get an appointment."

But I persevered. After two days in post production, living on Taco Bell, Krispy Kremes, gallons of iced tea, and no sleep, I went to my appointment with the assistant dean. I sat in a wood-paneled office opposite this well-tailored lady in a Chanel suit. My hair was greasy, I was unshaven, wearing sweats, and completely on edge. Generally, I would never have come to an important meeting this way, but I had no choice.

Peering over her bifocals, she said, "Yes, Mr. Yankee? And what can I do for you, today?"

I took one look at the school official and exploded in tears.

"I've done this short film about my Nanny and she's DYING!!!" I shrieked. "I'm going to see her tomorrow and you have to let me take my film off-campus this afternoon to get a copy!"

The poor woman must have thought I was crazy. "OK, OK!" she said, patting my arm. "You have my permission. Just stop crying!"

That afternoon, after a shower and a shave, I got the film to Lightning Dubbs in Hollywood just in time to return the master to the school and get on a plane for Connecticut. I had asked the people in the nursing home to wheel a VCR and TV in Nanny's room. She was fascinated as she watched it. At age eighty-six, she wasn't at her most lucid.

She sat there saying, "Is that supposed to be yer mummy? Is that supposed to be me?"

I showed her the six-minute film twice. On the second viewing, when she saw the woman crawling up the stairs, she grasped that her story had been preserved as a story of humanity. "When you told me you were gong to make a movie about me climbing up the stairs," she said, "I thought it would be a comedy. I couldn't imagine why you'd ever want to make a movie about me."

"Because," I said, "I remember you telling this story all through my childhood. I wanted to immortalize it—and immortalize you."

As she squeezed my hand, she said under her breath, "I still can't imagine who'd ever want to see a movie about me."

"You might be surprised," I said.

That was the last time I ever saw Nanny. One week later, she died of congestive heart failure.

Our family planned a lovely service at the Waveny Care Center, the nursing home where she had lived for the last four years, where she was loved and admired. She was the one who read newspapers to the patients who had lost their sight or told silly jokes to those who were having a bad day. Since her aneurysm as a young woman, she had been in pain every day of her life for more than forty-five years, but she never let it stop her from giving a smile to everyone she met.

Mama went to the local florist and ordered fifty lapel pins of fresh heather for everyone and I made a couple of photo collages of pictures from Nanny's life. As we all sat in the common room of the home on a crisp, October day, the service ended with a bagpiper in a full dress kilt playing *Amazing Grace*. He didn't stop playing, but walked slowly out the back door and into the yellow and burnt orange autumn foliage until the sound of his pipes disappeared into the distance. It was as if this lady with such generosity of spirit never really died. Whenever I hear someone with a Scottish accent or smell freshly baked cookies or see bit of tartan fabric, I am reminded of the power of unconditional love.

Heckie Hits Hollywood

JANE WYMAN, VAN JOHNSON AND EILEEN HECKART IN *MIRACLE IN THE RAIN*—1956.
MIRACLE IN THE RAIN © WARNER BROS. PICTURES, INC. ALL RIGHTS RESERVED.

ONCE MARK WAS BORN, Eileen's career really started to take off. Now that she was a mother, the idea that there was something more important in her life than her career had an even greater resonance. After the success of *Picnic*, Eileen Heckart seemed to be working constantly in theater, film, and television.

Sixteen months after Mark arrived, she gave birth to her second child. Since this was her third pregnancy, she took it in stride. On August 21, 1954, Philip Craig Yankee was born. Since Mark and Philip were less than two years apart, they were very close as children. They had the kind of relationship where they were the best of friends or trying to pound the crap out of one another. As Eileen's career continued to flourish, she found herself relying on Jack and Nan more than ever.

With her partial paralysis, Nanny wasn't sure she could handle the added task of caring for another infant. She had no intention of leaving the Yankees, but the stress of the added responsibility sent her into the hospital. The doctor called it a "false pregnancy." The day Eileen gave birth to Philip at St. Joseph's Hospital, she was sending flowers to Nan three floors below. Once she immersed herself in the practical matters of caring for another baby, Nanny handled it as she did everything else—one day at a time. She specialized in practicality.

By the end of 1953, Eileen Heckart had become a major player in live television dramas. She rehearsed several of these programs during the day while doing *Picnic* at night. Fred Coe, the producer of *Philco TV Playhouse*, saw how well the young actress had done with smaller, supporting roles and was one of the first television producers to give her a shot at a leading role. The teleplay was called *The Haven*, written by Tad Mosel. It was another "kitchen drama," where she played a slovenly, insensitive wife who broke your heart.

Mosel was a great writer in the days of live television. In later years, he won a Pulitzer Prize for the family drama, *All the Way Home*. Heckart and he did six projects together over the years and became lifelong friends. Mosel wrote many pieces specifically for her.

Syndicated columnist Faye Emerson wrote, "If Eileen Heckart had done the same performance in a movie as she did on *Philco TV Playhouse* in *The Haven*, she would have won an Academy Award. It was so real, so moving that the emotion stayed with me for days."

The night it aired, her phone rang off the hook. There were many calls from celebrities. Marlene Dietrich, whom she'd never met, sent her a basket of white orchids and geraniums.

"I'd never seen anything so elegant as basket of all white flowers," she once said to me. "The only two people I ever knew who were classy enough to send such a gift were Dietrich and Mary Tyler Moore."

Red Skelton, whom she'd also never met, sent a wire from Hollywood. Perry Como called and introduced himself, saying how moved he was by her portrayal. Strangers all over the country who had seen her performance looked up her phone number and called to congratulate her.

This performance also led to her winning the Sylvania Television Award as Best Supporting Actress of 1953.

On the strength of *The Haven*, Tad Mosel wrote other scripts especially for her, including *Other Peoples Houses*, about a family maid who must face putting her senile father into a rest home. One of their other projects was *My Lost Saints*, a family drama about a live-in housekeeper who is forced to bring her infirm mother to live in the home of her employers. On the third day of rehearsal, Eileen approached the writer.

"Tad, about the last line of the script . . . are you happy with it?"

"Well, Miss Heckart," he said, "I was. Obviously, I'm not anymore."

"Sorry honey," she said, "But it's just not right."

After he was able to put his bruised ego aside, Tad struggled with the line for several days. Finally, he came up with just the right nuance to capture the emotional journey of the leading character. He was forever grateful to her and learned the value of listening to "the talent."

"I've never had such a rapport in my life with a playwright as I did with Tad Mosel," she said. "If I stumbled over a line more than once, he'd ask me what was wrong. 'It's me,' I'd say. But Tad would go off in a corner, rewrite the line and bring it back."

Mosel always wrote the most eloquent letters. They were meticulously typed (by him, not a secretary) and full of rich detail. Whenever Mama received one, she was like a kid on Christmas. "I got a letter from Tad!" she said, beaming and waving it in the air. After she had read each letter three or four times, laughing to herself, she would read the whole letter to each of us again and again. As an adult, I received a few of them and cherished them as much as she had. There was a deep love and respect between Mama and Tad. I think it was one of the most important friendships of her life.

In a review of *My Lost Saints* in 1955, syndicated columnist John Crosby said, "The play was written especially for Eileen Heckart, one of the finest young actresses we have, and she was just immense in it . . . . She can do things with her eyes, this girl—not another muscle stirring—that will tear your heart out."

With reviews like this and the ones she had already garnered for *Picnic*, how could Hollywood not sit up and take notice? She was offered her first film, a supporting role in Warner Brothers' *Miracle in the Rain*, without a screen test.

"I wasn't important enough for them to give me a screen test," she once said to me. "Those tests are expensive to shoot, so they save them for the big stars in the leading roles. I was a character woman. Besides, they'd seen enough of me on television to know what I could do."

The young mother was reticent to leave her husband and two boys for nearly a month. She was relieved that part of the film was going to be shot on location in New York, so she could come home on her days off. This was a big break and she knew better than to turn it down. She and Jack would make it all work, with Nanny's constant support.

Directed by Rudolph Maté and based on a novel by Ben Hecht, *Miracle in the Rain* is a sappy love story with Van Johnson as a World War II pilot who falls in love with Jane Wyman. Mama played Jane's best friend. She described the plot like this: "First Van dies, then Jane dies and I'm left hanging on the altar at Saint Patrick's, mourning over the lot of 'em!"

Heckart was apprehensive about appearing in her first motion picture. While many successful stage actors have made the transition to the camera, just as many hadn't. Even with all that television work under her belt, she went to Karl Malden, her old friend from the Cambridge Playhouse, for advice.

"Heckie," he said, "this is the advice that Spencer Tracy gave me. There are really only three things you need to know in film. If it's a medium shot, you speak conversationally, just as we are speaking now. If it's a long shot, project as you would on a stage. If it's a close up, it's eyes left, eyes right. That's it!"

It was a credo she carried with her to the end of her days.

During shooting, she was terribly outspoken about how bad she thought the script was. One day, she was summoned to the Warner Brothers production office to explain her conduct. The young Miss Heckart was worried. She thought she'd blown her big chance and was about to be sacked. This was 1955 and the mood in Hollywood was sober and conservative. Eileen sat across the desk from this buttoned-down studio executive in a gray flannel suit with wire-rimmed glasses. His hair was slicked down and he was wearing too much Aqua Velva.

"Now, Miss Heckart," he said in a reprimanding tone, "you have been heard making disparaging remarks about this picture on the lot. We here at Warner Brothers take our films very seriously. What do you have to say for yourself?"

There was a long pause. The young actress started to snicker.

"Well, what do you *expect* me to say about this turkey?!"

She was really laughing by now. The studio executive looked shocked at first, and then he started to laugh with her.

"It *is* pretty terrible, isn't it?" he replied, starting to laugh himself. Soon, they were both in hysterics. "Just don't say it on the lot anymore, okay?"

"OK," she agreed.

He patted her on the head and she returned to work. No wonder she got more outspoken with time.

Eileen Heckart wasn't the only actress with strong opinions on *Miracle in the Rain*. She became friendly with her leading lady, Jane Wyman, who thought the picture was every bit as bad as Heckart did. Jane was a big Hollywood star, having played the leads in such films as *Johnny Belinda*, *The Yearling*, and *The Lost Weekend*. Jane was having a dinner party and was most eager for Eileen to attend her first real, Hollywood gathering. She was thrilled to be asked. Jane's ex-husband was there, an actor named Ronnie Reagan. He was with his second wife, an actress who had done a few small pictures named Nancy Davis. Eileen had never met Ronnie, but she knew his reputation as a star in many "B" pictures, like *Bedtime for Bonzo*, with an occasional smaller role in an "A" movie, like *The Hasty Heart*. He'd also recently served as president of The Screen Actor's Guild, so she thought he might be a good contact.

There were about a dozen people there for dinner and no one could get a word in except Ronnie. He spent the entire evening discussing every bill that was up for approval in the state of California, his views on every political figure of the day, and the state of the union. My mother wasn't interested in politics at that point in her life. In later years, she became addicted to CNN and *Meet the Press* and wrote her local congressmen every chance she got. But back in 1955, all Eileen wanted was some good, Hollywood gossip. Since Ronnie held the room captive discussing filibusters that no one else seemed to care about, the young actress didn't get a bit of the Tinseltown scoop she was craving. After dinner, Jane Wyman asked Heckart to accompany her to the kitchen to serve the after-dinner drinks.

Once out of earshot of the other guests, Eileen said to her hostess, "Jane, Ronnie seems like a nice man and all, but doesn't he ever talk about *anything* but politics?"

Jane grunted and rolled her eyes as she poured the crème de menthe. "Oh, my God, he's so BORING!" Jane said. "Why do you think I divorced him?"

※ ※ ※

In the early nineties, my mother and I were doing some Christmas shopping in Beverly Hills at Bullocks on Wilshire Boulevard. Many people were recognizing her and saying hello. As we walked through the soap department, I saw her grab a woman's arm and squeeze it.

"Hi!" Mama said to the woman. The man standing behind her looked alarmed.

"Hi," the woman replied quietly.

"How are you?" Mama said in a loud voice.

"Fine," the woman said.

She let go of the woman's arm and stood there, looking puzzled as the woman walked on.

"Mama," I said, "Don't you know who that was?"

"Well, I thought it was some character actress I'd met at Jane Wyman's years ago. I guess I was mistaken."

"Mama," I said, "Think about it. That character actress you met at Jane Wyman's was Nancy Reagan!"

"Holy shit!" Mama gasped. "No wonder that man behind her looked so upset when I grabbed her arm. That must have been the secret service. And here I just thought she was some old character woman I'd known years ago."

"Well," I said, "In a way, it was."

"Yeah," she said, putting back a box of lavender soap. "And in way it wasn't. Let's get the hell out of here. I need a cigarette."

⊗⊗⊗

While my mother was doing her costume fitting for *Miracle in the Rain*, she had one of her first brushes with Hollywood royalty. She was in a corner of the huge, costume warehouse trying on outfits with Betty, the wardrobe supervisor. She'd already chosen a dress and now she was looking for hats and overcoats. Neither she nor Betty could find anything that was quite right. As if from nowhere, this gruff-looking kid appeared and stared at my mother without saying a word.

"You're not going to wear that hat, are you?" the young man said to her.

She was mesmerized by him. He had sensuality and a power like nothing she'd ever experienced before.

"Um, no. I guess not," she said.

"Well, then take it off," the kid said.

He grabbed the hat off her head and threw it on the floor. After examining the shelves, he handed her a delicate, navy-blue cloche.

"Here," he said, "try this one."

Why had neither of the two women spotted it before?

"Okay, now the hat works," he said to Betty, "but haven't you got a better coat than that?"

The brash kid was acting like Harry Warner himself. The wardrobe supervisor started scurrying through the racks and returned with an armful of cloth coats.

He grabbed one from the center of the pile and sent the others flying. The two women were strangely titillated by him. The young Heckart put on the coat he'd chosen. The color matched the hat perfectly. The young man grabbed her by the shoulders and turned her toward the mirror.

"There," he said, "*now* you look like you belong in the movies!"

He disappeared among the racks as quickly as he'd entered. Heckart and Betty stared at each other.

"What the hell just happened?" Eileen said.

Betty shrugged her shoulders then started picking up the coats and hats he'd strewn around the room.

"Do you *know* that kid?" Mama asked.

"Yeah," Betty said. "I've seen him around the lot a few times. He's just finished doing a picture here. I think he's got one about to come out, too. His name's Dean. James Dean."

A few weeks later, *East of Eden* was released. They all knew who the kid was then. Who would have thought one of Hollywood's leading heartthrobs would have had such an eye for fashion?

Heckart was shocked to see herself ten feet tall for the first time on the big screen. Due to its very scope, film magnified every gesture and nuance in a way that television did not. Even so, movie critics called her performance in *Miracle in the Rain* "touching" and "engaging." Much as she hated being away from her family for weeks at a time, perhaps there was something to be said for making movies.

Smelling
Marlene Dietrich

MARLENE DIETRICH IN HER FAVORITE HOUSECOAT. THE FADED INSCRIPTION READS:
"TO MY DARLING, WONDERFUL, TALENTED EILEEN—FROM AN ADMIRER. WITH LOVE,
MARLENE." © 1978 JOHN ENGSTEAD/MPTV.NET

IN *MARLENE DIETRICH'S ABC's* under "Heckart, Eileen," it says: "If she were acting in Europe, she'd be the queen of the boards. In America, the typecasting barbarism deprives the world of her true talents."

When this was first published in the early sixties, my mother was so thrilled, she went out and purchased about seventy-five copies of the book to give as Christmas gifts to all of her nearest and dearest. But how did the two of them know each other in the first place?

While Eileen was cutting her teeth working in live television, she became friends with another young actress who also did a lot of TV work named Maria Riva. Maria was a warm, down-to-earth lady who enjoyed Heckart's wry sense of humor and respected her talent. Even though they were contemporaries, they were never up for the same roles. Maria played the sophisticated, "glamour gals" and Heckart tended to be cast more in the "kitchen dramas." Riva came by the glitz honestly—she was the daughter of Marlene Dietrich.

Recently, I have had the great fortune of becoming friends with Maria Riva. She now lives in Palm Springs, where I have a weekend home. Her daughter-in-law, Marilee Warner, runs a playwrights workshop where I have occasionally directed and showcased a few projects. When I found out Marilee was related by marriage to Maria, someone I'd heard my mother speak of so many times, I was eager to meet her. When you are in the presence of Maria Riva, it is almost like being in the company of Dietrich herself. She is strong, direct, imposing and, even in her early eighties, there is a sense of unmistakable glamour from a bygone era. But unlike her mother, Maria is tender, compassionate, and nurturing. There is a wisdom about her where she seems to look right through you.

Her 800-page biography of her mother, *Marlene Dietrich—by her daughter Maria Riva* is a brilliant book. It is thoughtfully written, meticulously researched, and delves into Dietrich's life with insight, candor, and sensitivity. When I told her about my one-man show and that it opened with me telling the story about how Mama and Dietrich met, she listened patiently.

"Well darling," she said, "if that's the story you want to tell in your little show, you go right ahead. But I know what *really* happened."

"Maria," I begged, "Please—that was my memory of what mother had told me. I want to know *your* story!"

Apparently, Heckart was invited to several soirees at Maria Riva's home and always in attendance was the grande dame, the legendary Miss Dietrich. You were never quite sure which role Marlene would be playing—the German *hausfrau* in the kitchen carving up the Black Forest ham or the Hollywood icon holding court in the salon for her fans.

Dietrich had seen Heckart's work on television and onstage, recognized her talent, and was always cordial to her. Mama was fascinated and terrified by Miss Dietrich—fascinated to be in the presence of a true Hollywood icon and intimidated by this formidable woman who was capable of turning on you at any moment. Marlene was extremely possessive of her only daughter and could be very jealous of Maria's friends.

After one of these parties, Marlene said to her daughter, "Why do you spend time with that strange Heckart woman? She's very talented . . . but she's *strange*."

What that meant in the parlance of Marlene Dietrich is that she didn't understand my mother. Dietrich didn't understand how anyone could be as talented as Eileen Heckart without being glamorous.

Maria responded to her mother with uncharacteristic firmness.

"I am very fond of Eileen Heckart and I am not giving her up as a friend."

This is where Maria's stories end and mine—as told to me by Mama—begin. Under the circumstances, Dietrich must have figured, "If you can't beat 'em, join 'em," so she set about befriending the young actress. She came to see my mother in *The Dark at the Top of the Stairs* on Broadway, four times in one month. It seemed like the stage doorman was saying with such frequency, "Miss Dietrich is here again tonight," it started to make the young actress very nervous.

Whenever Dietrich came backstage, she would always ask Heckart out to supper after the show. Mama always respectfully turned her down.

"Miss Dietrich," she said, "I'm honored by your gracious invitation, but I have a husband and two small boys waiting at home. If I don't catch the 11:06 out of Grand Central, there isn't another one until the milk train at 3 AM. So, thank you very much . . . but no thank you."

As important as family was to Dietrich, her ego was large enough that she hated being turned down for supper invitations. When Marlene learned that *Dark* was about to close, she came backstage and said to Heckart, "I am about to do my nightclub act at the Desert Inn in Las Vegas. Now that the play is closing, you *will* come and spend a weekend with me there."

This wasn't a request. It was a command.

Marlene kept badgering Mama about going to Las Vegas. She wouldn't let her off the hook. It wasn't that she didn't want to go—not entirely. But she didn't want to leave my father now that she finally had a little time off, even for a weekend. Also, Heckart knew that she was dealing with a chameleon-like presence. While the weekend would be memorable, it might not be all fun and games. By now, Dietrich had called the house several times, asking Eileen to pick a date.

My father said, "Honey, will you just go spend the weekend with Dietrich in Vegas, for Chrissake? It's the only way you'll ever get her off your back!"

Mama made the flight arrangements and arrived in Vegas around 3 PM on a Friday afternoon. She took a taxi to the Desert Inn.

When she checked in, the concierge informed her, "Oh yes, Miss Heckart, Miss Dietrich has been expecting you. She's in the theater and she asked that you meet her down there after you get settled."

Heckart went up to the glorious, four-bedroom suite. Even though she still felt a twinge of trepidation, Anna Eileen from Columbus was thrilled down to her socks. She was spending the weekend with true Hollywood royalty. Since she'd had little experience with the world of nightclubs, she was delighted that Marlene had invited her to come down to the theater and sit in on her rehearsal. Heckart looked forward to seeing the consummate professional at work with her conductor and musicians, so she quickly unpacked a few things, and proceeded down to the theater as instructed.

She opened the door to the theater gingerly, not wanting to interrupt Marlene's rehearsal. She slipped inside and started up the aisle. Not a sound. "Hmm, perhaps they're on a break," she thought. By now she was practically in the center of the large auditorium and there was no sign of any activity. She heard a faint scraping sound coming from the stage. As her eyes adjusted to the darkness, my mother saw a lone figure on her hands and knees with a scrub brush and a bucket scouring every inch of the vast stage floor. The woman's hair was wrapped in a scarf and she was wearing blue jeans and a faded, flannel shirt. As Heckart approached the woman, hunched over her bucket, she gasped as she saw her face.

"Marlene?" she called out.

Looking up, the woman shouted, "Hello darling! How was your flight?"

Still in disbelief, Heckart approached Dietrich. "Marlene, what are you doing? Surely they have a cleaning crew here at the hotel!"

Returning to her bucket, Dietrich balked, "Oh these stupid people! They don't know how to *scrub*! They never get this floor clean enough. I'm going to drag fifty thousand dollars worth of costumes around this stage tonight and it's got to be spotless!"

Apparently, Marlene Dietrich did this in every theater in which she performed.

After Marlene finished her charwoman duties, they went upstairs to the suite. Once champagne had been ordered, she turned to Eileen and said, "Now, my darling, of course, tonight you will come see my show. Tomorrow night, I can get you tickets for anything else on the strip. What would like to see?"

Without hesitating, Mama asked, "Do think you could you get me in to see Sinatra?"

"Of course," Marlene said, sipping her Dom Perignon. "My publicist will take care of it."

Unless she'd been reading *Variety* every day, how could Eileen have known that Frank Sinatra was the only performer on the Vegas strip who had box-office grosses higher than Marlene Dietrich?

That night, Eileen had a ringside table for Dietrich's show. It was the first time she had ever seen the star perform live and the sheer showmanship of it all, the grand illusion of making this middle-aged lady look like a glamorous star half her age, was awe-inspiring. Eileen cried as she sang "Lili Marlene" and her other signature songs. Yes, Heckart was an actress, but Dietrich was a consummate performer. Afterwards, she was summoned backstage and rhapsodized about the performance. Champagne and caviar were flowing like swans down the Danube and Eileen felt like she had stepped into another world.

After the hordes of well-wishers and fans bearing roses had subsided, as Dietrich was snapping orders at her maid, she turned to Eileen and said, "Now, my darling, I've arranged your ticket for Sinatra for tomorrow night. You must meet my publicist at the box office tomorrow at 4 PM sharp."

"That's wonderful, Marlene," she said. "Thank you for going to such trouble."

"Nonsense," Marlene replied.

The next afternoon, Eileen arrived at the box office at 3:40, not wanting to risk losing one of the hottest tickets in town. At 4 PM sharp, she went to the box office and asked for the publicist. A portly, middle aged man came out, looking stricken.

"Miss Heckart," he said, "I'm so sorry. I told Miss Dietrich I could only hold the ticket until two o'clock!"

Eileen knew she'd been had. She started to get angry, but then thought better of it. She returned to Dietrich's suite, where the star was signing a stack of headshots. Dietrich looked up from her writing desk.

"My darling, what happened?"

"You know Marlene," she said with smile, "I gave it some thought. I don't really want to see Sinatra. I'd much rather see your show again tonight."

Diva Dietrich beamed with joy as she opened her arms to accept an embrace from her loyal subject.

☒☒☒

In 1975, I got to meet Miss Dietrich myself. I was fifteen and I read in the paper that she was going to be doing her one-woman show for a week at The Candlewood Playhouse, a summer theater about thirty minutes from our home. I showed the ad to my mother.

I said, "Mama, don't you know her?"

"I sure do, honey," she replied.

"Can we go? Please?"

"Well, she can't have too many tours left in her. It would be nice to see her onstage one last time."

She discussed it with my father and bought tickets for the entire family. The audience, full of die-hard Dietrich fans, went wild the moment the curtain rose. Even though I wasn't that impressed with what I saw, I got swept up in the frenzy. At intermission, Mama said it was very sad for her to see the way Dietrich had become a parody of herself. The emotions were forced and the vocal and physical gestures were exaggerated past the point of believability. I remember one number where Dietrich came out onstage and stumbled. It wasn't exactly a fall—she seemed to get caught up in her own feet and tripped. Pretending it was deliberate, she then did an elaborate sweep of the stage as her musical director, the talented Stan Freeman shot her a look as if to say, "What the hell are you doing?" Dietrich gave him an embarrassed smirk and went on.

I leaned over to my mother and whispered, "Mama, is she drunk?"

"She's on her ass, honey," she replied.

It seemed the more missteps Dietrich made, the more the audience cheered. Even so, when she sang "Lili Marlene," Mama wept with the rest of them. Later, when I asked her why, she said, "Because I knew this was the last time I'd ever see her perform."

After the performance, the stage door entrance was so mobbed, they had put red velvet ropes around it. We were all longing to go backstage and meet the legend, but Mama was hesitant.

"Now listen," she said, "I'll do what I can. But this lady is so temperamental, I don't even know if she'll see *me*, let alone the rest of you. It will all depend on how she felt the show went and any number of other factors. I'll go back by myself and test the waters, but I'm not promising anything."

Mama gave her name to the stage doorman. The velvet ropes were pulled back and Miss Heckart proceeded backstage.

While we waited, my mother approached the green room backstage at the Candlewood Playhouse with trepidation. She was never quite sure what she was going to get with Dietrich and she was prepared for anything.

The grand dame entered in designer jeans with a matching jacket and a peach-colored silk blouse. When she saw my mother, she opened her arms and they shared a big hug. Dietrich was delighted to see her. The first hurdle had been crossed.

"How did you happen to come tonight, my darling?" Dietrich asked.

"Well, we only live a half-hour away," Heckart replied. "Did you think you'd get this close and I wouldn't come to see you?"

"But did you come alone?" Dietrich asked.

"Well, no," Mama replied, "I'm here with my family."

"Would they like to come backstage?" Dietrich asked.

"They'd adore it," she replied.

Dietrich wheeled around to face a barrel-chested prop man carrying a Grecian urn full of fake hydrangeas.

"Get Eileen Heckart's family back here!" she shouted.

The prop man jumped back in shock. "But Miss Dietrich," he stammered, "I don't know where they are!"

"Well FIND them!" she bellowed.

The stage door flew open and the frightened man shouted outside in a panic, "Oh my God! Where's Eileen Heckart's family?"

The velvet ropes parted once again for my father and brothers and me.

We were directed to the green room and I got my first glimpse of the great star. Onstage, she had looked ageless. Up close, you could see the artifice. Her lipstick was exaggerated way beyond the line of her lips and her false eyelashes were so thick, they reminded me of crow's wings. Even so, I knew I was in the company of greatness. She was meticulously put together. One look at her jeans outfit told you these weren't Jordache specials off the rack, but a denim suit custom-made with wide lapels and a tapered waist. My brother Philip kissed Dietrich's hand when he was introduced. When I went to shake her hand, she held it the entire time she spoke to us. Her perfume was so strong, I knew you could smell it a block away. For a starstruck kid like me, this was a religious experience.

Dietrich said, "Look at my legs!" She put her foot up on a chair and hoisted up the leg of her designer jeans. "Not bad for my age, eh?"

"Those are great legs, aren't they, boys?"

We all agreed, not knowing quite how to respond.

All the way home in the car, we talked about what incredible evening it had been. For three days afterwards, my hand still smelled like Marlene Dietrich. It was the only time I ever remember thinking, "I'll never wash my hand again." I sat there in algebra class holding my hand up to my face, letting the scent of Marlene waft over me. When I needed a really good whiff, I took the hall pass to the boys' room and stood there in front of the sink smelling every inch of my left hand and envisioning that I was still in the presence of one of the greatest, most glamorous stars the world has ever known.

Drunken Diva

THE FILM VERSION OF *THE BAD SEED* WITH MAMA AND PATTY MCCORMACK. *THE BAD SEED* © WARNER BROTHERS PICTURES, INC. ALL RIGHTS RESERVED.

AFTER THE SUCCESS of *Picnic*, as Josh Logan predicted, Eileen Heckart started to get lots of other offers. One of the best ones for a new play by Maxwell Anderson called *The Bad Seed*, based on a novel by William March. Anderson was the successful playwright of such works as *Winterset* and *Mary of Scotland*. By now, he had established The Playwrights Company with Sherwood Anderson and other notable playwrights, which enabled them to produce their own work. The Playwright's Company produced *The Bad Seed*.

The story revolves around a little girl who was born evil. Ten year-old Rhoda will stop at nothing to get what she wants. Having the outward appearance of a perfect, little lady, complete with blonde braids and Mary Janes, she kills a little boy in order to get his penmanship medal, which she feels she rightfully deserved. In the mid-fifties, the concept of an innocent child as a murderer was scandalous. This was long before *The Exorcist*, *The Omen*, or other films about diabolical children. *The Bad Seed* was the first of its kind and it created a sensation.

Nancy Kelly starred as Mrs. Penmark, Rhoda's doting, well-to-do mother. Heckart played Mrs. Daigle, the alcoholic mother of the boy who is killed by Rhoda. It was a wonderfully tragic part, with two, four-minute drunk scenes. When Mrs. Daigle shows up unexpectedly at the home of Mrs. Penmark, the bereaved woman is sloppily drunk and wondering how she can go on without her only son. In a rather talky script with lots of exposition as to how a child raised with every advantage could be born evil, Heckart's two scenes of drunken grief make an indelible impression. She received tremendous critical acclaim for the play and later, she won a Golden Globe and garnered her first best supporting Oscar nomination for the film. When Katherine Hepburn came to see the play, during the curtain call, she stood up for Mama and then sat down again. Clearly, there was only one performance Miss Hepburn felt warranted a standing ovation that night.

Brooks Atkinson in the *New York Times* said, "Eileen Heckart has two brilliant scenes as the desperate mother of the boy who was drowned. Miss Heckart plays them magnificently, never losing the private agony of the mother in the rush of drunken conversation."

Every stage mother in town wanted their little girl to play Rhoda, the perfect ten-year-old murderess. Director Reginald Denham said the auditions were frightening. The pushy mothers were far worse than the little girls ever thought of being. Finally, one little girl walked in all by herself.

"Where's your mother, dear?" the director asked.

"Oh, she's outside," the girl replied. "I conduct my own interviews."

Her name was Patty McCormack. Denham was so impressed by her professional demeanor and her simple, honest talent, McCormack won the role hands down. Of course, this was all designed by her mother to make her stand out from the crowd, and it worked. Behind the scenes, Patty McCormack's stage mother was every bit as controlling as all the others—she just did it from a distance. In later years, when McCormack started to develop into a young woman, her mother kept her small, developing breasts strapped down for so long that as an adult, she had to have corrective surgery. Little Patty couldn't play the perfect little-girl parts like Rhoda in *The Bad Seed* and Helen Keller in *The Miracle Worker* with bosoms, now could she?

A wonderful character actor named Henry Jones played Leroy, the handyman who is on to Rhoda's deviousness from the beginning. In the second act, he becomes another one of her victims when she traps him in a fire and burns him alive. As an opening-night present for Mama, Jones scoured the pawnshops on the Lower East Side of Manhattan until he found a child's penmanship medal, just like the one Rhoda steals from the little boy after she drowns him. He had it engraved with the name Claude Daigle and presented it to Heckart. He thought it was hysterically funny. While she liked Henry Jones, she thought it a sick joke and in extremely bad taste.

When she started getting so much attention for *The Bad Seed*, and many critics said that Heckart's eight minutes stole the show, Nancy Kelly was not pleased.

After all, as the leading lady she practically never left the stage. It was a work-horse part, while Mama had all the sizzle. One night, during the first scene where Heckart breaks down about how much she will miss her precious son, Nancy Kelly altered her blocking and crossed upstage to the bar cart. The only way Heckart could continue to address her would be to have her back entirely to the audience for her big scene. Heckart thought, "What the hell is she doing?" In the next instant, she figured out *exactly* what Kelly was doing: taking the focus off Heckart. She thought to herself, "Well, my character is drunk—I can just as easily talk to the fourth wall." She played the rest of the scene face front, not looking at Kelly once. It was the last time she ever crossed upstage during one of Heckart's scenes.

Even though the role of Mrs. Daigle was a small but flashy part, it took its toll on my mother. My brother Mark was almost the same age as Claude Daigle, the little boy who had been killed in the play. As hard as she tried not to make the substitution, the actress started to visualize her own son's face every night as the face of her little boy who'd been drowned. She imagined the inconsolable grief of her character and probably reflected back on the loss of Michael, her own stillborn child. As a result, each day around four o'clock she started to take on the mantle of loss and depression. By the time she got to the theater each night, she was in a dark mood of mourning, with shaking hands, and a tremor in her voice when she even bothered to speak to anyone in the company.

While Eileen Heckart often relied upon substitutions in her acting as part of her technique, she was always able to use them as needed, then release them. But this was different. She had never had a role overpower her like she did in *The Bad Seed*. As Mrs. Daigle talked about the loss of her son, she said, "He was such a lovely, dear little boy. He used to call me his sweetheart and say he was going to marry me when he grew up." It seemed there was no way Mama could play this line without thinking about her six-year-old, Mark. In a sense, she was mourning the death of her own son every night. No wonder her performance was so effective. And no wonder it nearly drove her crazy.

Jack insisted she see a doctor, but he could find nothing wrong with her. Jack was deeply concerned for his wife's well-being. She tried to put on a brave face for her two small boys, but it became increasingly difficult. Finally, Eileen Heckart did something she had never done before or since. Even though she had a year's contract on *The Bad Seed*, she quit after five-and-a-half months, leaving a successful play and walking away from one the biggest hits on Broadway, where she was receiving stellar reviews and being lauded with awards. The emotional pain was simply too great.

When *The Bad Seed* was optioned as a film, the producers at Warner Brothers had the good sense to take the majority of the Broadway cast to Hollywood. Heckart was asked to re-create her role as Mrs. Daigle. While Jack was hesitant to let her tread back into such dark, emotional waters, she knew that the concentrated, piecemeal process of shooting a film would not take the same toll as having to sustain a performance for two hours every night, eight times a week.

CLARK GABLE, MAMA, AND MERVYN LEROY ON THE SET OF *THE BAD SEED*

The movie was directed by film veteran Mervyn LeRoy, the prolific director of such hits as *Little Caesar*, *Tugboat Annie*, *Thirty Seconds Over Tokyo*, and *Mister Roberts*. Mama was crazy about Mervyn. He had a direct, no-nonsense approach and he got the job done quickly. LeRoy was also the man who was credited as discovering Lana Turner, Robert Mitchum and Clark Gable. She had mentioned to Mervyn that as a young woman, Gable was her biggest Hollywood heartthrob. Gable was on the lot doing some re-takes for *The King and Four Queens*, so LeRoy made a point of having him drop by the set. Heckart went weak at the knees.

Years later, Mama said to me, "Honey, I don't think I said four words the entire time. I just sat there and drooled."

The Hayes office, the powerful film censorship board, was outraged by the original ending of *The Bad Seed*, where the saintly mother commits suicide and the bad little girl lives. While this was completely faithful to the play, evil could not triumph over good in Hollywood in the fifties. Instead, the producers gave the film a tacky, contrived ending where Rhoda gets struck by a bolt of lightning. As if that weren't enough, they followed it with a Broadway-style curtain call, where the cast comes out one at a time and is introduced. The crushing blow is that after Nancy Kelly and Patty McCormack take the final bow, Kelly grabs the little girl, takes her over her knee and spanks her, for a true slapstick ending. It mars an otherwise strong film and takes it into the realm of camp, as if it were apologizing for itself. Mama hated the new ending. "Oh my God," she said, "that new ending is so

COURTESY OF UPA

'Henrietta High School.' Why couldn't the producers trust what they had and let audiences decide for themselves? But that was Hollywood in the fifties."

Heckart's moving performance as Mrs. Daigle worked even better in close-ups. She won the Golden Globe as Best Supporting Actress and was nominated for an Academy Award in 1956. Patty McCormack was also nominated in the Supporting category, while Nancy Kelly was nominated as Best Actress. None of them won. The best supporting Oscar went to Dorothy Malone for *Written in the Wind* and Best Actress went to Ingrid Bergman for *Anastasia*. On Oscar night, some overzealous publicity person took this photo of Mama standing in front of a large Academy Award statue with her fingers crossed. She hated cheesy stuff like this, but because of the studio, she felt she had no choice but to oblige.

It would be seventeen long years before she received another Oscar nomination.

Elvis and a Six-Pack

AN EARLY FIFTIES HECKART HEADSHOT

AFTER THE SUCCESS of *The Bad Seed*, Eileen got offered a number of film roles, but all of them were alcoholics. She was afraid that if she played another drunk right away, she'd be typecast for the rest of her life. She turned down one part after another, some of them very good, but all of them boozers. Finally, there was one script that didn't involve drinking. The film was called *Hot Spell* and was to star Shirley Booth and Anthony Quinn. The script was rather a weak rehashing of *Come Back, Little Sheba*, which had brought Shirley Booth an Oscar as well as a Tony.

Hot Spell is the story of Alma, a long-suffering wife (Booth) and her rogue of a husband (Quinn) who is having an affair and ultimately leaves her. Heckart played Fan, Alma's racy, next-door neighbor who teaches her how to win back her philandering husband by smoking cigarettes, talking like a "hep cat," and swilling Coca-Cola.

Eileen Heckart idolized Shirley Booth and was humbled to be playing scenes with her. This was the Shirley Booth before TV's *Hazel*, who was a Broadway star and a respected lady of the theater.

While they were rehearsing, Eileen kept referring to her as "Miss Booth," until the down-to-earth lady said, "You can call me Shirley, you know."

"Oh no!" Heckart replied, "I couldn't possibly!"

The film was directed by Daniel Mann, an old buddy of Heckart's who had directed her in several television shows. She told him that she had been offered nothing but alcoholic roles for the past six months and how happy she was to be working with him again.

"Hollywood can be so small-minded," Mann scoffed, shaking his head.

When the time came to shoot the scene where Fan teaches Alma how to swill a Coke and French inhale a cigarette, Daniel Mann said, "Darling, the producers want us to change this scene just a little. Instead of a six-pack of Coke, you're going to carry in a six-pack of beer."

Heckart froze. "No, I'm not," she said.

"Excuse me?" the director said.

"The contract I signed says I carry on a six-pack of Coke and that's what it's going to be!" she said.

Everyone on the set stopped in their tracks.

"Eileen, darling, what seems to be the problem?"

"Danny," she said, "I thought you knew exactly what the problem was, but obviously I was mistaken. I will *not* play a drunk in this film."

"Not, a drunk, Eileen," he said. "A drinker!"

"It's the same thing," she replied. "So, you work this out with management and I'll be in my trailer when you're ready for me."

With that, she left the set. Heckart sat in her trailer reading back issues of the *Hollywood Reporter*, which she had arranged to have delivered to her dressing room door every morning. So she sat. And sat. And read. And read—for three days. She figured they had changed the shooting schedule and didn't need her or had gotten delayed. She had no idea that behind the scenes, a huge battle was ensuing between her agent, the director, and Hal Wallis, the powerful head of production at Paramount.

Every now and then, the assistant director would come to my mother's dressing room and say, "Um . . . pardon me, Eileen. Would you agree to shoot the scene with beer if—"

"No honey," she'd say, barely looking up from her *Hollywood Reporter*. "The contract I signed made no mention of alcohol. That's why I took the part. I'm sorry, but I just cannot agree."

Later, Mama's agent told her that Hal Wallis screamed at him on the phone, "You cannot *have* Eileen Heckart in a picture without alcohol! It's what everyone *expects*, for Chrissake!"

Meanwhile, the actress at the eye of the storm sat in her trailer waiting to shoot her scene.

After three days, she was called to the set. Daniel Mann said, "Okay, Heckart. You win. Coca-Cola it is. But please don't ever put me through anything like that again."

"Like what, Danny?" she asked, completely unaware of the trouble she'd caused.

"Do you have any idea how I've been fighting for you for the past three days?" he said. "You damn near lost the part! If we weren't already behind schedule, Hal Wallis would have fired your ass!"

The irony is that while Mama was sitting there saying, "Not in the contract I signed," she had never actually signed one. There had been some mistake in the contracts office at Paramount and it had never been executed. Hal Wallis could have fired her at any time with no contractual obligation. But Heckart stood her ground and swilled Coca-Cola instead of beer.

Shortly after the Hal Wallis alcohol incident was resolved, she realized she was no longer getting her daily copy of the *Hollywood Reporter* on her doorstep. Since she was still getting billed for it, Heckart inquired at the studio mailroom. Yes, she was told, they had continued to deliver it. Something was wrong. After she hadn't received it for four or five days, one morning, as she was approaching her dressing room, she saw a burly, middle-aged man with a thick neck pick up the copy of the *Reporter* from her doorstep and saunter across the lot.

"Hey!" she shouted, "That's my magazine!" The husky man started running. Heckart followed him. He ran faster. She made a beeline down an alley to head him off at the pass, but then she saw him disappear into a bungalow. Outraged, she rapped on the door. The door flew open and she found herself standing nose to nose with Elvis Presley.

Every time my mother watched Elvis on television, she went gaga. She'd snap her fingers and sing along to "Hound Dog" or "Jailhouse Rock" and stare at the television in a daze.

"Isn't he the most adorable thing you've ever seen?" she'd say, sounding like a sixteen-year-old bobbysoxer. Elvis had just starting shooting on *King Creole* for Paramount and his bungalow wasn't far from Heckart's dressing room. She kept hoping she would run into him and now she was accusing his henchman of stealing her *Hollywood Reporter.*

"What seems to be the trouble, ma'am?" Presley said. "Is there a fire?" He flashed his megawatt smile and Heckart went weak in the knees.

"I . . . he . . . my . . . paper . . ."

She felt like the village idiot.

Elvis walked over to the coffee table where the large gentleman with the thick neck must have tossed the paper as he ran into the back room. He handed it to Mama.

"Is this what you're looking for, ma'am?" he asked.

"Thank you," she stammered, still transfixed.

"Ma'am, would you like to see my new car?" he asked.

"I'd love to," she said.

Presley led her out through the back of the bungalow where a shiny, cream-colored Cadillac was parked. After they walked around the car once, he opened the back door for her.

"I'm afraid you're going to have to take off your shoes before you step inside," he said. She kicked off her flats and he removed his loafers. My mother was always loyal to my father, but in that instant, I think Elvis could have asked her to take off whatever he wanted.

The car had ermine rugs on the floor, white leather seats and was appointed with a bar on one side and a dressing table on the other. Elvis was like a little boy showing off the bicycle he'd gotten from Santa. He pointed out all the special features of the car and showed her how the bar opened and the hidden switch for the vanity lights on the dressing table.

Once the tour was complete, he said, "Well ma'am, I guess we'd better get to work. I'm sorry about the confusion with your magazine. It won't happen again. You have a good day now."

He escorted her out of the car and around to the side of the bungalow. Anna Eileen from Columbus had renewed her faith in the magic of Hollywood.

Correcting Arthur Miller

GLORIA MARLOWE, VAN HEFLIN, AND MAMA IN *A VIEW FROM THE BRIDGE*. PHOTO BY
FRED FEHL, WITH PERMISSION OF GABRIEL PINSKI

In 1955, Mama was cast as Beatrice, the long-suffering Italian wife of a long-shoreman in the original Broadway production of Arthur Miller's *A View from the Bridge*. This play was originally two one-acts entitled *A Memory of Two Mondays* and *A View from the Bridge*. After this initial mounting, Miller re-worked the piece which was to become one of the modern classics of American Drama. After his tremendous success with *Death of a Salesman, All My Sons* and *The Crucible*, Arthur Miller was the preeminent American playwright of his day and Heckart was thrilled to be working with him. She found Miller to be a quiet man, placid and somewhat of a loner, but very much a gentleman.

A View from the Bridge is the story of Eddie Carbone, a gruff longshoreman, whose home is disrupted by two visiting relatives from Italy. One of them wants to marry his precious kid sister. Eddie is torn between wanting what is best for his sister and wanting to see her happy. One of the subplots revolves around his wife, Beatrice, with whom he has not had sexual relations in years. As Beatrice, the wife of Eddie Carbone (played by Van Heflin), Heckart never felt very secure in her Italian accent.

She said, "I sound about as Italian as Mickey Rooney."

Nonetheless, she felt the script was very strong and she had a good working relationship with the director, Martin Ritt. Ritt had started out as an actor and stage manager in such plays as *Golden Boy* and had gone on to direct a number of Broadway successes, including Clifford Odets' *The Flowering Peach*. A few years after *A View from the Bridge*. Ritt was destined for Hollywood, where he would become the director of such legendary films as *The Long Hot Summer*, *Hud*, and *Norma Rae*.

During rehearsals, there was a line that didn't ring true for Heckart. She discussed it with her director.

"Marty," she said, "I just don't think Beatrice would say something like this."

Martin Ritt agreed, but said he relied upon her talent to make it work. That wasn't the answer the actress wanted to hear.

"Arthur is here today," she said. "Will you ask him to change the line?"

Ritt looked stricken. "I can't ask Arthur Miller to change a line!"

"Why not?" she asked.

"Well . . . he's Arthur Miller!"

"What the hell does that mean? He's the playwright, for God's sake! If you won't ask him, then I will!"

Heckart marched to the back of the theater where Mr. Miller was chewing on his pencil and listening to the scene being rehearsed. Halfway up the aisle, her bravado left her.

"Oh God," she thought, "what if Marty's right? Arthur is such a quiet, sensitive man. What if I'm doing a terrible thing and I'm about to offend this important playwright?"

It was too late to back out now. She approached Arthur Miller, who smiled at her.

"Excuse me, Arthur," she said, "May I speak to you?"

Miller removed his notebook and script from the seat next to him and motioned for her to sit down.

"Well . . . um . . . it's about this line on page forty-three. You see . . . well . . . I just don't think Beatrice would say this."

Miller was taken aback by the statement, not accustomed to having people question his dramatic authority.

"Well, show me the line," he said.

The nervous actress opened her script to the folded page and placed it in the lap of the great American playwright. He read the entire page to get the proper context, teething his pencil the entire time. Removing the pencil from his mouth, he looked up at Eileen.

"Fine. What would you like to say instead?"

They agreed upon a suitable line and she walked away, totally satisfied. That moment for her affirmed the greatness of Arthur Miller. He had the sense to know that an actress playing one of his characters would have gotten inside the psyche of the character deeper than he had as the playwright. She wanted a new line and he was more than happy to give it to her. This story was one of Mama's favorite examples of the collaborative process of the theater.

Kazan, Inge, and "Old Archie"

MAMA AS LOTTIE LACEY IN *THE DARK AT THE TOP OF THE STAIRS*.
© BILLY ROSE THEATRE COLLECTION , THE NEW YORK PUBLIC LIBRARY
FOR THE PERFORMING ARTS—ASTOR, LENOX, AND TILDEN FOUNDATIONS

WILLIAM INGE was eager to work with Eileen Heckart again after her success
in *Picnic*, so he was very happy to have her play Lottie Lacey, the brash, wisecracking "Mother Earth" character in his new play, *The Dark at the Top of the Stairs*.
Dark was another memory play for Inge, based on his own unhappy childhood
in rural Kansas. The play centers around Cora, a fragile, young mother whose
husband walks out on her, leaving her to fend for herself and her two young children, not knowing if he will ever return. She confides in her sister, Lottie, who
gives the appearance of being a pillar of strength. When the two sisters share

a moment alone, Lottie confesses that her own husband has not been intimate with her in many years. He gives the appearance of being a good provider, but he is cold and distant with his wife. The leads in the play were Teresa Wright as the wife and Pat Hingle as her drifter husband. Mama forged lifelong friendships with both of them.

The director of *Dark* was one of the hottest directors in the American theater, Elia Kazan. Having directed such powerful plays as *A Streetcar Named Desire* and films like *On the Waterfront*, Mama was thrilled to be in such esteemed company. The quality in Kazan that impressed her most was his inventiveness.

"For every idea I had," she said, "he had five more."

During rehearsals, "Gadg" as his intimates called him (short for "Gadget," due to his love for props and set dressing), had weekly private, half-hour sessions with each actor to discuss character, motivation, and to explore new depths within each role.

"We all lived for those weekly sessions," Mama said. "It was the most exciting time of my life professionally and Kazan was the best director I ever worked with."

For whatever reason, Eileen Heckart became the "mother confessor" to the rest of the cast of *The Dark at the Top of the Stairs*. Perhaps it was due to the nature of the role she was playing (a good-hearted busybody), perhaps it was just her demeanor. Everyone came to her with their problems. Whether it was Timmy Everett talking about his troubled love life or Teresa Wright feeling overwhelmed by doing eight shows a week while trying to spend time with her daughter at Christmas, Eileen seemed to take on everyone else's baggage, while commuting to Connecticut on the train every night to Jack and her own two small boys.

During final rehearsals, Teresa Wright came to Eileen in tears. "Terry, what's the matter?" she asked.

"Oh, Heckie," she said in great distress, "I'm so upset about the curtain call. Gadg has Pat Hingle entering with me and leading me downstage, so I don't even get a solo bow!"

"I'll talk to him, Terry," she said.

The next night, Mama came in early on the train and made a point of going to Kazan before the preview performance.

"Gadg," she said, "Terry is really upset about the way you've staged the curtain call. I mean, she *is* the lead and she's not even getting a solo bow."

Kazan looked at her with annoyance. "I thought she was a friend of yours," he said.

"Well, she is, Gadg. That's why I'm speaking to you."

"So then why are you trying to sabotage her?" he asked.

"What do you mean?"

"Terry has the workhorse part. Pat Hingle comes on at the top of the play and the end in a very flashy part and is talked about throughout. Of course he's going to get a bigger hand. It's not because he's better. It's the way the role is written. So, do *you* want the applause to soar for Pat Hingle and dip for Teresa Wright? That's what'll happen if I give her a solo bow. Do you want to have to stand there onstage for eight shows a week and listen to that happen to your friend? It'll break her heart. Do you want that on your conscience? I sure as hell don't want it on mine!"

Mama knew Kazan was absolutely right, but she knew she couldn't tell Teresa Wright the real reason.

"I'm sorry, Terry" she said, "But Kazan said no."

Teresa was crushed and I don't know that she ever knew the real reason. She probably thought Kazan didn't feel she was worthy of it, which might have been worse. Her director was actually protecting her, but he didn't know how to tell her without making it seem like he was diminishing her talent.

The Dark at the Top of the Stairs was hugely successful and resulted in a Tony nomination for Mama. It became one of the hottest tickets in New York during the 1957 Broadway season.

John Chapman in the *New York Daily News* said, "There is a grand performance by Eileen Heckart as a woman who must remain a stranger to her husband—an expertly shaded performance which ranges from broad humor to pitiable loneliness."*

John McClain in the *New York Journal American* said, "Miss Heckart revels in the most rewarding role of her career. She is merely magnificent."

Kazan came back often and gave wonderful notes to the cast. One night, when Mama was getting ready to make her first entrance, she saw a distinguished looking older gentleman sitting onstage in the wings. She passed Kazan in the hallway and said, "Who *is* that?"

"Oh, don't worry about him," Kazan said. "That's just old Archie."

"Well tell 'old Archie' to get his ass off the stage!" she said.

Kazan laughed it off and went out the stage door. During her scenes in the first act, Mama watched the older gentleman in the wings as he laughed, reacted to the play, and had a perfectly grand time—in full view of the first five rows of the orchestra at the Music Box Theatre. It was incredibly distracting to all of the actors onstage, obviously throwing Teresa Wright and affecting her concentration. As she came off at the end of Act One, Heckart turned to the stage manager.

"What is he doing there?" she asked. "Did you see what it was doing to poor Terry out there?"

"Sorry, Miss Heckart," the stage manager replied, "But Mr. Kazan said it was okay."

"Well, to hell with Mr. Kazan!" she snapped. "He doesn't have to perform with some goon staring at him four feet away!"

Heckart marched up to the old man.

"Listen, your name is Archie?" she said.

"Yes," he said, beaming. "I think you're just wonderful!"

"Thanks, Archie. Look, I know you're a friend of Gadg's but you're sitting on the stage. The audience can see you!"

"He tried to get me a ticket," he explained, "but the show is sold out—and I can see why, it's so wonderful." He ran his fingers along his striped bow tie.

* *New York Daily News, L.P.* Reprinted with permission.

"Look, Archie," she said, "You've gotta go. It's nothing personal, but it's really affecting Miss Wright's concentration. Besides, I don't let anyone sit on my stage!"

"But I'll be just as quiet as a mouse for the next two acts!"

"That's not the point, Archie," she said. "Nobody sits on my stage. Now I'm sorry, but I don't want to see you there when the second act starts."

Archie picked up his program and shuffled out.

The next day, Mama could barely get into the green room. There was one of the largest floral arrangements she'd ever seen in her life. The huge basket of daisies, tulips, ivy, and snapdragons held a note which read:

Dear Miss Wright
Dear Miss Heckart:
  The flowers convey only admiration. The contrition is to be spelled out. I have
  only two excuses but they are complete—yourselves.
Forgive me,
Archibald MacLeish*

That night, she went home and said, "Jack, who is Archibald MacLeish?"

Jack laughed and shook his head. "He's only the Poet Laureate of America," he said. "Why do you ask?"

She proceeded to tell her husband the whole story about Kazan and Old Archie. He was horrified.

"Honey," Jack said, "Please tell me this didn't happen. Tell me you didn't throw Archibald MacLeish, one of the greatest literary giants of the twentieth century, *out* of the theater last night."

"Well, he was *sitting* on the *stage*, Jack!"

"I don't care if he took a dump in the middle of the orchestra!" Jack said. "You don't behave that way to one of the most important figures in contemporary American culture!"

Another time while she was performing in Philadelphia, she received a note saying "The Mellon family requests the pleasure of your company on their yacht this weekend." Never having heard of them, she threw the invitation away. Later, she said to my father, "Somebody named Mellon invited me out on a yacht."

"Oh my God!" my father said, "One of the richest, most important families in America. I hope you went."

"I most certainly did not!" she said. "I'd never heard of them. I wasn't going out on some stranger's boat on my only day off."

"Honey," Jack said. "You need to get out more."

Later in life, Mama was extremely well-read and politically aware. It's hard to think of her as ever being that naïve. Maybe Old Archie and the Mellons shook her up to the point where she started reading more.

---

* Courtesy of William MacLiesh. Reprinted with permission.

There was another incident where someone in the audience ruined her concentration during *Dark*, but she couldn't throw him out of the theater. The second act (the one Archibald MacLeish never got to see) opened with Mama as Lottie sitting at the piano singing and playing "When You're Smiling." There was a member of the Broadway Musicians Local in the wings doing the actual piano playing. One night, Jack brought five-year-old Mark and three-year-old Philip in to see the play.

As the second act began, Mama heard a tiny voice down front say, "She doesn't play!"

Her concentration was totally blown. Her hands flew off the keys and she went south on the lyrics.

From the mouths of babes . . .

Playing Catch with Marilyn Monroe

PHILIP, MARILYN MONROE, MAMA, AND MARK ON THE SET OF *BUS STOP*

MAMA WORKED with a lot of big stars over the years, but none bigger than Marilyn Monroe. Whenever anyone asked, "Eileen, what was it like working with Marilyn?" she would give two very different responses. The first was dismissive. With a wave of her hand, she'd say, "My God, she was so undisciplined. She was a star, not an actress!" She'd speak of a woman who was moody, making people wait for hours on end, and with the potential to be extremely vindictive to anyone who had crossed her on her rise to stardom.

Then there was the other response. Mama would get a wistful, faraway look in her eye. In a soft, maternal voice, she'd say, "What a sad, lonely young lady. She was adored by millions, but never believed that she was loved." At this point, Mama always got an expression on her face that said, "Don't make me go on, or I'm going to cry." For the rest of her life, whenever she spoke of Marilyn Monroe in this way, tears would stream down her face. I can't think of anyone else in the world who had that effect on my mother. As a child, it fascinated and frightened me. Who was this movie star who could make Mama cry like that? It wasn't anyone with whom she kept in touch and they hadn't remained friendly after they had finished working together. The pictures of her holding my brothers were all over the house. What was it about this blond lady with the nice legs that was so special?

By the late fifties, Eileen Heckart was closely associated with the works of William Inge. She'd made her mark in *Picnic* and received a Tony nomination as Best Supporting Actress for *The Dark at the Top of the Stairs*. In 1956, when the time came to do the film version of *Bus Stop*, his latest hit, the role of Vera (which didn't exist in the play) was written with Mama in mind. Inge wrote the first draft of the screenplay, which was then adapted by George Axelrod, who had written *The Seven Year Itch* with Billy Wilder for Marilyn. Joshua Logan was at the helm, and had directed Mama in *Picnic* a few years earlier.

Bus Stop is a sweet, simple story about a rancher named Bo Decker (played by Don Murray), who falls in love with Cherie (played by Marilyn), a third-rate nightclub chanteuse with delusions of stardom. Bo tries to persuade her to give up her singing career and move to his ranch in Montana to be his wife. Vera is the waitress in the club where Cherie performs. She is Cherie's best friend and confidante, so Mama was featured in the first half of the film. She and Marilyn had many scenes together and spent a lot of time hanging out on the set.

Show business can create strange relationships. In real life, Marilyn Monroe and Eileen Heckart were as different as night and day. They probably never would have become friends. But for all their differences they really bonded during this time together. I think Mama was able to see through Marilyn's pretense and sensed the frightened, little girl under the mask of mega-stardom.

Marilyn's behavior could be extremely unprofessional—coming to the set late, not knowing her lines, and then trying to blame others for the fact that she hadn't studied her script. She was always distracted by the fear that another starlet on the way up would dethrone her. Marilyn was a "method" actress and studied at the Actors Studio under Lee Strasberg. When Mama was starting out, she was flunked by the Actors Studio. The reason given: "insufficient talent."

"Can you *believe* that?" she said. "It wasn't for a part—they wouldn't even let me *study* there, for Chrissake!"

Paula Strasberg was one of Marilyn's mentors and was paid a tidy sum to be Marilyn's personal acting coach on the set of *Bus Stop*. One of Paula's jobs was to bolster Marilyn's fragile ego. Laurence Olivier told a story in his biography about

Paula and Marilyn on the set of *The Prince and the Showgirl*, her next film after *Bus Stop*, in which he also starred. While they were riding to the film location, Paula would whisper into Marilyn's ear, "Marilyn you are the greatest star that has lived. You are more famous than Jesus Christ." Olivier was appalled.

True to Strasberg's method, during the shooting of *Bus Stop* Marilyn spoke at all times with the hillbilly accent she used in the film. I'm not certain if her goal was to stay in character or that she was afraid that if she didn't cling to it with all her might, she might lose it.

There was an assistant director on the film with whom Marilyn had worked many years before. On the first day of shooting, he approached Marilyn just after the read-through. Mama was sitting right next to Marilyn and heard the whole exchange. He introduced himself as the one who would be responsible for getting her to the set on time. Marilyn put down her script and studied his face.

"Don't ah know yew?" she said in her heavy, Oakie drawl.

"Well yes, Miss Monroe," he said, pleased to be remembered. "We worked together on *All About Eve*."

"Uh hunh," she murmured. "Ah remembuh now." She stood and faced him. "Daaaawwwlin," Marilyn crooned, "We've known each other foah a laaawng time. When I was a bit playuh on that film, you were just as nasty as a snake to lil' ol' me. Well, sugah, things have changed. I'm in charge now. So, every time you come to mah trailer to give me mah call, you're gonna have to stand on yoah tippy toes."

The assistant director laughed it off and walked away. Two hours later, he knocked on the door of Marilyn's trailer. Mama, on her way to the set herself, overheard the exchange.

"They're ready for you on the set, Miss Monroe."

Marilyn sat at her dressing table with her blouse unbuttoned. The AD knew better than to avert his eyes—it was Marilyn's constant state in her dressing room. In fact, this was considered modest for Marilyn. She looked at him in the lighted makeup mirror as those infamously beautiful breasts heaved up and down. Not only did she make no effort to hurry, she started putting on her lipstick more slowly. She stared at the reflection of her prey in the glass, framed by fifteen incandescent bulbs. When Marilyn spoke, drawl or not, her tones were slow and measured.

"You heard me, daaaawwwwlin. On your tippy toes, or I ain't movin'."

They stared at each other for what seemed like an eternity while Marilyn fondled her tube of Max Factor Midnight Poppy lipstick. The fuming assistant director pointed his feet and stood on his toes. As his height increased by several inches, Marilyn broke into a sweet smile.

"That's better, sugah," she said in a whisper. "Now, say it again."

Through clenched teeth and even tighter fists, the assistant director hissed, "Places, Miss Monroe."

Beaming with a victor's pride, Marilyn buttoned her blouse, slipped into her four-inch black pumps, and strode out of the dressing room, the assistant director following a few steps behind. She made him do this every day for the entire shoot of *Bus Stop*.

Mama said she'd never seen anyone go through a photographer's proof sheet with more speed and dexterity than Marilyn Monroe. She would sit in her trailer with a grease pencil and mark two hundred photos in about a minute—and she was always right. Marilyn knew the camera better than anyone—and she knew every contour and angle of her own face.

One day, there were lots of entertainment reporters and gossip columnists on the set. As a result, Marilyn hadn't even looked at her dialogue for that morning's scene. Director Joshua Logan was shooting a scene with Mama, Arthur O'Connell as Virgil (the fatherly, older rancher), and Marilyn. Arthur had six lines in the scene, Mama had four lines and Marilyn had only two. They wound up having to shoot the scene thirty-seven times because Marilyn didn't know her two lines.

For the first three or four takes, Marilyn was apologetic and made a joke of it. She'd shrug her shoulders, titter and say, "I'm such a silly, ole ninny!" Since time and money are precious commodities on a film set, after a few more takes, the tension began to increase. Eventually, Marilyn needed a scapegoat. First she'd start on the makeup man. "Mah nose is shiny!" A willing participant rushed in and powdered Miss Monroe. Three or four takes later, it would be, "Mah curls are gone! How can I act when mah hair has fallen?" The on-set hairdresser rushed in with bobby pins and styling gel for Miss Monroe. A few takes later, it would be the continuity supervisor, the prop man, and on down the production chain— anything other than shouldering the responsibility herself.

Bus Stop was shot on location in Phoenix. There were many crowd scenes, especially at the rodeo where Vera and Cherie were in the stands together watching Bo compete. The extras were ecstatic to be sharing the same air with the sexiest, most glamorous movie star in the world. At the end of a long day of crowd shooting, everyone was tired and restless. Sweaty and exhausted, Mama and Marilyn started to head back to their trailers. As they walked, extras and locals who had been sitting in the rodeo stands all day started asking Marilyn for autographs and to pose for pictures. "Hey Marilyn!" one of them shouted. "Look over here!" Marilyn paused momentarily to indulge them and kept walking. And then a few more. And more still. With each request, those in the ever-growing crowd who felt they weren't getting their fair share started to get hostile.

"Hey, wait a minute!" a young woman shouted, "I didn't get a picture!"

Then a large man protested, "How come you signed *his* book and not *mine!*" Mama had never witnessed an angry mob before and it scared her.

Marilyn gave the appearance of total calm and never stopped walking. Finally, in an edgy whisper, she said to Mama, "Whatever happens, just stay beside me." She picked up her pace, scribbling autographs to as many of the outstretched arms as she could reach while she kept moving. Walking and signing, signing and walking, with ever increasing velocity. Through her panic, Mama thought, "How can Marilyn move that fast in four-inch heels?" She also wondered why there didn't seem to be a cop or a security guard in sight. By this point, the malevolent crowd was screaming, shoving and closing in on them. Marilyn grabbed Mama's arm and dragged her the last twenty feet to the trailer. Once they escaped inside, Marilyn locked the door and threw her body against it as the belligerent hoards pounded on the walls, practically overturning the Winnebago. Mama looked at Marilyn with panic. It was one of the most terrifying moments of my mother's life.

Mama's other set of Marilyn stories were about the vulnerable child in a woman's body who never believed she was loved. She was so afraid of disapproval, she sought adulation at all times. One day in between takes at the rodeo, Marilyn started talking about the many foster families who took her in when she was a child. She was bounced around to many different homes, and no one family ever kept her very long.

For once, she spoke without her Okie accent. As Marilyn looked at Mama with sadness and longing, she said, "I remember this one older couple . . . I really think they wanted to keep me. But they were already in their sixties and felt they were too old to have a small child. Oh, they were such sweet people. When they sent me back to the orphanage, they gave me a little straw hat and a matching straw suit-case. They were the nicest presents anyone ever gave me. I carried those with me for as long as I could. I really think that old couple may have loved me."

For the next forty-five years, every time Mama told this story, she would well up with tears and stifle the sobs that choked in her throat.

Marilyn adored children. She was desperate to have a baby herself. My two older brothers, Mark and Philip, went to Phoenix and spent time on the set. Mark was recovering from a bout of meningitis he'd gotten earlier that year. The doctor thought the dry, desert air would be good for him, so Mama packed up Nanny and the boys and off they went to Arizona.

Marilyn was crazy about my brothers. She loved to play a little game with them at night. Marilyn was constantly receiving elaborate gift baskets from agents, publicists, and studio types trying to gain her favor. After a long day of shooting, she removed the grapefruits and oranges from the baskets and went out onto her balcony.

She'd call down below, "Mark! Philip!"

Four-year-old Mark raced out onto the balcony with two-year-old Philip tottering close behind. They looked up at the pretty blond lady on the tiered balcony above.

"Wanna play a little catch?" Marilyn asked.

"Okay!" Mark would reply. And so began the nightly ritual of Marilyn Monroe playing ball with my brothers on the terrace, using grapefruits and oranges as their only sports equipment. First, Marilyn threw a grapefruit. Mark caught it with pride. Next, an orange to Philip. Of course at two, he couldn't catch anything, so the fruit rolled onto the balcony below and off the edge to the pool deck, five flights down.

"Marilyn," Mama would say, "It's very sweet of you to do this, but really, you don't have to."

"Are you kidding?" Marilyn replied. "It's my favorite part of the day! Besides, Vitamin C is very important for growing boys. They have to have their citrus!"

After a few days of this game, during her nightly phone call to my father in Connecticut, Mama remarked, "Oh, sure, Marilyn's playing catch with the boys on the terrace again. They're having the time of their lives. And guess who's gonna have her raggedy ass down at the pool at two in the morning picking up all those goddamn grapefruits and oranges? It ain't Miss Monroe, that's for sure!"

For all her foibles, Mama really loved Marilyn Monroe and saw how insecure and delicate she was. At the time of Marilyn's death, there was a piece in the *New York Times* stating that Eileen Heckart felt Miss Monroe was unprofessional and undisciplined. Mama was furious this was printed out of context. Had she said it? Probably. But she had also made many caring remarks about Marilyn. It was the only time in her life that Mama called the editor of the *Times* and demanded a retraction. They printed one a few days later, but the damage had already been done.

Years later, I was asked to attend a meeting of the Los Angeles chapter of the Marilyn Monroe Fan Club. Even after more than forty years, some die-hard Monroe fans were still really cross with Mama for these comments. I tried to tell her side of the story, but they weren't interested

Marilyn's death at the age of thirty-six helped insure her iconic status. More than forty years after her passing, she remains one of the most famous movie stars in the world. Mama got to see a side of her that not many people experienced— the insecure, vulnerable woman who desperately wanted a child. She witnessed the dichotomy between the movie star and the woman and what pain this obviously caused her. Marilyn Monroe seemed to want the security and stability that Eileen Heckart had, yet she seemed ensnared by the trappings of her own fame. I wonder if this is what made my mother cry so often when she spoke of her. I guess I'll never know for sure.

Birdcalls and Baby Brushes

MARGARET O'BRIEN, MAMA, AND SOPHIA LOREN ON THE SET OF
HELLER IN PINK TIGHTS

IN 1959, Mama did a Western called *Heller in Pink Tights.* It wasn't the greatest script, but the cast was very strong, with Sophia Loren, Anthony Quinn and Margaret O'Brien in the leading roles. Besides that, Heckart relished the opportunity to work with the legendary George Cukor.

Cukor was the original director on *Gone With the Wind*, served as a consultant on *The Wizard of Oz*, and directed *Camille* with Greta Garbo, *The Women*, *The Philadelphia Story* and a number of the classic Tracy/Hepburn comedies. He was one of the Hollywood greats, not to mention one of the best directors for women. Cukor had an incredible visual sense. In fact, *Heller in Pink Tights* is rather like marzipan—glorious to look at, but of no real substance. The great Italian producer Carlo Ponti packaged the film, based on a novel by Louis L'Amour, as a vehicle for his wife, Sophia Loren, in conjunction with Paramount.

Heller in Pink Tights is the story of a theatrical troupe touring the Wild West. Sophia Loren plays the troupe's leading lady, Anthony Quinn is the actor-manager, Margaret O'Brien plays the ingénue and Mama is the character woman (surprise, surprise). A handsome rogue of a gunslinger and gambler (played by Steve Forrest) gets into a poker game with Loren. Each thinks they are the better bluffer and when Sophia runs out of money, she bets herself. Of course, she is no match for the gunslinger. The rest of the film revolves around the theatrical troupe going on the lam from the man who is trying to collect on his bet.

Cukor had never done a Western and had always been intrigued by the notion of old-time theatrical troupes. He fell in love with the idea of a bunch of Indians getting their hands on a trunk full of old theater costumes and props and treating the tattered top hats and yellowed corsets like the treasure of Sierra Madre. He shared this idea with his longtime friend and design consultant, George Hoyningen-Heune, who took the concept and ran with it. Cukor himself said later that there was never much of a story, but the subject interested him. Unfortunately, the gorgeous images never made up for the lack of a script.

My mother really wanted to do this film. Lorna, the nineteenth century variation on the pushy stage mother, was a delicious role. There was, however, one tiny complication . . . me. Mama was two months pregnant and would be four to five months pregnant by the time they finished shooting. Since she was slim and hadn't shown much during her other pregnancies, she didn't think it would be a problem for her to fit into a corset, but she was a little concerned about all the scenes on horseback. Still, she was determined. And when Mama was determined to do something, there was no stopping her.

Sophia Loren is a blonde in this film, probably for no other reason than blondes were considered exotic in the Wild West. With her beautiful olive skin, she looks pretty silly in a big, flaxen wig. Margaret O'Brien at twentysomething was playing the aging juvenile in the troupe. A sterling child performer in such films as *Meet Me in St. Louis* and *The Canterville Ghost,* she was now trying to find her footing in Hollywood as a grown-up actress. In an interview about the film, Cukor said, "Margaret O'Brien is a real movie actress. She looks at dead bodies and you know they're dead, she feels cold and makes you feel the cold."

During the filming of *Heller,* Sophia and Margaret got very chummy and would spend a lot of time in Sophia's trailer exchanging beauty tips. One of the secrets that Loren divulged to the ingénue was that her stunning, almond-shaped eyes were enhanced. Sophia would purchase special, transparent tapes she had flown in from Sweden. She would attach them to the corners of her eyes. If she pulled the tapes taut, they became transparent. They helped avoid crow's feet and laugh lines, and accentuated her already stunning movie-star eyes. Margaret O'Brien was fascinated by this.

One day, Mama had a full morning of location shooting with O'Brien. She sensed something different about the ingénue, but couldn't figure out what it was. Two days later, Cukor was summoned to the editing room. Soon afterward, he returned to the set, ranting and raving.

"George," Heckart asked, "what's the matter?"

The enraged Cukor, happy to have an audience, bellowed, "Remember all that gorgeous location shooting we did on Tuesday? We have to reshoot the whole goddamn morning because Margaret O'Brien looks Chinese!"

The director hadn't noticed what his cinematographer had spotted. Margaret O'Brien had gotten hold of Sophia Loren's beauty tapes and had pulled them too tight. Hearing the commotion, Sophia Loren patted the director's arm.

"I'll take care of it, George," she said.

Sophia went over to O'Brien, waiting for her next shot, completely unaware that she has caused any consternation.

Sophia took the young woman's face in her hands and cooed, "How are you today, my darling?"

While the Italian star was caressing O'Brien's face, her thumbs moved along the young woman's temples. Feeling the tapes, Sophia led O'Brien by the hand and said, "Maggie dear, would you step into my trailer for a minute, please?"

Once alone, Loren was able to remove the tapes without embarrassment and everything was fine. Due to natural lighting, budgeting, and schedules, Cukor was unable to re-shoot any of O'Brien's scenes. If you are ever able to watch this movie, look closely at Margaret O'Brien's eyes. For three-quarters of the film, she looks perfectly normal, but in the last quarter, she looks a little like Madame Chiang Kai Shek.

Mama seemed to be of two minds about Sophia Loren. She admired this woman as the talented, sultry, screen siren that she was, but Heckart was never quite sure where she stood with her. At one end of the spectrum, whenever Loren and Anthony Quinn were together, they spoke in Italian, to the total exclusion of everyone else. Heckart found this extremely rude, especially since there were times she was convinced that the two stars were talking about her.

On the other hand, when my father and my seven-year-old brother Mark were visiting the set, Loren became the good, Italian earth mother. She said to the little boy, "Mark, would you like to sit on my lap while Mommy is shooting her scene?"

The happy child crawled into Sophia's lap, nuzzling his head between her breasts. Jack Yankee glanced over at his child with more than a twinge of envy. Sophia, catching his eye, looked down at Mark's head, turned to my father, and said, "There's nothing wrong with *this* one!"

It was the rainy season and flash floods hit the Arizona desert. Day after day shooting had to be postponed. The "suits" in the head office at Paramount were getting nervous. If they hadn't had half the film in the can already, the studio would have pulled the plug. George Cukor was scowling at the clouds, sitting on a wraparound porch at their rustic lodge of a hotel. Heckart had been waiting for days to ask him a question about the script and she figured there was no such thing as a good time anymore, so she plunged in.

"Excuse me, George," she said. "May I ask you a question?"

"What do you want?" he snapped. "We're four days behind schedule because of the weather. Paramount is ready to crucify me!"

Heckart took a deep breath and went for it.

"Well, George," she continued, "there is a reference in the script to my character doing birdcalls, and I was wondering . . ."

Cukor cut her off with no decorum.

"Oh for God's sake!" he barked. "Birdcalls? As if I haven't got enough troubles, you're talking to me about *birdcalls*?!"

He turned his back and walked away. On most days, Heckart had a great relationship with her director, so she chose not to take it personally and chalked it off to poor timing.

The next day, to everyone's relief, they were able to resume shooting on *Heller in Pink Tights*. About three days later, a peculiar little woman approached my mother on the set.

"Excuse me," the diminutive, soft-spoken woman said, "But, are you Miss Heckart?"

"Yes," Heckart answered, looking down at the timid creature.

"Well," she said, "I'm here to teach you your birdcalls!"

Mama cracked up. Cukor happened to be rushing past, just as this exchange took place. As he flew by, he shouted over his shoulder, "And they'd better be good, Heckart!"

She was delighted he'd come through for her after all. Now she had to come through for him.

This nervous, twittery lady from the Arizona Audubon Society was the perfect choice to teach birdcalls. Not only was she skilled at her vocation, she so resembled a bird, Mama could see why all the wildlife would flock to her. And it was obvious that working on a Hollywood Western with a Broadway star was the story she would take to her grave. She taught Mama how to imitate the call of a rose-breasted grosbeak, the whistle a whippoorwill, the coo of a morning dove, and several others.

The Bird Lady loved being on the set, but she started making my mother a little nervous. Every time Mama would finish another scene, she would appear from nowhere, fluttering about like a hummingbird, saying, "Miss Heckart would you like to try another bird call? Are you ready for one more?"

Finally, Mama had to say, "Thank you, I think I have learned more than enough!"

Heckart discussed with her director the place to incorporate the birdcalls and they found the perfect spot. There was a scene late at night where the theatrical troupe had a party and got drunk together after a performance. They were all partially in their stage costumes and had rifled through the wardrobe trunk to find suitable party attire. My mother wore a dilapidated, rhinestone tiara with half the stones missing. Here she saw a prime example of George Cukor's brilliance. As they were rehearsing the drunk scene, Cukor turned to the prop man.

"Take Heckart's tiara and loosen it," he said. "But only on one side."

As they continued the scene, whenever my mother turned her head, the tiara swooped down over her right eye for a moment and then returned to its precarious position atop her head. She didn't have to play drunk—the tiara did all the acting for her. As the party continued and she got more and more tipsy, Sophia Loren's character asked her to do some birdcalls. She did three of them, to the hysterical delight of the rest of the troupe. Unlike her drunk scenes in *The Bad Seed*, this one was hysterically funny.

Back in New York, when Mama was invited to see a rough cut of *Heller*, she discovered that this scene had wound up on the cutting room floor. While Eileen Heckart had certainly been around the business long enough not to take such things personally, she was still crushed.

Soon thereafter, I was born. To honor the occasion, George Cukor sent me a pair of monogrammed, sterling-silver baby brushes from Tiffany's. I still have them—they are among my most cherished possessions. I also still have the two letters that came with them, on the director's letterhead:

> *My dear Luke:*
>
>   *To welcome you on your arrival I send you every good wish for a long, long life and a happy one.*
>
> *With love from your old Uncle George—the wonderful gentleman that Mother's always raving about, I'm sure(?)*

Mama sent him back the following letter, in my name:

> *Dear Uncle George:*
>
>   *Thank you so much for my lovely brushes . . . but why did you have to cut my Mama's best scene in the film?*
>
> *Love,*
> *Luke*

Here was his reply:

> *Dear Luke:*
>
>   *Put those beautiful brushes down, get away from the mirror, and listen for a minute. It may have been before your day, but did you ever read "Little Lord Fauntleroy"? His mother was called 'Dearest,' cause she was serene, gracious, and ladylike at all times. So like your own dear mama. Would you please tell Dearest that I had nothing at all to do with the final cut of* Heller. *In fact, Paramount and I aren't speaking. (They don't seem too upset about this state of affairs.) That is why so much that was important was lost, including those birdcalls. Do explain this to Dearest. She happened to make mention of the cutting to me in her own delicate way. I was surprised she even brought the matter up, it's so like her to suffer in silence. I seem to have read in one of the columns that she is going to do a play. Please tell her that I'm at liberty and remind her that just a few short years ago, I was the best damned stage manager in Rochester. I'll have to close now, because this is my day to go to the unemployment office.*
>
> *A great big hug to you with love from your old Uncle George.*

I love that Cukor was able to have such a sense of humor about the cutting of *Heller in Pink Tights*, which had to have been devastating for him. I'm sure this was also one of the prime factors contributing to its being a total bomb. The story is rambling and slow and the film doesn't seem to go anyplace. Still, the cinematography is outstanding and the scenery and use of color is breathtaking. All of those scenes on horseback over mountainous terrain cannot have been easy for a pregnant woman. But, just like the character she was playing, Eileen Heckart was a trouper who kept working all through each of her pregnancies. She was about to learn just what a dangerous choice this had been.

Corsets, Caves, and a Complicated Birth

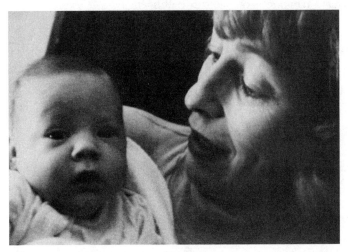

ME AT THREE WEEKS OLD—WITH MY PROUD MAMA

AT AGE FORTY, Mama found out she was pregnant for the fourth time. The news came as a total surprise and a bit of a shock. At first, she wasn't quite sure how to take it. Her acting career was in full bloom and she wasn't sure how she felt about having another child. Still, once she and Jack accepted the idea, they embraced it fully.

In 1959, forty was an advanced age for a woman to be having a child. The fact that my mother was a heavy smoker certainly didn't help. Dr. Joseph Barber, the no-nonsense obstetrician who had delivered Mark and Philip, cautioned her from the outset about the risks of having a child so late in life. Much as she liked and respected him, she argued.

"Look," she said, "if I have a bad seed, there's nothing I can do to save it. If I have a good seed, I could fall out of a second story window and be just fine. You can say whatever the hell you want, but I know I have a good seed and I am going walk out of the hospital with a healthy baby!"

I don't know where she came up with the facts, other than having done *The Bad Seed*, but she swore by them. If the actress was basing her knowledge on modern drama rather than medical science, as long as it worked, who cared? An abortion was never even considered. She was certain she was going to give birth to her third child just before her forty-first birthday and no one could tell her otherwise.

It was years before I knew I was a "surprise baby." When I was little and would look at a family portrait painted before I was born, Mama would say to me, "You were just an idea then."

She said that to my brothers as well, because she wanted all three of us to always feel that we were planned, expected, and welcome.

When Mama and Daddy told my brothers they were going to have another little brother or sister, at first the boys were ecstatic. After a while, Philip changed his tone. He was nearly six and liked ruling the roost. He didn't want any competition for his parents' affection other than what he already felt from his older brother.

At first, Heckart was well enough to keep working. Her next project was a television version of Henrik Ibsen's classic play, *A Doll's House*, for the Hallmark Hall of Fame with Julie Harris as Nora, Christopher Plummer, Jason Robards, and Hume Cronyn. One of Nora's children was played by a very young Richard Thomas.

Heckart played the role of Nora's best friend, Christine. It was a lovely supporting part and she was glad to be working with so many wonderful stage actors and old friends, including the prolific television director George Schaeffer. She was also relieved that her pregnancy wasn't showing yet, especially as she approached her fifth month. Being strapped into corsets and period gowns was even more difficult than in *Heller in Pink Tights*, since her preganacy was more advanced. While she wasn't showing all that much, the pressure of the corset on her tender belly was extremely uncomfortable. At least she didn't have to ride a horse this time.

The night before they were supposed to shoot the live presentation of *A Doll's House*, Jason Robards and Christopher Plummer, great drinking buddies from way back, went out on a bender. To say it was a rough night of carousing would be an understatement.

It began when Robards and Plummer had just come from the dress rehearsal and were loaded down with their gear, including a dressing gown from home Plummer was going to be wearing and didn't want to leave at the studio. Robards carried a fishing tackle box filled with his stage makeup.

Apparently, the men went from one dive into another, eventually winding up on The Bowery in a really shady gin joint.

A redneck sailor looking for a fight saw the dressing gown at Plummer's side and said, "Who the hell do you think you are, Winston fuckin' Churchill?"

Robards, so drunk by this point he could barely stand, glowered at him and staggered to his feet to defend his friend's honor.

"Hey, sailor!" Robards slurred, "You can't talk that way to my buddy! I'm gonna beat the crap outta you! Here Chris, hold my makeup!"

As Robards handed the tackle box to Plummer, the latch popped open and eyebrow pencils, blush brushes, and tubes of greasepaint spilled out over the sawdust-covered floor. The sailor started convulsing in loud guffaws.

"Jesus, what a pair of pansies!" the sailor said, roaring with laugher.

Robards punched the sailor in the stomach, knocking him to the floor. The sailor stumbled to his feet and hurled a chair across the bar, grazing Plummer on the forehead. The bartender started yelling and the next thing they knew, the actors had been tossed out onto the street, the spilled makeup case and dressing gown hurled after them. Before they left, Robards grabbed a parking stanchion out of the middle of the Bowery and hurled it through the plate glass window of the bar. As the police were about to arrive, the two men piled into an unsuspecting gypsy cab and somehow managed to avoid arrest.

The next morning in the television studio, the cast waited. And waited. Were the old boys going to make it in time for the taping? George Schaeffer was pacing, Julie Harris was wringing her hands and Eileen, being pregnant, was running to the ladies' room every few minutes.

"Oh, Eileen!" Harris said, tapping her fingers on her coffee cup, "What ever will we *do* if they don't show up!"

"They'll be here, Julie," Heckart said. "Something tells me they'll be here."

Minutes before the show began, Plummer and Robards stumbled in, looking like they'd spent the night in the middle of the West Side Highway. Robards had a bandage on his hand and Plummer had a gash on his forehead and dark circles under his eyes. Robards was still clutching his makeup kit and Plummer was wearing the dressing gown, which was tattered and stained. Fortunately, the wardrobe mistress had a backup, but that was the least of anyone's worries.

They managed to get into makeup and wardrobe just in time, but it was a harrowing moment for all parties concerned. *A Doll's House* came off remarkably well and is considered one of the classics from the golden age of live television. In the mid-eighties, it was rebroadcast on PBS, hosted by the now grown Richard Thomas. The presentation ended with a short documentary on the making of the show, including interviews with all the stars. Mama and Julie laughed about Jason and Chris and commented that the program came dangerously close to never happening at all. One of the elements of the piece that enchanted Heckart when she saw the show twenty-five years later was that she thought she looked really beautiful. She had the glow of a pregnant woman.

As Mama entered her third trimester, she became very ill. She was suffering from severe preeclampsia, a type of pregnancy-induced hypertension caused by excessive enzymes in the placenta. It can cause grave complications for the baby and the mother, including death. Dr. Barber told her that she must have total bed rest for the duration of her pregnancy and must be closely monitored. At first, her feet and hands became bloated. She was listless due to the heavy medication. Eileen felt terrible that she had to leave Jack and her darling boys entirely in Nanny's care at the holidays while she was flat on her back.

During this time, film director Delbert Mann telephoned. Del had won an Oscar for the film version of *Marty*, and he had worked with Mama in several live television dramas. He was also a considerate man whom she admired both personally and professionally. Del was slated to direct the film version of *The Dark at the Top of the Stairs* and wanted Mama to re-create her Tony-nominated performance as Lottie Lacey. There had been one delay after another in the shooting schedule. At last, the call she had been expecting for nearly a year had come.

"Heckie," Mann said, "We're ready for you. We start shooting next month."

"Well good for you, Del," she said. "I'm six-and-a-half months pregnant! Have a good time."

Eve Arden wound up playing Lottie in the film.

Eileen and Jack were very conscious of the boys' reaction to her illness. Philip felt he was being dethroned by Eileen's pregnancy and, as good parents, they went out of their way to be sensitive to his needs. At age six, the youngest Yankee became detached from his mother and clung to his father. The sicker his Mama became, the more the little boy blamed his unborn sibling. Mark seemed to have no problem with the situation. He was too busy trying to run interference from the strict nuns at St. Mary's School.

One day, a few weeks before Christmas, Mark came home after school and sat on Mama's bed.

"What did you learn in school today, darling?" she asked.

"Jesus was born in cave," he said.

"No, dear. He was born in a stable with other animals around."

"Jesus was born in a cave," he repeated.

That night, when Jack came home, Eileen asked him to get out the family Bible. She read to Mark all about the manger and the stable.

"You see, darling?" she said with a smile. "You must have misunderstood your teacher."

The eight-year-old boy shook his head of dark curls.

"Jesus was born in cave."

The next morning, Mama got up early and called his teacher, Sister Dorothea.

"Sister," she said, "I am very concerned. My son came home last night insisting that Jesus was born in a cave."

"Don't you worry, Mrs. Yankee," the nun said. "I'll take care of it."

That afternoon, when Mark came home from school, Mama asked, "Well did Sister Dorothea set you straight about Jesus and the cave?"

"Yes," he said, "And she asked me to show you this."

The little boy reached into his knapsack and pulled out a large art book of the great Renaissance masters. There were religious paintings by El Greco, da Vinci, and Rembrandt. Each one that depicted the nativity showed Mary, Joseph, and the infant in a dark, tomb-like structure.

"I'll be damned!" Eileen exclaimed, "I guess Jesus really *was* born in a cave!"

"Told you," Mark said.

Mama decided she needed to give the boys an outlet for their frustration over her illness and the pent-up feelings about the new baby.

She called them into the bedroom and said, "Let's draw nasty pictures!"

Mark loved this game. He drew pictures of the nuns getting slapped with large rulers, the bratty girls getting hit with water balloons, the playground bullies getting wedgies. He tore through ten sheets of paper in twenty minutes, laughing and joking the entire time. Philip, on the on the other hand, drew one picture meticulously. It was a picture of his father with a large, round belly.

Eileen said, "Tell me about your picture, Philip."

The five-year-old boy replied, "It's a picture of Daddy having a baby."

My mother felt it was a total denial of her. In her sensitive state, it took tremendous self-control not to burst into tears.

About five weeks before the baby was due, on a Saturday afternoon, Eileen was home alone. Jack was at the supermarket with the boys so she could rest and Nanny was having a well-earned weekend off, spending time with her niece in Rhode Island. All at once, her blood pressure shot sky high and she started having convulsions. Frightened, she managed to drag herself to a neighbor's house, who immediately called an ambulance.

In between the spasms surging through her weakened, frail body, she managed to sputter, "But-the-baby-isn't-due-for-five-weeks-yet!"

By the time the ambulance arrived at St. Joseph's Hospital, the paramedics had been able to stop the convulsions, but there was a new complication. Her water had broken. Terrified and alone, Eileen was admitted to the maternity ward. As she was going up in the elevator in a wheelchair, a young nurse recognized her.

"Oh Miss Heckart!" she gushed, "I think you're just wonderful! Could I please have your autograph?"

She thrust a pen and an empty writing tablet into Eileen's gaunt, pain-stricken face.

Eileen looked up at the nurse and said through constricted breaths, "Honey, I'm gonna be here for a few days. Do you think it could wait awhile?"

She was taken to a private room, but there was no time for her to rest. A gurney was waiting to take her straight to the OR. Just before she was taken into surgery, a nun came into the room. She leaned over the bedside table and started arranging the sacraments, setting out the anointing oil, the communion wafer, and the ceremonial wine.

"Wha . . . what are you doing, Sister?" Eileen stammered.

As the nun continued preparing, she said, "Mrs. Yankee, I'm the Mother Superior here at St. Joseph's. Because of the severity of your case, I've come to administer the last rites to you."

Eileen panicked.

"Thank you, Sister," she said, "but I don't need them."

"Don't you want to die in a state of grace?" the Sister asked.

"I'm already in a state of grace!" she shouted. "I'm having a child! Now, you get your ass out of here and call my doctor!"

The nun quickly gathered up her possessions and flew down the hall, never to be seen again. Just then, Jack entered the room. Not having the patience to wait for the elevator, he was winded from having run up four flights of stairs. He saw how hysterical his wife was and he leaned over the gurney, holding her trembling body.

When Dr. Barber came in, Eileen started screaming at him through her tears. "What the hell are you doing, sending that nun in here with the last rites?"

"Eileen, calm down," he said. "Your blood pressure is elevated as it is."

Jack chimed in. "Well why the hell didn't you think of that before you sent that fucking penguin in here to scare the crap out of my wife!"

"I didn't send her," the doctor replied. "Since this is a Catholic hospital, some administrator must have seen your file and told her to come."

Eileen bolted upright in bed, despite the pain. "Well, I don't ever want to see her again. Ever! You hear me! I'm going to walk out of this hospital with a baby and make all of you look damned silly!"

Dr. Barber spoke in hushed tones and gently pushed her back onto the gurney. "I hope that happens, Eileen. I really do," he said.

"It's happening!" she barked. "You can count on it!"

Just then, a young orderly came in to wheel Eileen away. Jack leaned over the gurney, stroking her hair.

"I'm not leaving," he said, gazing deep into her hazel eyes.

"Neither am I," she replied, squeezing his hand.

Jack followed the gurney through the maze of corridors, never letting go of her hand. As they took her into the OR, he said, "I'll be right here. I love you, sweetheart."

"I love you, too," she said, as she disappeared behind the heavy, swinging doors.

Before they began the procedure, Dr. Barber came to Jack, who was pacing in the waiting room. Jack held a cardboard cup of coffee in one hand and a rosary in the other.

"Jack," the doctor said, "I have to ask you this. You know how many dangers there are in this particular case. If we have to make a choice between your wife and the baby, who should we choose?"

Without hesitating, Jack said, "Save my wife at all costs."

Years later, my compassionate father told me this with great concern and considerable guilt, as if I wouldn't have understood. Eileen meant everything to Jack Yankee. He wouldn't have wanted to live without her. My brothers and I knew this instinctually from the time we were very small. And now, he was being asked to make a choice between his unborn child and the love of his life? There was no debate. His wife and the mother of his two boys was the most precious thing in the world to him.

The cesarean surgery was long and complicated. Eileen was in such pain, she had very little memory of it. Jack, on the other hand, remembered every long and tortuous hour. On Sunday, February 7, 1960, I was born. My mother used to say that she was so out of it, when they held me up, she couldn't even identify the parts—she had to ask the nurse if I was a boy or a girl.

We had both made it. Eileen knew she would prove the doctors wrong and she did. At five pounds and thirteen ounces, I was so small and frail, I had to be in an incubator for several days. But in every other respect, I was a perfectly healthy baby.

Mama was in the hospital for about a week. Once she was coherent enough to get phone calls, Philip started calling.

"Put the kid on!" he'd say.

"Well," she answered, "He's not here right now."

"He's not?" the little boy asked, not understanding that the infant wasn't with his mother every second.

"Can I give him a message?" Eileen asked.

"No," he said. "I'll tell him myself."

Every time Philip called, he had no desire to speak with his mother, not realizing she had nearly died. It was always, "Put the kid on!" Mama never found out what Philip's message was. She wasn't sure she wanted to know.

At the same time they brought me home, my father stopped at the toy store and bought Mark and Philip the biggest stuffed animal he could find. It was a large, plush elephant about the size of a Shetland pony. I wonder how my father even fit it into the car. This gift was intended to let the older boys know they were still special. Mark called it Ellie and played with it for hours.

Philip couldn't be bothered. He was fascinated by "the kid" and would stare at me incessantly. One day after school, Philip said, "Mama, I want to pretend that Luke is still in the nursing blanket, OK?"

"I suppose so," she said, handing him the blanket.

The six-year-old boy ran into the living room with the tiny nursing blanket and started beating the crap out of it. He punched it, choked it, wadded it up into ball and kicked it, stepped on it, and hurled it around the room. *Well*, Eileen thought, *at least he's expressing his feelings.*

As a little boy, I was fascinated by the story of my birth. It was so dramatic, so life-or-death, such a struggle to bring me into the world. And Mama told it with pathos, humor, and of course, a great sense of drama. This was probably when I first realized how my mother could hold a room captive by telling a story.

When we would be visiting a family friend, I would often say, "Mama, tell the story of when I was born."

In my early twenties, the guilt and the horror that my birth nearly killed my mother fully dawned on me. I spent years on the analyst's couch dealing with this. It was as if I had developed a hidden shame at being alive, a sense that I could kill people just by being who I am. It was the eighties, so this sort of self-actualization was all the rage. I tried meditation, chakra-cleansing, aura-fluffing, and energy-balancing. Once, I was doing a rebirthing workshop, a deep breathing technique for getting in touch with one's birth trauma. My experience was so intense, I realized how much negativity I was hanging onto surrounding my birth. I tried to bolt out of the room in the middle of the exercise, but the facilitator stopped me.

She said, "What's coming up for you?"

In my emotional state, I managed to blurt out, "I hurt my mother!"

As the pent-up energy was being released, it was manifesting itself physically in an alarming way. My mouth was contorted so that I could barely speak and my arms and legs were contracted into the fetal position. The facilitator gave me some exercises to release the tension and instructed me to continue with the deep breathing. When I completed the exercise, I felt a calmness wash over me like I'd never experienced before.

She looked down at me and said, "Now, look who let go?"

Clearly, I was carting around all this muck on a cellular level about nearly killing my mother.

As a little boy, whenever Mama would finish telling this Dickensian story of my birth, she always made it clear to me and to the other listeners that she would go through it all again if she had to.

"The pain was worth the prize," she said, beaming at me.

At that point, she held me close and I would know that I was deeply loved and wanted. While Eileen needed her career, she loved and needed her family far more.

Musical Moments

HECKART WITH BOB FOSSE IN *PAL JOEY*. PHOTO BY ALIX JEFFREY—THE HARVARD
THEATRER COLLECTION, HOUGHTON LIBRARY. REPRINTED WITH PERMISSION

ON THE STRENGTH of her work in the legitimate theater, Mama started to get
offered work in musicals. They terrified her, because she knew singing wasn't her
strong suit, but she did a few of them anyway. She had been studying for a while
with David Craig, the most renowned musical-comedy teacher in New York. All
of the top actors on Broadway studied with Craig, because he didn't teach voice,
but rather phrasing, body language, and most importantly, the way to act a song
and tell a story.

In 1961, the New York City Center was doing a revival of Rogers & Hart's *Pal
Joey* and they wanted Heckart to play the part of Melba, the newspaper reporter. It
is a cameo with one showstopping song. Melba comes to interview Joey, who insults
her. She lets him know that he is small potatoes in her book and tells a story of the
greatest interview she ever did, with the famous stripper Gypsy Rose Lee. She pro-
ceeds to sing "Zip," while performing a comic striptease, completely in pantomime.

The title role of Joey, the womanizing rogue, was played by an up-and-coming
musical comedy star named Bob Fosse. Before Fosse became a famous director/cho-
reographer, responsible for such Broadway masterworks as *Chicago*, *Pippin*, and the
film *All That Jazz*, he was a hoofer on Broadway and in Hollywood. Having understudied the role of Joey in a 1952 revival, he was now taking center stage.

The choreographer on this production was not very good and everybody knew
it. I'll call him Mitch. Fosse was such a brilliant dancer, he decided early on that

he would do his own choreography, occasionally asking Mitch for advice, as not to entirely undermine him.

Behind Mitch's back, however, Fosse would say, "To hell with him. I'm doing my own moves, anyway."

Heckart was incredibly frustrated with Mitch. Even as a non-dancer, she knew what he was giving her wasn't very strong. Still, it was such a good acting song, she focused on telling the comic story and making it work through her acting choices. She expressed her frustration to Fosse, who made a point of hovering in the rehearsal room one day while she was working on "Zip" with Mitch.

The following day, Bob Fosse approached Heckart at the top of rehearsal.

"Heckie," he said, "Gwen and I would like to take you out for a bite tomorrow evening after rehearsal. Would that be okay?"

"I'd love to, Bobby," she said. Mama was crazy about Fosse and his wife, the musical comedy star, Gwen Verdon.

The next night, they went to Downey's on Eighth Avenue and laughed, shared stories and had a delightful time. Gwen Verdon looked at her watch.

"Bobby," she said, "it's almost 7:30—we have to go."

"Oh," Mama asked. "Are you going to a show?"

"No," Fosse said, grabbing his coat. "C'mon Heckart. You're coming with us."

The three of them piled into a taxi and headed downtown. They arrived at a dance studio on West Eighteenth Street. Mama had no idea what they were doing there. Fosse led Heckart into a rehearsal room where an accompanist was waiting. They made small talk for a few minutes until Gwen Verdon re-entered in a leotard. Fosse motioned for Mama to sit in a chair in front of him.

"All right, Heckart," he said. "We are going to restage your number. Gwen is going to walk your part and I'm going to show you what to do." My mother stared at him, totally stunned.

"Oh Bobby," she said, "I am so touched that you would go to so much trouble, but I can't do that to this choreographer."

Fosse stubbed out his cigarette on the heel of his shoe.

"But he's no good!" he replied.

"I know that, Bobby," Mama said. "But I'm making it work as best I can. It would break Mitch's heart if I did that to him."

Fosse glared at her as she spoke. "It's your ass up there, Heckart! Who gives a shit about Mitch's heart, for Chrissake!" he said.

"Well," Mama said with a sigh, "I guess I do, Bobby. I want to thank you and Gwen for going to this much effort and the expense of renting the studio. I really do appreciate it—but no thank you."

Fosse raised his arm and pointed a bony finger at her.

"You know, Heckart," he said, "*that's* why you'll never be a *star!*"

Star or not, Eileen Heckart still stopped the show with "Zip." The applause she received each night after her mime striptease was so overwhelming, she worked out an encore. She came back onstage and mimed picking up all the clothes she had taken off—gloves, stockings, garters. It got almost as big a hand as the number itself. The kids in the chorus were so in love with her, they made her an honorary Broadway gypsy, and presented her with the traditional gypsy robe made out of purple taffeta and pink marabou feathers. She loved that robe and kept it for more than twenty years. They also presented her with a poster-sized scroll she had framed. It was a tongue-in-cheek proclamation from "Ass. Bog, Ltd" (the Association for the Broadway Order of Gypsies, Limited). It was signed by each member of the company with a declaration of her role as a lifelong honorary Broadway gypsy. The final line read "Henceforth and hereafter let it be known that HECKIE is a GYPSY!" It was one of her favorite honors of her entire career.

Mama received such acclaim for *Pal Joey*, within the year she was asked to star in her first Broadway musical, *A Family Affair.* Once she realized what she'd gotten herself into, she was scared stiff. In *Pal Joey*, she had one showstopping number in a tried and true Rodgers and Hart musical. Here, she was a leading lady carrying an original piece.

While *A Family Affair* was rife with problems, there were several things that distinguished it. It was the first show to be directed by Harold Prince, who took over for Word Baker when he was fired during previews. Prince (whom I would later assist on another flop, *Grind*) knew the show would most likely fail, but his mentor, George Abbott, convinced him to do it and get the credit for directing a Broadway musical. A few years later, he was to direct *Cabaret, Company*, and win more Tonys over the course of his career than anyone in theater history.

It was also the first musical for John Kander, who wrote the music to John and William Goldman's lyrics. This was before Kander hooked up with Fred Ebb and created showbiz history of their own with shows like *Cabaret, Chicago*, and a little ditty called "New York, New York."

A Family Affair was the story of a big, Jewish wedding and the backstabbing that goes on among the father of the bride (played by Shelley Berman) and the mother of the groom (played by Heckart). The rest of the cast included Larry Kert as the groom (hot off his success as Tony in *West Side Story*), Rita Gardner as the young bride and the classical actor Morris Carnovsky as Heckart's long-suffering husband. Since one of the scenes opened with Carnovsky and Heckart sharing pillow talk before turning in for the night, Carnovsky loved to tell people in later years, "I once shared a bed with Eileen Heckart." As listeners raised an eyebrow, he couldn't keep a straight face.

The script for *A Family Affair* never really worked. There were some wonderful songs (not to mention a few that were less than wonderful) and the talented company was trying their utmost to turn this lemon into lemonade. When Heckart, as the overbearing Jewish mother Tilly Siegel, learns of her son's engagement, she sings a big, brassy production number called, "My Son the Lawyer." As she calls

HECKART LOOKING VERY UNHAPPY IN A FOOTBALL SONG FROM *A FAMILY AFFAIR.* SHE WAS DESPERATE TO BE CUT OUT OF THE NUMBER AND AFTER MUCH GNASHING OF TEETH, SHE WAS. PHOTO BY BOB GOLBY

everyone she knows to tell them of the impending nuptials, the chorus girls and switchboard operators all dance around her with telephones while she remains center stage, singing and doing high kicks.

Walter Kerr in the *New York Herald Tribune* said, "Though Miss Heckart honestly hasn't much of a singing voice, she is not impervious to the proud, busy beat of 'My Son, the Lawyer.' You believe in her pride so much, you also believe she is singing."

Norman Nadel in the *New York World-Telegram* said, "Eileen Heckart can do just about everything except sing, which makes her almost the ideal Tilly Siegel . . . her musical failings are more than compensated by her superb showmanship."*

Perhaps critic Richards Watts, Jr. said it the best in the *New York Post*: "The brilliant Eileen Heckart seems less happy than usual as the meddlesome mother."

* Courtesy of Norman Nadel. Reprinted with permission.

One day during rehearsals, Stanley Lebowsky, the musical director, asked Heckart to come to the theater early to hear this girl who was auditioning for the role of understudy to the ingénue, played by Rita Gardner. Mama hated going in early. She always wanted to spend as much time as possible with the family, especially with a new baby less than a year old. But Lebowsky had been so patient with her as a non-singer that she agreed. The actress coming in to audition was forty-five minutes late. When the girl finally showed up, she was dressed in ratty clothes from the Salvation Army with stringy hair in her face, no makeup, and she was carrying voluminous shopping bags. Mama thought to herself, "What the hell am I doing here? Why should I give a damn about the understudy to the ingénue, anyway?"

As the ditzy girl propelled into the rehearsal room, she threw down her packages and started apologizing profusely.

"I'm so sorry I'm late," she said. "I'm about to open at the Rainbow Room and I couldn't decide on the right shoes so I bought the heels and the flats and I have to return one of them by six thirty, so which ones do you like better?" She started rifling through her shopping bags and pulled out one of each and held them up. Mr. Lebowsky, who was totally stymied by this behavior, shot Heckart an apologetic look.

Mama said, "Honey, for the Rainbow Room, you'd better go with the heels."

The ditzy girl replied, "Oh, thank you so much Miss Heckart. I'm such a fan of your work! Thank you!"

She then proceeded to sit down and unlace her combat boots and put on the black pumps. While she was going though this rather bizarre spectacle, Mr. Lebowsky said, "Were you planning on singing something for us today, dear?"

The girl looked up as if she'd forgotten why she was there. "Oh, yeah, of course. I'd like to sing "Soon It's Gonna Rain" from *The Fantastiks*. How do you like the shoes?"

She beveled her left leg towards them. Lebowsky mouthed, "I'm so sorry," in Heckart's direction. The ditzy girl took her music out of her bag and walked over to the accompanist, who had finished three crossword puzzles by now. She pushed her hair out of her face and the voice of an angel burst through. Mama was aghast. She'd never heard an instrument quite like it. Lebowsky seemed relieved that this hadn't been an exercise in futility. Once the girl had gathered up her shopping bags and scurried out the door, Lebowsky turned to Heckart.

"Well, Heckie, what do you think?"

"What do I think?!" she echoed. "She's neurotic as hell, but my God, what a voice! Much as I love Rita Gardner, you should give this girl the part. What's her name?"

Lebowsky looked down at headshot on the table.

"Her name is . . . Barbra Streisand!"

Just as Lebowsky was about to offer her the understudy, Arthur Laurents cast her as Miss Marmelstein in *I Can Get It For You Wholesale*, the role that catapulted Streisand into the spotlight.

Heckart found Shelley Berman, the leading man, to be moody and temperamental. He was a very popular stand-up comic at the time and while he sang well, she did not consider him a strong actor. Heckart was a respected actress, but not really a singer. Their relationship was strained at best. In the book scenes, Berman tended to fall back onto his nightclub *shtick* and excelled in the musical numbers. Heckart found the truth in the flimsy book scenes and acted the songs, but had little musicality. He often got impatient with her when rehearsing the songs, which made her feel she was bringing the show down. When Berman would roll his eyes or snap his fingers to get her back on the beat, she laughed it off with a sarcastic comment. Inside, she was dying.

There was a kid in the chorus of *A Family Affair* who was making her Broadway debut. Mama noticed the way she stood out and was very impressed with her. Whenever the director or choreographer was in doubt about who should get a featured bit. Heckart shouted, "For God's sake, give it to her!"

As a result, this chorus girl wound up with about six featured bits. Her name was Linda Lavin. Fourteen years later, when Mama had a guest spot on the sitcom *Alice* playing Linda's mother-in-law, Lavin told this story to the studio audience.

She said, "I might not have had a career if it hadn't been for Eileen Heckart's generosity." They worked together several times over the years and always had a great fondness and affection for one another.

There was a lot of talent involved in *A Family Affair*, but they just couldn't get it to fit together. It was as if many of the players involved were cutting their teeth on this show before stepping into their greatness. It ambled along on Broadway for sixty-five performances. Mama was incredibly relieved when it closed.

Even so, there were many times in my childhood when we were having company that she would ask Jack to warm up the hi-fi and put on the original cast album of *A Family Affair*. As much as it terrified her, she loved being able to play that record for people and tell them the story as they listened to each of her five numbers. It was as if a part of her was saying, "By God, I actually did a musical!"

In 1985, when I assisted Hal Prince on *Grind*, a musical starring Ben Vereen, as we were introduced he shook my hand and said, "Luke, I feel as if the wheel has come full circle."

For Heckart, *A Family Affair* had the opposite effect. She was terrified to try another musical and turned many of them down, including *Company*. She was sent the script before all of the music was even written, when it was a series of vignettes about married life. When Elaine Stritch attained iconic status for doing the musical, Mama thought twice about having dismissed the piece so hastily.

The whole nature of "this song is out and this one is in tomorrow at the matinee" was too scary for her as a non-musical person. In a play, she would live with a new scene, work on it for a few days, and make it better. In a new musical, a number she may have spent weeks rehearsing could be cut on the spot. Occasionally Heckart would sing a number in a show, but a full musical? Never again.

My Mother, the Star

MAMA'S IDEA OF A CHIC FAMILY PORTRAIT—ALL DRESSED UP AND BAREFOOT. PHOTO BY ROBERT SATTER

FOR ALL HER SUCCESS, being a wife and mother was far more important to Eileen than anything that happened inside the spotlight. Even while she was acting on Broadway, she was the type of mother who would do a matinee and evening performance and then come home and fill Easter baskets until 3:00 in the morning. She would give us elaborately themed birthday parties, backyard picnics with fireworks for the Fourth of July, and school parties to rival anything produced by David Merrick. Mama loved any excuse for a party. She had a knack for turning an ordinary event into something special, something grand.

She had a large, dog-eared book, filled with ideas for children's birthday parties. Each year, a few months before my birthday, she would dig out the book and say,

"Now let's find something really special for your party this year!" When I was in first grade, it was a hobo party. She wrote the invitations on the torn-out classified pages of the newspaper, telling everyone to come in shabby, old clothes. When all the little boys arrived, she presented each with bindle sacks with chips and sandwiches and we played games like "kick the can." Another year it was a pirate party where everyone had eye patches, plastic swords, and mustaches painted on with burnt cork. When Mark was seven, she threw him a cowboy party where everyone had cowboy hats, and cap-gun pistols. There was even a milking contest with a clothesline full of rubber gloves filled with milk. All the kids in school looked forward to our parties.

I recently saw a guy I'd gone to grade school with by the name of Bob Festo. He told me that after one of my celebrations, he came home and said, "Mom, that was the best birthday party I've ever been to!"

"That's wonderful, dear," she said. "Tell me about Eileen Heckart."

"She wasn't there," he said. "But Mrs. Yankee was really cool!"

In our hometown, Mama was famous for saying, "Oh honey, up here in New Canaan, nobody knows who I am. I'm just plain Mrs. Yankee."

There was nothing plain about her. How many Connecticut housewives do you know who go into the supermarket wearing dark glasses, a full-length black mink coat with a cigarette holder, and copy of *Variety* tucked under her arm to read in the checkout line? *Plain* Mrs. Yankee? She couldn't be plain if she tried. The ladies in the supermarket or the beauty parlor buzzed about it for days if she stopped in. And if she had been on television the week before, she couldn't get through the checkout line without half a dozen people commenting on it. She sincerely believed that no one in New Canaan knew or even cared who she was. But that was part of her charm. She never thought of herself as a celebrity or saw her theatrical, larger-than-life behavior as anything out of the ordinary. She just thought her wardrobe was a little jazzier than the other wives and mothers. I loved going to the grocery store or running errands with her, just to watch the townspeople gush.

Of course, there were a number of people who treated her like plain folks. "How ya doing, today Mrs. Yankee?" Peter, the stock boy at the supermarket said. "How many cartons of True Blues this week?"

Part of the fun was seeing where the mother and the diva would intersect. When I was a sophomore in high school, she had just learned she was nominated for an Emmy for her first episode of *The Mary Tyler Moore Show*. This was her second Emmy nomination out of seven she received in the course of her career. Since the previous nomination for the PBS teleplay, *Save Me a Place at Forest Lawn* had been nine years prior, she was really delighted.

I waited for her to get off the phone with her agent. I didn't mind, because I could tell from her tone that he was sharing some great news with her.

"Guess what?" she said, putting down the phone. "I just got nominated for an Emmy!"

"That's wonderful, Mama!" I said, "Congratulations. I'm sorry to bug you with something so dumb at a time like this, but I need a sick note for my math teacher. I skipped algebra yesterday to go into New York for that Pepsi audition."

"That's right," she said, reaching for her stationery.

Whenever I skipped a class to go in for an audition and I needed a good excuse, she'd say, "Tell them you had dysentery. Nobody will ever question that."

As she wrote the sick note, she was still basking in the glow of her Emmy nomination.

The note read:

Dear Mr. Levai:
   Please excuse Luke from Math class yesterday. He had the stomach flu.
Thanks for watching!
Eileen Heckart

Her signature was big and florid and took up half the page. My math teacher *loved* it! I think he framed it.

Back in those days, she came home from the theater at night and left her false eyelashes on the edge of the bathroom sink. On several occasions, my father stumbled into the bathroom for a pee at 4 AM and started swatting at her eyelashes, thinking they were bugs. When he realized they weren't moving, he flushed them down the drain.

In the morning, she said, "Jack have you seen my false eyelashes? I left them on the bathroom sink last night."

"No," he replied. "But you'd better call the exterminator. We're having a terrible problem with spiders in there."

"Really?" she said. "I hadn't noticed."

When the exterminator didn't find any trace of spiders and Mama lost four pairs of expensive false eyelashes in the course of a month, she figured out what was going on.

"Jack!" she hollered, "Will you wear your goddamn bifocals when you go to the loo in the middle of the night! Maybe you'll stop flushing my eyelashes down the drain!"

When Mark and Philip were very small, Eileen's mother, Grandma Esther, came to visit from Ohio. Mama had been trying to get Esther to come for years, but she always refused. She said it was because she was afraid to fly, but I think it was more out of a sense of jealousy over her daughter's success. Finally, Mama convinced her. She took the train from Columbus. It was a long trip and Esther was not in good humor when she arrived. After she unpacked, she came down to the kitchen and saw two-year-old Philip in his high chair eating an artichoke. He had a little ramekin filled with drawn butter and he was stuffing the leaves into his mouth and scraping the ends with great gusto, hurling the eaten leaves onto the floor. Never having seen an artichoke, Esther was horrified.

"Anna Eileen!" she said. "Are just gonna let that child eat the plants!"

"Mama," she replied. "It's an artichoke!"

"Well, it can't be good for him!" Esther muttered.

She turned the corner into the Colonial dining room and started back up the stairs. Just at that moment, Mark was coming down with his red stool. Because of Nanny's partial paralysis, she couldn't carry things in her hands as she went up and down stairs. She had to go down backward holding onto the railing. Nanny carried the babies in an Indian-style papoose, but with the dirty clothes from the master bedroom hamper, she wrapped the laundry up in a sheet and tossed it down the stairs. At age four, Mark thought that was how you got things up and down the stairs. Just as Grandma Esther was turning the corner, Mark sent his little red footstool careening down the stairs. It missed Esther's permanent wave, but as she lunged to avoid the incoming projectile, Mark managed to bean her left shin. She ran back into the kitchen, screaming at the top her lungs.

"That child tried to kill me!" she bellowed.

"No he didn't, Mama. He was just moving his stool to the kitchen," Eileen replied.

"Don't you tell me!" she screamed. "I know malicious intent when I see it! That child tried to kill me!"

"Mama," Eileen said, "he's only four. I don't think there's much malice in him."

"He tried to kill me . . . and I'm going home!" Esther shouted.

"But Mama . . ."

"I'm going HOME!" she said.

With that, Esther bolted up two flights of stairs, packed her bags, and took the next train back to Columbus. She spent thirty-six hours on a train for a ninety-minute visit.

Once again, Mama had been rebuffed by her mother. She was deeply hurt. Their relationship was a complicated one, tied up in childhood resentments and petty jealousy. Esther must have been aware of her shortcomings as a mother and having to face her oldest daughter brought them leaping to the fore. Mama would call Esther and say, "I'm going to be in a TV movie tomorrow night at nine o'clock on NBC." Esther wouldn't even turn on the TV. I never understood what this was about, but I know it wounded my mother. She and Esther spoke on the phone about once a month, exchanged Christmas gifts and birthday cards, and that was about the extent of their relationship. Until she moved into a nearby nursing home in her final years, I had very little sense of my mother's mother.

※ ※ ※

When Mark and Philip were seven and five, one Mother's Day, the family went into Manhattan. They saw Disney's *Sleeping Beauty* at Radio City Music Hall, had a fancy dinner at Luchow's, and strolled along Fifth Avenue on their way back to Grand Central Station. Eileen was so protective; going into New York with the boys made her a nervous wreck. She had been firm with them about not getting lost or being out of her sight, even for a second. Mama was looking in the windows of FAO Schwartz with Mark as he recited his entire birthday wish list for the next three years. Meanwhile, little Philip saw an old Hispanic woman on a street corner selling orchids. They had pink, satin ribbons on them which read, "Happy Mother's Day." Philip had to have one. He had saved his allowance for months and asked his father if he could go across the street to buy an orchid for his mama. Jack agreed and watched him cross the street while Eileen was preoccupied with Mark in the toy store window. Once Philip was out of sight, Eileen turned around in a state of maternal panic.

"Jack, where's Philip?" she shrieked.

"Oh, don't worry. He's around someplace," Jack replied, thrusting his hands into his pockets.

"What the hell does that mean?" she demanded. "Where is he?"

Just then, Philip came back around the corner of West Fifty-Seventh Street with a broad smile, hiding his treasure behind his back. Eileen was so frightened, that without even thinking, she slapped him hard across the face.

"Don't you ever run off like that again!" she screamed. "You could have been hit by a taxi—or worse!"

As the tears ran down his assaulted cheeks, the devastated little boy reached behind his back and handed his mother the orchid. She clutched him to her breast as they both stood there on Fifth Avenue crying their eyes out. Eileen never forgave herself for that.

⊗⊗⊗

There was a dance instructor in New Canaan by the name of Walter Schalk. Mr. Schalk was not your typical small-town dance instructor. He was tall and macho, with an intimidating presence. He taught ballroom dancing in such a way that he combined etiquette, manners, and athleticism. Schalk convinced the jocks in the town that it took as much stamina to execute a foxtrot as it did to throw a lateral pass on the football field. What's more, the foxtrot taught you how to interact with girls. If a teenage boy showed up for Walter Schalk's class without his shoes shined or his tie on straight, he had to get down in the middle of the room in front of God and everyone and do ten push-ups. If a girl wasn't in a skirt or a dress, she was sent home or reprimanded in front of all her peers.

Schalk also managed to seduce the parents and city council into believing it was *the* thing for a young teenager to do in New Canaan. He was feared, revered and very wealthy. The best part of all was that at the end of the school year, he put on a spectacular dance revue with elaborate costumes, lavish sets, and a full orchestra. It was always sold out and the parents mobbed the place to see how their gawky teenage son or daughter had transformed into a junior Gene Kelly or Cyd Charisse.

Mark and Philip were thrilled to be taking Walter Schalk's class when they were twelve and thirteen respectively. They came home from dance class and could talk of nothing else for the next two days. Two months before the recital, Philip asked, "Mama, will you come to our final dance revue on June fourteenth?"

"Are you kidding?" she replied. "I wouldn't miss it for the world!"

About one month before the big day, Milton Goldman called with an amazing offer. It was a plum role in a movie for television with a first-class director and a stellar cast. Paying top dollar, it was shooting on location in Toronto for a month.

"Wait a minute, Milton," she said, "When does it finish shooting?"

"June eighteenth. Why?"

"Sorry, Milton," she said, "but I can't do it."

"What are you talking about, Heckie?" he said. "It's the lead, and didn't you hear the cast list?"

"I heard it," she said. "But I promised the boys I'd be there for their dance recital."

"Look," Milton said, "I'll see if they can come back with more money, but I—"

"It's not the money, Milton," she said. "I promised my boys."

"Heckie," Milton said, "do you mean to tell me you are going to turn down this great role with an all-star cast for your kid's *dance* recital?"

"I'm sorry, Milton," she said. "I made a promise."

Jack was chagrined about it, too. It was great money and with three boys, they were feeling a bit stretched financially when Eileen didn't work for a while.

"Jack, if you really need me to do it for the money, I will," she said. "But I promised Mark and Philip."

She and Daddy grappled with this for a few days. In the end, they decided that her word to the boys was sacred. She desperately wanted to do this part and she even went so far as to see if they could adjust the shooting schedule around her, but no dice. Mark and Philip were torn about it, too. As much as they wanted both their parents there to see them dance, they knew how important Mama's career was to her.

When the movie for television came on, we all sat down in the family room to watch. "Are you sorry you didn't get to do it, Mama?" Mark asked.

"A little bit," she said. "But I got to watch you dance and that's far more important."

After that, whenever one of us had an upcoming event, and we asked if she'd be there, she'd say, "If I'm free, I'll be there."

Even though she didn't regret her decision, she always built in an escape clause for the future. We weren't always thrilled about this, and she felt terribly guilty when she had to enforce it due to an acting job. At least we could never say she had broken a promise.

When I performed in the Walter Schalk dance revue six years later, she was there, too. But I was so klutzy and awkward, I was the one who always had to get sent out into the hall with the dance hostess for special help. I almost wish she'd gotten another TV movie.

⊗⊗⊗

Before Mama and Daddy moved out of our wonderful childhood home on Comstock Hill Road, we had what became known in our family as The Mother of All Garage Sales. It wasn't so much that they needed the money, but the practical side of her wanted to get rid of stuff, so why not make a few bucks by cleaning out the basement and the attic? One of my parents' favorite hobbies on the weekend was driving around to every yard sale in Fairfield County, hunting for bargains and antiques. Mama loved it when she could get a bunch of hardcover mysteries for a quarter each. As a child of the Depression, Anna Eileen loved a good sale.

My brothers and I spent weeks sorting, tagging, and displaying our worn out stuff in the driveway and the three garages, praying it wouldn't rain that weekend. My parents ran an ad in the local paper and people came from far and wide to see if Eileen Heckart's yard-sale crap was better than anyone else's.

The local antique dealers started arriving at 6:30 in the morning. My father was furious. Some of them were incredibly pushy and insisted on being given a preview. He started screaming at them, saying, "The doors open at 9 AM and you may NOT come in until then!"

By 8:30, nearly fifty people had congregated, so he caved in and let them enter early.

While Daddy, Mark, Philip and I were manning the garages, Mama sat down at the foot of the driveway making the cash transactions. Plain Mrs. Yankee was posted there at a card table with a calculator, a cigar box full of change, two packs of cigarettes, a pitcher of iced tea, and a box of Entenmann's glazed donut holes. That was enough to keep her going all day long.

Late in the day, a paunchy man with a large mustache came down the driveway hauling a folded Oriental screen. As he plopped it down in front of "Plain Mrs." and her cash box, he spoke like an agent making a deal for a client. With a cigarette still dangling from her lips, the lady of the house stopped counting her dollar bills and eyed him suspiciously.

He said, "You're Eileen Heckart, aren't you? Saw you on that TV show once. Listen, about this Oriental screen, you've got it marked five dollars. I'll give you a buck-and-a-half for it, whaddya say?"

Putting down her wad of singles, my mother studied the folded screen and weighed the proposition. Drumming her fingers on the card table, she said, "Well, it's the end of the day and we're trying to get rid of stuff. Okay, a buck and a half."

As the stocky man reached for his wallet, he pulled out a pen instead and thrust it in her face.

"Hey, will you autograph it for me too?" he said.

She flicked her ashes and without even looking up, replied, "Not for a buck and a half."

⠿⠿⠿

When I was a little boy, Mama would go into the major department stores in New York at the start of the holiday season. She'd case out the Santas to see which one had the best routine that particular year so she knew where to take me. When I was seven, she decided it was Macy's. We waited in line for Santa, and when we finally got up to the front of the line, just before this picture was taken, Santa turned to my mother and shouted, "Heckie! My God, it's been ages! How are you?"

ME WITH THE UNEMPLOYED ACTOR SANTA

Santa was an unemployed actor. My mother looked at him in shock, ready to kill the son of a bitch who had just ruined Christmas for her fair-haired baby boy and probably had scarred him for life. But I took it another way. I knew that only Mama's really close friends called her Heckie. And if Santa knew her well enough to call her Heckie, I was getting *everything* on my Christmas list that year!

Mama showed me the Christmas tree at Rockefeller Center, and then took me to Sardi's for dinner. Vincent Sardi made a big fuss over me. He took her caricature off the wall, showed it to me up close, and brought me my ginger ale in a champagne bucket with a swizzle stick. I felt so grown up and important.

From across the dining room, Soupy Sales blew my mother a kiss. In 1967, *The Soupy Sales Show* was the hottest kids' show on television. He was my hero, my idol, my whole world.

As I reached for another onion breadstick, I turned to my mother said, "Mama, do you *know* Soupy Sales?"

"Well, as a matter of fact, I do," she said. "Would you like to meet him?"

My jaw hit the floor.

"Meet him? Could I really?"

She beckoned the maitre d', who requested that Mr. Sales stop by Miss Heckart's table. A few minutes later, Soupy Sales came by. He kissed my mother's hand.

"I loved your last play," he said, "You are such a wonderful actress."

Wow—I thought if Soupy Sales thinks she's a good actress, she must be!

"This is our youngest son, Luke," she said, "He's a big fan."

"How do you do?" he said, shaking my hand.

"Hi, how's Pookie?" I asked, referring to one of the puppet characters on his show.

"Pookie is just fine!" he said. "Miss Heckart, it's always a pleasure to see you and I can't wait for your next play. Merry Christmas to you both."

I was starting to see my mother in a different light. As Soupy left, I turned to her and said, "Now, Mama, tell me the truth. Did my older brothers *ever* meet anyone as important as Soupy Sales?"

Years later, she told me in that moment she thought to herself, Marilyn Monroe, Debbie Reynolds, Laurence Olivier . . . to name a few.

She turned to me and said, "No, darling, they never did."

That was the first time I really know my mother was somebody. Soupy Sales and Santa Claus in the *same day*? I could have died happy at age seven!

Competitive Colleagues

DADDY, MAMA, DEBBIE REYNOLDS, PHILIP AND MARK ON THE SET OF *MY SIX LOVES*

IN 1963, MAMA DID A FILM with Debbie Reynolds and Cliff Robertson called *My Six Loves*. It was one of those fluffy, romantic comedies along the lines of *Pillow Talk* or *Please Don't Eat the Daisies* about a Hollywood movie star (played by Reynolds) who adopts a family of six orphaned children. Cliff Robertson played the local preacher who, of course, falls in love with Debbie Reynolds in the last ten minutes of the film. Mama played Ethel, Debbie's personal assistant and "Gal Friday." The film was directed by Gower Champion, the celebrated Broadway director who was trying to parlay the success of *Bye, Bye Birdie* and *Carnival!* into a career in Hollywood. He was better off on Broadway. The following year, Champion would direct the legendary Broadway musical, *Hello Dolly!* After directing many other Broadway shows, he died on the opening night of *42nd Street*, one of his greatest triumphs.

Champion had the good sense to fill all of the supporting roles in *My Six Loves* with solid, Broadway character actors, including Alice Ghostley, Marty McCarty, Max Showalter, and David Janssen as Reynolds' cigar chomping Hollywood agent.

At the height of her stardom, Debbie Reynolds took to my mother immediately. They appreciated one another as professionals and no-nonsense, "call 'em as you see 'em" broads.

As the film was getting ready to wrap, Debbie told Mama that she was having a dinner party the following week for all the principal actors on the film and would she mind coming early in the day to help with table arrangements and place cards.

As Mama approached the elegant Bel Air home, Debbie Reynolds' butler greeted her at the door in a tailcoat.

"Yes, Miss Heckart," the butler said, "Miss Reynolds is expecting you. She's in the grand salon."

My mother hadn't yet dressed for the party and she was very conscious of being in her blue jeans and flannel shirt in front this elegant servant. As they went through one beautifully appointed room after another, she was relieved to see that Debbie was also in her jeans.

"Thank God you're in slacks,' Mama said. "I was feeling so self-conscious in front of your butler."

"Oh please," Debbie replied, "I *pay* him to dress up!"

They went into the elegant dining room and Debbie started consulting with her friend about who should sit next to whom. Mama was very impressed with the grand marble table, set with Waterford china, Steuben crystal, Baccarat water tumblers, and the best sterling silver. There was one item, however, that Mama recognized immediately. At each place setting was a glass bottle in the shape of a cluster of grapes. One grape cluster held a glass and a half of red or white wine (or cranberry juice if you were a friend of Bill W.) and each guest could refill their own wineglass as needed. My mother loved these inexpensive novelty bottles and she bought them by the dozen.

"Oh Debbie," Mama said, "Aren't those glass grapes just Heaven? I think they make them in Tijuana for about a nickel. I get them at the Pottery Barn in Connecticut for sixty-nine cents a piece. How much do you have to pay for them out here on the coast?"

Debbie stopped dead in her tracks and glared at her guest across the marble dining table. Her face was uncharacteristically pinched.

"Heckart," she said, "Tonight at the party, I am telling everyone I had them flown in from Switzerland. If you say a word, I'll kill you!"

That night, none of the dinner guests commented on the Steuben, the Waterford, or the Baccarat. All they wanted to know about were the glass bottles from Tijuana.

"Oh Debbie!" Gower Champion said. "Aren't those fabulous! Where did you ever find something like that?"

Sipping her Beaujolais, she said, "Why, thank you, darling. I had them flown in from Switzerland. Isn't that right, Heckart?" Debbie shot a steely gaze across the table.

"Mmmmhmm," Mama agreed, shaking her head. "Switzerland! A glassblower just outside of Zurich!"

⊗⊗⊗

One of Mama's favorite roles was Regina, the domineering Southern matriarch in Lillian Hellman's *The Little Foxes*. She had played the role in summer stock for Tec D'Acosta back in Milwaukee and was so eager to do it again, she went back to her alma mater, Ohio State University, and did it as a guest artist in a student production in the early sixties. As a young boy, I saw the film starring Bette Davis and completely understood why she loved this story of deceit and intrigue among a wealthy family in the 1800s fighting for control of their cotton plantation. When I was in high school, Mama and I talked about the play and the character of Regina.

"Is Regina the Bette Davis part?" I asked.

"Excuse me!" she said. "It's the Eileen Heckart part!"

"Oh! I'm so sorry!" I said.

It was one of the first times I saw the Mom turn into the Diva because of something I had said. It was a little scary. More was to come in my later years.

In 1956, she did a TV version of *The Little Foxes* for the *Hallmark Hall of Fame*, playing the supporting role of Birdie, the alcoholic sister-in-law. Greer Garson played Regina and Franchot Tone played Horace, her husband. It was directed by the great television director, George Schaeffer. Mama was disappointed not to have been cast as Regina, but Greer Garson was a big movie star at the time, so she bit her lip and played the plum, smaller role.

On the first day of shooting, Mama was delighted to see that the assistant director was Bob Hartung, an old friend from her days in live television. The two of them made plans to go out to lunch that day and have a lengthy catch-up and gabfest. When the break arrived, as the two of them headed for the door, Greer Garson approached them.

"Where are you going for lunch?" she asked. "May I join you?"

Heckart and Hartung looked at each other. They knew if Greer joined them they wouldn't have their dish session.

"Well, Greer," Mama said, "There aren't a lot of nice restaurants in this neighborhood. We're just going to some tacky little Irish pub around the corner. It's probably not up to your standards."

"That sounds fine. I'm half Irish, you know," Garson replied.

They were stuck. Gallantry or rudeness were the only options.

"Won't you join us?" Bob Hartung asked.

Heckart gave him a knowing look as if to say, "It's okay, we'll catch up another time."

They sat in the Blarney Stone Pub on Seventh Avenue as businessmen were wolfing down steak-and-kidney pies and old rummies sat at the bar. Greer Garson was dressed to the nines and dripping with jewelry. Her cloche hat with the amethyst brooch couldn't have looked more out of place. As they were having a subdued and polite meal, a young woman raced up to the table with an autograph book.

"Oh, this is my lucky day!" she exclaimed.

Garson flashed her best Hollywood smile and reached for the woman's fountain pen.

Not offering it, the young woman continued, "I just saw *The Bad Seed* for the fourth time. Miss Heckart, you are one of my favorite actresses. May I please have your autograph?"

As Mama reached for the pen and started to sign, Hartung turned to the young woman and said, "And you know who this is, don't you?"

Garson grabbed his arm. "Let Miss Heckart have her day," she said.

Whenever Mama repeated this story, she remembered Greer Garson as saying "Let Miss Heckart have her little moment." Interpreted that way, it's a very bitchy comment. She had thought Greer Garson was putting her down as a bit player having one small taste of glory. Years later, when I finally met Bob Hartung while I was directing in Albuquerque, I heard his version of the story. In his rendition, Greer Garson's response is gracious and elegant. She doesn't want to steal Eileen Heckart's thunder. Mama already had a certain amount of animosity towards Garson for playing Regina when she believed she was the better actress and more suited to the part. I guess I'll never know which one is accurate, but I choose to believe the gracious version of the story.

There was another incident on *The Little Foxes* regarding Greer Garson that I am not quite certain how to interpret, either. The producer hired a limousine and driver to pick up the cast each morning and return them home at the end of the day. The rigorous television shooting schedule was erratic, so the driver usually hung out on the set. Since he always picked up Greer Garson first, Heckart assumed this was her limo and that she was graciously transporting the other principal actors. At least she felt Garson was leading everyone to believe this was the case. One day during shooting, Heckart developed a terrible ear infection and was in great pain. She'd had mastoid surgery a few years before and knew she had to get to the emergency room. There was no one available to take her to the hospital except the limo driver. Holding a towel to her ear, which was bleeding profusely, Mama went to Greer Garson.

"Greer," she said, "I've got an emergency here and I have to get to a hospital. Would you mind if your limo driver took me to the hospital?'

"Darling, you must!" Garson replied. "The rest of us can take taxis home today. Don't give it another thought!"

Fortunately, it was nothing serious and she was back at work the next day. In the production office, she said, "It was awfully generous of Greer to let me take her limo. I want to thank her and pay for the driver's time yesterday."

"Miss Heckart," the associate producer said. "That's not *her* limo. It's for use by all of the principal actors. You have as much right to that limousine as she does anytime you need it."

Once again, I don't know how to read this story. Did Greer Garson *really* lead everyone to believe she got a limousine in her contract because she was a Hollywood star—or did Mama just interpret it that way? She'd never been a fan of Garson's and from the time she made her legendary five-and-a-half minute acceptance speech at the Academy Awards when she won for *Mrs. Minniver*, Mama had viewed her as a selfish, Hollywood phony. I'm certainly not saying that my mother was lying, and I never met Greer Garson to get my own take on her as a person. But I do know that she may have chosen to see the actress in a rather skewed way due to her own feelings of regret and animosity at not getting to play one of her dream roles on television. As far as I can see, Greer Garson was always considerate and benevolent with Heckart. If I hadn't met Bob Hartung and heard another version of the autograph story, I never would have questioned any of this. In spite of all her success, I interpreted these incidents with Greer Garson as more examples of Mama's insecurity. I felt sorry for the fact that whether it was as an actress, a wife or a mother, much of the time she felt she wasn't up to the challenge of juggling all three roles in her life. Often, she felt that at least one had to suffer for the sake of the other two. It wasn't true, but I know she saw it that way.

Where I saw this type of animosity for another actress the most was in my mother's reaction to Elaine Stritch. Heckart and Stritch were very similar types and they were up for many of the same roles. Most of the time, if it was a musical it went to Stritch—if it was a straight play, it went to Heckart. Because of her work in such groundbreaking shows as *Company*, Stritch received something akin to cult status in the American musical theater, which really annoyed Eileen Heckart. Even though they were on equal footing, she often viewed Stritch as the bigger star, which drove her crazy. Over the years, the word, "Stritch" became like a curse word in our household, especially the way my mother said it.

"You know that Woody Allen movie I was up for?' she said. "*Stritch* got it!"

She had a way of stretching out the "r" and hitting the "t" so the name rhymed with "bitch."

Elaine had a reputation for being very difficult. Heckart, on the other hand, had a reputation for being tough, but a consummate professional. She could be demanding and speak her mind, but always in the context of the work. When Mama was inducted in the Theatre Hall of Fame in 1994, the mistress of ceremonies for the evening was Elaine Stritch, who was not yet a member. I think this pleased Mama almost as much as the honor itself.

I was present at the ceremony, as were my father and brothers. We were all beaming with pride.

Afterwards, Elaine said to my mother, "You know, Heckie, back in the late forties when I had first arrived in New York, you and a couple of your friends invited me out for coffee one afternoon. I called my parents back in Michigan and I was so excited, I said to them, 'I just had coffee with some *real* actors.'"

There was a sweetness and a vulnerability about Elaine's statement that stopped my mother in her tracks. Was this jealousy one-sided?

Just as Mama was dying, Elaine Stritch was achieving great acclaim with her one-woman show, *Elaine Stritch at Liberty*. Because of her name being a dirty word in our household, I boycotted the show for a long time. My absence didn't hurt its success, especially in the theater community. When I finally saw it in Los Angeles, I was blown away. It was honest, funny, biting, tender, and one of the most exciting one-person shows I'd ever seen. I bought the double-CD recording of the show and played it in my car until I had committed it to memory. The humanity as well as the humor of it moved me so deeply, I tried to fashion my own one-man show after it.

In a strange way, seeing her show felt like being with Mama, yet hearing all new stories. I wondered if perhaps what Mama had criticized in Stritch all these years were really just the parts of herself she didn't like—the wisecracking, tough persona that covered a lot of old wounds. Perhaps Stritch held a mirror up to her—one she didn't always want to see. They were both cynical, call 'em-as-you-see 'em kind of broads and not exactly a picture of feminine gentility. In fact, this was a quality they both seemed to hold with disdain.

When I saw Stritch's show, I went backstage to speak to her afterward. I knew she'd never remember me, but I wanted to tell her how moved I was.

"Miss Stritch," I said, "You were just brilliant. I am Eileen Heckart's son."

She peered through her thick, black-rimmed glasses and stared at me, trying to find traces of my mother.

"You're Heckie's son?" she said softly.

I saw a lifetime of memories dance across her face.

"I miss her," she said.

"So do I, Miss Stritch."

Our Neighbor, Ethel Mertz

THE AUTOGRAPHED PICTURE VIVIAN VANCE SENT ME AFTER THE CHRISTMAS PARTY.
COURTESY ESTATE OF VIVIAN VANCE—REPRINTED WITH PERMISSION

MY MOTHER LOVED RITUALS. Whether it was the pomp and majesty of the Catholic church or the lore of the Native Americans, she was fascinated by the traditions that were passed down from generation to generation. Maybe it was the grand theatricality of them, or maybe it was something more. But she loved any excuse for a party or a celebration.

One year, as she was planning how to decorate the house for Christmas, she decided she wanted to follow an American Indian ritual and line the exterior of the house in *luminarias*: paper bags weighted down with sand, with a candle in the center to give off a soft glow. My older brothers hated those brown paper bags. There must have been fifty of them lining the driveway and another twenty-five edging the flat roof over my parents' bedroom.

During the entire Christmas season, every time my parents had company (which seemed particularly excessive that year), my brothers had to go out in the freezing Connecticut night air, through ice, snow, and single-digit temperatures and light the seventy-five *luminarias*. The ones on the icy, flat roof were particularly treacherous. Mark nearly fell off the side of the house more than once. But it was all for the sake of art, beauty and the holidays, so Mama had to have them. Thank God I was too little to go out in the snow and play with matches.

My mother was great friends with Vivian Vance, a native of Albuquerque, who told her about the *luminarias*. Much as we all came to love Viv, I don't think my brothers ever forgave her for planting that idea in Mama's head. Viv and her husband, John Dodds, often came to the house. That year, she taught my brothers and me how to fold the paper bags to make the *luminarias*. At first it seemed like a fun project, but the reality of it soon set in.

Viv was a warm, caring, sincere lady. She was Ethel Mertz without the cynicism. John Dodds was a major literary agent in Manhattan. He was an elegant man in cashmere sweaters and tweed suits who doted on Viv. She had seen my mother on *The Goodyear Television Playhouse* in the fifties and sent her the following note:

> *Dear Eileen Heckart—*
>> *I wrote you a fan letter last year after watching you on Kraft and never mailed it. I'm going to mail this one. You are, without a doubt, the greatest actress I ever saw. I admire you greatly.*
> *Vivian Vance*
> *"I Love Lucy"*

Mama was so touched by this letter, she wrote her back and a correspondence quickly blossomed into friendship. Since Viv and John lived in Stamford, two towns away, she and Mama would often run into each other on the train. They had never had any cause for more than a polite nod in the past. Now, whenever they met, they talked incessantly for the fifty-minute ride from Grand Central Terminal.

The first time Viv and John came to the Christmas party, I must have been about four. I was so nervous that Ethel Mertz was going to be in the living room. It was one thing to have Mama and her other actor friends around. But this was someone I watched on TV *every* day—and she was going to be in the *house*?!

I was afraid to meet her. As she sat in the living room, folding the Stop & Shop grocery bags that would be filled with sand and candles to line the driveway, I stood behind the door and peered at her. Yup, it was Ethel Mertz all right. How thrilling it was to see her up close! Of course, I had seen Mama on television any number of times, but that was different. This was one of the stars of *I Love Lucy*. Finally, she saw me peeking through the crack in the door.

She smiled, and said, "Hi!"

I started to run away, but bumped into Mama entering with another tray of canapés. "Come and meet Viv!" she said.

She took me in and intro-
duced me. My television idol
couldn't have been sweeter.
Viv sat me on her lap and
showed me how to fold the
luminarias. For the rest of
the evening, I wouldn't leave
her side. When I learned
that she lived on Long
Ridge Road in Stamford,
two towns over, I was beside
myself.

"Does that mean you'll
come again?" I asked.

"It sure does, honey, she
replied. "And maybe one
day, you'll come over to our
house, too!"

I couldn't believe that

THE DIVAS AND THEIR HUSBANDS AT HOME: MAMA, JOHN DODDS, GARY
MORTON, LUCILLE BALL, VIVIAN VANCE, AND DADDY

Ethel Mertz was inviting me
to her house. For a fleeting moment, I wondered if Fred would be there . . . then
John Dodds walked by.

One night, Mama and Daddy were at a dinner party at Viv and John's home
with Lucille Ball. Viv and Lucy remained the best of friends for the rest of their
lives. Lucy had always respected Eileen Heckart's work, but I think this was the
first time they had actually met. She was married to producer Gary Morton at the
time and, as successful businessmen, the three husbands got on famously. As the
ladies and their spouses were laughing, joking, and drinking, Lucy had one highball too many.

She turned to my mother and said, "Who the fuck knows Eileen Heckart? I could
make you a household name!"

The silence in Vivian Vance's Colonial living room was deafening.

After taking a sip of scotch, my mother replied, "Well . . . thank you . . . but, for
starters, I don't think I want to be a household name. There's an awful lot of baggage
that goes along with that."

Lucy scoffed at her, lighting another cigarette.

"Besides," Mama continued, "My husband's job is here in Connecticut. I couldn't
just up and move to the West Coast."

Lucy glanced across the room at my inconvenient father and waved her hand in
the air. "So, we'll make him an executive at Desilu. Husbands are expendable!"

That comment didn't exactly endear her to anyone in the room, least of all my
father. Mama looked Lucy right in the eye and said, "No, thank you."

After an awkward pause, my father reached for his car keys.

"C'mon honey, get your coat."

John Dodds walked my parents out to the car with an embarrassed smile. Viv called the next day and told Mama how sorry she was. "I guess Lucy had one too many last night," Viv said apologetically. "Please tell Jack how bad John and I feel. Should I call him myself?"

Mama assured her that it wouldn't be necessary. She also realized how difficult it could be at times for Viv to be "second banana" to a star as powerful as Lucille Ball.

⊗⊗⊗

In 1968, Vivian Vance did something incredibly generous for my parents. By now, she and John had moved from Stamford and had bought a ranch in Santa Fe. This was before Santa Fe had become the trendy, touristy destination it is today. It was a charming little Southwestern town where people went to get away from it all. Viv and John loved their place out there and were always after Mama and Daddy to come for a visit.

My father was going through an emotionally difficult time. I had never known Daddy to be anything other than strong and focused. Now, he was sullen and depressed. He was going through what Mama called his *What's It All About, Alfie?* period, otherwise known as midlife crisis. At age forty-seven, he was questioning whether or not selling insurance and raising three kids was all he had to look forward to for the rest of his life. He and Mama had some long, heavy talks, but it didn't seem to help. One night, Viv called and wanted to have a lengthy catch-up chat with Mama.

"So Heckie," Viv said, "tell me everything. How are the boys? How's Jack?"

"Well, Jack's not so good," Mama replied.

"What?" Viv responded, "Nothing's *ever* wrong with Jack. What's up?"

After Mama explained the situation, Viv said, "Send him to Santa Fe."

"Oh, but Viv, we couldn't possibly impose . . ."

"Honey," Viv repeated, "send him to Santa Fe."

Dad got on the phone and spoke with Viv for a few minutes. Maybe it would be a good thing after all. He was very fond of Viv and he and John were both successful businessmen with wives in show business. Perhaps it wasn't the worst idea.

My brothers and I were terribly confused when Mama explained that Daddy was going away for a few days by himself. At age eight, I was too young to fully comprehend it all, but I knew something wasn't right. Mama was the one who went away, not Daddy. And alone? This was very peculiar. Mama explained that he needed a little vacation. She spoke to us the way the dentist does when he says, "Now, this won't hurt a bit," before he yanks out your bicuspid without Novocain. Philip immediately assumed they were getting a divorce. I wasn't sure what that meant, but it didn't sound good. They both assured us that this wasn't true—Daddy just needed to go away on his own for a while and think some things through.

Behind our backs, Mama was quite nervous about it all. She'd never seen her husband so distraught. Had he had enough? Was dealing with the transient lifestyle of an actress too much for him? After being raised in such a broken home, one of the golden rules Eileen lived by was to sustain her marriage at all costs. She figured she'd better let him go off to Santa Fe and find himself, for better or worse. A few days later, Daddy boarded a plane for New Mexico.

Mama was so unaccustomed to Daddy being away, it really threw her off her stride. She insisted that Mark sleep on Daddy's side of the king-size bed, because she was afraid to be alone at night. She seemed to be smoking more than usual and was edgy and anxious. Daddy called us every night and told us about the natural beauty of the place, how he and John went horseback riding every night at sunset while Viv prepared wonderful Mexican dinners. Jack had many heart-to-heart talks with Viv and John. After he spoke to each of us, he and Mama would talk for a long time. My brothers and I tried to eavesdrop on the extension phone, but they always heard us breathing and made us hang up. We knew this was a major event in our parents' lives and that the outcome could drastically affect us.

After five days, Daddy came home. He seemed calm, energized, and possessed a renewed sense of purpose toward life. He and Mama were happier than ever. I never knew exactly what occurred during that time in Santa Fe, but I know Vivian Vance and John Dodds were instrumental in patching up a hole in my parents' marriage— or at least one in my father's heart. Nothing was ever said of it again, but I know that neither Mama nor Daddy ever forgot the consideration that Vivian Vance and her husband showed my father as he reached his proverbial fork in the road.

America's
Not-So-Sweetheart

THE CAST OF *TOO TRUE TO BE GOOD*—BACK ROW: RAY MIDDLETON, ROBERT
PRESTON CYRIL RITCHARD, DAVID WAYNE. FRONT ROW: LILLIAN GISH, SIR
CEDRIC HARDWICKE, MAMA, GLYNIS JOHNS. PHOTO BY FRED FEHL—WITH
PERMISSION OF GABRIEL PINSKI

THE CAST OF theatrical stalwarts assembled for the all-star revival of George
Bernard Shaw's *Too True to Be Good* (1963) included Robert Preston, Glynis Johns,
Cyril Ritchard, David Wayne, Ray Middleton, Sir Cedric Hardwicke, Lillian Gish,
and Eileen Heckart. Too bad they couldn't get anybody good. It consisted of two
one-act comedies and with this stellar cast, it became one of the "must-see" events
of the Broadway season.

During this time, Mama rekindled her friendship with Lillian Gish. Having
toured with her sister Dorothy in *Over 21* while Jack was overseas during the war,
they had kept in touch periodically over the years and were delighted to be working

together. One day, Lillian overheard Mama on the telephone backstage. She was trying to make arrangements for someplace to stay before the matinees so she didn't have to commute from Connecticut on two-show days. All of her options were going bust.

She explained this to Lillian, who said, "Then you must stay with Dorothy and me!"

"Oh Lillian," she replied, "That's very generous of you, but I couldn't impose."

"Nonsense!" Lillian replied. "We have converted Mother's suite into a guest room. We'd be delighted to have you."

For the entire three month run, every Tuesday and Friday night, Mama had a sleepover with two of America's first silent-film stars, Lillian and Dorothy Gish. The Gish sisters were complete tea totallers. They never touched a drop of alcohol, but they purchased a pint bottle of scotch they kept on hand for their guest. Whenever she arrived, Lillian scurried around putting out ashtrays and fluffing pillows.

Lillian said to Mama, "Mother used to say one could always tell if a girl was good because she wore panties and she didn't smoke cigarettes. Eileen, dear, you're *half* good!"

One Friday evening, before her second weekly stay-over, Lillian came to Mama's dressing room.

"Eileen, dear, Dorothy and I have been invited to supper after the show at '21' with some old friends and we were wondering if you'd like to join us."

"That's very sweet of you, Lillian," Mama said. "Who are the friends?"

"Mary Pickford and Buddy Rogers."

My mother couldn't believe what she was hearing. Would she care to dine at '21,' one of New York's most exclusive restaurants, with four of the biggest silent screen stars of all time, the first movie actors and her childhood legends? Boy, she thought to herself, this kid from Columbus has done good! She had a girlhood crush on Buddy Rogers ever since she saw *Wings*, the very first Oscar-winning picture, and she had always loved Mary Pickford, America's sweetheart. Surely, this would be an evening to remember.

Heckart and the Gishes arrived at '21' first. The ladies ordered their glasses of tomato juice and Mama had a scotch on the rocks. When Buddy Rogers entered, he looked as handsome and dashing as ever. Mary Pickford was on his arm, looking pale, delicate, and fragile. Ten years his senior, she looked considerably older and more like his mother than his wife. Buddy Rogers was charming. He flirted with the Gish sisters, who loved male attention. Mary Pickford sat quietly in the corner drinking double old-fashioneds like they were soda pop. While Dorothy's attention was diverted, Lillian followed Mama to the ladies' room. When she came out, Lillian cornered her as she walked through the bar, speaking in an urgent whisper.

"Eileen, dear," she said. "May I have one of your cigarettes, please?"

"You want to *smoke*, Lillian?!" Mama asked.

"Shhh!" Lillian said, stomping her tiny foot. "You mustn't let Dorothy know I smoke!" Mama looked at Lillian and considered this for a moment.

"Wait a minute. You're *how* old, Lillian?"

"Seventy," Lillian replied.

"And how old is Dorothy?" Mama asked.

"Sixty-five."

"Lillian," Mama said, fishing out two cigarettes, "don't you think you're old enough to do as you please?"

"Oh, no!" Lillian gasped. "She's my baby sister. It would destroy her if she knew. You must promise me you won't tell."

"I promise, Lillian. Scout's honor." Eileen laughed to herself as she lit both cigarettes and handed one to Lillian. They stood there in the bar at '21' puffing away. Lillian felt terribly wicked, even though she never inhaled.

As they returned to the table, Mary Pickford was on her fourth double old-fashioned and was slumping in the banquette. Buddy Rogers leaned over, attempting to adjust her. She slapped his hand away. As the rest of them proceeded to have a sumptuous meal of filet mignon with asparagus and baked potatoes, Mary Pickford just kept drinking. She contributed nothing to the conversation unless someone spoke directly to her.

"Mary, darling," Dorothy said. "Tell Eileen about Pickfair!"

"Oh yes," Mama said, "I've heard so much about it!'

The estate Mary Pickford had built with Douglas Fairbanks in Beverly Hills was legendary. Mama had read about it in movie magazines as a young girl and had often fantasized about this grand, movie-star palazzo. Pickford said nothing. After an awkward pause, Buddy Rogers started regaling the ladies with tales about the estate.

Mary Pickford chimed in from behind her highball glass.

"Pickfair!" she screamed at her husband. "You're never getting your hands on Pickfair! I'm leaving everything to the State of California and to the Motion Picture Home and you can go fuck yourself!"

Dorothy Gish turned white. Lillian dabbed her forehead with her napkin.

"Oh dear Eileen," Lillian said, pursing her lips, "It's a tragic evening! Just a tragic evening!"

From then on, whenever Mama got together with the Gish sisters, it was for afternoon tea in the Palm Court at the Plaza Hotel. It was a far safer choice.

Barefoot in the Confessional

BAREFOOT IN THE PARK—1965. © BILLY ROSE THEATRE COLLECTION, THE NEW YORK PUBLIC LIBRARY FOR THE PERFORMING ARTS—ASTOR, LENOX AND TILDEN FOUNDATIONS

IN SEPTEMBER 1965, my mother was asked to replace Mildred Natwick as the mother in Neil Simon's *Barefoot in the Park* on Broadway. This was Neil Simon's third major comic success, following *Come Blow Your Horn* and *Little Me*. It was a sweet comedy about newlyweds in a tiny, New York apartment. The conservative, widowed mother of the bride comes for a visit and discovers new love herself with the rakish older man next door. Mama had been offered the role of the mother originally and turned it down for several reasons. First of all, she was hesitant about working with an unproven Broadway director. The guy they had hired was part of a popular comedy duo, but he didn't have a track record directing for the theater. His name was Mike Nichols. I wonder whatever happened to him?

The second reason was that the leads were to be played by Elizabeth Ashley and Robert Redford. Heckart knew of Bob Redford's fine reputation as a hard-working young actor who had done several solid, supporting roles on Broadway in the past few years. In fact, an agent friend of Heckart's, a flinty, fast-talking show-business broad named Jean Thomas, had been trying to help the young Redford break into television commercials. Jean worked very hard for the up and coming actor and had no luck getting anyone to give him the time of day. When Jean sent Redford to one arrogant casting director, the woman whined, "He's got a mole on his face! I can't use an actor with a mole on his face." Jean was furious that the powerful casting director wouldn't even consider Redford. A few years later, this same casting director (having no memory of the incident) called Jean Thomas and said, "I'm looking for someone with a lot of talent—a real Robert Redford type."

Jean shouted into the phone, "You wouldn't know if Robert Redford had talent if he was on top of you fucking you!"

The main reason Heckart didn't want to do *Barefoot* when it was first offered was because of Elizabeth Ashley. For all her talent, Mama had heard that Ashley had a reputation for being difficult. She had come up to the house one evening when I was quite young as a guest of actress Jean Arthur. I was four years old and when it got to be nine o'clock, Mama said, "Luke, its way past your bedtime."

Jean Arthur and Elizabeth Ashley had both said, "Wait a minute! We're enjoying his company and we're not ready for him to go to bed yet!"

"Well, neither of you are his mother, are you?!" Heckart snapped at the two ladies.

Jean Arthur never stopped talking about herself and Ashley occurred to my mother as a woman who seemed insecure and deeply troubled. When Mama's agent, Milton Goldman, called to offer my mother the role of *Barefoot in the Park*, Heckart said to Milton, "Well I hear Redford is charming—but I've met Miss Ashley and I don't think I'd feel comfortable working with her."

"Heckie, that's not your province," Milton replied.

"The hell it isn't!" she said. "I have to face her eight times a week while you sit back and collect your ten percent?! You're fired!"

Mama slammed down the phone and didn't speak to Milton Goldman, a good friend and the best agent she ever had, for nearly a year. She found another agent in the interim and eventually she reconciled with Milton, but she was so angry over the Elizabeth Ashley incident, it took awhile for their relationship to regain its former level of trust and camaraderie.

Barefoot was a huge success. It ran for 1,530 performances on Broadway, playing over three-and-a-half years. Once Ashley and Redford had completed the initial year, the producers started casting replacements and turned to Heckart. By then, she knew that Mike Nichols was more than a stand-up comic and she was hoping that he would come back and work with the replacement cast, but he had no interest in doing so. In fact, although Nichols directed many long-running plays over the years, he never returned to a show after opening night. The stage manager or the assistant director would maintain the show and put in replacements. Once the initial thrill was over for Nichols, there was no fun in it for him and he never went back. Mama ran into him in Shubert Alley one day before rehearsals started.

"Mike," she said, "Won't you please come back, even for a few days?"

"Oh Eileen," he said, "I thought about it when I heard you were going to be taking over, but I just can't."

The stage manager put Heckart through her paces with the two young actors, Penny Fuller and Tony Roberts, playing her daughter and son-in-law. Mama was crazy about Penny and Tony. She kept in touch with both of them for the rest of her life and they became cherished family friends. Penny became one of the daughters Mama never had. She came up to the house many times and often turned to Mama for career advice. Mama was so proud of her success, especially when Penny was nominated for a Tony as Eve Harrington in the musical *Applause*. A few years before Mama died, she learned that Tony Roberts was going to be playing the role of George, the embittered, middle-aged college professor in Edward Albee's *Who's Afraid of Virginia Woolf?* at the Berkshire Theatre Festival.

"No!" she cried. "He's way too young!"

In Heckart's mind, Tony Roberts would forever be twenty-four. I wonder how she'd feel to know he just opened on Broadway as Mr. Velasco, the rakish love interest to the mother in a revival of *Barefoot in the Park*.

My older brother Mark got his sexual education from watching *Barefoot*. The first act ended with Tony and Penny as the young newlyweds, stripping down to their underwear and getting ready for bed. Mark later told me that when he was thirteen and saw Penny Fuller backstage in her bra and panties, all sorts of things arose—and questions, too. Mark has always had a special place in his heart for Penny, as have I.

During the run of *Barefoot*, an ardent fan of Mama's, who ran a sporting goods store, came backstage. Knowing Heckart had three sons, he gave her three pairs of metal baseball cleats in varying sizes.

"If they don't fit," he said, "they'll grow into 'em!"

She thought this was a rather strange gift, but thanked him all the same.

A few days later, Mama was in the kitchen doing dishes while I, at age six, sat peacefully in the combination dining room and family room watching cartoons. With the kitchen door open, Mama could keep a watchful eye on her youngest. Twelve-year-old Philip came barging in.

"Get out!" he said. "I want to watch *F-Troop*."

"No!" I whined. "I was here first and I'm watching Bugs Bunny!"

Mama overheard the exchange and was turning around to intervene just as she saw Philip pick up one of the metal baseball cleats. He put it on his hand like a glove and whacked me in the back of the head. I screamed like a stuck pig, more from the injustice than from the actual pain. Mama witnessed the whole scene and she was seeing red. It was one of those times when a parent observes her child doing something so rotten, so unconscionable, that, for a moment, she thinks no punishment is too great. Philip was frozen in shock as Mama bolted into the dining room. She immediately came over and comforted me, to make sure I wasn't bleeding or scarred. Once she knew my skin wasn't broken, there was one thing on her mind: to make Philip pay. She turned to the twelve-year-old with fire in her eyes and started chasing him all around the dining room. Philip ran as fast as he could, darting behind the chairs, under the table, and across the floor on his belly. The boy was so small and wiry, he knew he could outrun his mother, until she got him cornered behind the rattan sofa, where I sat screaming my head off. By this point, I wasn't yelling in pain, but so that my older brother would get in more trouble. As the youngest, I'd learned this technique at an early age.

The entire time Mama was chasing Philip around the room, she was shouting, "How could you do such a terrible thing to your brother? I am going to spank you so hard when I catch you! You are in big trouble, mister!"

Her prey was trapped behind the furniture in the corner of the room, but she still couldn't get to him. He was crunched up in a tiny, unreachable ball. As a last resort, she kicked at him. Even in her rage, she was aware her toes weren't making contact with anything. But she was so furious, she had to express her anger physically and kicking in his general direction was as close as she could get.

After the incident was over and Philip had been banned from watching TV for a whole month, the guilt set in.

"How could I have behaved so badly?" she said to herself. "No matter what my child did, that was beyond the pale." Being a good Catholic, she figured she'd better get to confession, and fast.

The next day was Wednesday, a matinee day for *Barefoot in the Park*, so this was perfect. Every Catholic actor on Broadway knew that the Monsignor Phillip Nolan, the old priest at Saint Malachy's on West Forty-Ninth Street, was a big theater lover. He'd give you absolution and get you in and out of confession in record time. After the matinee, Mama ate a quick sandwich at her dressing table while putting her hair up in rollers for the evening show. Wearing full stage makeup, including two pairs of false eyelashes, she wrapped a shocking pink scarf over her curlers like a babushka, donned a white mink coat with pair of dark glasses, and trotted off to confession.

As she sat in the tiny chapel at Saint Malachy's waiting her turn, she saw good ol' Monsignor Nolan exit the confessional. He was replaced by a young, red-headed Irishman. He was around twenty-five years old and looked like he'd just stepped out of the seminary and off the plane from County Cork.

"Hmmm," she thought to herself. "Must be the changing of the guard. Well, I hope this kid can still get me in and out pretty fast."

When the curtain was pulled back on the confessional, she removed her dark glasses and knelt in the booth, crossing herself. She began the familiar prayer.

"Bless me Father, for I have sinned. It has been three weeks since my last confession." She paused before she continued, not wanting to speak the next words aloud. "Father," she said, "I kicked my child."

The young priest tried to remain impassive.

"Ya kicked yer child?" he repeated, in an Irish brogue so thick you could cut it with a butter knife.

As bad as it was when she said it, to have someone else repeat it made the offense seem even worse.

"Yes, Father," she said. "I kicked my child." The young priest leaned forward and peered at her through the lattice-work grate that separated penitent and confessor. He studied her for a long time, focusing on her heavy makeup, curlers, and white mink.

"Are you a working girl?" he asked.

"Yes, Father, I work," she answered, not understanding his implication.

He nodded his head. "What part of town do ya work in?" he asked.

"Around Times Square," she said, referring to the Theater District.

The young priest scowled at her.

"And what hours do ya work?" he demanded.

"Mostly in the evenings," she replied.

"And who takes care of your children while you're workin' in the evening?" he asked.

"My husband," she replied.

"Oh, and yer husband approves of yer work, does he?" he asked.

"Well, not really, but I love it so much he knows he can't stop me."

She fingered her rosary beads. She'd never had a priest grill her like this at confession.

"And ya kicked yer child?" He spoke slowly, measuring out each word.

Eileen glanced at her watch. "Father," she said, "Is this going to take much longer? I have to get back to work."

"Oh ya do, do ya?" Now he was sounding angry. "And what exactly is it that ya do?"

"I'm an actress, Father!" she said. "What did you think?"

The priest looked nervous and confused. "Well . . . what show are ya in?" he asked.

"*Barefoot in the Park*, Father," she said.

"Good God!" the priest shouted, "You're gonna be late for the evenin' show! Say one Hail Mary and get the hell outta here!"

The Automat and
Forest Lawn

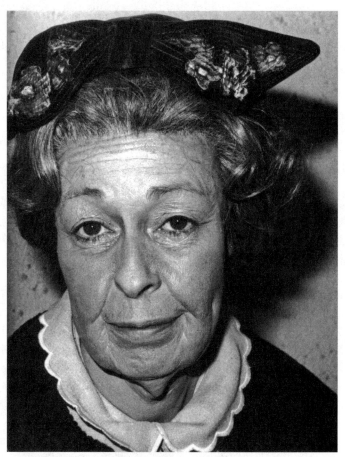

MAMA AT FORTY-SEVEN, WEARING SEVEN HOURS' WORTH OF OLD AGE MAKEUP FOR
THE PBS TELEPLAY *SAVE ME A PLACE AT FOREST LAWN*

EVER SINCE MAMA had worked with Teresa Wright in *The Dark at the Top of the
Stairs*, she and her husband, Robert Anderson had remained great friends. She was
delighted when she was asked to do Anderson's new play, *You Know I Can't Hear
You When the Water's Running* on Broadway. It consisted of four one-act comedies
dealing with sexual situations which were quite shocking at the time. Directed by
Alan Schneider, the cast included Heckart, Martin Balsam, George Grizzard, and
Melinda Dillon. The production was very successful, running for 756 performances.

While she was doing *Water* on Broadway in the fall of 1967, Mama was sent a script for a PBS special. It was to be part of a series called *The New York Television Playhouse*, where plays were filmed for broadcast. The third in a trilogy entitled *Acts Before Dying*, the piece was called *Save Me a Place at Forest Lawn.* Since she was already in a hit Broadway show, the schedule was impractical, the money laughable, but she simply had to do it.

Forest Lawn was a thirty-minute one-act play about two old ladies sitting at a table in the automat planning their funerals while they eat their lunch. It was funny, touching and utterly charming. Maureen Stapleton had been cast in the other role and a young television director with a theater background named Glenn Jordan was set to direct. Jordan would go on to become one of the formost directors and producers of dramatic movies for television.

Aside from being crazy about the script, at forty-seven, Heckart relished the chance to play a crusty octogenarian. Written by a woman named Lorees Yerby, the play had been produced Off-Broadway starring Margaret Hamilton and Mildred Dunnock. The script was well received from the outset. For PBS, the choice was made to go with younger actresses playing older women.

Mama did lots of research for *Forest Lawn.* She went into the theater early almost every day and had dinner at Horn & Hardart or Chock Full o' Nuts, two of the few remaining automats in New York City. "I have to find my lady," she said.

Sometimes she came home with very sweet stories about the old ladies and gentlemen who were the regulars at these cafeterias. At other times, she said to me, "Darling, there's so much loneliness in the world. It's so sad."

Mama loved doing this research. Dad was a little disappointed that she was home even less now, but he knew how important this role was to her. She wrote notes when she could do so without being conspicuous. Mostly, she just observed and remembered.

One night, Mama came home absolutely thrilled. "I found my lady today!" she announced.

"Really? That's great," I said. "What was she like?"

"Tall, wiry and crazy as a loon," she replied.

The whole family congregated in the living room to hear the tale.

"Well," Mama said, "she was impeccably dressed in clothes from the early forties that reeked of moth balls. She sat there stuffing a Kleenex into her fist and talking into it like she was communicating with the mother ship or something. She was wearing a tired, fox stole and an awful hat with a rhinestone brooch that was missing half the stones. Whenever anyone got too close to her, she'd start screaming at them. It was usually something like, 'Godammit, can't you watch where the hell you're going?'"

"Then she'd stuff her Kleenex deeper into her fist and talk about it into her hand, like she was holding a telephone. The whole thing was so comical, I couldn't help but laugh."

"She caught me and said, 'I guess you think I'm pretty funny don't you?'"

"I had no choice but to say, 'Yes ma'am, I do.'"

"She came back at me with, 'Well ya know, it's all Calvin Coolidge's fault!'"

"I said, 'I beg your pardon, ma'am?'"

"She went on a tirade, saying, 'He let all those goddamn foreigners in here! Gotta get a boat! Get 'em outta here! Might take two boats!'"

"As she was ranting and raving, I was thrilled. She was so feisty and ornery, I said to myself, 'That's my lady.'"

Mama had great respect for Maureen Stapleton and was delighted that she was going to play opposite her. After she found her lady, she phoned Maureen to share her enthusiasm for the project.

"Mo, isn't it a wonderful script?" she said into the phone.

"Well, I guess so, Heckie," Maureen said, "I'm just not sure I'm up to it."

"Why, Mo?" Heckart asked. "What's the matter?"

It seems the well-known character actor with whom Maureen Stapleton had been living had run off with Zora Lampert, a hot, young character actress.

"Heckie, I've been so depressed, I just don't know if I feel like doing anything right now," Maureen said. "Call me at the end of the week."

This was quite a blow. It was the most excited I'd ever seen my mother about a project and her co-star in a two-character play was apathetic at best. It didn't bode well. When she called Maureen at the end of the week, she went on and on about her breakup, but still hadn't made a decision about *Save Me a Place at Forest Lawn.* It was less than a week before the shooting was to begin. Mama was getting anxious. Finally, with the support of her director, she used a little reverse psychology on Maureen.

"Mo, I know you'd be wonderful in this part. Together, I think we could play the hell out of it. I've spoken with Glenn Jordan about your situation and if you really don't think you're up to it, he's lined up Ruth White to replace you. We both still want you to do it, but he needs to have an answer by Monday."

It's amazing how quickly the idea of expendability can cure all ills. Maureen was fine on Monday. The two actresses were wonderful in *Save Me a Place at Forest Lawn* and both won regional Emmy Awards for their work. Dick Smith, the renowned Hollywood make-up artist, spent seven hours perfecting old-age makeup on my mother, including a turkey waddle and bags under her eyes. Since Maureen was heavy at the time of the taping, all she did was put a few gray streaks in her hair, and they looked the same age.

When they both showed up for the awards ceremony, Maureen was thin as a rail. This is the delicate Maureen Stapleton we think of in films like *Airport*, which was filmed two years later. Mama hardly recognized her.

"Mo, you look wonderful!" Mama said. "What happened?"

"It wasn't easy!" Maureen said. "They locked me in a funny farm for six months!"

Save Me a Place at Forest Lawn was one of the most satisfying pieces of my mother's career. It was sweet, funny, and brimming with heart. The combination between Maureen Stapleton and her was perfect.

Flash forward to 1998. I was looking for a small film project in which I could direct my mother. I got in touch with Michael Dutton, the son of deceased playwright Lorees Yerby, and took an option on *Save Me a Place at Forest Lawn* to adapt it into a movie for television for Mama and Julie Harris. With a letter of commitment from Julie, I started working on the script. I'd do reading after rewrite and I just couldn't get it to work. Maintaining the delicacy and intimacy of the original while expanding the story and adding more characters was more difficult than I had thought.

"I don't know how I feel about doing *Forest Lawn* again, honey," Mama said. "When I was in my forties, I could have a sense of humor about being eighty. Now I'm not so sure."

I assured her that she had retained her sense of humor and would add a different dimension to the project that wasn't there thirty years ago. She remained skeptical.

When I made the mistake of showing a few of my early, unfinished drafts to Mama, she encouraged me at first, then said, "Honey, you're never going to get that piece to work. Just give up on it."

When I brought in an old friend, Jim Bontempo, as a co-writer, she said, "Are you still working on that damn *Forest Lawn* piece? Jeee sus, you're more stubborn than the Republicans!"

After a while, I stopped talking to her about it, but quietly kept working on the script.

Finally, Jim and I were ready to do a first-class reading in Los Angeles. Under the new title, *A Place at Forest Lawn*, after nearly two years of work we felt we had a viable script. Julie Harris was recovering from a stroke and it was unclear if this great lady of the theater would ever work again. My heart ached for her. I offered to fly Mama out to do the reading.

"You'd better send me the script first," she said.

"Of course," I replied.

"You'll have to blow it up pretty big, you know. My macular degeneration has gotten even worse since I saw you last."

By the time I enlarged the seventy-five-page script to a size she could read, it was well over two hundred pages. Jim and I referred to the draft as "Heckielawn."

She called me a few days later.

"I'm pretty bummed out," she said.

"How come?" I asked.

"Because I hate turning down a good script," she said. "And *A Place at Forest Lawn* is a good script. Darling, I'm sorry, but I'm just not well enough to work at the moment. Listen, you've taken this and made it a viable script for a couple of old broads. See if you can get someone like Anne Bancroft. You don't need me anymore, honey. Go do this project without me."

It was a tremendous rite of passage.

We rented the Coronet Theatre. I cashed in a lot of favors and assembled a cast that included Marion Ross in Mama's role, Betty White, Marcia Cross, Steven

Culp, and John Glover. I filled the place with agents, producers, and studio types. The reaction was electric.

One Hollywood mogul after another said, "Here's my card. Call me in the morning. The script isn't quite there yet, but I can see the potential. Call me tomorrow and we'll discuss it."

I was over the moon. I woke up the next morning, ready to spend the day on the telephone when I turned on the news. It was September 11, 2001. Timing is everything. I do not pretend for a moment that what happened to me that day compares in any way to the loss and devastation suffered by so many others, but it was lousy timing.

After 9/11, no one was interested in a script about dying with dignity and assisted suicide. In the interim, we decided to rewrite it as a play, figuring we'd have a better chance of getting it produced as a full-length theater piece. After five more readings and ten more rewrites, it got its first professional Equity production in Arvada, Colorado in the fall of 2005. Even with all the wonderful actresses who have done staged readings of the script, including Pat Carroll, Frances Sternhagen, Elizabeth Wilson, Millicent Martin, and Barbara Rush, it's hard for me not to hear Mama's voice in the leading role.

The Christmas Party and Merman's Martini

THE FAMILY IN FRONT OF THE EILEEN HECKART CELEBRITY CHRISTMAS TREE AT HALLMARK GALLERIES

MAMA LOVED THE HOLIDAYS. In fact, she was such a Christmas lady that Martin Richards, the producer of *Chicago* and many other Broadway hits once commented, "Luke, sometimes I think Christ was born just so your mother could have her party."

Sacrilegious as the comment was, I saw Marty's point. On Thanksgiving Day, before the we could have our turkey, my brothers and I had go out to the garage and carry in the twelve refrigerator boxes full of wreaths, lights, garlands, and enough ornaments to decorate a medium-sized village. As a little boy, this gave me a real sense of magic and wonder about Christmas. The house was totally transformed. There were gold swags running down all the staircases, a nativity scene in every corner, evergreen wreaths, and garlands aplenty and, the grand centerpiece of the house, a fourteen-foot Christmas tree with exotic lights and handmade decorations.

One year on Christmas Day, one of my friends commented, "Don't sit still too long at the Yankees. Eileen is liable to put a wreath around your neck!"

Mama even went so far as to put a little crown on top of her Oscar and a ring of fake holly around his feet. Even her Academy Award had a special holiday outfit.

The Hallmark Greeting Card Company had a gallery on West Fifty-Seventh Street, connected to one of their larger New York stores. They had different seasonal exhibits, including a celebrity Christmas tree display. The Hallmark executives requested a handful of celebrities each year to describe what their ideal Christmas tree would look like, then their designers created it and put it on display. The photo at the start of this chapter is Eileen Heckart's perfect Christmas tree. She hired a photographer and made special arrangements for us to have our photo taken in front of it.

In New York theatrical circles, you knew you had arrived when you were invited to Eileen Heckart's tree trimming party in Connecticut. This was the one, big party my parents gave every year. Most of the time, some pretty major celebrities turned up. Everyone in our family would talk about "the Christmas Party" in hushed tones, with a sense of reverence. In addition to the tree trimming and house decorating, it was a sit-down dinner for thirty-five people. Considering our tiny, family dining room could comfortably hold twenty at most, bodies were crammed in elbow to jowl. As far as I was concerned, the best part of all was that I got to play host to the biggest stars on Broadway. I was nervous, excited and the king of the world.

Mama was a fabulous hostess, always trying to outdo herself. One year, she wanted to serve a delicacy she had seen at Marlene Dietrich's house. It was a *croque en bouche* (French for "crisp in the mouth"), an elaborate pastry made out of a tower of profiteroles (a fancy word for cream puffs) in the shape of a Christmas tree.

She telephoned caterers all over Fairfield County searching for anyone who even knew what she was talking about, let alone was willing to make one for her. By the time she got to caterer number fifteen, Mama said, "Honey, do you have any idea what a *croque en bouche* is?"

"Of course I do," the woman said.

"Thank God!" Mama said, slapping the counter. "Can you make me one for a party on Sunday the fourteenth?"

Mama heard the woman flipping pages in a date book. "Yes," she replied. "If your party is on Sunday, I'll have it ready on . . . Thursday."

"Perfect!" Mama said. "You're saving my whole Christmas!"

Mama called the caterer on the appointed day. "Hello, this is Mrs. Yankee."

"Who?" the harried woman said into the phone.

"Mrs. Yankee?" Mama replied. "I'm calling about my . . ."

"Oh, of course, you're the *croque en bouche*," the caterer replied.

"Yes," Mama said. "May I pick it up today?"

"Oh no," the woman said. "I couldn't possibly have it for you today. Check back tomorrow."

Mama was a little put off, but called back the following afternoon.

"Nope, not yet," the caterer said. Her voice was edgy and tired. "I have a dinner for 200 guests from the UN tonight. I'll have it for you tomorrow."

""You *do* realize that my party's on Sunday?" Mama said.

"I'm aware of that. You'll have it," the woman said, and hung up the phone.

When Mama called back on Saturday and it still wasn't ready, her annoyance turned to panic.

She whimpered like a puppy who'd been beaten with a hairbrush. "I've planned my whole meal around this goddamn *croque en bouche*," she said. "It's my only dessert. If that fucking caterer doesn't have it ready in time, I'm going to cry!"

By now my father, brothers and I had learned to take such crises in stride. Mama always got a little hysterical the day before the Christmas party, so she was right on schedule. Still, we understood her disappointment. As a backup, she had me run to Gristede's Market and buy three chocolate Yule logs and six quarts of Neapolitan ice cream.

The morning of the party, Mama the called the caterer one last time. "Hello, this is Mrs. . . . ."

"It's ready," the woman replied.

My mother was a wreck, what with all the other party preparations, but she stopped everything and asked me to go with her to carry the *croque en bouche*. I had visions of coming home for the weekend that summer from Manhattan as my father and I would be served Neapolitan ice cream and chocolate Yule logs all through the reruns of *Columbo* and *M*A*S*H*.

We arrived at the stylish, Fairfield County clapboard house with the long, winding driveway and found our way to the oversized kitchen with beamed ceilings and hanging copper pots. I expected some round, elderly lady to emerge from a storefront. Instead, a youngish, blond, country-club matron glanced our way as she applied purple rosettes to a white cake from a pastry tube.

"May I help you?" the woman asked, not looking up from behind her large cake.

"I'm Mrs. Yankee?" Mama said, drumming her fingers on a rustic ladder-back chair.

"It's on the counter," the woman said, returning to her pastry tube. Her shrill voice had no emotion whatsoever. I thought that if she were a warmer person, she would be very pretty. She was wearing a white butcher's apron over a lavender blouse and gray slacks. There was something almost regal about her.

"You can just leave the check in the basket by the door," she said.

As Mama scribbled out a check, I reached for the *croque en bouche*.

"Gently!" the woman said, as I started to pick it up. I carried it like a newborn infant, afraid to even breathe in its direction. Mama studied the precious cargo in my arms, wrapped in yards of cellophane.

"It looks beautiful," Mama said as she placed the check in a bleached wicker basket.

The caterer managed a pained smile for the first time. "Glad you like it," she said, still without looking up. As we were leaving, she mumbled, "Have a nice party."

Once in the car, I clutched the pastry tower for dear life, terrified I would smash the delicate tree of cream puffs. Oh my God, I thought to myself, if I were to break this thing now, I'd be grounded for the rest of my life. I started to reach for my seat belt, but was afraid it might dent the side of the *croque en bouche*, so I wrapped both my arms around it and clutched the armrest for support. My fingers were turning purple, but I didn't dare loosen my grip.

Mama reached for a True Blue before turning on the ignition. "Ooooh," she said as she exhaled a large puff of smoke, "That caterer was such a bitch! I will *never* do business with that woman again!"

A few years later, I was at a wedding and that same blond lady was the caterer. In front of the guests, she was all smiles, but I caught her coming out of the kitchen reducing one of the waiters to tears. I was glad not to know what was going on behind the scenes.

When Mama posted her Christmas list the following November, there was a book on it called *Entertaining with Martha Stewart*.

I said, "I'd like to get you that *Entertaining* book for Christmas—as if you need another one."

She said, "Oh, but Martha Stewart is all the rage, even if she was so rude to me."

"Why?" I asked, "What did she do?"

"You were there, too," she said.

"I was?"

"Of course—the *croque en bouche*, remember?"

I nearly dropped my coffee cup.

"Martha Stewart was the snooty lady who made the *croque en bouche?*"

"Of course," she said, "Who else?"

I hadn't known her name at the time, but the entire world knew it now.

⊗⊗⊗

About seven years earlier, Paul Newman gave me some pointers at the Christmas party on how to upstage my co-star in children's theater. I was doing the two-character, psychological thriller *Sleuth* in the basement of the YMCA. Never mind the fact that I was thirteen playing a thirty-five-year-old womanizer. My co-star, Robbie Drinkwater, wouldn't learn his lines. He was too busy trying to French kiss Erica Barton in the boiler room. Sometimes they let me watch, but I got bored. Clearly, Robbie didn't take the play as seriously as I did and I was really ticked when he still hadn't memorized his script a week before we were supposed to perform. I was sharing my frustration with one of the neighbors at the Christmas party and Paul Newman overheard it.

Mr. Newman turned to me with a warm, fatherly smile. He said, "Listen guy. When I'm working with an actor who doesn't know his lines, here's what I do. Rather than saving his ass and throwing him an ad-lib, I just stare at him with a sort-of shocked expression. I give him a look that says, 'Well, it ain't me, buddy! If you don't know where you are in the scene, I sure as hell can't help you!' I'm telling you, Luke, it works every time."

I hung on his every word. As I was taking it in, I was saying in my head, "Holy shit! I'm getting acting lessons from Paul Newman!"

Outwardly, I kept my cool. I said, "Thanks a lot, Mr. Newman. I'll give it a try."

I couldn't wait to get to rehearsal the next day and try it on Robbie Drinkwater. Secretly, I hoped Robbie hadn't been studying his script all weekend. Of course, he hadn't. When he missed his first cue and I just stood there staring him down, we both wound up standing onstage looking like assholes. I doubt that ever happened to Paul Newman.

While I could certainly be a starstruck kid, it was hard to be bowled over by these people when they were just being regular folks, hanging out in Mama and Daddy's living room helping put up the Christmas decorations. Earlier that evening, Mr. Newman had been telling Daddy how he could built a go-kart track around the greenhouse for my older brothers. Mark and Philip loved the idea. Mama didn't.

While I was getting my acting tips that night, Joanne Woodward was sitting nearby stringing popcorn and cranberries. One of the servers came up to her and said, "Aren't you Mrs. Newman?"

"Not when I'm working," she replied.

Another regular at the Christmas party was Mama's agent, Milton Goldman. Milton was an institution in the entertainment world. Aside from his deal-making (I often saw him on two phones at once), he was famous for the way he introduced people. "That's Larry Olivier—he does Shakespeare." "This is Agnes De Mille—she dances." "Meet Otto Preminger—he's in love with a stripper." Milton knew that the way to a mother's heart was through her kids. He used to laugh and joke with me all the time, especially when Mama was present. In fact, sometimes he introduced her by saying, "This is Luke Yankee's mother. She acts sometimes, too." Whenever he did this, I'd giggle as if he'd said something terribly naughty and give him a big hug.

When I was ten, Milton asked Mama if he could bring a guest to the Christmas party. The guest was Ethel Merman. I had just seen *Hello, Dolly!* starring Miss Merman. I had gone nuts over the show. It was my first big, Broadway musical and I was hooked. I played the original cast album nonstop for two months. I was only sorry it wasn't Miss Merman on the recording. Instead, it was some woman with a funny voice named Channing. Mama went to Sam Goody's and got me a 45-rpm record of Louie Armstrong singing *Hello, Dolly!* and I played that twice as much.

Russell Nype, the actor playing Cornelius (one of the supporting roles), was an old friend of Mama's, so she had asked him to arrange a house seat for me. It was about a month and a half before the show was going to close. Mama was playing across the street in *Butterflies are Free*, so I rode back and forth with her and her driver. She'd told me to go backstage afterwards and thank Russell Nype for arranging the ticket.

As the stage doorman waved me up the stairs, I felt like I was going into a parallel universe. This was the first time I was going backstage on Broadway by myself. I was grinning from ear to ear.

"Luke!" he called. "I'm up here!"

I kept trudging up the steep, linoleum steps to the fourth floor. Russell Nype greeted me at his dressing room door in his white briefs and a T-shirt.

"Hi, Luke!" he said, "I'm Russell. Did you enjoy the show?"

I didn't know where to look. I'd just seem him onstage in a bowler hat and a three piece suit.

"Oh, I loved it, Mr. Nype!" I said. "Thank you so much for arranging the ticket." I looked either directly into his eyes or at the floor. He must have watched my face turn red and caught on.

"Forgive me for not being dressed," he said. "Even in November those wool suits are murder under the lights."

"Oh, that's OK, I understand."

I waved my program in the air nonchalantly, and dropped it on the floor. As he stooped to retrieve it, he said, "Would you like to go downstairs and meet Ethel? Maybe we could get her to sign this for you."

Wow, I thought, he actually calls her Ethel!

"That would be wonderful, Mr. Nype," I said.

He disappeared into the dressing room and re-emerged in a tattered, gray terry-cloth robe with several makeup stains on it.

"C'mon," he said, grabbing my hand. "I hope we haven't missed her."

By the time we raced down the three flights to her dressing room, Miss Merman was gone. Trying not to show my disappointment, I unfolded my curled program, which I'd been clutching so I wouldn't drop it again.

"Oh well," I said, with forced casualness. "Would you sign it for me instead, Mr. Nype?"

He smiled broadly as I reached down and grabbed the program.

"What a little gentleman you are!" he said, as he leaned against Miss Merman's door to sign his autograph.

He handed it back to me saying, "Thanks for coming, Luke. Give my love to your mom."

As I was coming back though the alley behind the St. James Theatre, I ran into Mama. At age ten, I was a little nervous to be going through the alley by myself at night, which is why she'd come to meet me. She was wearing a brightly colored patchwork skirt with a white blouse and she had long, flowing ribbons in her hair. As we nearly walked past each other in the alley, we started to laugh. Mama looked so glamorous at that moment. Eileen Heckart was one of the hottest stars on Broadway at that time. Maybe I didn't get to meet a Broadway legend that night, but I was driving home with one.

With Milton bringing Miss Merman to the party, I was not only going to get another chance to meet her, I was going to be her host. I tried telling my classmates at school, but they just didn't get it.

"Who?" Larry Serven asked as he swung on the jungle gym. "Ethel Mertz?"

"Well, yeah," I said, "She's going to be there too, and her real name is Vivian Vance. But this is Ethel *Merman*. She's a huge Broadway star!"

Sometimes I got really frustrated that nobody else in the fourth grade cared about the same things I did. Occasionally, one of the teachers would be interested, especially my music or art teacher. If I sensed an opening, I'd talk their ears off. But rhapsodizing about Broadway musicals sure as hell didn't make me the most popular kid on the playground. I got the crap pounded out of me more than once. When I talked to my parents about it, my father encouraged me to fight back, but it wasn't in my nature. Mama suggested I try to laugh it off instead.

When I did my first show in children's theater, the dramatics instructor made programs that folded up to look like oversized tickets with comedy and tragedy masks on them. I brandished them around on the playground like my very own Tony Awards. One of the school bullies, Darren Lawlor, asked me if he could see them. I handed them over with hesitation, delighted he was taking an interest. Darren grabbed the programs and spat on them, pretended to wipe his ass with them, tore them to pieces, and stomped them into a mud puddle.

I was so afraid of getting beaten up, I forced a smile through my tears and said, "That's OK, Darren. I can always get more."

After that, I'd learned when and where to keep my mouth shut.

At my ten year high school reunion, I said to Darren Lawlor, "Do you remember the time . . ."

As I told him the story, he looked at the floor. "Luke," he said, "I was such an angry little boy. Can you ever forgive me?"

Even after all those years, the apology meant a lot to me.

Around the house, I couldn't stop jabbering about Ethel Merman coming to the Christmas party. Mama got so sick of hearing it, she sat me down for a talk.

"Now, listen," she said, "You mustn't gush over Miss Merman. Big stars don't like that."

"They don't?" I asked, looking confused.

"No, darling," she said. "You may tell her how much you enjoyed her performance—once—but you must be very respectful."

I was afraid Mama might call Milton Goldman and tell him not to bring her.

I barely slept the night before the party. I had to get Mark to help me button my red velvet Christmas vest. I was far too antsy to do it myself.

While Milton Goldman was schmoozing Christopher Plummer on the sun porch, I approached Miss Merman in the front hallway with my heavily rehearsed opening line.

"How do you do, Miss Merman," I said. I was so excited, my body was swaying from side to side. "I really enjoyed your performance in *Hello, Dolly!* It's such a pleasure to meet you and my mother would like to know if I could fix you a drink."

Merman was charmed. With my pale-blond, Prince Valiant haircut and my dimpled cheeks, I was pretty cute.

She looked down at me, smiled, and then boomed in that voice you could hear in the second balcony of the Winter Garden, "Sure, kid, I'll have a martini!"

I furrowed my preadolescent brow and started swaying faster. I must have looked like a human metronome, but she pretended not to notice.

"Well, Miss Merman, I'm only ten. I'm afraid I don't know how to make a martini . . ."

"Ten, huh? Well, it's time you learned. Come on, I'll show you!"

She reached out and touched my shoulder. As if on cue, I stopped swaying. The next thing I knew, Ethel Merman had taken me by the hand and led me over to the bar. Philip was on bar duty. At sixteen, he felt very sophisticated to be tending bar. To his chagrin, Miss Merman shooed him away and proceeded to show me exactly how to make the perfect Ethel Merman martini: two olives, just the right amount of Tanqueray, pass the vermouth bottle over the glass lightly. This was one of the true *Auntie Mame* moments of my life. My chin practically touched the bottom of the bar and I really had to stretch to reach the silver ice bucket. Maneuvering the ice tongs at this angle wasn't easy, but I knew better than to use my fingers for the ice cubes of a Broadway legend. With my sweaty palms, I was terrified I was going to drop the heavy, dark green, half-gallon bottle of Tanqueray onto Ethel Merman's foot.

Oh, no, I thought, she'll be out of *Hello, Dolly!* on crutches for the rest of the run and it will be all my fault!

But I was damned if I was going let anything as stupid as a heavy liquor bottle stand in the way of my moment of triumph. I poured the Tanqueray just as she requested without spilling a drop. Next, I drizzled the vermouth over the glass, speared two olives onto a toothpick and, in one fell swoop, I snagged a cocktail napkin with a reindeer on it and handed her the glass. Miss Merman took a small sip. She licked her lips and looked toward the ceiling. After a moment, she looked down at me.

"That's pretty good, kid," she said. "Tell ya what—you can be my bartender all night!"

I preened with a satisfied smile.

For the rest of the evening, whenever anyone would say, "Merm, can I freshen your drink?" she'd cup her hand over the top of her martini glass and say, "No, thank ya, Luke's taking care of me!"

Vivian Vance had arrived an hour or so before. I was in rehearsals to play King Arthur in *Camelot* in my children's-theater group and I couldn't wait to tell Viv. As Mama was passing a plate of hors d'oeuvres, I broke the news.

Viv replied, "Well honey, if you need any help with your acting, you give me a call, 'cause God knows you won't learn anything around here!"

Mama laughed so hard, she nearly dropped a tray of caviar and toast points.

Merman and Viv were old drinking buddies. They sat on the sofa for hours and got so loud, it seemed like they were trying to out shout one another. The two of them had been reminiscing about TV shows they'd done together and had very different— and very vocal—opinions about times and events. I can still hear Viv shouting across the living room, "Merm honey, you are so full of shit, it's not even funny!"

But Viv said it with such love, you couldn't help but laugh at it. Even so, I didn't like Viv telling my new best friend and the lady for whom I was personally tending bar that she was full of shit.

As the party wore on, I thought of the perfect way to cement my friendship with Miss Merman. I'd share something special with her, something that meant the world to me, and that I only shared with my closest friends. But first, I approached my mother to ask her permission.

"Mama, do you think it would be all right if I asked Miss Merman to come up to my room and see my puppet collection?'

My mother thought for a moment before responding.

"You may ask her," she said. "But you have to understand Miss Merman is a very important lady. There are a lot of people here who want to talk to her and if she says, 'No,' you mustn't get your feelings hurt."

The first hurdle had been cleared. I knew I had to pick my moment carefully, but I had to act quickly. People were finishing their after-dinner drinks and starting to leave. The window of opportunity was narrowing. Finally, I saw my opening. Vivian Vance was in the loo and Miss Merman was sitting alone on the brocaded living room couch covered with the embroidered, Saint Nicholas throw, which was inscribed: "Santa Believes in the Yankees." My palms were sweating again. I tried not to sway this time, but my feet seemed to take on a life of their own. My voice was smaller and quieter than usual, so I stood very close to her.

"Um, Excuse me Miss Merman, do you think, if you're not too busy, I could invite you up to my room to see my puppet collection?"

Merman bit her lip and looked toward the ceiling. She spoke more slowly than before.

"Ummm . . . well . . . maybe . . ."

"Oh, no, that's all right," I said. "I understand you're a very important person and a lot of people here want to talk to you. You don't have to."

I walked away, feeling ridiculous. How dumb, I thought to myself. Why would a big star like Ethel Merman want to come upstairs and see my stupid puppets, anyway? My skin felt hot and prickly. I knew I was turning red, so I went into the bathroom and splashed some cold water on my face. When I returned, I started helping people with their coats, which was one of my jobs at the party. The men's overcoats smelled of Old Spice and wet mohair while the ladies' coats had an odor of Chanel No. 5 and damp mink. A few minutes later, Milton Goldman came in and requested his coat and Miss Merman's.

I followed Milton back into the living room, holding Miss Merman's leopard jacket. "Hey Merm, c'mon." Milton said. "The limo's due any minute. Put on your coat."

Miss Merman looked down at me. As if remembering something, she said, "Wait a minute, Milton! I gotta go upstairs and see Luke's puppets!"

I don't know which got bigger, my eyes or my mouth. I quickly took Miss Merman by the hand and led her past the fourteen-foot Christmas tree and up the gold-swagged stairs to my room. I chose quickly as I showed her the purple wizard, the carved, wooden dragon, Wilfred the clown, and Cassandra, the blond ice skater. She was very gracious and said that she was sorry she didn't have time to see more, but the car was waiting. I thanked her for coming up to see them and told her again what a pleasure it was to meet her. As the limo drove off, her gloved hand waved to me from the rear window.

About a week later, I received a Christmas card in the mail. It has a picture of Santa writing "Merry Christmas" repeatedly on a chalkboard, like a naughty schoolboy.

Inside, it read:

Dear Luke,
   Thank you for taking such good care of me at your parent's party.
   Good luck in "Camelot."
Merry Christmas & Love, Ethel Merman.

I shrieked with excitement. I showed it to all my friends and kept it on my bulletin board for months afterwards. To this day, I have it framed in my study. Miss Merman will always have a place in my heart . . . and I can still make a fabulous martini!

Divas and Democrats

MAMA AT THE WHITE HOUSE MEETING PRESIDENT LYNDON B. JOHNSON—1967

IN 1967, MY PARENTS were invited to lunch at the White House. Needless to say, they were thrilled. Lady Bird Johnson was a real theater lover and had seen Mama's current Broadway play, *You Know I Can't Hear You When the Water's Running*. Lady Bird had come backstage and was extremely warm and gracious. Still, Mama was surprised and delighted when the engraved invitation to a luncheon arrived. Even though she wasn't a fan of President Johnson, an invitation to lunch with the president and first lady was an event.

She shopped for weeks for just the right outfit. Mama found a simple, dark brown dress at Bonwit-Teller. It had rhinestone buttons on the sleeves and it was elegant, tasteful and not too flashy. She also bought a pair of white gloves. Even though my mother wasn't exactly the white-glove type, this was proper formal etiquette for the period. She called a friend who was a diplomat and asked a few questions about protocol. For instance, should she keep her glove on when she shakes the president's hand or should she take it off? It was determined it would be best if she removed the glove to go through the receiving line and then replace it.

As she was about to meet LBJ, she became terribly nervous. Those butterflies had a strange effect on her.

"How do you do, Miss Heckart?" President Johnson said.

"Well, Lady Bird came to my matinee two weeks ago. Where were you?" she replied.

Putting on his best politician's forced smile, he said, "Well ma'am, we were havin' a little problem with the Russians that day. I had to go to a summit meeting. I'm sure sorry I missed it."

Heckart shot him a disappointed look that seemed to sear him like a pig on a spit.

All during the luncheon, he kept looking at her out of the corner of his eye. As they were getting ready to leave, LBJ ran up to my mother and said, "Miss Heckart, I think I could make it to the evening show on the twenty-sixth, would that be all right with you?

"Thanks, Mr. President," she said. "That'd be just fine.

God forbid LBJ should lose a single constituent.

⊗⊗⊗

Another political moment for my mother occurred in July 1969, the night Ted Kennedy made his famous Chappaquiddick speech. My mother and father were out for the evening to a dinner party at the country home of Jan Miner. As Madge the Manicurist, the longest running character on a television commercial in history, Jan dubbed those famous "you're soaking in it" commercials in many languages around the world. As a result, money was never an issue. This afforded her to go to Yale Rep and do a new play for $250 a week or to take on whatever theater projects she chose. Jan was Mama's best friend for years. Her husband, Dick Merrell, was a set designer, so their home was elegantly overdecorated. They were loving and generous to all of us and since they had no children of their own, Jan and Dick often showed up for our birthday parties, summer picnics, or other special occasions. They were important members of our extended family.

Dressed in her best Abercrombie and Fitch wardrobe, Mama walked into the home with more antiques and faux rustic quaintness than the set for *The Farmer's Daughter*. As she entered, she spotted a woman sitting in a tufted, wing-backed chair, engulfed in a large cloud of smoke generating from the ashtray full of Chesterfields by her side. When the haze cleared, my mother saw that it was Bette Davis. Davis was a neighbor and Mama knew that Jan had recently done a featured role in a TV movie with her, but the two had never met. Mama was taken aback to see the legend in the flesh. Being the only other smoker in the room, she joined

Miss Davis for a cigarette before the hostess beckoned everyone into the gingham-upholstered study to watch Senator Kennedy's speech.

Even at a cozy dinner party, it seemed appropriate to turn on the television to see how Ted Kennedy would attempt to address the many concerns and questions facing him. Besides, Davis was such a staunch Kennedy supporter, she'd rather have licked the lint off the baseboards than miss a Kennedy moment.

In brief, Ted Kennedy had driven off a bridge in Martha's Vineyard, in the town of Chappaquiddick. There was a young, female intern in the car with him who was killed in the accident. Rumors were flying that he may have been having an affair with this woman and there were many accusations of foul play. Some thought it was an attempt on Kennedy's life, others thought it was rigged by his opponents to ruin any hopes he might have for a run at the White House, while still others speculated it was intentional to silence the young intern before she started spilling the beans. It was the biggest political scandal of its time.

My mother was a strong Kennedy supporter. She was very active politically at this time, and even did a bit of campaigning for some senators and congressmen when she could make the time. She got very active in the McGovern campaign for the presidency in 1972 as well as that of a Connecticut senatorial candidate named Joe Duffy. When she was a guest on *The Dick Cavett Show*, she had specifically asked if she could plug Duffy on the air. Cavett agreed, but George Jessel, the guest before her, wouldn't shut up and monopolized most of Mama's interview time. Cavett had her pitch Duffy after they had already ended the program and then went back and had it re-edited, cutting out one of Jessel's war stories to make room for Mama to pitch her candidate for senator. She was forever grateful to Cavett, which made her even more crushed when Duffy wasn't elected.

My mother was a staunch Democrat and liberal. She was an advocate for women's rights (especially the right to choose) and she was addicted to the Sunday morning political talk shows. When the Watergate hearings were televised, you couldn't tear her away from the television set. Much as she supported the Kennedys, she had a lot of questions regarding the Chappaquiddick incident.

As they all reconvened in the living room, Bette Davis turned to my mother.

"What are you going to say in your telegram, Heckart?"

Mama stared at her.

"I beg your pardon, Miss Davis?" she said.

"We were all so moved by Teddy Kennedy's speech, we're sending him telegrams of support and congratulations. What are you going to say in yours?"

There was a palpable silence in the room.

After a thoughtful pause, Mama replied, "Well, Miss Davis, to tell you the truth, I had a few qualms with Senator Kennedy's speech and I don't think I care to send a telegram at this time."

Those famous eyes bulged out of their sockets.

"Just what kind of a hate-monger *are* you, anyway?" Davis screamed at my mother.

Mama stared at her in shock as Bette Davis spewed a torrent of abuse at her, reducing her to tears in a matter of seconds.

Finally Bette blurted out, "What sign were you born under?"

My mother knew that Miss Davis was into astrology at the time and through heaving sobs, she stammered, "Aries . . . the same as you!"

After a shocked pause, Bette Davis replied, "Well . . . then all I can say is that you must have been born on the shitty end of the cusp!"

My father, who had been in the bar, walked in at this point, ready to pounce.

"I don't give a shit who you are lady, nobody talks to my wife that way!" Jack said.

Jan Miner, who had been hovering in the doorway of the kitchen, said, "Can we just put all this behind us and come to dinner, please?"

The conversation at the table was incredibly strained. As Jan was clearing the soup bowls, Mama followed her out into the kitchen.

"Jan," she said, "I don't want to ruin your dinner party, but I am so upset. I've never been spoken to like that by anyone in my life."

"I don't blame you, darling," she replied. "I was in the kitchen and didn't hear all of it, but I heard enough."

"We'll stay through dinner, but will you forgive me if Jack and I leave right after the meal?"

"Of course, Heckie." Jan said to her good friend, touching her cheek. They returned to the dining room, but once again, Davis bested them by leaving the minute the lamb brochettes and summer squash were finished. Her driver appeared at the door. Bette Davis gave a quick and cursory, "Thank you," and was gone.

I rarely saw Mama get as agitated as when she told that story.

※.※.※.

Flash forward to 1976. Mama was cast in a cameo opposite Burgess Meredith in a Gothic horror movie called *Burnt Offerings*. Based on a popular novel, it was the story of a family who moves into a house that is possessed. Heckart and Meredith played the owners of the house. The young couple was played by Karen Black and Oliver Reed. The role of their kindly, old aunt was played by Bette Davis. Mama almost turned the role down when she heard that Davis was doing the film, she was still so terrified of her. But they just had one tiny scene together, so how bad could it be?

When Heckart arrived at the hotel outside of Carmel where they were filming, there was a note waiting for her. It read:

Dear Eileen–
  Join me for dinner in the hotel restaurant at 7 PM.
Love, Bette

"*Love*, Bette?" Mama said to herself in utter disbelief. Was this the same woman who had reduced her to a blubbering mess over her political beliefs seven years earlier?

The family was particularly proud of Mama at this moment, not for any career achievement, but because for the first time in her adult life, she'd managed to stop smoking. She'd tried Smoke Enders, placebos, carrot sticks, yoga, and now hypnosis— and the hypnosis seemed to be working. She hadn't had a cigarette in nearly two weeks and even though it was still touch and go, we were thrilled for her progress. She knew that having dinner with the ultimate chain-smoker would be a real challenge. Besides, one didn't just say "no" to a dinner invitation from Bette Davis.

They met in a quiet corner of the hotel restaurant and Miss Davis was charming. She embraced Mama as if nothing had ever occurred between them and as if they were the best of friends. Davis puffed away on her Chesterfields and Mama devoured the contents of two breadbaskets and more than her usual quota of J&B. As the evening wore on, Bette started to show her true colors. Much of the conversation went like this:

"Have you ever worked with John Smith?" Miss Davis would say.

"Oh, I adore him," Mama would reply. "He's one of my dearest friends."

"He's an asshole . . . and he can't act!" Bette would reply.

This went on for the bulk of the evening, with Bette Davis vilifying almost everyone in show business my mother loved and admired. Finally, as Mama's agitation increased and the waiter emptied Davis's ashtray for the third time, Mama said, "Bette, could I have one of your cigarettes, please?"

"I thought you'd never ask!" Davis replied.

"Well, actually, I was trying to quit," she said.

"In God's name why? You've earned the right to do as you please. Light up!" Bette said, sliding her Zippo across the table.

Mama's anxiousness subsided, enough to enjoy the rest of the evening. They sat there and chain-smoked for another two hours and even sent the busboy out for more cigarettes. So much for hypnosis.

✖✖✖

Four years later, in 1980, Mama was cast in a small but fun role as a crafty bag lady in a television movie called *White Mama*, starring Bette Davis and an up-and-coming, African-American actor named Ernest Harden, Jr. Davis winds up befriending the young man, who for a time pawns all of her possessions, until she is reduced to being a bag lady. At the end, he wins a prizefight and is able to earn back all her belongings and her apartment. Heckart plays another homeless person who befriends Davis and shows her how to survive on the street.

Jackie Cooper was directing *White Mama*. My mother loved the affable nature of the former child star and found him to be a very competent director. She shot her first scene in a crowded location in Watts, the roughest part of urban, inner-city

THE PHOTOGRAPH BETTE DAVIS AUTOGRAPHED FOR MY MOTHER, WHICH READS, "DEAR EILEEN—NEXT TIME NOT A BAG LADY—LOVE, BETTE." COURTESY OF MICHAEL MERRILL

Los Angeles. The set was teeming with about 150 extras. Staring right at Bette Davis, Jackie Cooper and Eileen Heckart, one of them asked, "Hey man, you anybody famous?"

As she saw my mother approaching the set across a sea of extras, Bette Davis shouted, "Heckart! You and I are the only two here who know this isn't acting, it's stunt work!"

As Mama tried not to laugh, Jackie Cooper just shook his head and sighed, saying to the lighting grips, "It's going to be another long day, boys."

Davis was no spring chicken and her health was deteriorating. Because of her physical limitations, she had strict rules about how late she would work. At the end of a full day of shooting, the assistant director came to her and said, "Bette, I know you're supposed to be done for the day, but if you wouldn't mind shooting one more scene with Ernest, then he'd be fresh for the fight scene in the morning."

Davis looked at the poor assistant with fire in her eyes. "So Ernest will be fresh for the morning?" she repeated. "Who's carrying this fucking picture, anyway?" she screamed. "Mr. Harden's name is *not* over the title. There is only one name over the title and it's Bette Davis. I did not work all these years so that Mr. Harden could be fresh for his fight in the morning. I am more than three times the age of Mr. Harden and you should be more concerned about whether or not Miss Davis will be fresh in the morning . . . or even if she'll still be breathing in the morning! Good night!"

Bette Davis's terrible temper was legendary in show business. God knows my mother had gotten more than a taste of it. There was one scene in *White Mama* where Heckart was able to keep Mount Bette from erupting. It was a moment where the two disheveled bag ladies go into an upscale coffee shop for a meal. The hostess says, "Table for two?" and escorts them through the crowded restaurant to the back door. She quickly ushers them out saying, "We won't be serving the likes of you in here tonight." Davis and Heckart share a pitiable look and exit.

The pretty, thirtyish blond actress playing the hostess was very nervous. She was chattering to the other extras, drinking lots of coffee, and subsequently racing to the ladies room.

While Ms. Davis was finishing her makeup, the young woman said to my mother, "This is the greatest day of my life! Will my grandchildren ever believe that I once played a scene with Bette Davis and Eileen Heckart?"

Mama was moved by the woman's earnest enthusiasm. When Bette Davis arrived on the set, it was obvious she was in one of her moods. Rather than a stage set, they were filming at an actual restaurant. It was an awkward move for the actress playing the hostess to hold the heavy glass door open with one arm and make it wide enough so that both actresses could get through while still remaining in the shot. It was a clumsy bit of staging for a woman who didn't have much strength in her upper body.

After the hostess blew the first three takes, Bette Davis turned to my mother and said with exaggerated, clipped speech, "Raaaaather inept, isn't she?"

Heckart looked the other way and was grateful the young actress wasn't within earshot. She screwed up two more takes. Bette was sighing and shooting daggers at the hostess. The more times she messed up, the more Davis seemed to linger in the doorway at exactly the spot where the poor woman didn't have the strength to hold it open. In one take, she nearly slammed the door on Bette. You could feel the air getting thicker on the set.

When the two bag ladies were back on their opening marks, Davis turned to Heckart and said, "If that stupid bitch doesn't get it right this time, I'm going to let her have it!"

Heckart grabbed her arm. "Now Bette," she said, "Give the kid a break. She said this was the greatest day of her life to be in a scene with Bette Davis and Eileen Heckart. Please don't ruin it for her."

Davis looked at Heckart in total disbelief. "Did she really say that?"

"Yes, Bette. Before you came to the set."

Just then, Jackie Cooper said, "Okay, ladies, can we take it from the top, please?"

Bette Davis turned to the director and said, "Jackie, wouldn't it be easier for the hostess if we stopped before we got to the door? It's a very awkward move and then the poor girl wouldn't have to hold it open so long!"

The young hostess looked at Miss Davis with gratitude and humility.

"Good point, Bette," Cooper said. "Let's try it that way. Roll 'em!"

The actress got it on the next take. Even Bette Davis could be compassionate when someone reminded her.

One of the few people I ever heard of who had the nerve to stand up to Bette Davis and win was Jack Cassidy. He was doing a movie called *Bunny O'Hare* with Davis, a most unfortunate comedy about an aging hippie. Cassidy started shooting a few days after her and everyone was calling him with reports from the set about what a terror she was.

Friends said, "Oh Jack, she'll eat you alive. Get out now while you still can!"

Cassidy was undaunted. He was known for being quite the ladies' man, so he decided to play his game, not hers. As he strolled onto the set, he sauntered up to the sixty-three-year-old Miss Davis and exclaimed in front of the entire cast and crew, "Bette, I'll bet you've got one good fuck left in you and I want it!"

Davis fell on the floor laughing and they were the best of friends for the rest of the shoot. She was as good as gold to everyone.

On the last day of shooting on *White Mama*, while both ladies were in their full bag-lady regalia, Davis beckoned the staff photographer. "Come, on Heckart," she said, "I want a photo to use as my Christmas card!"

My mother cracked up. Irascible and difficult as she could be, she was still Bette Davis, the stuff of Hollywood legend. The ladies flashed their biggest smiles and posed for the camera as if they'd always been the best of friends.

Balloons, "Butterflies," and Sneakers

ME AT NINE IN MAMA'S DRESSING ROOM—OPENING NIGHT OF *BUTTERFLIES ARE FREE* ON BROADWAY. PHOTO BY L. ARNOLD WEISSBERGER

IN THE SPRING OF 1969, I found myself without any playmates for the summer. As the time came to make plans for the long school vacation, the most important time in any nine-year-old's life, Bobby Prentice told me with great excitement that he was going to off to sailing camp and would take part in *regattas*, whatever they were. Vicki Butler was thrilled to be going to a Catholic girls' camp where she'd play volleyball, learn macramé, and sing folk hymns. I think I'd rather have had my catechism instructor, Sister Adrienne Marie, rap me across the knuckles with a ruler and lock me in the broom closet until Labor Day. Jimmy and Tommy Moore were going to a baseball clinic. Given my total aversion to any and all sports, I wondered if this was a place where one went to get cured of a desire to play base-ball. While I had no interest whatsoever in partaking in the summer activities of my friends and neighbors, I still began feeling a little anxious. What was I going to do while all my chums were away?

I voiced this concern to my parents at dinner that night. As luck would have it, Mama wasn't working that summer. This was a good thing for me, but not necessarily for her. She had done a Broadway play called *The Mother Lover* back in

February that had opened and closed on the same night. Since then, she had done a guest spot on *Gunsmoke*, but nothing else was on the horizon.

On the rare occasions when Mama was going through one of these dry spells, after a few months she got a little edgy. When someone asked, "Eileen, what's the matter?" she'd reply, "Honey, I haven't got anything a job won't cure!"

It seemed strange that with all her acclaim, she was going through a fallow period, but this was part and parcel of a career in show business. At times like this, she reminded me (and herself) of the time Bette Davis was taking out full page ads in *Variety* and the *Hollywood Reporter* saying "For your consideration—Miss Bette Davis. Available for employment." It comforted her that she was in such good company when it came to a lack of work.

In lieu of a new Broadway play, taking charge of her youngest son's social calendar for the summer seemed a handy alternative. A few days later, Mama offered up the perfect solution. She waltzed in and announced that the two of us had season tickets for the Wednesday matinees at the Westport Country Playhouse, one of the oldest and most renowned summer theaters in America.

Mama handed me the season brochure and I pinned it up right over the head of my bed. I would stare at it for hours, wondering who all those glamorous people were and what these wonderful plays would be like. We would not be watching kiddie matinees of *Puss in Boots* and *The Emperor's New Clothes*. This was a full compliment of sophisticated, adult dramas and comedies. There was Betsy Palmer in *The Prime of Miss Jean Brodie*, James Whitmore and Audra Lindley in an elegant, new comedy called *The Chic Life* (I pronounced it "the Chick Life" until my mother set me straight), next was some guy who had been on a TV sci-fi show named William Shatner in the comedy *There's a Girl in My Soup*. To my mind, they were all in a class with *Death of Salesman* and *Oklahoma!* I was going have a summer of high art and culture, surrounded by grown-ups. What could be more thrilling?

Some of the shows were listed as "Prior to Broadway." When Mama explained what that term meant, I was even more excited. We were going to see these shows even *before* they went to New York and made theatrical history? This was getting better and better. She told me that this didn't necessarily mean they would end up on Broadway, only that they hoped to. The biggest thrill of all was that Mama knew someone in almost every show, so we'd get to go backstage and meet all the stars. And in the plays where she didn't know anyone, she could probably have Jim McKenzie, the summer theater producer, make an introduction.

I carefully removed the thumbtacks from my imprinted, green-and-blue-cardboard season schedule, making certain not to tear even a corner, and took it in for Show & Tell. I was extremely animated as I described the theater season to the other kids, as if I were giving a performance.

"I'm going to see twelve plays this summer!" I gushed.

All I got were blank stares. Mrs. Dalcher, my third-grade teacher, was a theater lover, so at least she appreciated it. She'd even seen Mama on Broadway a few times. But the rest of the third graders thought plays were stupid and boring. A few of the girls seemed mildly interested and one or two of the boys thought it was cool that I might get to meet Captain Kirk, so I pretended to be excited about the possibility in order to appease them. I didn't like outer space stuff and I'd never seen his TV show, anyway. At least the other boys and I were sharing a common interest for once.

There had been one time in the past where I'd gotten the attention and respect of my classmates by going to a play. The previous Christmas, Mama and Daddy had taken us all into New York to see *Hair*. Since my brothers were six and eight years older, Mark and Philip were longing to see it. At first Mama and Daddy thought it was over my head and they were going to leave me at home with Nanny, but I made such a stink about it, they finally relented. At age eight, I didn't know why *Hair* was such a big deal—only that if my big brothers wanted to see it that much then by golly, so did I.

The kids at school thought I was really cool then. The fact that I'd seen THE groundbreaking event that everyone was talking about, with naked people in it, no less, made me hip for a few days.

The next day on the playground, my classmates gathered around me by the jungle gym and wanted to hear all about it. I was really digging the attention, not to mention my five minutes of fame.

"So, Luke," Frankie Gallo asked me. "Were there *really* naked people in the play?"

"Well, yes, Frankie," I replied, sounding like a miniature Alistair Cooke. "There *is* a brief nude scene, but it's very tastefully done."

"What the heck does that mean?" Annalise Masten asked. "Did you see naked people or not?!?"

"Yes," I said, "they were naked for a while, but that wasn't the point of the play."

They couldn't have cared less about dramatic structure or sociopolitical commentary. The fact that I had actually seen a dozen penises and vaginas onstage singing and dancing was both titillating and scandalous to them. I looked around to make sure no teachers were in earshot as I leaned in and spoke in hushed tones to my new compatriots.

"To tell you the truth," I said, "my parents were kind of bored by it. They said it seemed to be about nothing more than fucking and the flag!"

Everyone squealed with laughter and horror. The fact that I actually said the "F" word—and that I was quoting my *parents* as I said it—more scandal, more shock, and more acceptance. I loved being part of the "in" crowd, however fleeting it was.

Back at Show & Tell, I couldn't understand why adult comedies and dramas at the Westport Country Playhouse didn't grant me the same status as *Hair* had. Still, I was thrilled with my new, grown-up summer-vacation plans, and no one was going to take that away from me.

The first production was Eddie Bracken in Robert Anderson's *You Know I Can't Hear You When the Water's Running*. Mama had originated this play on

Broadway two years before and could think of nothing more boring than sitting through a summer stock production of a piece she'd originated and played for over 350 performances.

As we were discussing our summer plans, she said, "Well, we don't have to see *that* one. You've already seen it!"

"No I haven't!" I protested. "You wouldn't let me!"

One of the scenes in *Water* included a frank discussion of masturbation. When Mama was doing *Water* in New York, I was considered way too young at age seven to see it. But now, at the ripe old age of nine, I was pushing the envelope. My mother was starting to wonder what can of worms she'd opened with these theater tickets. She figured most of the adult material would go over my head and she was going to explain as little as possible, unless I asked a direct question. Nonetheless, she coached me beforehand.

"Now, in the second act," she said, "the mother will say, 'Timmy is playing with himself.' Do you know what that means?"

I sat there wordlessly, shaking my head and waiting for an explanation. Mama was treading gingerly. She didn't want to give me more than I was ready to handle.

"Well" she continued. "It means playing with your peenie and kind of . . . rolling it around."

"Oh . . . you mean like in the bathtub?" I asked.

"Why not?" she responded, and quickly changed the subject.

Going to matinees with my mother was a little different from going with just any Connecticut housewife. The silver-haired, matinee ladies and assorted Fairfield County matrons were huge fans of hers, and when they weren't elbowing each other and exclaiming, "Look Marge, there's June Havoc!" they could be very sweet. The one exception was the lady who knew my mother from the unemployment office. She seemed to have contempt for the fact that Mama was collecting unemployment, yet spending her money on something as luxurious as theater tickets. It probably never occurred to her that this could be a tax write-off for an actress. All this made us less than anonymous, and I loved every second of it. I lived from Wednesday to Wednesday in the summer of 1969, always asking Mama who she knew in each play and if we could meet them afterward. My mother was a major Broadway star at this point. To have her come backstage at a summer-stock theater and pay her respects was a big event for many of these actors, as it was for me.

One of the mid-season "prior to Broadway" tours that summer was a comedy directed by Joshua Logan called *Why I Went Crazy*. It starred Imogene Coca, Richard Castellano, and Arnold Stang. Josh Logan was considered show business royalty. He had directed my mother in *Picnic,* her first major Broadway success. He'd done many other groundbreaking shows, including the musical *South Pacific.* Despite Mr. Logan's brilliance, he had directed a spate of flops in the mid- to late sixties and this play was no exception. I don't remember much about the convoluted story, except for the fact that all the men played women and all the women played men in the first act, then they all switched roles in Act Two. I can still see the beefy Richard Castellano, best known for playing mafia "hit men," in a blonde wig and housecoat while tiny, birdlike Imogene Coca strutted around in a three-piece pinstripe suit telling the little woman she had spent too much money at the Grand Union on pork chops. *Why I Went Crazy* was attempting to be an absurdist comedy and missing the mark by a country mile. I doubt it ever would have been produced in the first place if Joshua Logan hadn't agreed to do it. His name still had a certain caché with investors and audiences alike.

At one point in the play, a young woman gets pregnant and Mr. Castellano (now out of drag and playing her uncle) hands her a couple of unwrapped condoms. Arnold Stang was playing the child. A burlesque style comic with a rubbery face and a small frame, he looked rather obscene at fiftysomething in blue knickers and a white pinafore.

He saw the condoms and exclaimed, "Oh boy! Balloons!" and he took them off-stage to blow them up.

Mama and the other matinee ladies howled with laughter.

I leaned over to my mother amidst the audience's guffaws and said, "What's the matter with the balloons? Why is everyone laughing?"

"I'll tell you later," she whispered.

I promptly forgot about it, as children do, until three days later we were driving home from Caldor's department store. The top was down on the olive-green, '67 Mercury Cougar convertible, and the summer breeze from Long Island Sound was wafting across my face as I sat next to Mama in the front seat. I spoke with businesslike authority.

"Now . . . about Arnold Stang's balloons!"

She laughed as she took a long drag on her True Blue. No doubt she had discussed the matter with my father and after all the questions she'd been dodging with moderate success since week one of the theater season, she felt it was time.

As we turned off the Merritt Parkway, she said to me, "Well . . . what do you know about sex?"

"Not much," I replied.

Mama opened what was to become an ongoing discussion about the facts of life. With each play that summer, I learned a little bit more. By the middle of the theater season, I was piecing it all together.

"Ohhhh," I said, "So that's why the man from *Star Trek* and that lady from *Cabaret* were rolling around in the bed together in their underwear!"

"That's right, honey," she replied.

Show by show, I got my whole sex education that summer. By the end of the season, I was asking questions about *You Know I Can't Hear You When the Water's Running*, the first play, from a different vantage point. I didn't entirely understand what masturbation was, but I knew it was more than rolling your peenie around in the bathtub. The one play she would not let me see that season was *The Boys in the Band*. If I was just learning about what men and women did together, she certainly didn't want to open the topic of homosexuality. Mama took Nanny to see that one instead. I don't think she understood it much more than I would have. Still, if it hadn't been for those Wednesday matinees at the Westport Country Playhouse, I might still be in the dark.

Toward the end of the summer, Mama's agent, Milton Goldman called her.

"Listen, Heckie," he said, "there's a new play at Westport. I want you to go see it."

"Well, Milton, as a matter of fact, Luke and I have tickets to the matinee tomorrow. What is it?"

"It a new comedy," he said. "They want to bring it into New York and the producers want to replace Maureen O'Sullivan. It's called *Butterflies are Free.*"

All at once, our theatergoing had a higher purpose. I knew what a lean year Mama was having work-wise and that she was desperate to find a good, new play. She made me promise not to tell the other matinee ladies the following day. I was crushed. After all, this was big news!

"Not even the nice lady who gives me a stick of Juicy Fruit every week?" I asked.

"No," she said, "not even her. It would be terrible if word got back to Maureen O' Sullivan, who may not even know she's being fired."

I understood and agreed to zip my lip.

Mrs. Baker, the mother in *Butterflies are Free*, is one of those characters who is talked about all through the play, enters at the end of the first act and doesn't have a single line until Act Two. At the act break, as soon as we were out of earshot of the other ladies, I asked, "Well Mama, what do you think?"

She looked down at me and laughed as she puffed on her intermission cigarette.

"Honey, she hasn't *said* anything yet! Give me a chance! But I do like the play so far. It's a sweet story . . . and the girl is very nice."

The "girl" was an ingénue who would be making her Broadway debut in this play. Her name was Blythe Danner.

Maureen O'Sullivan did some wonderful film work over the years, but she seemed very ill at ease onstage in this role. It seemed like she didn't know what to do with her hands, so she took her gloves on and off a great deal and raised her folded hands to her mouth in a prayer-like pose at regular intervals. Even so, we could both tell it was a marvelous part in a sweet and touching play. She called Milton and told him she wanted him to move forward with the negotiations. That afternoon wound up becoming a very important day in my mother's life. I was thrilled to be the one to help her "discover" her next major Broadway role.

She went into New York the following week to meet with the producer, Arthur Whitelaw, the playwright Leonard Gershe, and the director, Milton Katselas. At the end of the meeting, she turned to them with her characteristic directness and said, "Well, do you people want me or not?"

Producer and playwright both said, "Yes."

Katselas said, "I'd like to think about it."

She came home that night and cried to my father, "Jack, the director doesn't want me!"

The next day, Arthur Whitelaw telephoned.

"Hello . . . is this Mrs. Baker?" he said.

"I'm sorry, you must have the wrong number," Mama said.

"No, I don't think so," Arthur said, laughing into the phone.

Mrs. Baker was the character's name. Exit Maureen O'Sullivan . . . enter Eileen Heckart.

Butterflies are Free wound up being one of the longest running shows of Mama's career. And while my parents sometimes cautiously invested in my mother's plays, *Butterflies* is the only one where they made their investment back and even turned a profit. My parents didn't discuss money issues in front of the kids. I know they invested in other shows of Mama's prior to *Butterflies*, but I don't know which ones. My father was a good businessman, so he didn't mind cautiously investing in his wife's productions. Still, it was nice to see one actually show a return.

While the show was in previews, she was having an early dinner between shows at Sardi's. Cab Calloway was doing the same.

"How's the show?" Calloway asked.

"It's simply marvelous," she said. "And if the critics don't like it, they're just assholes!"

Cab Calloway got a pained expression on his face and motioned behind her. She turned around and saw Walter Kerr and Richard Watts at the next table—two of the most important theater critics in town.

Butterflies opened on Broadway on October 21, 1969. It was also my first Broadway opening and I was elated. Daddy had taken my brothers and me to Stamford and rented tuxedos for all of us. The diva was going to be sure that her men dressed the part as much as she did. Since this was the first time all of the Yankee men were in formalwear, Mama insisted Daddy get out the Polaroid before loading us all into the car to drive into Manhattan. I loved getting dressed up. Not only was I going to my first Broadway opening, we were attending a private party at Sardi's afterward to wait for the reviews. I couldn't imagine ever having a more thrilling evening in my life.

At seventeen, my brother Mark was at the zenith of his hippie phase. He rarely changed out of the same pair of ratty blue jeans and denim work-shirt with patches on the elbows. He was not at all pleased about having to wear a tux for the opening, but he finally agreed, with one concession. He would wear his sneakers with it. This was considered the cool thing to do in 1969.

At first, Mark and my parents had several lengthy discussions about his choice of footwear for the big night. In the end, Mama gave in, saying, "Listen, if they're looking at my son's feet, my performance is in terrible trouble."

When Mama mentioned this to the chic, elegant, and charming Arthur Whitelaw, the producer wore his sneakers as well. It was a loving gesture in support of my brother and more importantly, it put his leading lady at ease. Arthur and Mark made a big deal out of their hip solidarity, but the next day, my brother said, "Mama, nobody looked at my feet the entire night!"

The energy at Sardi's as we waited for the reviews was electric. They turned on the TV in the tiny bar and we all crowded in to see the television reviews. Leonard

Harris on WCBS said, "Welcome *Butterflies are Free*. It'll give you two hours of laughter and in the end it'll break your heart. It's the funniest, tender play I've seen in years."

The other television critics were equally good. I quickly learned in this game that the only review that really mattered was the *New York Times*. Arthur Whitelaw had a friend in the dispatch office at the *Times* who was going to bring a copy over the moment it was off the press. Arthur stood quietly next to the cloakroom reading it for himself. Mama spotted him and grew increasingly nervous. We followed her gaze and tried to study Arthur's impassive face as he read. It was the longest three minutes of my nine-year-old life. Finally, Arthur broke into a huge smile as he strutted into the main dining room and read Clive Barnes' review to the expectant crowd. It was a rave.

It said, "The wonderful Eileen Heckart, acid-tongued and with computerized comic timing, sails regally into her own." He went on to say what a fine comedienne she was, revealing "a delightful, sly warmth."

Butterflies Are Free ran for 1,128 performances.

In addition to Mark's opening night wardrobe, my mother had her own memorable encounter with a pair of sneakers during the run of *Butterflies*. One Sunday evening, while she was fixing dinner for the family on her night off, as she opened the refrigerator door, a watermelon came careening out and landed on her right foot. Philip had precariously jammed it in there so it would be chilled for a school picnic the next day. It was a wonder it didn't break the shelf of the fridge, let alone my mother's metatarsal arch. She screamed in pain and my father ran her to the emergency room at Norwalk Hospital. Fortunately, the foot was only bruised and swollen, but there was no way Mama would be able to wear high heels for Tuesday night's performance. She did manage, however, to slip into a pair of yellow canvas tennis shoes. She could even walk on the injured foot without too much discomfort. But how could she play this matron from Scarsdale in her sneakers?

Arthur Whitelaw himself came to the theater that night to make the curtain speech. "Hello, ladies and gentlemen," he said. "My name is Arthur Whitelaw and I am the producer of the play you are about to see. I regret to inform you that Miss Eileen Heckart . . ."

As if on cue, the audience emitted a communal groan, assuming the producer was about to announce that the star they had paid to see would be played by an understudy.

"Now, wait a minute!" Arthur continued, "Miss Heckart has injured her foot, but she *will* perform—as long as *you* can suspend your disbelief enough to see her in a $600 navy-blue-and-white Chanel suit . . . with a pair of $7.95 yellow Keds on her feet!"

The audience burst into spontaneous applause. On my mother's curtain call that night, it was the only time her footwear ever got a hand. By the next performance, the costumer had gotten a pair of bedroom slippers and dyed them to match her dress and no one was the wiser until her foot was healed.

The story of *Butterflies are Free* revolves around a young man named Don Baker who was born blind and has been raised as a normal child in every respect. Completely adjusted to his handicap, he has recently established his independence and moved to Greenwich Village, away from his domineering yet well-intentioned mother. He meets Jill, the kooky girl next door and they start to have an affair.

MAMA AND KEIR DULLEA IN *BUTTERFLIES ARE FREE* ON BROADWAY—1969. COURTESY OF MARTHA SWOPE

After their first sexual encounter, as they are basking in the afterglow, his mother unexpectedly arrives to pack him up and take him home. A comedic parent-child battle ensues filled with ribald zingers and witty one-liners. At the heartfelt conclusion, the mother finally accepts her son's hard-won independence. During the moment of acceptance, her eyes brimming with tears, Mrs. Baker turns to her son and says, "You know, Donnie . . . it's hard to adjust to . . . not being needed anymore. But I can do it now . . . and you get on with your own life."

For me, this became my mother's signature line. The many times I saw the play, and even more times I watched the film, I always imagined she was saying this to me. She spoke this simple line with such emotional honesty, depth, devotion, and tender vulnerability, how could she not have been thinking about her own children? As I grew into my teens and early twenties, naturally we would argue about silly, adolescent issues where I had to be right. Like Don Baker in *Butterflies are Free* (a role I later played in community theater), I was desperately trying to establish myself as a separate entity from this gigantic force in my life known as my mother.

Yet, whenever I would see this scene in *Butterflies*, it was as if she were right there saying, "There's another side to this story, Luke. There is someone who loves you so much it hurts, someone who would do anything for you, someone who would even give her life for you." How often do parents feel this, and how rarely do children see it? The truth in her performance was holding a mirror up to nature, and it was one I didn't always want to see. To this day, all I have to do is think about that scene and I start to cry.

I saw the play many times on Broadway before I had this revelation about the final scene. At age ten or eleven, it's hardly the thing a child thinks about. When I got tired of sitting in the audience or simply wasn't in the mood to see the play again, I would hang out backstage. Mama had two funny little dressing rooms at the Booth Theatre. There was no large star dressing room, so she had one room for dressing and one for napping, with a fridge and a cot in it, which she used on matinee days. I became great friends with Mama's dresser, Alva Gandolfi, a soft-spoken, Italian woman who took me under her wing and treated me like the child she never had.

One night while I was backstage with Alva, Mama came offstage with tears in her eyes after playing her final scene. She was subdued and speaking quietly.

"Mama," I said, "What's the matter?"

"My child has just told me he doesn't need me anymore," she said.

"What do you mean?" I asked. "Did you have a fight with Mark?"

"No darling," she said. "In the play."

This was the first time I understood what acting was. It was also the first time I sensed the depth of my mother's talent.

For years, Mama had a round table in the corner of her dressing room with a floor-length tablecloth. When celebrities would come backstage to pay their respects, she'd ask them to sign it. The tablecloths varied in color over the years, depending upon her decorating whims. Later, her dresser would embroider the names with black thread to preserve them. Whenever I would go into her dressing room, my favorite game was to see what names had been added. I would trace the letters with my fingers and imagine who these grand people were with such large, flowing signatures: Katherine Hepburn, Helen Hayes, Bette Davis, Marlene Dietrich, Julie Harris, Jessica Tandy, Paul Newman, Jason Robards, George C. Scott, and so many others. Even if I didn't recognize their names, I knew if they were good enough to sign the tablecloth, they were to be respected and honored.

When Mama was doing a play on Broadway, the house took on a different tone. Since she didn't get home until well past midnight, she would usually sleep late in the mornings while Nanny fixed our breakfast and got us ready for school. My father told us repeatedly to be very quiet as we went past their bedroom door. And if we had to enter the inner sanctum to get our lunch money off Daddy's dresser, we had to tiptoe. Secretly, I wanted a morning visit with Mama. I wouldn't intentionally try to wake my mother up, but sometimes if I coughed too loudly or jangled the change as I took it out of the silver cup where Daddy had placed it for us the night before, I would relish the times she would roll over, stretch a flannel arm from beneath the covers, and sit up, sleepily reaching for the waiting thermos of coffee and a sweet roll placed there by my father. There was always the lush smell of expensive perfume and, in the earlier years, the antiseptic odor of Max Factor stage makeup. If time permitted and I wasn't going to miss the school bus, I would be allowed to sit at the foot of the bed and hear a wonderful story about what had happened at the theater the night before or which celebrities had come backstage.

For my mother's entire life, this was the ritual. I'd sit at her feet while she was in bed holding court, propped up by dozens of pillows and always laden with True Blues and Sanka in the morning and Dewars or Nestea at night. In the evenings, when there wasn't the pressure of time, these often became deep, soulful conversations. To this day, the scent of Norrell perfume tinged with stale tobacco is one of the most comforting smells in the world to me.

In the afternoons, Mama always made a point of being in the kitchen as we came home from school. Whenever possible, she'd find some domestic chore to do between three and three-thirty, just so we could see those familiar blond locks through the kitchen window as the school bus rounded the corner. When she wasn't able to achieve this due to appointments, auditions, or interviews, she made sure Nanny did it. Mama felt it gave us a sense of security.

When working on Broadway, she usually had dinner alone around four-thirty or five. I would often sit with her and get a preview of what Nanny had prepared that night for the family. Afterward, the driver came around six o'clock to take her to the theater. For years, she grappled with the New Haven railroad and took the train into Manhattan, but she grew tired of the public nature of this dreary commute, not to mention the undependable train schedules. If it hadn't been for the bar car where she could smoke and have a scotch and water in a paper cup after the show, she never would have made it.

More than once, she had been followed late at night getting off the train. Fortunately, the cops at the South Norwalk train station got to know her and kept a watchful eye. Finally, she'd had enough. From *Butterflies* on, Mama had it in her contract that she got a car and driver when she was doing a play, or no dice. She lost several roles because of this, especially in Off-Broadway productions where the producers didn't have the budget to hire a car and driver, but she stood firm.

At the Tonys that year, both Eileen Heckart and Blythe Danner were nominated as Best Supporting Actress in a Play for *Butterflies are Free.* It seemed peculiar that they were nominated in the same category, since Mama's name was over the title. Perhaps since Mrs. Baker didn't come in until the second act, the nominating committee considered it "supporting" when it was really a lead. She actually thought this helped her chances. She loved and adored Blythe. But Eileen Heckart was ready to win the Tony.

"I mean, for God's sake," she said, "how many times can you sit there and be a good sport?"

Mama really thought this was going to be her night. When they announced Blythe Danner as the winner, she was thrilled for Blythe, and mad as hell. She and my father put in an appearance at the reception, but left the party as quickly as possible.

At the party, Mama said to Blythe, "I'm happy for you, honey, I really am. But you've got a lot of years left. My time is running out. I don't begrudge you anything, Blythe, but this one is very, very difficult for me."

Back in New Canaan, Mark, Philip, and I sat piled on my parents' king-sized bed watching the telecast. Generally, we would have been sticking popcorn in each other's ears, giving each other whacks in the head and mildly terrorizing one another the way brothers do, but not this night. All three of us sat there glued to the fourteen-inch, black-and-white Sylvania TV, the largest one in the house. When they announced the winner, we were thrilled for Mama's sweet and charming co-star. At the same time, we knew how much this meant to our mother and how terrible she must have felt. I screamed "Yay!" for Blythe as Mark yelled "Shit!" and Philip hurled the *TV Guide* at the set. Just barely of legal age, Mark went off to a bar and Philip and I watched the rest of the show in silence.

With the Broadway run still going strong after a year, Arthur Whitelaw asked Mama if she would go to open a London production of *Butterflies* at the Apollo Theatre in the West End. This was a dream come true for her. She'd always wanted to go to London, but Mama had promised herself when she finally went, it would be with a play. I was very concerned about my mother being gone for so long. I was nearly eleven years old and incredibly dependent on her. Because of my interest in theater, I didn't have many friends at school. There was no one I could talk to the way I talked to Mama. I loved my father, but the relationship was more reserved. While I knew we would all miss her terribly, of the three boys, I believed I would miss her the most.

Once again, she had the perfect solution. If the show was a hit, I would fly over and spend the year attending the American School in London. I lay in bed at night with my mind racing about my upcoming trip to a foreign country. Mama and I made all sorts of plans—a trip to Harrod's to buy puppets, excursions to Buckingham Palace and Hampton Court—I was ecstatic.

At the same time, she said, "Now, there's a chance it may *not* be a hit in London, darling."

"But why wouldn't it?" I asked. "They loved it in New York. They still do!"

"Yes," she said, "but sometimes British humor is very different. Remember that play we saw at Westport with Edward Mulhaire called *The Secretary Bird*?"

"Oh yeah," I answered, turning up my nose. "Pee-ew! It wasn't funny at all!"

"That's exactly my point," she said. "That was a big hit in the West End. *Butterflies* could be the same thing in reverse."

My stomach felt queasy. Maybe this wasn't such a sure thing after all. Difficult as it was, we'd just have to wait and be patient. We completed the application procedure and I was accepted to the second half of the fourth grade at the American School in London. At least that hurdle was crossed. I waited with baited breath to hear the news from abroad. After the opening night, she sent me a telegram which read, "Darling—fourteen curtain calls—stop. Pack your woolies—stop. Love, Mama."

I had been sworn to secrecy until this moment. Now, I was telling the world. Much to my chagrin, it turned out to be a false alarm. Apparently, numerous curtain calls are a matter of course in the West End, like in opera or ballet. They are no criteria for success or failure. The London critics hated *Butterflies are Free*. With their history of boarding schools and reserved politeness, the Brits didn't understand how a son could be so disrespectful to his mother and they simply didn't find it funny. I think I was more disappointed that Mama was. The critics uniformly panned it, and then at the end of the season, the *London Daily Mail* named *Butterflies are Free* the Best Foreign Play of 1971. Go figure.

When Mama returned from London in early December, we all went to JFK to welcome her home. As she went through customs, my father, brothers, and I all stood behind a second-story, plate-glass window watching suitcases being unloaded and a beehive of activity below us as several thousand people were being checked in. Mama saw us, waved and blew kisses, then headed over towards a large animal crate.

"What do you suppose is in that box?" my father asked us, with a tinge of concern.

A customs official opened the box and Mama held up an adorable, little ball of black-and-white fluff with a pink nose. It was an Old English sheepdog she had purchased near Windsor Castle, named Amanda. My brothers burst out laughing as I squealed with delight. My father held his hand up as if to say, "Stop! Send it back!" We already had two dogs and my father thought a third was too much. They had many such battles about family pets over the years, but he never won. Jack Yankee was such a softie at heart. He managed to get over his outrage after Amanda threw up in his brand new Mercedes sedan on the way home from the airport. By the time we arrived in New Canaan he was in love with her, too.

The other extravagant purchase my mother made in Great Britain was an authentic London taxicab for my father. It arrived by boat a few weeks later and he loved to chauffeur his sons and his new Old English sheepdog around in it. But the car was a lemon and no one in the States knew how to repair it, so he wound up selling it for parts. Amanda, on the other hand, was with us for many years and had more personality than many people I know. Whenever anyone would sing, dance or tell an animated story (a frequent occurrence in our household), Amanda would bark shrilly until she was once again the center of attention.

Keir Dullea had played the leading role of Don Baker, the young blind man in *Butterflies are Free* on Broadway and in London. He and Mama adored one another. When a rather strange offer came to do the play for John Kenley, an eccentric summer-stock producer in Ohio, Mama thought, well, my mother never saw it, because she won't fly. If I were to do it in Columbus, playing practically in her backyard, she'd have no excuse.

The role played by Blythe Danner on Broadway was to be played in this production by Sue Ann Langdon, a popular sitcom actress of the moment who was too old for the part and who, according to Heckart, was a nice lady but tended to land all the jokes with a sledgehammer. Needing some support onstage, Mama implored Keir to do it with her for a few weeks touring Ohio. Keir agreed, largely out of respect and admiration for Heckart. She told the producer she would only agree to do it if he would cast Dullea. Opening night in Columbus, the Ohio Yankees, Heckarts, Starks, and other assorted relatives came from far and wide to see their Anna Eileen. It was a major homecoming. There was, however, one conspicuous omission—Esther. My mother phoned her the next day.

"Mama, where were you last night? Were you sick?" her daughter asked.

"No," Grandma Esther replied through pursed lips.

"Then why weren't you there?" she asked.

"The seats are too hard in that theater," she answered.

"Mama," her daughter retorted, "I'll get you a cushion. I'll get you two cushions. The only reason I agreed to do this in Columbus was so that you could see it! Now what about tonight?"

"Anna Eileen," she snapped, "you know I can't sit still that long!"

And that was that. Mama had agreed to do this second-rate tour of a role she had played for a year and a half and was sick to death of playing for one reason— so her mother would come see it and offer her a bit of support and perhaps even some acknowledgement of her talent. But it wasn't to be.

My Moment Inside the Spotlight

THE CAST OF *REMEMBER ME*—FRONT ROW: MARIAN SELDES, ROBERT STACK, AND MAMA

IN 1972, MAMA DID a play on the New England summer-stock circuit called *Remember Me* by Ronald Alexander. Ronnie had two moderate Broadway hits: *Time Out for Ginger* in the early fifties and *Nobody Loves an Albatross* in the early sixties. He was hoping that *Remember Me* would be another success. Sadly, he was mistaken. It was a convoluted, Gothic murder mystery starring Mama, Robert Stack and Marian Seldes. It must have been one of those times where the actors read the roles instead of the play. Even though they couldn't get the script to work, it had two things going for it: there were three juicy, scenery-chewing roles for the leading actors and a fabulous touring schedule. It was playing those gorgeous, summer resort towns in Cape Cod, Maine and all over the New England coast.

At twelve, I got be a theater brat and spend my summer vacation traipsing around with Bob Stack's kid and Marian Seldes's kid and Ronnie Alexander's three kids. We'd all go to the beach during the day and hang out at the theater at night. Ronnie's girlfriend was a kooky, free-spirited lady named Amanda, who went by the affectionate nickname of Panda. While everyone else would be rehearsing new material, hoping to come up with the magic formula that would turn *Remember Me* into a successful play, Panda would drag this gaggle of kids to the beach, the museum or whatever local attraction was in the town of the week.

Remember Me was a twisted murder mystery about a wealthy New England society couple, Charles and Catherine (played by Robert Stack and Marian Seldes). They have the outer appearance of a happy, upscale life until Martha, a woman from Charles's past (played by Mama) shows up. It seems that when he was young and hungry, he worked for Martha, who ran a sex circus. She has tracked him down and wants to live with him and have him take care of her in her declining years. She doesn't want money—she wants to move in. Secrets are revealed, including the fact that Martha used to celebrate a black mass and Charles was the celebrant; in other words, he had sex with dead people. Martha threatens to let the cat out of the bag unless Charles lets her live in his guesthouse. Charles winds up having to tell his wife, who is appalled, and warns him that if the children ever find out, she will cut him off without a cent. Martha gets drunk one night and starts shooting off her mouth. Tempers flare and Charles winds up strangling her. The rest of the play is about how he can hide the body from his wife and children, and live with the guilt of what he has done.

Martha was a funny, colorful part. Even though the play didn't work, I could see why Mama wanted to play this brash, loudmouthed drunk who wore tarty clothes and was basically an aging madam. The critics praised Heckart's work and most of the acting, but they all said the play was sordid and confusing at best. Mama had no respect for the director. He left after the first performance, in Skowhegan, Maine. They had no budget to replace him, so the producer tried to step in, which was an even bigger disaster. Occasionally, they tried to put in new material Ronnie Alexander would write, but for the most part, the cast was trying to grin and bear it for the rest of the summer.

My father and I drove up to the Cape Playhouse in Dennis, the heart of Cape Cod, and spent the week with Mama there. After that, I continued on with Mama to Ogunquit, Maine, then back to our beloved Westport Playhouse, right near home. The last stop was to be in the Pocono Mountains where they would complete the tour.

Even though it had been several summers since my sex education at the Westport Country Playhouse, there were certainly a lot of things about *Remember Me* I didn't understand. Mama's character ran a sex circus? Bob Stack's leading man had been a celebrant in a black mass? Mama's answers to these questions were particularly vague. I knew they were bad things, so I didn't ask too many questions. All I knew was that Mama's character walked away with the show because she was hilarious, flamboyant and the best aspect of this troubled play. Eileen Heckart found a way to make this terrible woman totally lovable. That was one of the elements upon which my mother built her career. Heckart was famous for showing the audience the humanity and charisma of the seemingly despicable characters she often played.

While *Remember Me* had to have been one of the least successful plays on the summer stock circuit that year, Mama won the Straw Hat Award as Best Actress in a play for her wickedly outrageous performance as Martha. The Straw Hat Award was sponsored by the Council of Summer Stock Theatres and honored outstanding performances in summer touring productions. It was one of the best looking awards Mama ever received—a small, gold-plated straw hat in a Lucite cube on a mahogany base. The award was presented to her by one of her favorite Hollywood icons: Cary Grant. At the time, he was a spokesperson for Fabergé Cosmetics, one of the underwriters of the award.

She said to me, "Honey, there he was—Cary Grant! He looked so sexy, so debonair, my knees damn near buckled as I went up to the dais to receive the award!"

Afterward, Grant offered to give her a lift in his private plane wherever she needed to go. She thanked him for the offer and told him with a tremendous degree of disappointment that she had a car coming for her. The way she talked about it afterward, I wouldn't have been surprised if she'd cancelled her car and driver just to take a ride with Cary Grant.

Sometimes, if a show was listed as "Prior to Broadway," the savvy critics from the larger cities nearby would make a special trip down to get the first scoop on a new show. This was the case with Kevin Kelly, the acid-tongued reviewer on the *Boston Globe*. Kevin Kelly had a field day with *Remember Me*. He gave it a scathing notice, attacking the actors and the weak direction every bit as much as he did the play. Usually in a situation like this, a critic will spare the cast and blame a bad script and unfocused, poor direction. Not so with Kevin Kelly. He noted that Heckart barreled onto the stage like an aging roller derby queen. Stack, according to Kelly, looked like rigor mortis has already set in, while he likened Seldes's stage movements to that of "a spastic gazelle."

Daddy and I sat with Mama in the kitchen of the little beachfront cottage the theater had rented for her and howled over this review. Mama didn't just laugh it off—she was in hysterics over these ludicrous and unwarranted remarks. Marian Seldes never read reviews and didn't want to hear about them until after the run of a show was complete. Robert Stack, however, considered it a personal affront. He hadn't done a play in a number of years and was deeply hurt by the critic's words. After all the wonderful reviews this cast received that summer for rising above a mediocre script, isn't it a shame that this is the one that everyone remembered.

At age twelve, I was already a star in my children's theater group, having done a number of leading roles the year before: King Arthur in *Camelot*, Tevye in *Fiddler on the Roof*, Littlechap in *Stop the World, I Want to Get Off*, and the Poet in *Kismet*. My preadolescent Tevye, complete with prayer shawl, yarmulke and lots of glued-on facial hair, was something to behold. I also imitated Lily Tomlin's character Edith Ann constantly. The character was a smart-alecky six-year-old who told everyone where to go and what to do, occasionally revealing wisdom and deeper truths through sidesplitting humor. Tomlin had made this character famous on *Laugh-In* and I thought it was the funniest thing ever. I saved my allowance to buy the LP of her comedy routines and proceeded to commit them to memory. Whenever I was in the presence of grown-ups or, for that matter, anyone who would listen, I performed one routine after another verbatim. I got laughs, I was told I sounded just like Edith Ann and if one was foolish enough to encourage me, I would perform the entire album until asked to stop. I drove the *Remember Me* cast crazy with them. The only way they could ever shut me up was when they started reciting the routines along with me.

That summer, I also traveled with a wonderfully crafted hand puppet named Tuni—Mama had given him the name, short for Petunia. Tuni was all handmade— a tramp clown with lots of personality. He was a soft-spoken, lovable clown with a soothing voice. Looking back, he was probably my alter ego. I could amuse myself for hours with Tuni and would sometimes talk through him to convey my real feelings to the other adults in the company. How Mama could deal with me all summer and still handle eight shows a week on tour, the constant rewrites and everything else that was involved in making a flawed play work is beyond me.

One of my particular chums in the cast of *Remember Me* was Marian Seldes. For all her loving gentleness, it's very difficult to describe Marian to someone who has never met her. There is an otherworldly quality about her. A tall, willowy actress with a mellifluous voice and graceful gestures, Marian doesn't walk into a room—she sweeps in and claims it. There is a presence and an energy in her like none I have ever encountered. To say she is grand would be an understatement. If she is congratulating someone for a performance she enjoyed, she is honoring them by bowing at their feet. Often, when people first meet her, they think, "Who is that eccentric lady? She can't be for real!" But if one is fortunate enough to go deeper, you realize it's not an act. It's Marian. When she finds a role that is suited to her unique and unusual qualities, as she did with Edward Albee's *A Delicate Balance* or Tina Howe's *Painting Churches*, among many others, it is mesmerizing. And she adored the twelve-year-old me. She respected me as a person rather than treating me like the son of her co-star. Many years later, she directed me in *King Lear* at Juilliard and later still, she did a staged reading of my first play. No one could take his eyes off her. Through her own grandness, she elevates everyone around her and makes them feel grand.

The night *Remember Me* opened in Westport, Connecticut, all the know-it-alls and savvy theater folk from New York came up to see it. This was the closest the tour was coming to Manhattan and if there was any chance to bring this play into New York, this was it. Mama knew it was a lost cause, but Bob Stack and some of the other cast members hung onto the vain hope. By this point in the tour, I came and went freely backstage without the stage doorman even giving me a passing glance. I noticed that Mama had a lot more opening night flowers in her dressing room than anywhere else. After the curtain call, I flew backstage to play host and greeter to Mama's entourage. I stood in the green-room hallway outside Mama's dressing room door, waiting for the star to emerge.

As I waited, the first face through the door was my buddy, Milton Goldman. As we exchanged pleasantries, he got a predatory look in his eye. He was in high "agent mode," thinking of a deal he'd been negotiating earlier that day.

"Hey Luke," he said, "they're doing a new Jean Kerr play on Broadway called *Finishing Touches.* There's a role in it for this precocious, loud-mouthed fourteen-year-old. You'd be perfect for it."

I couldn't believe what I was hearing. On my mother's opening night, one of the most prestigious agents in New York was suggesting a role in a Broadway play for *me*? This was a dream come true. I could barely contain myself as other well-wishers and local friends flooded into the tiny, sparsely furnished green room. Fortunately, Milton didn't seem to be in any hurry that night. Once Mama had greeted everyone and the guests had started to subside, I grabbed her arm.

"Mama, Milton says there's a role I'm perfect for in a new Broadway play!"

The star looked at her agent like she wanted to strangle him.

"Now Milton," she said, "You know Jack and I don't approve of kids in show business—especially *our* kids!"

"But it's a nice little part, Heckie," Milton said. "It's only a couple of scenes. And he really is right for it. You could at least let him audition!"

"No, Milton!" she barked.

Mama looked down at me with a steely glance.

"Luke, we will discuss this later," she said.

As she walked Milton to the stage door, I heard her say, "Jesus, you sure opened a can of worms this time—on *my* opening night!"

I could barely sleep that evening. I tossed and turned, wondering if there was any possibility I could change my mother's mind. I took her coffee and sweet roll into her the next morning and we talked about how well the play had gone the night before. She said how nice it was to be back in her own bed and wasn't it wonderful that this leg of the tour was only fifteen minutes from home.

She knew what I wanted to talk about. She took my hand as I sat on the edge of her bed.

"Look," she said, "I'm really not doing this to be mean. You know how your father and I feel about children in show business. It ruins them, they don't have a childhood and you are *not* going to be like that. I have watched too many young people be destroyed and I am not going to let that happen to you. You are too young to understand the way this business can eat people up, but I have seen it happen."

"So . . . I can't even audition for it?" I asked.

She thought for a moment.

"Well, since you seem determined to go into this crazy, effing business, it might not be bad for you to have the experience of a professional, Broadway audition. Would you like that?"

"Oh yes!" I said.

"Let me discuss it with your father," she said. "Since Milton opened his big mouth, if your father agrees, we will let you audition."

Later that morning, she had a private phone conversation with my father at his office. Afterwards, I was summoned to the living room.

In a formal tone, she said, "Your father has agreed. I will call Milton and have him set up an audition."

As I started to move in for an excited embrace, she stopped me.

"Now, wait a minute!" she said. "I want to be sure we understand the rules. You'll be competing against professional children from the High School for the Performing Arts and all the other training schools. These are kids who have been acting a lot longer than you. In the remote possibility you should get the part, for all the reasons I've already told you, your father and I would not let you do it. But if you want to have the experience of a professional audition, you may read for it. Are we clear?"

"We're clear," I said.

Milton Goldman made the necessary arrangements and Mama took me into New York on the train on her day off from the show. I was given the sides for the role of Hughie, the son. Mama and I sat in the lobby of the Edison Theatre with thirty or so other young boys and their mothers. Mama kept her distance for fear anyone would recognize her. She hated pushy stage mothers with a passion and being in the company of so many of them was almost as bad as being perceived as one.

"Let's find a quiet spot in the lobby of the mezzanine," she suggested. "There won't be as many people there."

We found an unoccupied settee outside the ladies' lounge. Thinking back on how flawlessly I had memorized all those Lily Tomlin routines, she gave me line readings and asked me to parrot them back to her. Naturally, her choices and instincts were impeccable. I did exactly as she instructed and felt incredibly lucky to be getting this sort of coaching from a bona fide Broadway star. I think she was twice as nervous as I was.

The director was a distinguished gentleman of the theater named Joseph Anthony. The original director of such Broadway hits as *The Rainmaker*, *The Most Happy Fella*, and *Rhinoceros*, he had also directed Jean Kerr's *Mary, Mary*, which had been a big commercial success. The playwright had requested him on this largely unfinished play in hopes of creating the same magic. Ironically, Joe Anthony had also been one of my mother's first acting teachers in New York. I had been instructed to be totally businesslike and professional. As my name was called, I approached the stage, script in hand, without saying a word to anyone. Later, my mother (who was hovering in the darkened balcony watching the proceedings) told me that as I marched past the creative team without even introducing myself, Mr. Anthony had put out his hand and said, "I'm Joe, Luke." I was oblivious to anything but the task at hand. I read with the stage manager, a thirtyish man with a bushy, walrus mustache. After I read, Joe Anthony consulted with two other people, most likely the casting director and an associate producer. He called to me onstage.

"Luke, do you think you could come back in two hours and read for Jean Kerr and the producer, Robert Whitehead?"

Having prepared for this possibility by my coach, I said yes.

We went to a coffee shop on Eighth Avenue where I devoured a turkey sandwich, absolutely thrilled that I was about to read for the playwright and the producer. Mama let me know that Bob Whitehead was an incredibly powerful man on Broadway and also a dear friend of hers. She figured he would probably recognize the Yankee name, but didn't want nepotism to play any part in this. She sat there nursing a cup of coffee and a pack of cigarettes, having far too many knots in her stomach to eat anything. I didn't understand why I was so calm and she was so nervous. We worked a little bit more on the script and returned to the Edison Theatre for my callback.

This time, I knew better than to bolt past the people sitting in row G. I stopped, shook hands and exchanged pleasantries with Jean Kerr and Robert Whitehead and then went up onstage. We were on the set for a musical called *Don't Bother Me, I Can't Cope*, which was currently running at the Edison. It was filled with platforms and modular levels. After I read, Joe Anthony asked me to run all over the stage. He kept shouting different directions.

"Now left, now right, now grab onto that pole and swing around!"

Mama had insisted that I do this audition totally on my own. Coaching and line readings were one thing, but she was not going to interfere or influence my actual time with the auditors. She learned this lesson from Patty McCormack years ago during the Broadway auditions for *The Bad Seed*. No mention had been made of my famous parentage. We both figured Milton Goldman had clued them in, but it wasn't going to come from us. Luke Yankee was standing on his own merits. He certainly wasn't getting a callback because he was Eileen Heckart's son.

As I was walking off the stage, Joe Anthony called to me. "Luke," he said, "Where's your mother?"

A familiar, gravelly voice in the darkness boomed, "She's about to throw herself off the balcony!"

They all howled with laughter. She came down and chatted for a few minutes and then we got on the train and went back to Connecticut.

"Now, this is always the hardest part," Mama said. "You gave a very good audition and now you need to put it out of your mind as much as you can. That was the whole point of this. You achieved it and you can be very proud of yourself."

Put it *out* of my *mind*? How could I possibly do that?

Two days later, Mama and I drove to the Pocono Playhouse, which was the final stop on the tour. The Pocono Mountains were gorgeous and the theater was a rustic, old barn in need of repair. As we were unpacking in our cabin, the phone call I had been waiting for, and Mama had been dreading, came through.

It was Milton Goldman. Mama took the phone into her bedroom and asked me to wait outside.

I guess somewhere in the back of my young mind I thought that if I actually *got* the part, we could work *something* out. It was only an hour into New York on the train and once the show opened, I could still go to my regular school in Connecticut, except for Wednesday matinees. I was a good student and I knew I could keep up. Would she reconsider?

"Heckie," Milton said into the phone, "they want to negotiate Luke's contract. What do I tell them?"

"Tell them 'No, thank you,' Milton."

"But Heckie . . ." Milton said.

"Tell them 'No thank you,' Milton," she repeated. "You and I discussed this before he ever auditioned. You know how Jack and I feel. Blame the whole thing on me and tell them 'No.'"

Mama called me into the bedroom and told me about Milton's call. I'd been doing my best to eavesdrop, and even though she was speaking softly into the phone, I'd already figured it out.

She said, "Congratulations, darling. You got the part. Even though your father and I won't let you take it, at least you have the satisfaction of knowing they wanted you. Out of all those professional children, they thought you were the best. No one can ever take that away from you."

I stared at the frayed edge of the tufted bedspread in the rustic cabin. A thousand thoughts flooded my mind. My life could have changed a moment before. I could have been on Broadway, playing in the same world as my mother, in the same theaters where she received recognition and adulation every night. They wanted *me* for my talent, not because I was anyone's son. My mind flashed on *my* opening night, *my* name on a Broadway marquee, *my* chance to stand in the spotlight. It was an opportunity to step out of the shadows and be someone on my own, not the kid hanging out backstage, but the kid *on* stage. It was all I ever wanted, all I ever dreamed of and it was being offered to me . . . and taken away. I thought my mother loved me. How could she do this to me?

We studied each other for a long time. Neither said a word. I ran my hand against the wooden slats on the back of the scratched, oak headboard and shuffled my feet on the braided, Colonial rug.

Finally, I broke the silence.

"Mama," I said, "let me show the picture I drew in the car on the drive up."

I ran into the other room and came back with a large newsprint pad.

I showed her a drawing I had done of about seventy-five faces in a crowd. I made up a story about every face, chattering like a magpie. When I finally took a breath, I felt two hot tears roll down my soft cheeks.

Wiping away the tears on my sleeve, I turned to my mother and said, "You know, I'm talking so fast so it won't hurt as much."

"I know, darling," she said, squeezing my hand.

A little while later, she called my father and a long, private conversation ensued. Were they doing the right thing? Should they relent? Would I grow up hating or resenting them for refusing me this opportunity to be on Broadway? Daddy asked to speak to me. Mama handed me the phone and he offered a few awkward, well-intentioned words of support and encouragement, reinforcing what Mama had said. I appreciated the attempt, but at the moment, nothing helped. As parents, they had never been in a situation like this before and they didn't know how to handle it.

Word had spread quickly through the *Remember Me* company. Several other members of the cast had been up for roles in *Finishing Touches* as well. Everyone was buzzing with the news that Luke had been offered a role, but Heckie wasn't going to let him do it. People kept asking me how I felt. The truth was I wasn't sure how I felt. I honestly believed that my parents knew best. When Mama told me her fears about bratty showbiz kids, I knew what she meant. Was she really afraid I would turn into one of *those*? It wasn't in my character and even if it had been, she and Daddy would have cut me down to size at the first trace of that behavior. I was crushed, but I accepted their decision. What choice did I have?

That night at the Pocono Playhouse, after the show, Robert Stack called me into his dressing room. He sat me down at his dressing table as he took off his makeup. The room smelled of musty playbills and Brut cologne.

"Luke," he said, in that deep and authoritative "good cop" voice, "I want you to know I think your parents made the right decision. Obviously, you're a very gifted young man. Whatever talent you have now, you'll have it and more by the time you're twenty, and then you can make your own choices. But for now, you need to listen to them."

I thanked him and he shook my hand firmly. Mama must have told him how concerned she was about me. He wanted to put in his paternal two cents as a fellow actor and parent. I had tremendous respect for Bob Stack and this made it increase tenfold. Not only was he a member of the Hollywood elite, he was a tender, compassionate man.

I knew Mr. Stack was right. And I knew in my heart Mama and Daddy were right. Still, to this day I wonder how my life might have been different if I'd been allowed to do that Broadway play and follow a professional career as a teenager.

When *Finishing Touches* played its pre-Broadway tryout in New Haven that Fall, Daddy took me to see it. The boy playing my part was a young man with bright, red hair named Scott Firestone. Of course, I hated him. My father said he'd never seen me so angry. It was as if I took all my anger and resentment at my parents and directed it toward him. I'm sure Scott Firestone was perfectly fine in the part. Under the circumstances, it seemed totally justified to focus my aggression on the usurper.

With Barbara Bel Geddes and Robert Lansing in the leading roles and a very weak script, *Finishing Touches* limped along on Broadway for about four months, and then closed. *Remember Me* was never resurrected after the summer tour. The only footnote it ever received was Mama getting the Straw Hat Award from Cary Grant.

A few years ago, I was at my dry cleaner on Melrose Avenue in Hollywood. The red-haired guy in line ahead of me was having some difficulty. They had misplaced his order.

"But you *must* have it," he said to the employee behind the counter. "It's under the name Firestone. Scott Firestone!"

I hadn't thought of that name in thirty years.

As he started to exit with his armful of pressed shirts and trousers, I turned to him and said, "Excuse me, but didn't you do a play called *Finishing Touches* on Broadway?"

"Good God!" he exclaimed, "How would you know that?"

"It's a long story," I said. "Maybe I'll tell you sometime. I'm glad they found your dry cleaning. So long."

Mama Wins an Oscar

MAMA IN THE FILM VERSION OF *BUTTERFLIES ARE FREE.* ©1972, RENEWED 2000
COLUMBIA PICTURES INDUSTRIES, INC. ALL RIGHTS RESERVED. COURTESY OF
COLUMBIA PICTURES

WHEN COLUMBIA PICTURES bought the film rights to *Butterflies are Free* and
announced it as a vehicle for Goldie Hawn, Mama was chomping at the bit. Would
she get to re-create her stage role in the movie? She figured she probably wasn't a
big enough film star and she didn't stand a chance. Historically, there are so few
film roles for actresses of a certain age and many names were discussed for this plum
role. Ingrid Bergman, Olivia DeHavilland, and Angela Lansbury were the top three
contenders. Each time another name was kicked around in Liz Smith's or Army
Archerd's column, Mama would get anxious. She called her agent about it frequently.

Milton Goldman kept reassuring her. "Heckie, no one has been signed yet. I'm
working on it—just hang in there."

As fate would have it, Mike Frankovitch, the film's producer at Columbia, was
a major theater lover. Despite pressure from the studio, he wanted Eileen Heckart
to recreate her stage role. The offer was made and accepted. Mama was overjoyed.

She shot for six weeks on location in San Francisco and Hollywood and fell in love with Goldie Hawn and Edward Albert Jr., who were playing the young couple. Goldie was particularly delightful in the film. A veteran of TV's *Laugh-In*, she had a three picture deal at Columbia. Having made *Cactus Flower* and *There's a Girl in My Soup* (ironically, the play with William Shatner at Westport that had taught me the facts of life), *Butterflies* was to be the third. The giggly blonde was the perfect comic foil for Heckart's uptight suburban matron. Out of the many ingénues Eileen Heckart worked with during her career, there were three she valued as the daughters she never had: Brenda Vaccaro (with whom she had appeared on Broadway in 1961 in John Patrick's comedy, *Everybody Loves Opal*), Blythe Danner, Penny Fuller, and Goldie Hawn. Over the years, she kept in touch with them whenever possible. Her love and admiration for these ladies never waned.

Edward Albert, Jr. played Don, the role originated by Keir Dullea. He was the son of film actor Eddie Albert, someone Mama had known for years. Many times, if Mama was on location with a young man around the age of her boys, she made him her surrogate son. She took him under her wing, cooked for him, gave him maternal advice, and treated him like one of her own. It made her feel less homesick. On *Butterflies*, she chastised Eddie for smoking and counseled him on his love life. Having known his parents for so long, she was able to advise him on the best way to handle them.

The film version of *Butterflies* was extremely faithful to the play, with one exception. They changed the locale from the east coast to the west coast. No doubt this was done to save on location costs. Instead of Greenwich Village, Don Baker's apartment was in the Haight-Ashbury section of San Francisco. Instead of Scarsdale, his mother was a suburban matron from Hillsboro. In practically every other respect, the script was the same.

The film was directed by Milton Katselas, who had guided the play successfully and was doing his first film. Film crews are always wary of a situation like this. Will the novice director try to bluff his way through and be a tyrant when he doesn't understand the intricacies of the camera—or will he defer to those with a lifetime of experience? The cinematographer, grips, and gaffers were on their guard. On the first morning, Katselas called a meeting with the technical heads of each department.

"Folks," he said, "this is my first film. I know actors, but I know very little about the camera. If we're going to get through this and stay on schedule and on budget, I desperately need your help."

"You got it, Milton!" they said. "Anything you need!"

Mama was so secure in her role as Mrs. Baker, after a particularly strong take, she'd shout "Print it!" before Katselas had a chance to say a word. After a few days, he came to her and said, "Heckie, I appreciate your enthusiasm, but as the director, I really wish you'd let me be the one to say 'Print it,' okay?"

It takes a secure individual to handle situations like that with such grace.

The film version of *Butterflies are Free* was released to enthusiastic reviews—especially for Mama.

AL HIRSCHFELD'S CARICATURE FOR THE FILM OF *BUTTERFLIES ARE FREE* WITH MAMA, EDDIE ALBERT JR. AND GOLDIE HAWN. ©AL HIRSCHFELD/MARGO FEIDEN GALLERIES LTD., NEW YORK. WWW.ALHIRSCHFELD.COM

Rex Reed said in the *New York Daily News*, "Eileen Heckart gives one of the most exquisitely detailed performances you are ever likely to see on the screen, avoiding all the clichés in a magnificently sensible reading of a 'mother' role that would be easy to dislike in less craftsmanlike hands."*

Tom Costner in the *Village Voice* said, "Eileen Heckart's turn is an acting lesson which many character actors would do well to study. Just hearing her version of the suburban-matron whiskey tenor is worth the price of admission."**

Once again, Mama had taken a character that was not easy to embrace and made the audience see her vulnerable side so that we laughed with her and understood her pain.

When the Academy Award nominations were announced for Best Supporting Actress of 1972, the list consisted of Geraldine Page in *Pete 'n' Tillie*, Susan Tyrell

* Courtesy of Rex Reed. Reprinted with permission.
** Courtesy of Tom Costner, the *Village Voice*. Reprinted with permission.

in *Fat City*, Jeannie Berlin in *The Heartbreak Kid*, Shelley Winters in *The Poseidon Adventure*, and Eileen Heckart in *Butterflies are Free*.

When Mama was nominated for the Oscar, it was as if everyone in the town of New Canaan was nominated as well. Many friends and colleagues, both in and out of the business, were living vicariously through her success.

Billy Reid, one of the bullies I feared the most at New Canaan Country School, sauntered up to me on the playground. Billy and I had known each other since kindergarten and he had gotten meaner over the years. Billy was a very angry boy and he liked to take out his aggression on me. One of his favorite tricks was to wait until someone had gotten off the school bus in the seat directly behind me. Billy would then move into the empty seat and quietly read for a few minutes. When I least expected it, he would lean over me, put his fingers to his lips, and whistle with a shrill, piercing force directly into my ear. Sometimes, I couldn't hear out of that ear for a couple of hours afterward. I was so scared of him, I never fought back. Instead, I sat there saying, "Goddamn you, Reid!" snapping my fingers in front of my ear in hopes of regaining my hearing. He thought this was hysterical.

On a cold January day, shortly after the Oscar nominations had been announced, Billy Reid approached me on the playground. My body tightened and I kept my distance.

"Hey, Yankee," he said. He spoke in a monotone and hardly opened his mouth. "I hear your old lady's nominated for an Academy Award."

"That's right, Billy," I replied, shifting my weight and trying to hide the tremor in my voice.

"She gonna win?" he asked, sticking his thumbs in the belt loops of his Levis.

"Well, I don't know, Billy," I said, "I certainly hope so."

"When are the awards?" Billy asked, stepping in closer.

"On March twenty-seventh," I said, stepping back.

Billy quickly moved in and stood nose to nose with me. "Well, she better win," he said through clenched teeth. "If she doesn't, on March twenty-eighth, I'm gonna kick the crap outta you!"

"But Billy," I said, "I have no control over it!"

"I don't give a shit!" he said over his shoulder as he walked away. "She better win . . . or else!"

Of course, after she won, Billy Reid wanted to hear every detail and smiled at me like I was his new best friend—for about an hour. At least he wasn't kicking the crap out of me.

Ten days before the Oscar ceremony, we went on a family vacation to Naples, Florida. We were to stay at a friend's condo on the beach for a week and then afterwards, the boys would fly home and Mama and Daddy would fly to L.A.

Mama's strongest competition for the Oscar was Shelley Winters. *The Poseidon Adventure* was a popular disaster movie and Winters even got to die onscreen— one of the factors that weighs heavily on voters. All the pundits said Shelley Winters had it in the bag. For Jimmy the Greek, the biggest oddsmaker in Las Vegas at the time, my mother was his only upset of the entire evening. He had also placed his bet on Winters, as did most of the Hollywood soothsayers and columnists.

My mother's Hollywood agent, Ina Bernstein, sarcastically summed up Shelley Winter's performance.

"Now, Heckart," she said, "there is no way you can win over that performance. You have to take a big bucket of popcorn and go see it. Shelley Winters does an underwater ballet in her bloomers for ten minutes, during which she saves Gene Hackman's life. She surfaces, grabs her left tit, and dies. Now, how can you possibly top that? All you do is *act* in *your* movie, for Chrissake!"

One night in Florida, we were in a seafood restaurant with mounted swordfish on the walls and autographed photos of Frank Sinatra, Joey Bishop, and Sheckie Green. Mama got very depressed and cried over her lobster tail.

"I'm not going to win the damn thing!" she said through choked sobs. "Shelley's going to win the damn thing. I've never won a goddamn thing my entire life!"

Of course, this was untrue. As she sank deeper into her self-pity, Philip said, "For God's sake! I hope you *do* win now, just so you have to apologize to all of us!"

The first thing Philip said to me after she won was, "Mom owes us an apology."

When my parents arrived in Los Angeles, it was star treatment all the way. Robert Stack and his wife Rosemarie wanted to give a cocktail party in her honor at their sumptuous home in Bel Air. The party was very grand with many Hollywood "A"-list players. After Mama won, Stack joked, "She had to win. We gave her a party."

The day of the ceremony, my mother was a nervous wreck. With Mike Frankovitch and Columbia Pictures picking up the tab at the Beverly Hills Hotel, she and my father went all out. She had strawberries and cream for breakfast and had her nails wrapped. Daddy got a massage. By noon, she was sitting with her head in the toilet, vomiting from the sheer terror of it all. She managed to calm herself by the time the limo arrived to pick them up.

All her life my mother was extremely nearsighted and needed glasses for distance. As Diahann Carroll was singing one of the nominated songs, "Strange are the Ways of Love" from *The Stepmother*, Mama took off her glasses and placed them in my father's lap.

"What are you doing?" he whispered, knowing she couldn't see.

"I'll tell you later," she whispered back.

She was preparing. She had a sense of calm and an awareness that she was going to win.

"It's mine," she said to herself.

She looked at the back of Shelley Winters' head sitting in front of her and she said to herself, "Sorry, Shelley. It's not your turn. I'm going to win tonight."

She told me once that from the time she was a young girl, whenever she had trouble falling asleep, she visualized herself winning an Academy Award. She saw every detail clearly in her mind as the she walked to the stage and the crowds cheered. Now, what she had seen in her mind's eye for more than forty years was coming to pass.

As Cloris Leachman and Robert Duvall ascended the podium, a hush swept over the crowd. This was the first major award of the evening. Duvall read the names of the nominees. When he got to Shelley Winters, he burst out laughing and seemed to guffaw over her name. It was a raucous, unattractive laugh, and there was no hiding it. The appearance was that his laugh was saying isn't it funny that Shelley Winters was nominated for *The Poseidon Adventure?*

What was Robert Duvall laughing at? He had locked eyes in the audience with James Caan, who was his pal from *The Godfather*, which they had recently filmed and for which they were both nominated as Best Supporting Actor that night. (Both men lost to Joel Grey for *Cabaret*, along with their other co-star, Al Pacino.) Duvall and Caan were great friends. Just as Duvall was announcing Winters' name, Caan caught his eye and made some obscene gesture, which was one of their private jokes on the set. Duvall totally lost it on live television being broadcast around the world. The appearance to the international audience was that he was laughing at Shelley Winters, which was not the case at all. Needless to say, Miss Winters was *not* pleased. He called the next day and apologized, but the damage was already done.

Generally, nominees are seated on or close to an aisle. That way, when they win, they have a clear shot to the stage. Not Miss Heckart. I guess the folks doing the seating at the Dorothy Chandler Pavilion didn't expect her to win, either. Shelley Winters was seated in front of her on an aisle, but Mama was about six seats in. So, when they called her name, she had to awkwardly crawl over all these other people in the row in order to get to the stage. She moved very fast because she was terrified they'd stop applauding before she reached the podium. Her fears were in vain.

Her acceptance speech was vintage Heckart. In other words, "Say it and get off." She said, quite simply, "I'd like to thank the first man who ever recommended me for this part, Howard Otway, and a darling crew . . . and of course, you. Thank you." That was it. Not Dad, not her agent, not her co-stars or director—just an old friend from her days in summer stock.

It was two days before her fifty-fourth birthday. Her only regret was that she forgot to add, "You sure know how to give a girl a birthday present!"

Howard Otway had built the Theatre 80 St. Marks down on St. Marks Place in Greenwich Village. He had appeared with Mama right out of college doing summer stock in Milwaukee with Tec D'Acosta in the mid-forties and they had remained close ever since. Howard was a sweet, rather eccentric man who was not good with money. When he had it, he spent it. When he didn't have it, he spent even more. He'd sunk every penny into building this theater, his lifelong dream. Just before it was completed in 1967, we were having Easter dinner with Howard and his family. Before we sat down to eat, he couldn't wait to take us on a tour of his new child, Theatre 80 St. Marks. As we crawled over paint cans and maneuvered around sheets of drywall and spackling knives, he led Mama onto the stage. He disappeared into the wings and returned with a huge diva bouquet of bright red roses, which he presented to her.

"You are the first actress to ever walk across my stage," he said, as he knelt at her feet with the bouquet. She spontaneously burst into tears.

Howard was great friends with Arthur Whitelaw, the Broadway producer of *Butterflies are Free*. When the show was coming into New York, as it became evident that they needed to replace Maureen O'Sullivan, Howard Otway said to Arthur, "For God's sake, get Eileen Heckart!"

MAMA AND CLORIS LEACHMAN AT THE 1972 ACADEMY AWARDS. COURTESY OF CORBIS/UPI

Mama had never forgotten that he was the first one to mention her for the role. As a result, Howard Otway was the only person she thanked when she won the Oscar. At that time, Theatre 80 St. Marks had gone from being a legitimate theater (opening with *You're A Good Man, Charlie Brown*, which had been a huge hit) to becoming one of New York's premiere revival movie houses, showing classics like *The Women* and *The Philadelphia Story*. Even so, Howard Otway was not making ends meet. He was deeply in debt and on the verge of closing. When my mother mentioned his name at the Oscars, he gained an instant degree of celebrity. Shortly thereafter, his film distributor extended his credit for another six months and the bank offered him a second mortgage. Sometimes, the power of Hollywood is simply amazing.

When Cloris Leachman called Mama's name, Daddy was so excited, he grabbed her face in her hands and planted a big kiss on her. The only problem was that he did it with such force that as she went up to the stage, he looked down and noticed that he had skin under his thumbnail. Daddy said to himself, "Oh dear God, what have I done?" But he quickly forgot about it in the excitement of the moment.

By the time Mama was having her publicity photos taken backstage with Cloris Leachman, as they were being mobbed by reporters, Cloris said to her, "Eileen darling, is your chin bleeding?"

Not having any idea what my father had done, Mama thought Cloris was referring to a discoloration.

"Oh no," Heckart replied. "It's just a birthmark. I've had it all my life."

If you look closely at some of the photos taken backstage that night, you can see a spot of blood on my mother's chin where my father gouged her as he gave that congratulatory kiss. If her head were up, you would see a trail of blood. She had no idea that she had this big gash trickling down her chin. She was fond of saying that she was the first bloody Oscar winner in history.

This was the year of *Cabaret*, which swept many of the awards, including Joel Grey as Best Supporting Actor, Liza Minnelli as Best Actress, and Mama's old friend, Bob Fosse as Best Director. It was also the year of Marlon Brando winning for *The Godfather* and sending a young Indian woman, Sacheen Littlefeather, in his stead to refuse the award and make a political statement about the plight of the Native Americans and how they are depicted in film. Later, Sacheen

THE FIRST BLOODY OSCAR WINNER IN HISTORY! PHOTO COURTESY OF CORBIS/UPI

Littlefeather was identified as an actress named Maria Cruz. Mama always said this event put a bit of a pall on the evening, though she tried to rise above it.

At the end of the telecast, John Wayne got up onstage and suggested all the winners and presenters come out and take a bow. As everyone joined him, he said, "Now why don't all of you out there on TV join with us in singing "You Oughta Be in Pictures."

While Liza, Bob Fosse, and Joel Grey were all up front, Heckart hovered in the second row with the people who had won the technical awards. Many years later, she confessed to me she was thinking she didn't deserve to be up front with all those big stars and important people. But once her old friend from Broadway spotted her standing behind him, Bob Fosse grabbed her hand and yanked her down front, shouting, "Heckie, C'mon! Stand by me!" Even one hour after winning the Academy Award, Eileen Heckart didn't really believe she was a star.

Back in Connecticut, my nanny, my brothers and I were reveling in our own sort of glory. At age thirteen, I was watching the telecast with Nanny in her cottage across the driveway. Philip was over in the main house with his best buddy, a stocky boy named Fuzzy Kidd, who had an outrageous personality to match to his name. Mark was in a local dive in downtown New Canaan called the Heritage Bar & Grill and happened to step out of the men's room just at the crucial moment. When Cloris Leachman announced Mama's name, I started screaming so loud and jumping so high, Nanny couldn't help but think, "He's going to have a heart attack and die and Eileen is going to blame me!" She was leaning so far back in her bed, I couldn't tell if she was fainting or giving me a wider berth.

Within seconds, I had to stop leaping and shouting, because the phone started ringing off the hook. Nanny had an extension phone to the main house in her room so I could grab it before Philip. For the rest of the evening, I became Oscar Central, the conduit to what was *really* going on in the star's home the night she won the Academy Award. Of course, it was impossible for us to watch the rest of the telecast. Occasionally, in the middle of a call, I'd glance at the TV and say into the phone, "Joel Grey just won for *Cabaret*" or give a similar update. As the calls kept pouring in from neighbors, family friends and reporters, sometimes my brother would pick up the phone in the main house at the same time.

I said, "Who's calling? The *New York Times*? It's all right Philip, I've got this one."

I proceeded to give interview after interview. I was in that early adolescent stage before pimples and puberty where one is fearless and thinks he knows everything. Nanny marveled at how smooth I was with all these reporters at age thirteen. The next day when I went to school, my eighth-grade class gave me a round of applause.

Over in the main house, Philip and Fuzzy broke into the liquor cabinet and polished off two bottles of champagne. Under the circumstances, they didn't think Dad would be too upset. Besides, it was the Korbel Brut, not the Dom Perignon.

Downtown at the Heritage Bar & Grill, everyone was buying drinks for Mark and writing congratulatory notes to Mrs. Yankee. The last few were such drunken scribblings, she could barely decipher them. Ultimately, Mark had to stay at a friend's house in town and couldn't even think of going into his job as a dog groomer the next day, he was so hung over.

Back at the Governor's Ball, it seemed like every celebrity in the history of Hollywood was there. As my parents were making the rounds, my father pulled my mother aside.

"Oh honey," he said. "I know this is your night to be in the spotlight, but there is only one person here I *really* want to meet . . . and she's coming down the stairs right now."

Entering the room was Mae West. She was resplendent in black sequins and flanked by two beefy boys who practically carried her. She looked as though she were held together by mascara, bobby pins, and voluminous false eyelashes. At that advanced age, Mama figured she was probably good for about an hour a day and this was it. She dragged my father over to the table where Miss West was holding court. She looked at my mother vaguely for a moment, and then seemed to grasp it all. In that infamous, sultry timbre, she spoke.

"Ohhhh, Miss Heckart. Congratulations on your award."

After a slight pause, she looked my father up and down and purred, "But it looks to me like you already *had* the prize."

My father was so excited, he nearly peed himself.

Mama also congratulated Rosalind Russell, who had received the Jean Hersholt Humanitarian Award that night. My mother had always been a little jealous of Rosalind Russell, because she had played Rosemary in the film version of *Picnic*, Mama's first Broadway triumph. In fact, Russell's husband, producer Frederick Brisson, had bought the property for her. Besides, in the early fifties, the name Eileen Heckart meant nothing in Hollywood.

Now a victim of severe and crippling arthritis, Russell's face was all bloated from cortisone injections. She was in a wheelchair and extremely frail. Mama waited in line to pay her respects. The minute Russell saw my mother, she reached for her with outstretched arms and took her face in her hands.

As she cradled my mother's face, she said, "Oh, if I'd let you play your *Picnic*, you'd have had your Oscar years ago."

Russell reached forward and kissed her on the forehead as tears streamed down my mother's face. Any trace of former jealousy or resentment immediately vanished.

When Mama and Daddy got back to their suite at the Beverly Hills Hotel, the room was stuffed with congratulatory flowers and a large stack of messages and telegrams. The one on the top read, "Call Marlene. Regardless of the hour, call Marlene."

Underneath the famous first name, it referenced a phone number in Paris. When you get a call like that from Diva Dietrich, you don't mess around.

Mama was thinking, "Won't this be thrilling? My very first phone call after winning the Oscar will be a congratulatory message from Marlene Dietrich!"

The excited actress reached the overseas operator, who put her through to that distinctive, one-of-a-kind sound.

"Hello?" the husky, German voice said.

"Hello, Marlene! It's Eileen."

"Darling! Your makeup was terrible!"

"It was?" Mama asked.

"It was in the movie, too," Dietrich replied.

For the next ten minutes, Marlene Dietrich proceeded to berate Heckart for her deplorable fashions, her awful makeup, her nondescript hairdo, and her total lack of style. Two hours after winning the Oscar, my father listened to the other end of this conversation in utter disbelief as his wife sat there saying into the telephone, "Yes ma'am . . . all right . . . mmm hmmm . . . yes, Marlene . . . I won't do that any more . . . Yes ma'am . . . Uh-huh."

But, in her staunch, Germanic style, that was the only way Dietrich could congratulate her. That was Marlene's way of expressing her love—by showing my mother that she cared enough to criticize her. While Dietrich had a great deal of respect for my mother, I don't know that she really understood her. In the world of Marlene Dietrich, if you were going to be a star, that meant glamour, mystery, and Hollywood mystique. These were her stock in trade, but not Eileen Heckart's. In her heart, perhaps Dietrich knew she needed this allure, because she never believed she was a great actress. Marlene Dietrich was a bigger star than my mother ever thought of being. But Dietrich knew a great actress when she saw one and she wanted my mother to behave like a star. While Dietrich could be just as happy in a pair of blue jeans making scrambled eggs for Maurice Chevalier or slinging hash at the Hollywood Canteen, she sure knew how to work an ermine stole or a gown by Adrian. While Mama could turn on the glamour when she wanted to, Dietrich personified it.

After several days of parties, fetes, and soirees, as they were on their way back to their beloved boys in Connecticut, Mama turned to my father on the plane.

"Jack," she said, "What's today's date?"

"The second of April," he replied. "Why?"

"And tomorrow is Monday . . . oh, my God!" she said, "I'm due at the unemployment office tomorrow!"

He said, "Why not have a little class and wait until Tuesday?"

When she went in to pick up her check on Tuesday, everyone in the office burst into applause. Unemployed or not, they knew a star when they saw one.

Miss Le "G"

EVA LE GALLIENNE. ©NANCY RICA SCHIFF—1982. REPRINTED WITH PERMISSION

AT THE SAME TIME that Milton Goldman told me about *Finishing Touches*, he had also mentioned that Eva Le Gallienne was looking for a teenager to play a role in a new play called *The Dream Watcher*. He didn't know any of the particulars, but said he could arrange for me to meet her if I was interested. If I was *interested*? I thought.

Mama suggested that Milton find out a few more details before things went any further. *The Dream Watcher*, written especially for Eva Le Gallienne, was going to be done at the White Barn Theatre in Westport—fifteen minutes from home. The White Barn Theatre was a wonderful, old, summer theater built by the Broadway producer Lucille Lortel to workshop and premiere new plays before taking them elsewhere. Shows there usually had pretty short runs, a month or so, tops. Since the play would not be presented until the following summer, Miss Le Gallienne would not start meeting with potential actors for at least six months.

After the *Finishing Touches* experience, I wasn't sure I wanted to audition for another play if my parents wouldn't let me do it. It was too hard on me emotionally and I couldn't help but think it would somehow hurt my reputation as a young actor if I kept auditioning for roles, getting them, and turning them down. Under the circumstances, Mama said yes, I would be able to do this role if I got it.

"But this is a little different, darling. It's the lead opposite Miss Le Gallienne."

Just who *was* Eva Le Gallienne, anyway? I didn't have a clue. All I knew was that my mother spoke about her with a sense of reverence, so she must be someone pretty special. Eva Le Gallienne was one of the great ladies of the American theater. An actress, director, producer, and writer, she founded the Civic Repertory Theatre and later co-founded the American Repertory Theatre. She was one of the foremost translators of the works of Ibsen and Chekhov and never stopped working and teaching. And, at twelve, I was being considered to play the lead opposite her in the pre-Broadway tryout of a new play.

The following year, in late February, Mama drove me over to the White Barn to meet Miss Le Gallienne. I was surprised that even my mother called her this.

"You mean, you don't call her Eva?" I asked.

"NO ONE calls her Eva!" Mama replied. "And neither will you!"

Wow, I thought to myself, *this must be some fancy dame.*

Miss Le Gallienne taught master classes at the White Barn from time to time and we were to be at the theater promptly at 1:45 when she would be on a lunch break. As we drove up past the vast, green lawn dusted with snow, the place was buzzing with activity. There were lots of college-age actors and actresses milling about in scarves and overcoats rehearsing scenes, vocalizing, and shoving sandwiches into their mouths while studying scripts. A few acknowledged my mother respectfully. Tiny, birdlike Lucille Lortel was scurrying about. Miss Lortel was a big fan of Mama's, having produced a tour she'd done in Germany in the fifties. As we entered the green room, she greeted Mama warmly, shook my hand and went to retrieve Miss Le Gallienne.

My first memory of the lady was how small and delicate she was in appearance and yet, there was a majesty about her. I was reminded about what people said when they saw Yul Brynner in *The King & I.* Even though he was a slight man, he seemed taller than anyone in the room. The same was true of Eva Le Gallienne. We shook hands and she embraced my mother. They talked about some of the theater people they had in common. While I doubt she used these words, I had a sense of her saying, "Oh, my *deah*" to my mother, with grandness that wasn't forced, but a part of who she was.

She turned to me as if she were sizing me up.

"Tell me, Luke," she said, "How old are you?"

"I just turned thirteen, ma'am," I replied.

She studied me for a moment, then said, "Have you ever played a leading role before?"

"Well," I said, trying to hide the slight tremor in my voice, "I just played Tevye in some workshop scenes in my children's theater."

She looked at me quizzically. "Tevye the Milkman?" she asked. "In *Fiddler on the Roof*? At thirteen?"

I nodded.

"How extrawwwwdinary!" she exclaimed and threw her head back in a warm, full-bodied laugh.

She had tiny slits for eyes and skin so white it was almost translucent. I couldn't tell how old she was, but from my adolescent perspective, she was *really old*. She said she wanted me to read the play and would arrange to get me a copy of the script. Her break was over, and Lucille Lortel beckoned her back into class. All in all, it was about a seven-minute meeting. I didn't quite know what to make of it- neither did Mama.

A copy of the play arrived a few days later. *The Dream Watcher* was a very sweet piece. Based on a young-adult novel by Barbara Wersba, who had also written the script, it was the story of a misfit teenager with no self-esteem who befriends a neighbor, an eighty-year-old woman who tells him about her career as a great Shakespearean actress. She quotes Olivia in *Twelfth Night* and Juliet to him, gets him drunk on sherry and introduces him to the finer things in life. At the end of the play, after she has died, he finds out it was all a fabrication. She had never been a great actress in London. Yet through her grandness and passion for life, the young boy has discovered his own passion. It was marvelous part and I desperately wanted to do it.

A week later, one afternoon the phone rang for me. The phone was ringing a great deal these days, because it was three weeks before the Oscar ceremony the year Mama was nominated. My brothers and I had grown unaccustomed to phone calls not being for us.

A distinctive, clipped voice on the other end of the phone said, "Hello Luke, this is Eva Le Gallienne."

"Oh . . . um . . . hi," I stammered, trying to sound casual.

"Well," she continued. "We're going to be doing *The Dream Watcher* this summer at the White Barn with Ellis Rabb directing. If you're still available, I'd like you to come over and read for me next Sunday afternoon. Would that be acceptable?"

"Yes," I said, "that would be just fine."

"Two o'clock," she said. "Until then."

I hung up the phone and bolted into the living room where my parents were having their evening cocktail.

"Mama! Daddy!" I shouted as if the house were on fire, "Eva Le Gallienne wants me to read with her next Sunday!" My parents looked at each other as if to say well, here it goes.

"That's wonderful, darling," Mama said. "Did you ask her which scenes you should prepare?"

My excitement waned.

"No, I didn't think of that."

"Well, then," Mama said. "You'll have to call her back, won't you?"

Just as she had done with the *Finishing Touches* audition, my mother was making me handle this as a total professional. I called Miss Le Gallienne back, who told me to look at the first two scenes and the final scene.

When I told this to Mama, she said, "But you'll prepare the whole script—just in case."

"Really?" I asked.

"Yes. Really," she repeated. "You don't want her to ask you for something else and come off half-assed."

I knew good advice when I heard it. Mama coached me on the scenes, sometimes giving me line readings, sometimes letting me find it for myself. She was starting to trust me more as an actor. With the Oscars less than a month away, she was up to her eyeballs in interviews and television appearances, but she made the time to work with me.

The following Sunday, Mama was a nervous wreck. She had arranged to spend the afternoon visiting her good friend Burry Fredrik, who lived right up the street from Miss Le Gallienne. Burry had started out as the assistant stage manager on *The Dark at the Top of the Stairs* and had been one of the producers on *Too True to Be Good.* She and Mama did many projects together over the years and were very close. The plan was that Mama would hang out at Burry's and I was to call her there to come and pick me up afterwards.

In addition to working on the script, Mama also made sure I had done my homework on Miss Le Gallienne herself. I knew she had actually met Sarah Bernhardt on one of her farewell tours and had one of the foremost collections of memorabilia of the great Italian actress, Eleanora Duse, in the world. Miss Le Gallienne greeted the two of us and Mama excused herself. She gave me a tour of her elegant, rambling Colonial house, which she had designed herself. Everything was meticulously in place. We wound up in her study, which was lined with musty, antique books. She showed me some of her Duse artifacts and seemed genuinely impressed that a boy of my age had heard of Duse. She took a large volume off the shelf, which was a copy of Sarah Bernhardt's autobiography. She explained to me that as a girl, she couldn't afford to buy the book, so she borrowed it from a library and transcribed the entire book, word for word.

She flipped to the end and said, "I felt very good when I was able to write *that* word," she said, pointing to the final word in the manuscript, *finis.* I laughed with her and was awestruck.

One of the qualities I admired most in Miss Le Gallienne was that she never treated me like a child or talked down to me. Perhaps it was because she had such respect for my mother or perhaps it was because her character in the play is enchanted by this young boy, and vice versa. Whatever the reason, I greatly appreciated it. We read every scene in the play together that afternoon. My mother's coaching about preparing the whole script had served me well. Toward the end of the afternoon, she said, "Well, I'm not certain when Ellis Rabb will be available to direct, but in the meantime, if you'd like to keep working with me on our scenes, I think you'd be just fine. Would you like that?"

I beamed at her like a kid on Christmas morning. "Oh yes!" I shouted.

"That's what I thought you'd say," she replied, throwing her head back once again in that warm, throaty laugh.

By the time I called Mama at Burry's after more than three hours, she had gone through two-and-a-half packs of cigarettes, a large bottle of Perrier and a half-pound of sharp cheddar cheese.

"My God, what were you doing for so long?" she asked. "I was so nervous, I smoked and ate Burry out of house and home!"

"Miss Le G and I read the whole play," I said, "and she wants me to do the role."

"Miss Le G?" she repeated.

"That's what her intimates call her and she said that if we were going to work together, I could call her that, too." I said.

"How do you like that, Burry?" she said, shaking her head. "Her *intimates* call her that!"

For the entire summer, Mama or Daddy would drive me over to Miss Le Gallienne's home in Westport. We would rearrange the furniture in the study into a mock stage and rehearse. Ellis Rabb remained unavailable to direct and we seemed no closer to an actual production, but I was having the time of my life working every Sunday with one of the first ladies of the American theater.

The scene where the old lady gets the young boy drunk on sherry comes early in the play. As he enters her house, she says, "Do come in dear boy, I have an exquisite bottle of Amontillado in the cupboard."

One afternoon while we were rehearsing off book, she seemed to go up on her line. She said, "Do come in dear boy, I have . . ." and stopped abruptly, raising her hand to her forehead. I waited, then fed her the line.

"An exquisite . . . ?" I offered.

Miss Le Gallienne turned to me sharply. "I *know* the line,' she said, "I was *thinking* about the line! You don't *think* about your lines, did you know that?!"

As she stared at me, I could feel my face turning scarlet.

"I . . . I'm sorry," I mumbled.

She threw her head back in a gale of laughter and embraced me quickly. It was an important acting lesson and the last time I ever corrected Miss Le Gallienne on a line.

When I returned home, Mama wanted to know every detail about our rehearsals. She was as curious about what occurred as she was about how I behaved. When I told her the story of the line correction, she was shocked. "You *never* correct another actor on a line!" she said. "That's what the stage manager is for."

"But Mama," I said, "We don't have a stage manager yet. We don't even have a director yet."

"It doesn't matter," she said. "It's not your place to correct another actor on his lines—ever!"

Those Sundays were an enchanted time for me. We would walk around Miss Le Gallienne's vast estate, putting out salt licks for the deer, filling the bird feeders, watering the lilacs and hydrangeas, and talking endlessly about art, theater, and the pursuit of lofty ideals. She would tell me about her career, about doing plays by Ibsen and Shaw, and what it was like being one of the first actresses to play *Peter Pan* in America. The thing that astonished me was that she actually seemed to value my opinions.

One afternoon, I asked, "Miss Le G, did you see Laurence Olivier do *Long Day's Journey Into Night* on television last night?"

"Certainly," she replied.

"So, what did you think of it?" I asked.

She stopped mixing the suet with the sunflower seeds and stared at me.

"What did *you* think of it?" she asked.

"Well," I started, "to tell you the truth, it put me to sleep."

"Me too," she said with a smile. "Now, you may put this suet into that pie tin for the cardinals and then we'll get to work!"

The following week, she told me she would be going to upstate New York for a while to visit relatives and to teach some master classes at the Chautauqua Institute, so we wouldn't be meeting for a few weeks.

"Perhaps," she said, "by the time I return, Ellis will have a better sense of his schedule and we'll know what's what."

I was disappointed, but I certainly understood.

Because of the pending production, I had bowed out of the summer show at my children's theater group. When a few weeks went by and I didn't hear a word from Miss Le G, I managed to worm my way back in, playing a smaller supporting role in a full production of *Fiddler on the Roof*. Since I'd played Tevye in some workshop scenes earlier that year, I might have had a shot at the lead, but came in after most of the roles had already been cast. Instead, I played Fyedka, the Russian who marries the youngest daughter.

Mama was starting preliminary work on a new play she was going to be doing on Broadway that fall, Ira Levin's Gothic thriller, *Veronica's Room*, ironically to be directed by Ellis Rabb. One of her multiple characters in the play was an Irish housekeeper with a thick brogue. She hired Elizabeth Smith, one of the best dialect coaches on Broadway, to come up for the weekend and teach her an authentic Irish dialect.

"While she's here," Mama said, "Why don't we get her to teach you a Russian accent for *Fiddler* as well?"

"Geez, Mama, would that be okay with her?" I asked.

"I'm wining and dining her for the weekend and paying her a small fortune," Mama replied. "It'll be just fine!"

That weekend, the top speech coach on Broadway taught Mama an Irish brogue for her Broadway show at the Music Box and taught me a Russian dialect for my children's theater show in the basement of the YMCA.

A few more weeks went by and the phone rang one Thursday evening. Mama answered.

"Luke!" Mama called to me, "It's Miss Le Gallienne!"

I grabbed the phone while my parents hovered in the next room, as anxious to know the outcome as I was. She told me that due to the many delays, the White Barn Theatre had already spent the money in the budget allocated for *The Dream Watcher*, so there wouldn't be a production anytime in the foreseeable future.

At first, I was professional and matter-of-fact about it. "Well, I know these things happen in the theater, Miss Le Gallienne," I said.

She explained the business particulars to me, and even though I interjected an occasional "Mmm-hmm," I wasn't listening. As the conversation was drawing to an end, I started to cry.

"I just want to tell you," I choked into the phone, "that working with you has been the greatest experience of my life."

"Oh, my dear Luke," she replied, "I've liked it, too. I'm sending you a hug over the phone, all right?"

As I hung up, my parents, who had heard every word, ran into the room and embraced me.

As I dried my eyes, Mama said, "Oh darling, you've certainly learned a lot this year about the cruelties of show business, haven't you?"

"Are you sure you still want to be an actor, buddy?" my father said, putting his hand on my shoulder.

"More than ever!" I said.

I took a walk in the garden just as the sun was setting. Both my parents offered to go with me, but they respected my desire to be alone. The sun was a blazing, bright orange ball, lowering itself behind the forsythia and Japanese maple trees. I cried a bit more as I stood there, not from disappointment that the production wasn't going to happen, but from knowing that my afternoons with Miss Le Gallienne had come to an end. I reflected on the times we shared and how much I had learned about acting, poetry, and the classics. As I watched the sun disappear into the garden, I knew that this had been a summer I would never forget.

I saw Miss Le G a few other times over the years. *The Dream Watcher* finally got a production at the White Barn Theatre two summers later, when I was too old and too tall to do the part. Having worked with Eva Le Gallienne wound up being quite a calling card. It impressed the great acting teacher Herbert Berghof so much, he took me into his adult acting class at HB Studios in Greenwich Village when I was only sixteen. And it certainly raised a few eyebrows when I auditioned for Juilliard. Miss Le Gallienne came to the school and actually gave a guest lecture to my acting class.

When I spoke to her afterward, she said, "Gracious Luke! You've gotten so frightfully tall!" and she threw her head back in one of those throaty laughs I remembered so well.

One of the only films that Eva Le Gallienne ever made was *Resurrection*. In it, she played Ellen Burstyn's grandmother, a prairie woman in a gingham apron. Her acting is extraordinary. In her final scene, as Ellen Burstyn is leaving the old woman to make her way in the big city, Miss Le Gallienne has tears running down her cheeks.

"Why are you crying, Grandma?" Ellen Burstyn's character asks.

"Because I know I'll never see you again," Le Gallienne replies.

I can never watch this scene without bursting into tears myself. That was the way I felt the day she said goodbye to me. Not many people in my generation have even heard of Eva Le Gallienne. But when I encounter someone who knows and truly understands her greatness, there is a sense of wonder and awe.

Necrophilia at the Public Library

WITH REGINA BAFF IN *VERONICA'S ROOM*. COURTESY OF CORBOS/UPI.

MAMA'S NEXT PLAY on Broadway after winning the Oscar was a Gothic thriller by Ira Levin called *Veronica's Room*. Once again, the play didn't entirely work, but it was a fascinating concept and an incredible role for Eileen Heckart. Ellis Rabb had just directed *A Streetcar Named Desire* at Lincoln Center starring Rosemary Harris, which had gotten significant acclaim. With the horror cult classic *Rosemary's Baby* five years prior, Ira Levin was the era's hottest writer of that genre.

The preliminary ads read, "From the author of *Rosemary's Baby* . . .and the director of *A Streetcar Named Desire* . . . starring last year's Oscar winner . . . VERONICA'S ROOM." Somebody in the PR department was certainly doing his job, because this ad campaign generated a strong buzz in the theater community.

This was the first time I could remember that my mother wouldn't tell me anything about her new show. She kept the whole thing shrouded in a sense of mystery.

"Oh, you'll see," she said.

I was going crazy! To not *know* what my mother's new Broadway play was about? How could I brag to the kids on the playground? Since she had won the Academy Award six months before, I had a new-found respectability at school. Now the kids wanted to know what she was doing, although they really only seemed interested in her next big movie.

That summer, she had done a film with Gene Hackman and Liv Ullman called *Zandy's Bride*. It was about a male order bride in the Old West. The role of Gene Hackman's mother was not a substantial one, but she knew this was going to be a first-class production, with a hot new Swedish cinematographer-turned-director named Jan Troell. Troell had done a number of films with Liv Ullman, as a cinematographer for Ingmar Bergman, and Heckart was eager to work with one of this new breed of European directors. Besides, Liv Ullman and Gene Hackman were huge stars at the time, so she was keeping good company all around. Since it was a pioneer story, the location was brutal. They shot in the mountains of northern California, surrounded by rattlesnakes, grizzly bears and poison sumac. Heckart found Gene Hackman to be moody and temperamental, but she loved working with Liv Ullman. They became very friendly and she thought the talented Swedish beauty was both approachable and warmhearted. All in all, however, it was not a very happy experience and Mama never even saw the film until many years later on television on *The Million Dollar Movie*. When she did, she was quite impressed. "We all knew the script was a turkey," she said, "but the cinematography was breathtaking."

Because of shooting *Zandy's Bride*, she didn't have the time to do the research on *Veronica's Room* she would have liked, so she sent me, her thirteen-year-old son, to the New Canaan Public Library.

"Excuse me," I asked Mrs. Seymour, the ancient librarian with her bifocals on a chain and a little, white flowered sweater.

"Yes, dear? Can I help you?" she wheezed.

Beaming up at her, I asked, "Do you have any books on incest and necrophilia?"

I had no idea what either word meant, just that Mama was studying both. I knew they weren't nice things, so Mama told me to be careful how I asked and to make it sound very professional. She'd even written down the proper spelling of the two words for the librarian.

When the shocked old lady peered up at me and gasped, I replied, "Oh, they're not for me . . . they're for my mother!"

Mrs. Seymour assured me that the New Canaan Library did *not* carry any books of that nature and I might want to try somewhere else—like 42nd Street.

That night, I told Mama what had occurred and she decided she'd better explain to me what *Veronica's Room* was all about. We sat in the sun room, the new addition to the house on Comstock Hill Road. Earlier that year, Mama and Daddy had taken the plunge with something they had wanted to do for a long time and had converted an open porch into a beautiful solarium, with plants and a tile floor. It even had a vaulted ceiling with a skylight, the perfect spot for a fourteen foot Christmas tree. Because of the low ceilings in the house, Mama had never been able to have a tree over eight feet. She was absolutely thrilled that this year, she'd get to have the tree of her dreams. When the skylight was installed, she was crushed to see it was opaque, white Plexiglas rather than clear acrylic.

"But I want to be able to see the snow falling in the winter!" she whined.

"But lady," the architect replied, "you'd also have to see the bird shit in the summer!"

As we sat there in the sun room on a warm spring evening, she told me the story of *Veronica's Room*. It was a dark and sordid tale of an old, Irish housekeeper (played by Heckart) and her husband, the gardener (played by Arthur Kennedy), who lure a young girl to an old mansion, saying she looks just like Veronica, the rich girl who had lived and died there. They convince her to dress up like Veronica in 1934 in order to help Veronica's sister, who is terminally ill. Once the girl is dressed in period clothes, the old couple returns elegantly dressed as Veronica's parents. They try to convince the girl that it is 1935 and that she is Veronica. They then proceed to tell her they are going to keep her incarcerated there as a punishment for killing her sister and having sex with her brother. She has disgraced the family name and must pay for her sins. Once Heckart's character strangles the young girl onstage, the audience learns that the woman masquerading as the mother and the housekeeper really is Veronica herself, and she is indeed having incestuous relations with her brother, the character played by Arthur Kennedy. They have also given birth to a boy, now grown, who strips the clothes off the body of the young girl and carries her offstage to have his way with her. At the end, Veronica has a schizophrenic mad scene, displaying her multiple personalities.

After Mama explained the plot to me, she told me what incest and necrophilia were. Then she said, "Would you like to see some of the play?"

"I'd love to!" I said.

She proceeded to act out a number of the monologues. Even though it was my mother joyously sharing her current project with me, part of me was thinking, "This is a great actress doing a command performance for me alone!"

The woman had a three-page monologue to the young girl before she killed her. Mama stood there in the living room acting to any empty chair. It was a spellbinding performance. I had never seen her so excited about a role before. Mama was dazzling in *Veronica's Room* and got outstanding reviews. The confusing plot fared less well.

Richard Watts in the *New York Post* said, "There are no better players on our stage than Eileen Heckart and Arthur Kennedy and they work heroically as the sinister couple."

Edwin Wilson in the *Wall Street Journal* said he felt Heckart and Kennedy were giving their all and giving full characterizations, playing their parts beautifully.

With this winning combination of talent, everyone thought the play was a surefire hit. It was even playing at the Music Box Theatre, which Mama called her "hit house." She'd had some of her greatest triumphs there, including *Picnic* and *The Dark at the Top of the Stairs*. Irving Berlin was the owner of the Music Box. The great American composer was close to ninety, but he still came down to the theater every day to check the box-office receipts. When he heard that Eileen Heckart was taking over the star dressing room, he gave her carte blanche to redecorate it however she pleased. She'd never been offered this before and she was beside herself. The British thriller *Sleuth* had been playing there for many years and the English gentlemen who had occupied it had not paid much attention to the battleship-gray walls and peeling paint. It was in dire need of a makeover.

Heckart did her best to save money wherever she could, but she still did it up right, with cobalt-blue lamps, a sleeper sofa for naps on matinee days, and lime-green, shag carpeting—all the rage in 1973. The window in her dressing room overlooked the Royale Theatre, where the fifties musical *Grease* was enjoying a lengthy run across the street. There was one chorus boy whose window overlooked hers and he would bow to her every night at half hour. Sometimes, she would put little messages in the windows for him and at the holidays, he was delighted when she put a tiny Christmas tree in the window with working lights.

When *Veronica's Room* closed after less than two months, Mama was very disappointed. On occasion, I watched my mother read roles rather than plays. The role of Veronica was a tour de force and with such estimable talent involved in the production, she thought it was certain to succeed. Aside from her sadness that the show was closing, this was another show in which she and my father had invested. It wasn't enough to break the bank, but enough to feel a pinch when they lost it all. After this, my father insisted on being much more cautious when it came to investing in Mama's plays.

My mother learned that the next inhabitant of her fancy dressing room would be her old friend, Sandy Dennis. Sandy had understudied the ingénue in *The Dark at the Top of the Stairs* and she was a neighbor in Westport. They had also played opposite each other in the film *Up the Down Staircase* in 1967 and were extremely fond of one another.

Sandy was opening in Alan Ayckbourn's British comedy, *Absurd Person Singular*. "If I have to give up this gorgeous dressing room so quickly," Mama said, "I'm glad it's at least going to someone who will appreciate it."

A few months later, when we went backstage to see Sandy Dennis after the Actors Fund Benefit performance, she hugged my mother tightly and said, "Eileen!

Thank you so much for my dressing room!" People like Sandy who really *knew* Mama knew that she preferred to be called Eileen rather than "Heckie."

One morning at breakfast while Mama was in rehearsals for *Veronica's Room*, I told Nanny about Mama acting out the scenes for me in the living room and about my experience with the librarian. Nanny wanted to know what incest and necrophilia were. Later, when doing an interview for the *New York Times*, my mother shared this story with the journalist. The article ended with a paragraph about Miss Heckart's family and mentioned how I had helped Mama do research on the play. The story concluded with the line, "And when his Scottish nanny asked him what necrophilia was, don't you think he told her?"

Berlin, Brecht, and "Mother Courage"

THE FAMOUS SILENT SCREAM FROM *MOTHER COURAGE AND HER CHILDREN.*
PHOTO BY CLIFF MOORE—REPRINTED WITH PERMISSION.

IN 1956, MAMA WAS INVITED to Berlin on a goodwill tour sponsored by the Theatre Guild. A number of theatrical luminaries were performing short pieces, including Ethel Waters and Thornton Wilder. Mama was asked to re-create a one-act play she had done Off-Broadway at the Theatre DeLys, Eugene O'Neill's *Before Breakfast.* It is essentially a fifteen-minute monologue in which a shrewish wife berates her offstage husband (played by James Daly) while he is shaving in the bathroom. At the end of the piece, she goes offstage to find he has slit his own throat as a means of escaping his terrible wife. Mama was very excited to be going to Germany with this group of fine performers.

The one phrase of German she learned on the airplane was *bitte onschnöllen*—"please fasten your safety belt." She seemed to get all around Berlin on that one phrase. When Mama wanted to buy toy trains for Mark and Philip, she went to the largest department store in Berlin. She went into the toy department, said "bitte onschnöllen" to the floorwalker and he called for the buyer, who spoke English and got her the trains. One evening, she took the wrong subway and wound up on the edge of the Communist zone, right by the checkpoint for the border of the Iron Curtain. There were austere looking policemen with attack dogs all around. She was so scared, she started to cry. With tears in her eyes, she went up to a man in a trench coat and glasses.

In a quivering voice, she said, "Bitte onschnöllen?"

He handed her a subway token and pointed towards the correct train platform.

One night, Thornton Wilder took her to see Bertolt Brecht's *Mother Courage and Her Children*. The production starred Brecht's wife, Helene Weigel, in the title role. It was a life-changing experience for the young actress.

"There I was," she told me, "in an ornate theater with cupids and flying buttresses and onstage there was a tattered sheet for a curtain. All the wires and gears were exposed. The acting was so raw, so honest. Even though I didn't speak a word of German, Weigel's work just knocked me out. It was one of the most powerful performances I had ever seen onstage."

Eileen Heckart vowed then and there that she would one day play Mother Courage. She was fascinated by the strength and fortitude of this character who sacrifices everything, even her own children, in order to survive. For Heckart, the notion of anything coming before her family was a foreign concept. Perhaps that was one of the reasons she wanted to play the role so badly. Bertolt Brecht's concept of Theater of Alienation, where the audience is supposed to be a spectator, devoid of feeling and never forgetting they are watching a play, is not everyone's cup of tea. But Mama related to the guts and toughness of Mother Courage. Since the character practically never leaves the stage for three hours, she saw it as one of the greatest acting challenges of her career.

In the fall of 1959, she was given an opportunity to do a staged reading of *Mother Courage* at UCLA with a wonderful cast of respected character actors, including Edie Adams, Dean Stockwell and Jack Albertson. Even though it was supposed to be a reading where all the actors would carry scripts, Heckart was so thrilled to be finally playing Mother Courage, she decided to go ahead and memorize her part.

When Jack Albertson saw her without a script, he grumbled, "Well, if Heckart's got the title role and she's not carrying a book, neither am I!"

Edie Adams followed suit. One by one, all the actors put down their scripts. It was early in her pregnancy with me, so she didn't tell anyone she was expecting—

except Edie Adams. She and Edie had bonded immediately and knew each other from television, though they had never actually worked together. Every time Mama came offstage (which wasn't very often), Edie would scream, "Put your feet up!"

Adams was constantly bringing her chicken soup and nourishing foods to maintain her strength. At the end of the play, when Mother Courage pulls her otherwise horse-drawn wagon around the stage, Edie was greatly alarmed at the sight of this pregnant woman exerting herself.

In the early nineties, Edie Adams did a tour of *The Best Little Whorehouse in Texas* that played the Westport Country Playhouse. Unable to attend to production, I sent a note backstage to Ms. Adams saying, "My mother always spoke so highly of you and how you took such good care of her during *Mother Courage*. Perhaps, in a small way, I owe my very existence to you." She was so touched by the letter, she printed it in her biography, *Sing a Pretty Song*.

In 1974, Mama was given the opportunity to do a full production of *Mother Courage and her Children* for Michael Kahn at the McCarter Theatre in Princeton, New Jersey. Kahn mounted the production especially for her and even cast my brother Philip in the role of Swiss Cheese, Mother Courage's simpleton son. Philip had been studying acting for a few years. Mama knew he wasn't a self-starter and that she'd have to give him a hand getting work. She asked Kahn if he could audition. It was a supporting role and Kahn knew how to keep his star happy. Philip acted in a few shows and wound up becoming a very good stage manager. He discovered he was better suited behind the scenes.

A friend of Mama's who was a theater professor at Harvard found out she was doing the role and helped her procure a copy of Bertolt Brecht's *Couragemodel*. It was a visual breakdown, scene by scene, of the original Bertolt Brecht production she had seen in 1956 in Berlin starring Helene Weigel. It was Brecht's blueprint for how to stage the play authentically, the way Brecht intended. She and Kahn used it as their production bible.

William Glover, syndicated columnist for the Associated Press said, "Casting Eileen Heckart in *Mother Courage* was probably not only theatrically inevitable but imperative."

Glover complimented her ability to stay within the austerity of Brecht's style and even intensify it.

Mama received stunning reviews across the boards for her *Mother Courage*. She only regretted that it was a limited engagement, running for six weeks. She felt that she was just beginning to really play the complicated role to its fullest by the time the show closed. Even so, she had gotten to play one of her dream roles and had scored a huge home run in doing so.

Holland in the Holocaust

ME AT 14 MAKING MY FILM DEBUT IN *THE HIDING PLACE*

WHEN ASKED TO PLAY the leading role of a film called *The Hiding Place*, a moving story about the Holocaust based on the award-winning book by Corrie ten Boom, my mother had serious reservations. It is the true saga of two sisters who hid Jews in the back of their father's watch shop during the Nazi invasion of Holland. The women are caught and sent to Ravensbrük concentration camp, where only one survives, through the strength of her faith. The film was produced by World Wide Pictures, Reverend Billy Graham's film company. Because his films always carried a heavy-handed spiritual message, they were shown in church basements and on retreats and did not receive commercial distribution. With Eileen Heckart, an Academy Award winner, in the leading role, Graham hoped the film would be picked up by one of the major studios. The other sister, Betsy, was to be played by Julie Harris and the father was to be played by Arthur O'Connell, who had played opposite Mama in *Picnic* and who had worked nonstop in Hollywood in strong character roles ever since.

The more Mama read the script, the more daunted she was by the project. The role of Corrie was incredibly demanding. She would have to ride a bicycle across cobblestone streets, haul boulders in the concentration camp, and be beaten by Nazi soldiers. Aside from the physical demands, she had qualms about such a long location shoot—two months in Holland and at least a month in London. She hated being away from her family for that long. Upon rereading the script, she discovered the supporting role of Katje, a nurse in the camp who dealt in the black market and smuggled in supplies for the inmates. It was a wonderfully flashy part and the sort she was famous for playing. She called the director, Jim Collier.

"Listen, Jim," she said, "I've thought it over and I really don't want to play Corrie. But if it's not already cast, I'd love to play Katje."

The director was crushed. He'd been carrying around 8x10s of Eileen Heckart and Julie Harris for weeks, saying, "Would you like to see my two leading ladies?" However, having Eileen Heckart in a supporting role was better than not having her at all. After a bit of fancy footwork on the part of the producer and casting director, it was agreed that Mama would play Katje and Jeannette Clift, a wonderful regional theater actress who had done several other roles for Graham's company, would play Corrie ten Boom.

Most of Mama's work would be shot at an army barracks outside of London, where they were re-creating the Ravensbrük work camp. She also had a few exteriors in Haarlem, outside of Amsterdam, the actual location of the watch shop. As it happened, Mama's week in Holland coincided perfectly with my spring break from eighth grade.

"So, how would you like to go with me to Amsterdam on your spring break?" she asked.

"Oh, WOW!" I shrieked.

"Who knows?" she said. "Maybe one day we can get you a little walk-on in the movie, too."

"Really, Mama?" I said, barely able to contain myself.

"Now, I'm not promising anything," she said. "But when we get over there, I'll talk to the director and we'll see."

We arrived in Amsterdam the last week of March, about a month before the tulips were in bloom. Mama only had two days of shooting, so that meant we could play for the other five days. Julie Harris, Arthur O'Connell, and Jeannette Clift had already been there for over a month and they were delighted to have two new dinner companions at the lovely, five-star hotel where the film company was housing us. As a boy of fourteen, I'd never experienced waiters in tails and white gloves who called me "sir" and held the door for me whenever I entered or left the room. The cast and crew were all warm and gracious to me. Mama had done several projects with Julie Harris over the years, most notably the TV version of *A Doll's House* when she was pregnant with me. And she and Arthur O'Connell went all the way back to *Picnic*, where he played Howard, her suitor, and the film of *Bus Stop*, where he played Virgil, the rancher. Although Mama and Jeannette Clift had never met, they had an immediate rapport. Clift was a serious theater actress and had just finished playing the lead in a production of Brecht's *The Life of Galileo* at the Alley Theatre in Houston. She had heard of Heckart's *Mother Courage* and they had many conversations about the craft of acting, especially the rigors of performing the works of Brecht.

I certainly hadn't forgotten Mama's offer to try to get me a small part in *The Hiding Place*, and mentioned it to her every day as we traipsed around to the Van Gogh Museum, the Anne Frank House, and the other wonderful tourist attractions of Amsterdam. She assured me that she was just waiting for the right moment to broach it with Jim Collier, the director. One night at dinner, she made an excuse for me to leave the table, saying she had left her glasses up in the hotel suite. While I was away, she popped the question to Jim, who said he would take it under consideration.

The next night, Mama and I were a little late for dinner, after having been at the Rijksmuseum all afternoon. As we entered the dining room, Julie, Jeannette, and Arthur were all beaming at us.

Arthur O'Connell started chanting like a schoolboy, "We know something you don't know!"

We stared at them all, confused.

Jim Collier pointed at me and spoke like a boardwalk huckster.

"Luke," he said, "You've got a part in the film tomorrow if you let us cut your hair!"

Without missing a beat, I put my head down on the table, and grabbed a fistful of my blonde locks.

"Take it all!" I exclaimed.

The role was actually quite lovely. It was a little scene with Julie Harris. She is out in front of the watch shop on a stepladder washing the windows. In my wool cap and knickers, I say sweetly, "Good morning, Miss ten Boom!"

"Bert!" she says, smiling at me.

"For your window," I say, handing her a sign that reads: *Jews are NOT Welcome in This Shop.*

Without looking at the sign, she says, "Thank you."

I tip my cap, smile, and say, "Good day."

The most chilling moment of the scene is as I walk away. She reads the sign and abject horror crosses her face. Julie Harris gazes at me, this nice neighborhood boy, and then looks back at the sign, then back at me. In this silent moment, you see her realize for the first time the pervasive and diabolical nature of the Nazi occupation.

I was so excited to be making my movie debut in a scene with Julie Harris. Not only that, I had a dialect coach, a make-up man, a hairdresser, and a costumer all fussing over ME! Mama stood on the sidelines, smoking like a chimney. I was a little tentative the first few times and Jim Collier kindly gave me one or two runs at it just to get comfortable in this strange, new world. Julie couldn't have been more caring and supportive, telling me after each shot what a wonderful job I was doing. I nailed it after a couple of takes. I even got paid thirty guilders, which I think was equivalent to about fifty bucks.

I had a bit of a cough on the day of the shoot and I was terrified I would blow a take by hacking. That morning, Julie had given me a jar of honey for my throat. I ate the honey and affixed a label to the inside of the jar which read: "In this jar, on March 30, 1974, I received 30 ml of Dutch honey from the esteemed actress, Miss Julie Harris while on location in Holland shooting *The Hiding Place*, my first film."

Two months later, Jim Collier wrote me a letter, saying that due to timing, my scene had wound up on the cutting room floor. I was heartbroken, not only for me, but for Julie's searing reaction shots in the scene. The director did, however, manage to secure the raw footage for me. Mama spent a fortune having it transferred to sixteen-millimeter film so we could watch it, which I did repeatedly.

When we went to the premiere of *The Hiding Place*, I was unprepared for what I saw. The scenes in the concentration camp were brutal and graphic. There was one scene where the Nazi guards catch Katje, Mama's character, stealing from the infirmary and they beat her with the butts of their guns. By now I was fifteen and I certainly knew that this was a movie and not reality. Still, watching Nazi prison guards beat Mama black-and-blue gave me nightmares for two weeks afterward. To this day, it is difficult for me to watch that scene.

There was another scene I watched them shoot where the Nazi guards were herding several hundred women onto a train to transport them to Ravensbruk. Heckart, Harris, and Clift were featured as they try to keep from getting separated in the throngs of frantic women. These were local day players, mostly Dutch housewives and young businesswomen. Even though almost none of them was a professional actress, each time the director shouted "Action," they were crying real tears and screaming with hysteria that seemed anything but contrived. Heckart commented to the assistant director, "I've never seen extras so effective."

"Of course," he replied, "they all lived through it."

It suddenly dawned on Mama that the terror of the Holocaust was not an acting exercise for these women. It was a part of their lives.

The Hiding Place was top-heavy with Christianity, including an epilogue where the real Corrie ten Boom talked about her faith in God and how that kept her alive amidst the atrocities of the Nazi regime. Several major studios told Billy Graham that if he would cut the epilogue and soften the religious dogma, they would pick up the film for major distribution, but he refused. Instead, it went the same route as his other films, and was rented for church retreats and Bible study classes. It's a shame, because it's quite a good film and the performances are wonderful. Even so, there is a certain group of Mama's fans who know her only for *The Hiding Place* and talk about what a profound effect the movie had on them.

The Diva Critiques

ME AS ELWOOD P. DOWD IN *HARVEY*—AGE 17

MY MOTHER WAS a woman who spoke her mind. A lot of people loved that about her. There were no grays with Mama; good or bad, you always knew where you stood. She had a direct, often blunt, shoot-from-the hip, take-no-prisoners attitude which many found refreshing. In a world full of bullshitters and Hollywood "yes" men, I can see how that quality could be thought of as endearing. But to be on the receiving end of one's own mother's criticism wasn't always a happy experience. As many times as she would say, "That's a nice tie, Luke," or "You look so handsome in that blazer," there were just as many times when I would walk in with a new haircut and the first thing out of her mouth would be, "Jesus, did you get scalped!" Or "Darling, you didn't *really* pay good money for that shirt, did you?" When it came to expressing an opinion, my mother was famous for going, "Fire—ready—aim." She would speak, and *then* she would think about what she'd said.

In 1972, while she was shooting the film version of *Butterflies are Free* in San Francisco, young Goldie Hawn was still very much in her hippie phase. The cast was all meeting in the lobby of the stately St. Francis Hotel to be chauffeured to the shooting location. Goldie bounced up to Heckart, all bubbly and full of energy, wearing green hot pants, purple fishnets, a hot pink sweater, and a jacket of bright red foxtails. Mama adored Goldie and the feeling was returned. Mama felt this sort of camaraderie gave her the liberty to tell the truth.

"Good morning, Eileen!" Goldie cooed. "Did you sleep well?"

"I'm not sure," Heckart replied. "I think I might be still having a nightmare."

Goldie looked at her quizzically.

"Goldie," Heckart said. "This is a very elegant hotel. Please tell me you didn't come down in the elevator dressed that way!"

"Oh, Eileen, you're so funny!" she giggled, waving a heavily bangled arm in the air. "Of course I did!"

As Heckart kept looking up and down Goldie Hawn's tiny, multicolored frame with an expression of utter disbelief, finally the wide-eyed ingénue asked, "What's the matter—don't you like my outfit?"

"My darling," Heckart replied. "It is a study in ugliness."

Goldie held my mother in such high regard, she tried not to show how crushed she was. "But I just bought it yesterday in Haight-Ashbury!"

Mama took her by the arm and started leading her quickly through the lobby.

"I'm sure you did, dear. Now, let's hope we can get you out of here without us getting us tossed out of this hotel on our asses!"

⊗⊗⊗

My mother was most vocal when she was critiquing my work as an actor. This was one instance where the melding of Miss Heckart and Mrs. Yankee was not always a good thing.

When I was eleven, I played the Master Toymaker in the operetta *Babes In Toyland* for my fifth-grade school play. While the other mothers were baking brownies for the concession stand and sewing costumes, I was getting acting coaching at home from the Diva. When she first started to work with me, she would give line readings and I would parrot them back to her. This was the first time over the course of my lifetime when she would coach me. She had many requests to teach acting and she always declined, saying she had nothing to teach. It simply wasn't true.

After our first session, I remember being happily surprised that I felt real emotion. There was a scene where the Toymaker yelled at the villain, the evil Mr. Barnaby. After I listened to Mama read the line a few times, I felt really angry myself as I read it. When I told her this, she explained to me calmly, "Yes, that's what acting is, darling."

I must have really tried her patience, but she didn't show it.

When I went back to school, the other kids were so impressed that there was some real *acting* happening in the East School auditorium. Every time I came offstage after that scene, people would stop me in the wings and whisper, "Wow, that was really good, Luke!"

How different that felt from having some bully shove me to the ground for messing up in a game of kickball. It went straight to my head. Within days, I started offering Miss Eiserer, the music teacher and director, my own suggestions for the other actors.

"Excuse me," I said, "but why does Mary fidget so much while she's singing her solo? Can't you just tell her to put her hands in her pockets?"

"She doesn't have pockets, Luke," she said, peering over her glasses at me.

"Well, then why not give her some? And when Kevin says the last line of the play, 'Let happiness reign in Toyland forever,' he doesn't say it like he means it. Would you like me to coach him on it?"

Sometimes, Miss Eiserer was my ally and took my suggestions. At other times, she just ignored me. I must have made her crazy, but she never let on. Mama created a gray beard for me and held it on with floral clay. Spirit gum would have been too rough on my tender, young skin. Toward the end of the play, I was sweating so much, I could barely move my head for fear my beard would cascade onto Miss Eiserer's music stand in front of the stage. Mama praised me for my stillness and the simplicity of my choices—which meant I didn't overact. I was a triumph in *Babes in Toyland.* The acting bug had bitten me good and hard.

The following year, I was enrolled in a children's-theater class in the basement of the local YMCA. It was run by Alan and Lillian Matthews, a wonderfully crusty old couple. They transformed the basement of the Y into a black box theater. For the next three years, this became my haven. Other than home, it was one of the few places where I felt accepted, loved, appreciated, and free to be completely who I was.

Al and Lil Matthews had professional careers in supporting roles in summer stock when they were young. That was their only claim to fame. To those of us under their tutelage, they were Laurence Olivier, the Barrymores, and the Fondas all rolled into one. Teaching drama to kids at the Y was probably augmenting their Social Security, but not by much. Al Matthews was a stocky man with large glasses, an unkempt fringe of silver hair around his balding head and yellow teeth. His gruff exterior masked a huge heart. Al loved to pontificate about dramatic theories and gave us simplified concepts of the work of the great Russian director, Constantin Stanislavski. His wife, Lil, was a gentle lady in an ill-fitting blonde wig. She always wore heavy pancake makeup and clothes that looked like they came from the thrift shop. She was very warm and maternal with affected speech from "the theatah."

The best thing about Al and Lil was that they treated us gawky teenagers like total theater professionals. They had us doing classic scenes from Tennessee Williams, absurdist plays by Ionesco, the works of Thornton Wilder, Oscar Wilde, and workshop scenes from current Broadway musicals. I remember Lil looking at Robbie Drinkwater, a round boy of fourteen with a toothy smile, and saying,

"Robbie, dear, I'd like you to try a scene from *The Rainmaker.* How do you feel about doing love scenes with your shirt off?"

Since the question was asked with utter seriousness, he could only respond with, "Um . . . sure . . . why not?"

He'd barely hit puberty and he was going to be bare-chested and French-kissing Sheri Scott onstage. Most of the other boys were jealous, but not me.

The first fully mounted show at the Y was the musical *Camelot* and I was cast in the leading role of King Arthur. A few years prior, Mama had been to a fire sale at the Stratford, Ontario Shakespeare Festival while doing a TV movie in Canada and she brought home some outrageous Shakespearean costumes. They were exquisitely detailed, beaded, and braided Elizabethan outfits. Among them were a flowing purple velvet cape, a couple of chain-mail headdresses, colorful, Venetian robes, and a few gauntlets. Considering she did almost exclusively contemporary plays, it wasn't exactly like she was keeping a costume on hand for her next portrayal of Lady Macbeth. What had possessed her to buy all this stuff, anyway? No one knew, but it sure was fun to play with. My favorite piece was a black, velvet tunic with Elizabethan sleeves that flared out and draped to the floor, lined in pale blue satin. It fit me perfectly, and she let me wear it as King Arthur, along with a gold, jeweled medallion of a Maltese cross and a gold, Gucci belt with a knight on it she had worn in the film of *Butterflies are Free.* I was the best-costumed kid in children's theater. She always saw to that.

On the rare occasions she didn't have what I needed in her arsenal, she went to Brooks Van Horn, the largest theatrical costume rental shop in New York. One time, she rented a full clown suit for me, complete with baggy pants and the only pair of flap shoes west of the Mississippi. If I was going to be onstage, Miss Heckart *and* Mrs. Yankee made sure that I did it right.

We were going to be opening *Camelot* in a few weeks and Mama had asked casually if I'd like her to watch a run-through and maybe give me a few pointers. I immediately said, "Yes. Please!"

She'd been so helpful with *Babes in Toyland* and since this was a better script and a meatier role, I expected more—and better—line readings. I had no idea what was in store.

We drove home from the run-through on a chilly Connecticut afternoon in late November. It was only 5:30, but it had already been dark for nearly an hour. My memory of the event was that it was pitch black and I could see nothing in the car except the glowing tip of her cigarette and the oncoming traffic reflected in her oversize prescription glasses. I was pumping her for information about the rehearsal. The other students and teachers had praised me for my performance and I was certain that she would do the same. She spoke deliberately as she drove in the olive-green Mercury Cougar Daddy had given her as a birthday present.

"I see great potential in you as an actor, Luke," she said.

"Do you really, Mama?"

"Yes," she replied, speaking in measured tones. "You have a wonderful speaking voice and you seem to feel at home onstage."

"Oh, I do!" I said.

She took another drag on her True Blue. "Now," she said, "we can handle this in one of two ways. I have a lot of notes, but I will only give them if you want me to. I can be a supportive mother and simply show up on opening night with your father and the other parents, and we can leave it at that . . . or I can tell you things to make you better. It's up to you."

There was a long pause. I rubbed my chilled hands together over the car heater as I weighed the two options.

In a small, still voice, I replied, "I want to be better."

"Are you *sure* that's what you want?" she asked.

"Yes," I answered. "I want to be better."

She took another drag on her cigarette and the floodgates opened. "For starters," she said, "your posture is terrible. We have to get you something different to wear, because you can't even stand up straight in that damned long-sleeved thing. Let's try my black satin tunic with the red velvet sleeves. It will be much better. Now, on your first entrance, what the hell are you thinking about? You have no sense of nervousness or anxiousness. It's your wedding day, for God's sake. Why are you so placid? It's a boring choice—and the worst thing you can ever do onstage is bore an audience. And why were you rushing so much in the scene with Merlin? You weren't thinking about what you were saying. It's *your* scene, you have the focus. Take your time!"

Mama's critique went on and on and on. Her notes were excellent, but it was far too much for me to absorb all at once. The fifteen-minute ride home seemed to last for hours. Around her third or fourth sentence, I started to cry. It was so dark in the car, she didn't notice as first. As soon as she heard my breath catching in my throat, she stopped, reached over and touched my cheek with her gloved hand.

"I love you," she said.

Though muffled sobs, I said, "I love you, too."

"I'm not doing this to be mean, you know," she said. "I'm doing this to make you a better actor."

"It's OK," I said, wiping my cheek on my wool scarf. "Go on."

Once I stopped crying, she continued. She went line by line, moment by moment, scene by scene, treating me as though I were Laurence Olivier rather than her twelve-year-old son.

I learned so much about acting that afternoon, it was better than any master class I've ever had since. Part of me just wanted her to be a loving, supportive Mama, like all the other mothers who served on the PTA and praised their children. But deep in my heart, I knew this wasn't her style. It probably wasn't even possible. Besides, who better to toughen me up for the cold, cruel world of show business? From that moment on, whenever we talked about acting or the theater, I was no longer her child—I was a peer. I was being treated like a professional, but not like a son. Since I had requested it—demanded it, even—I had to be responsible for my own choice.

The next day at *Camelot* rehearsal at the Y, the black velvet tunic with the floor-length sleeves was out and the shorter, black satin tunic with the red velvet sleeves was in. It *did* look more showy and king-like, anyway. While my mother was doing *Butterflies* on Broadway two years before, a fan had come backstage one night and given her a beautiful medal of St. Genesius, the Catholic patron saint of actors. The silver medal was about the size of a half-dollar and depicted a curly headed man in theatrical robes pulling back a curtain with the engraved inscription, "Saint Genesius, Guide My Career." The woman who had given it to Mama had said, "Miss Heckart, I am very religious. Please don't ever give it away."

"I won't," Mama replied. "But one day, it will go to our youngest son, who is an actor." From that moment on, I would open the black leather jewelry box on her dresser and stare at it as if it were some sort of a magic talisman. A few weeks later, the night I opened as King Arthur in *Camelot*, she presented the medal to me with a note on her embossed, Eileen Heckart stationery from Tiffany's. This was the good stuff, reserved only for special occasions. At first, it felt odd to be getting a note from Mama on her Eileen Heckart paper, but when I read the note, I understood the significance.

It read, "Dear Luke, Go out there on that stage tonight and feel glad to be alive. I love you, Mama."

I was in the fraternity now.

When I returned home from the performance, there was big bouquet of lilies and snapdragons from Mama and Daddy on the living room cocktail table. It was filled with satin ribbons with handwritten messages on them, proclaiming, "Viva La King!" and "Arthur and Guinevere!" She sure knew how to make me feel special.

The next production at the Y was a series of workshop scenes from different musicals. I was cast in some of the best leading roles. I was performing scenes from *Kismet* in the first act and *Stop the World, I Want to Get Off* in Act Two. *Stop the World* is the musical that put Anthony Newley on the map. The lead, an Everyman character, is a circus clown named Littlechap. His journey through life is used as a metaphor for the various phases of emotional and spiritual development. It is a tour de force role, with showstopping songs, including the now-famous ballad, *What Kind of Fool Am I?* So, there I was, at age thirteen in clown white with a painted smile, wearing black leotards and sitting in a pin spot singing "What Kind Fool Am I?" I was too young to really grasp what the song was about, so I sang it from my heart, with no pretension. Mama thought I was just wonderful, but she said very little to me. Many years later, she told me she had chosen to withhold any praise because she was afraid I might get self-conscious and destroy the simple, honest work I was doing. I was desperately seeking her approval. That was the only thing that really mattered. She had the keys to the kingdom, but I couldn't find the door.

Kismet is a Broadway musical from the early fifties based on the tales of the Arabian Nights. The beautifully melodic score is almost operatic and very difficult to sing. It also boasts flashy, storybook characters straight out of Omar Khayam. At the Y, I played the leading role of the Poet, a charming rogue, thief, and story-teller. It was played onstage by Alfred Drake and in the film by Howard Keel—a real swashbuckler with panache. Mama had gone through her wardrobe closet and we'd come up with a fanciful costume of a leather vest, burgundy balloon pants, lots of clunky, Moroccan jewelry, and leather boots. I doubt many other mothers in New Canaan could pull such garb out of their closet at a moment's notice, but one of the many things I loved about my Mama was that she could. Over the years, she developed this reputation with neighbors, especially around Halloween.

One year, a local lady called and said, "Eileen, I know this may sound like rather an odd request, but would you happen to have a red fez?"

"Of course," Mama replied. "Doesn't everybody?"

Our Halloween costumes always won the prizes—Mama saw to that. She was known all over for the clown makeup she created. My brothers and I would stand still for nearly an hour in the master bathroom while she gave us each a white face, a large red mouth and nose, and huge eyebrows. She used a white nurse's stocking with bright yellow fringe sewn onto it for hair. With a ratty tailcoat, a derby, and a large, polka-dot scarf tied in a bow, my brothers and I all came home from the Halloween parties with blue ribbons. She also did hobos, pirates, exotic gypsies, painted ladies. If she didn't have it in her wardrobe trunk, she created it.

I thought Mama was sheer magic. There was nothing she couldn't create.

My mother's finest hour in my children's theater career was when I played Sammy Fong in *Flower Drum Song.* The sight of all those WASPy Connecticut kids doing an obscure Rogers and Hammerstein musical about Asian-American immigrants in San Francisco's Chinatown seemed an odd choice to the other parents, but not to my Mama. She took the train into Manhattan to Bob Kelly's Theatrical Make-Up Supply Store and bought an entire case of Chinese Yellow greasepaint sticks. Then she checked a makeup book out of the New Canaan Library and taught all the other mothers at the YMCA theater group how to apply it as she demonstrated on me.

"First, you block out the existing eyebrows with Clown White," she said, dabbing my face with a small, natural makeup sponge. "Then you apply the Chinese Yellow. Next, you apply the eyeliner in an almond shape and finally, you paint on a less curved eyebrow than the one you whited out."

The mothers were enrapt and the kids were ecstatic. Of course, considering the tiny, black box theater sat about fifty, the makeup for *Flower Drum Song* looked heavy and artificial. With all her good intentions, Mama had designed something to be seen from the second balcony of the Winter Garden. The basement of the New Canaan YMCA only had four rows of seats about six feet away from the stage. Even so, she came to every performance and, with an army of mothers, helped create the Asian looks on forty-three scrubbed blond and blue-eyed little faces. She even put black spray all over my hair. It ruined my pillowcases at night, but it was all for the cause.

The intensity of her critiques of my work seemed to increase with age. The older I got, the more my mother demanded, and the more she felt I could take. When I was a junior in high school, Mama came to a run-through of *Harvey*, Mary Chase's comedy about a man whose best friend is a twelve-foot rabbit that only he can see. I was playing the leading role of Elwood P. Dowd. I was seventeen and playing a role made famous by Jimmy Stewart when he was forty-two. The day Mama came, she sat in the back of the New Canaan High School auditorium in a full-length, black mink coat with a matching hat. Of course, she also wore the standard-issue movie-star dark glasses. Actually, they were prescription glasses, but they didn't look like it. She sat all alone in row Q, scribbling my acting notes on the back of an envelope with an eyebrow pencil. She wore a heavy gold charm bracelet which tinkled like an ice-cream truck through the acoustically perfect auditorium every time she raised her hand to write. The rest of the cast thought the Good Humor man was circling the parking lot, but I knew better.

As members of the cast peered out into the darkness, I started hearing furtive whispers in the wings.

"Mrs. Yankee is out there! Luke's mother is watching the run-through!"

No one cared when Joanne Jaworowski's mother was out there, or Ailey Smith's—except maybe Joanne or Ailey. By now, everyone knew that when you talked about "Luke's mother" or "Mrs. Yankee," you were referring to the local celebrity. They were all thrilled and nervous to have an Academy Award winner watching a rehearsal of their school play.

On those occasions when my mother was watching a run-through, Peg Sherry, the high school English teacher and director, had difficulty keeping everyone in check. As for me, I just got more and more uptight. I knew I wasn't really right for this part and at this moment, doing my best didn't seem even close to being good enough. I did lots of shows with Miss Sherry and we remain friends to this day. Years later, she told me that it reached a point where she could tell if my mother was in the audience just by watching my body language. This particular day was the first time that radar kicked in. As my voice began to crack and my gestures became stilted and mechanical, I was transformed into even more of a gangly teenager than I already was. I became all arms and legs and did not have a clue what to do with any of them.

One of the ironies of this bizarre situation is that Mama actually thought she was being inconspicuous. Later at dinner when I told her the rest of the cast was so excited that she'd been there, she looked at me incredulously.

"What are you talking about?" she said. "Nobody knew I was there!"

"Are you kidding?" I shrieked. "You were about as inconspicuous as the *Hindenburg*!"

"I don't know why you make this stuff up," she scoffed, fingering her filter tip before lighting another True Blue. "I was quiet as a mouse. And no one came near me the entire time."

"Of course they didn't, Mama!" I said. "They're all scared to death of you!"

"That's the silliest thing I ever heard," she replied, waving her cigarette in the air.

When we got around to her notes, they were really good. I sat there with my heart in my mouth, so eager for her approval, I didn't realize that I was getting it all along. It took me years of psychotherapy to see that the way she showed her support and her love was by treating me like a professional, not by pandering to me because I was an adolescent.

The one note I remember the most vividly from *Harvey* was when she said, "Harvey is an invisible rabbit—it's also the title of the play. You are the only one who sees him. He's funny. He's your best friend. He says things to make you laugh. You're not really seeing Harvey or talking to him. You need to make Harvey real."

It was invaluable advice and it made my performance ten times better overnight.

When I was in my early twenties, I was putting together an audition demo reel for agents and asked her if she would be willing to do a scene with me from *The Corn is Green*. Mama had played the role of Miss Moffat, the English school-teacher, as a guest artist at St. Edward's University in Austin, Texas a few years earlier. She was wonderful in the part and I figured it would be pretty damn classy to have Eileen Heckart on my demo reel. I thought it might get the attention of a casting director or two, so she agreed to do it with me.

In the scene, Morgan, her protégé and a young student she plucked from the coal mines, has just returned from applying for a scholarship to Oxford. After having a taste of the finer things in life, Morgan is excitedly chattering to Miss Moffat about his future.

Ken Lewis, a dear friend of the family who worked in television, agreed to block the scene for the camera. I had rented a soundstage in New York for the actual taping, but she and I would rehearse the scene on our own at home. We ran lines together a few times, but every time I suggested we rehearse the scene on its feet, she hesitated. This seemed strange to me for someone who was such a perfectionist at her craft.

One blustery spring afternoon, I asked her if we could walk through the scene the way we were going to do it on camera. She was watching *Another World*, one of her favorite soap operas, and she seemed annoyed at the question.

"I'm watching my show," she said. "And after this, I have to take some stockings up to Mama."

Grandma Esther was in a nursing home about forty-five minutes away in Stratford. Mama had moved her there a few years prior, after Van had died and she had become too infirm to care for herself. Given their relationship, Mama wasn't thrilled about having to take responsibility for her mother, but she knew no one else would. As the oldest daughter, it was expected. At age ninety,

Grandma was fairly out of it, unless she happened to need a bottle of clear nail polish or another pair of L'eggs Knee Highs.

"Well OK," I said, "but we go into the studio in a few days . . . I hope we have the time to work the scene out before then."

The actress understood that studio time was expensive.

"Fine," she said. "Go set up the chairs in the living room. I'll come in on the next commercial. We can work for a few minutes before I go see Mama."

"Are you sure?" I asked, knowing there was nothing worse than asking her to do something she didn't want to do.

"Go set up," she repeated. "I'll be there in a minute."

I rearranged the furniture in the center of the Colonial living room, pushing back the sofa a few feet and putting two delicate, wooden chairs with embroidered cushions and an oval table on what was now center stage.

The actress swept into the room. "All right, let's get on with it!" she said, sitting across from me on the makeshift set.

Since this was for my audition tape, I'd chosen a scene that was heavily balanced toward Morgan, where the teacher only had a few responses. Miss Heckart was listening intently to her co-star as I launched in to the first monologue. Halfway through my long speech, her eyes glazed over.

"Uh-oh," I thought, "I'm losing her." I felt as if I were a cardiologist in the ER and she was about to go into coronary arrest. She interrupted me mid-sentence, turning her head sharply.

"What the fuck are you doing?" she said.

I was so startled by the question, I didn't know how to answer it.

"What do you mean? At that moment in the scene?"

"Of course that's what I mean!"

My tongue turned into a brass paperweight.

"Uh . . . um . . . well, I mean . . . I . . . I was trying to play the moment where he's trying to express his feelings to his teacher and . . . um . . . "

"Well, I guess you haven't thought out that moment very clearly, have you? You better figure it out before we get into the studio. Keep going!"

She snapped her fingers and looked away as if she were summoning a head-waiter at The Plaza.

I felt I didn't have any choice but to continue with the scene. I had no idea what I'd done wrong and she wasn't about to tell me.

When I reached the end, she stood up and said, "You have got a LOT of work to do before we get into the studio, buster! You'd better start by getting clear on your intentions. Since this is going to camera, I don't want you to look like an asshole."

She sauntered out of the room as noiselessly as she had entered it. I sat there on our makeshift set for a long time without moving. I wasn't exactly sure what I had done wrong, but I knew I wasn't good enough to do this scene— and no way was I good enough to be playing a leading role opposite Eileen

Heckart. I wasn't an inexperienced actor at this point. I'd been working onstage for more than ten years and I'd finished two years studying acting at Juilliard, one of the top drama schools in the country. I knew about beats, intentions, and finding the truth in a scene. I sat there with my fist held up to my mouth as it rested on the lacquered, cedar table. I chewed on the knuckle of my index finger as I rethought every second of the scene, trying to fill in the holes in my performance.

As I sat there, engrossed in finding my missing intentions, Mama came in. It was not Miss Heckart this time—it was Mama. She was wearing her beige, cloth coat and had her purse slung over her arm. I could see the two plastic eggs containing Grandma's L'Eggs Knee Highs sticking out of the top of her paisley print leather handbag. This time she entered the room carefully, not wanting to interrupt my reverie. She walked over to where I was torturing myself and quietly kissed me on the crown of my head. Then she patted me on the shoulder, and exited. This simple gesture seemed to say, "It's all right. I know you'll figure it out."

As her silver, Buick Skylark darted out of the driveway, I realized this was another invaluable acting lesson. Without saying a word she let me know—in no uncertain terms—that my performance wasn't working and that I had to fix it. When we got into the studio the following week, I asked her if my intentions in the scene were clear now.

She said, "Of course," as if there was never a doubt in her mind.

When I look back on these critiques, I am reminded of Stephen Sondheim, whose father figure and mentor was the legendary composer, Oscar Hammerstein. Sondheim has said in many interviews that when he showed his first musical to Hammerstein as a teenager, he expected him to say, "This is incredible! I am going to produce it on Broadway." What he got instead was, "This is the worst thing I've ever read—now, let me tell you why." Sondheim was crushed—and said he learned more about the craft of writing a musical from Hammerstein in that one afternoon than from anyone else in his entire life.

I guess my experience could be similar. While I would never presume to put myself in the same league as Mr. Sondheim, we have this in common.

⊗⊗⊗

Just after I turned eighteen, I came out to my parents. I was too afraid to look them in the eye as I told them, so one spring night, I sat them down in the living room and read them a letter I had written. It was very difficult for them. For all their worldliness, homosexuality was something they just didn't understand. My father was quietly hurt. Mama was extremely vocal about her anger and disappointment. It was one thing for most of Mama's closest friends to be gay, but it was quite another for her fair-haired golden boy. Underneath the showbiz demeanor and the brashness, she never lost the simple innocence of Anna Eileen from Columbus. It was as if she took it personally and felt I had chosen this rather than it having chosen me. It was the only time in her life she ever went to a psychotherapist.

"I think therapy is a crock of shit!" she said to the doctor. "I don't believe in it and I never will. But I love this child so much and I don't know how to handle this. I need you to give me some answers." The doctor gave her some counsel, but it didn't really help. She had to figure out this one for herself.

For many months it became the moose in the living room we didn't discuss. It was the only time in my life there was ever a serious, long-standing rift between my parents and me. The emotional pain was excruciating.

When Mama finally felt she could, she said, "You're only eighteen. You're awfully young to make a decision like that, darling. Just promise me you'll keep your options open."

That summer, just before I started at Juilliard, I performed in a community theater production of Robert Anderson's *Tea and Sympathy*. I was desperate to do this role of a young man struggling with his sexual identity and who is accused of being gay simply because he likes art, poetry, and music. The director of the production gave me very little help, so I was left to my own devices. I also gave him considerable guidance in casting, including the role of the boy's father, which I suggested would be a good part for Jack Yankee.

This was a painful example of life imitating art. How perfect that Daddy and I were doing *Tea and Sympathy* together. In one of his two scenes, the father comes to his son's boarding school to confront him about the rumors that he is gay. We were practically living this scene offstage and we couldn't talk about it. While doing this play could have been cathartic for us, instead it wound up being an exercise in frustration. Daddy had to say things in the scene I knew he was feeling. Rather than pouring his unexpressed feelings into the lines, instead they became stilted and awkward. The same was true for me.

When Mama came to the opening night, the minute the curtain came down, she gave me hell.

"What in God's name are you doing on that stage?" she said. "You're doing all these big, phony sobs and overacting up a storm. It's bullshit! You go to your opening-night party and we'll have a long talk about this tomorrow. You've got to get rid of some of these mannerisms, and fast!"

Needless to say, I had a terrible time at the opening night party. Everything I hadn't been getting from the director of *Tea and Sympathy* came crashing down on me. On some level, I'd known it, but didn't know what to do. But did she have to tell me so harshly backstage on opening night? Surely, the actress should have known better.

The following afternoon, I sat at the kitchen table with a pitcher of Nestea and a note pad.

"Honey," she said, "I'm sorry I was so hard on you last night. But you're *acting* up there and you don't need to."

"I'm not sure I know what you mean," I said.

"Look," she said, "you will probably never again in your life play a role that is closer to what is going on in your life right now. If you cut all the phony tears and overacting and just go out there and play Luke Yankee—simply and honestly—I guarantee your performance will be two hundred percent better overnight."

I grasped what a difficult thing this was for her to say. She was acknowledging my homosexuality, something she hadn't been able to do until now. And I knew she was right about my performance. She came to see the play again toward the end of the run.

"Yes," she said. "Now *that's* more like it!"

While these acting lessons were rough on my psyche but invaluable to my professional growth, I never once heard the words, "Luke, I'm proud of you."

Did she feel it? Absolutely. Did she tell other people? Everyone. In moments of strength, I tried asking her for the words.

She would always dismiss it with, "Oh, for God's sake, I say it to you all the time!"

And my mother honestly believed that she said the words—but never once. The St. Genesius medal, the Chinese Yellow, the rented costumes, the opening night flowers—this was how she said it. In the last years of her life, I started telling her all the time how proud I was of her. There was a bit of solace in giving her the words she couldn't give to me. It's not that she didn't *want* to give them. For whatever reason, she didn't have the capacity. But she gave me so many other things. I'm still coming to grips with the simple fact that even though she couldn't *say* she was proud of me, she felt it with every fiber of her being.

When I was in my thirties, one of my Christmas gifts for Mama was quite unique. I had done a self-help seminar called "Launching the Future" which outlined ways to achieve what you wanted to manifest in your life. A powerful tool the workshop leader mentioned was a gratitude letter, a simple expression of thanks to someone who has made a difference in your life. I was going through a period where I was grappling with Mama's critiques: the good intentions behind them versus the way I was hurt by them. I figured this was the perfect time to write her a gratitude letter.

We always opened our Christmas stockings first thing in the morning on December 25. When we were little, we even slept with them next to our pillows. That year, before I went to bed on Christmas Eve, I handed Mama a pale, blue envelope. "This is in lieu of a stocking," I said. "Open it on Christmas morning." In it, I listed everything she had done that was really special to me—Tuni, the handmade clown puppet she had given me for Christmas when I was twelve, making Beef Wellington and chocolate mousse for my birthday, instilling a love of the theater and a respect for acting in me. It included every large and small thing I could think of that had impacted my life. It went on for four and a half typed pages.

Later that morning, she said, "Oh, darling, I cried so much when I read your letter. As a parent, you always wonder if you're doing the right thing. Then you get a letter like that from one of your children and you say to yourself, 'Maybe I didn't do such a bad job after all.'"

In that instant, any resentment or anger I had about the critiques, the outspokenness, or the unintentional hurts, melted away. It didn't matter anymore. It wasn't what was important.

Eight months later, I gave Daddy a gratitude letter for his birthday. He kept it in his top dresser drawer for the rest of his life and read it over again and again. I had learned an important lesson in giving thanks to the people I love.

Heckie Goes Solo

MAMA AS ELEANOR ROOSEVELT. PHOTO BY JOE F. JORDAN—REPRINTED WITH PERMISSION

MAMA PERFORMED in two one-woman shows over the years. Once she got over the fear of being all alone onstage for ninety minutes or more, she found it extremely gratifying. The first, which she performed on and off for three years starting in 1975, was a piece about Eleanor Roosevelt, simply called *Eleanor*. My mother steeped herself in research, spending time at the Roosevelt library in Hyde Park, reading every book and seeing every interview she could get her hands on. When she was younger, Mama always thought of Eleanor Roosevelt as a rather homely woman who wore funny hats. Once she began her research, she was amazed to find out how much Eleanor had done for racial equality, women's rights, and a myriad of political and humanitarian causes.

The script was by Arlene Stadd, a writer for television who had done very little work in the theater. This was her first foray into the difficult format of a one-person show. She and Heckart worked closely to transform the play from a history lesson into a theatrical event. While Mama received wonderful reviews for her work, the material itself didn't always fare as well.

Heckart requested Michael Kahn as director, who had done her successful production of *Mother Courage* at the McCarter Theater in Princeton and *Our Town* at Stratford. At first, the idea of doing a seventy-eight-page monologue terrified her. She felt she would never learn it all. Of course, she did and had many wonderful, dramatic moments in the play. The piece spanned from Eleanor's girlhood to her time as First Lady and beyond, when she worked at the United Nations.

Eleanor Roosevelt was famous for her high-pitched, reedy voice. Eileen Heckart was famous for her deep, baritone voice. As a result, Mama knew she couldn't go for a duplication, nor did she want to. Instead, she strived to reveal Roosevelt's essence, emphasizing her compassion and her indomitable spirit. She wore body padding and had buck teeth specially made. Vocally, while she used the upper-crust, mid-Atlantic speech, she used her own voice in every other regard.

One moment I remember in particular was the end of the first act. By now, Heckart had spent nearly an hour onstage as this unflappable woman, amiable, energetic, open, and deeply influenced by the Victorian credo to never reveal one's darker emotions in public. She turns on the radio and listens to the opening of FDR's Pearl Harbor speech, announcing the start of the U.S. involvement in the Second World War. After she hears the famous opening lines, she looks at the floor and switches off the radio. Looking up to the audience with tears rolling down her cheeks, she says in a very small voice, "I have never . . . in all my life . . . been so tired."

As many times as I saw her perform *Eleanor*, this moment always moved me to tears. There was a simple, honest vulnerability about it that was positively gut-wrenching. *Eleanor* was one of the many performances of my mother's over the years which I considered a lesson in fine acting. The more I learned about the craft, the more I tried to watch and study her technique.

Whenever anyone asked her about this, she said, "Oh, honey, I don't have a technique. I just get up and act."

But, like most consummate professionals, that's what makes them so good. You cannot see the technique, but it is there, just the same. It is the sum of the whole that moves you to laughter or tears, not the bits and pieces.

Glenna Syse in the *Chicago Sun-Times* said, "Eileen Heckart's portrayal of Eleanor Roosevelt has them all beat . . . her performance is indelible, with the effortless grace that has always been my definition of consummate skill. A class evening in all respects . . . I wish she'd run for office."

Chicago television-critic Wanda Wells said, "Eileen Heckart has captured Mrs. Roosevelt's seemingly boundless energy and makes this one-woman show a night of sheer enchantment."

One of the problems with doing a one-person show, aside from the fact that it's your hide out there and no one else's, is the issue of loneliness. There are no fellow actors to have a bite with in between shows, no one who was out there with you to discuss how it went. There was only Mama, her stage manager Walter Mayer, and her dresser Donald Draper. But in this case, there was an exception.

One of the most famous White House pets of all time was Fala, the Roosevelt's Scottish terrier. There was a reference in the script to Eleanor walking in with Fala at one point in the play. The producers debated as to whether or not this stage direction was to be taken literally, since it was a one-person show. Clearly, they didn't know what sort of animal lover they were dealing with in Eileen Heckart.

The entire time I was growing up, we always kept two or three animals at once, mostly dogs. They included a collie named Mr. Pushkin, a golden retriever named Charlie Brown, two German shepherds (Lance and Gretchen), a Hungarian Poolie (Gypsy), two cats (Egypt and Mister Socks), Amanda, the Old English sheepdog, two beagles (Turk and Morgan), three rabbits (Champagne, Punch, and Peter), a duck named Shemp, and iguana named Leroy. Mama would have taken in every stray animal she ever saw if my father had let her. Considering her passion for animals, it's surprising she wasn't a vegetarian.

The only animal that she ever refused to adopt was one Paul Newman tried to give her. It was a rare albino boa constrictor.

"Heckie," he said, "the boys will love it."

"I'm not so sure how I feel about snakes, Paul. What does it eat?"

"That's one of the great things about it," he said. "You only have to feed it once every two weeks."

"But what does it eat, Paul?"

"You just go to the pet store and get a little field mouse . . ."

"A live *mouse*?" she asked. "I'm going to feed a living thing to a white snake? Absolutely not!"

Heckart insisted that they use a real dog in *Eleanor* and said she would take full responsibility for it after the show closed. My father had other ideas. He didn't want the expense and responsibility of another dog. It was agreed that Mama would take Fala on the road with her but after the run of the show, well, we'd see.

The tour of *Eleanor* opened in Greenville, South Carolina. The reviews were mixed for the play but stellar for its star. And most nights, the dog got a hand as Mama led it on and offstage. She and Fala quickly became inseparable. Having a puppy to take care of on the road gave her companionship and kept her from being so lonely. A week later, Mama got a call from the kennel where Fala had been born.

"Oh, Miss Heckart, we've made a mistake," the woman said. "We were supposed to give you a male Scottie and we've given you a female. If you bring the dog back, we'll exchange it for you."

"Bring the dog *back*?" Mama said. "I've already bonded with this one. I'm not going to swap him . . . or her!"

Anyone who knew anything about the Roosevelts knew that Fala was a male, so Mama was very careful onstage to say "he" and "him" when referring to the dog. During the run, Fala had to be spayed in between engagements. When they resumed the tour in Chicago, the minute Fala came onstage, she rolled onto her back, revealing the stitches up her belly—not to mention her true gender—to the entire audience.

When the show played Ford's Theatre in Washington, D.C., Daddy and I went down for the opening and to spend a long weekend with Mama. He was still adamantly opposed to keeping Fala, but figured he'd better meet her first. I wasn't particularly fond of small dogs, but I thought she was adorable, a scrappy, little fireball with lots of personality. Daddy refused to warm up to her. One of Fala's toys was a blue, rubber, figure eight. You were to grab onto one end and twist it with your wrist while the dog had the other end between her teeth. It was a wonderful tug-of-war which Fala usually won. The first evening, I played this game with Fala for hours, but my father would have none of it. The next morning, Mama awoke to hear Fala growling in the living room of her hotel suite. She walked in and there was Daddy on the floor playing with Fala. The dog held one end of the rubber toy firmly in her mouth and Jack held the other end in his mouth. They were practically nose to nose and he was growling right back at her.

"Jack!" Mama said, "What are you doing?"

Daddy took the rubber ring out of his mouth and looked up at her.

"She likes it better this way," he said.

"Well maybe she does, darling," Mama said, "but I don't think your teeth are as strong as hers. If you're not careful, your molars will wind up all over the carpet."

In that instant, we all knew we'd be keeping Fala.

When Mama did *Ladies at the Alamo* on Broadway the following year, Donald Draper was her dresser once again. Donald and she had become great friends by this point and he had really trained and raised Fala. During the run of *Alamo*, Mama took Fala in one night to play with Donald while she was onstage. Every time she returned to the dressing room, Fala ran to the door and stood by her side, wondering when it was her turn to go on. When they left without her having been in front of the audience, Fala was very depressed. She must have remembered her time in the limelight and wanted it back. I've worked with many actors like that. On subsequent visits, Mama made a point of taking Fala out onstage before they opened the house and walking her across the proscenium. She didn't get the applause, but at least she got her theater fix. She was always a happy puppy after being onstage. Clearly, this dog belonged in our family.

Mama's other venture into one-person shows was in 1994. The producer Terry Hodge Taylor offered to commission a solo production for her on whatever character she chose. Heckart suggested Margaret Sanger, the founder of Planned Parenthood and one of the first activists for a woman's right to choose. Mama was a firm believer in women's rights and staunchly pro-choice. She used to say, "I never really had to worry about women's lib. Jack allowed me to have a career and always treated me like an equal. He was always there changing the diapers whenever I needed him to. He was an advocate for women's lib before it was even fashionable." Still, she knew he was the exception to the rule.

Like Heckart, Sanger was a gutsy, no-nonsense Irishwoman. She wasn't looking to make a political statement as much as she was searching for an interesting character to play who still had social relevance. With Sanger, she got more than she bargained for.

Heckart chose Jerome Kilty to write the excellent script, entitled *Unfinished Business*. Kilty had written the successful two-character play *Dear Liar*, based on the letters between George Bernard Shaw and Mrs. Patrick Campbell. He understood how to make an historical figure spring to life and he did it eloquently with *Unfinished Business*. When the show opened in Westport, there were picketers. The right-to-lifers were out in force to stop a show about a woman in favor of legalizing abortion.

"Do not support this show!" the protesters chanted.

"Turn around and go home!" they said to patrons as they parked their cars.

There was even the threat of a bomb scare, but it turned out to be bogus. For her part, Mama was thrilled to be creating such a sensation before she even uttered a word. She knew that Sanger was a controversial character, but she had no idea she would provoke this sort of response. As a result, the ticket sales were brisk. She was wonderful as Margaret Sanger and really enjoyed doing the play. Alas, the producer ran short on funding and defaulted on payment to a number of people when they played Fort Lauderdale, so the run was truncated. While she was disappointed, Mama never was one to look back. While she still wanted to work, at this point in her life she was starting to slow down and enjoyed having time to herself—as long as it wasn't too often.

Mary's Aunt Flo

MICHAEL KAHN WAS ONE of Mama's favorite stage directors. In the mid-seventies, Michael was running the financially troubled American Shakespeare Theatre in Stratford, Connecticut. Trying to put as many stars as possible into his productions in order to pump up the box office, he asked Heckart to play Mrs. Gibbs in his production of Thornton Wilder's *Our Town* in 1975. Fred Gwynne (best known as TV's Herman Munster, but also an accomplished stage actor) would be playing the leading role of the Stage Manager, Kate Mulgrew was cast as Emily (long before her television success on *Mrs. Columbo* and *Star Trek Voyager*) and Geraldine Fitzgerald would play the other mother, but Heckart had first choice of the two roles. She said she would do it under two conditions. First, he had to give her an "out clause" in case a more lucrative TV or film project came along, with an under-study at the ready. Secondly, while this was not a "deal breaker," she wanted him to consider finding a small part for me to play in the large cast. Since this was a summer production, the timing was perfect.

Michael agreed to both and a week later, Mama drove me up to Stratford to audition for the role of Joe Crowell, the paper boy who opened the show. It was a sweet little part with two scenes. I read with the stage manager in the lobby of the famous, Elizabethan-style theater, surrounded by photos of Eva Le Gallienne, Jan Miner, and so many actors and actresses who were already a part of my life. I was a tall fifteen-year-old and my height almost prevented me from getting the part, but my voice hadn't fully changed, so I still sounded youthful and could get away with playing a young boy. He offered me the part and an Equity contract to boot.

Behind the scenes, there was considerable debate as to whether or not I would be on a full, union contract or be deemed what they called a "local jobber." At this point, it was very difficult to join Actor's Equity and a *Catch-22* situation prevailed. Basically, you couldn't audition for an Equity role unless you were a member, but you couldn't become a member without being offered a contract first. This was before Equity had established a membership candidate program where you could earn points through apprenticing.

Years later, I learned that Michael Kahn had no intention of paying me the Equity salary of one hundred and twenty-five dollars a week, plus benefits. He wanted to hire me as a local jobber at a salary of thirty dollars per week, which he was paying the other actors who played the townspeople. Knowing how difficult it was at that time for a young actor to obtain an Equity card, Mama pulled rank with the director.

"Michael," she said, "I want Luke to have his Equity card."

"Eileen," he said, "I'm afraid we can't afford that. But I'd be happy to hire him as a local jobber."

"Take it out of my salary if you have to," she said, "but if you want me to do the show, Luke gets his card."

I had no idea this arrangement had been made. I thought I was being made a full Equity member because the theater was trying to reach a quota. This may have been a way for Mama to alleviate her guilt over refusing to let me do the Broadway role in *Finishing Touches* the summer before, where I was certain to have gotten my card. Whatever the reason, at fifteen I was now a professional actor and making a huge salary for a teenager.

While I was only in one show, most of the actors were part of the summer repertory company, also performing *Twelfth Night* and *The Winter's Tale.* The company included John Glover (who later won a Tony for *Love! Valour! Compassion!*), Powers Boothe, and many fine regional theater actors. This time, I was treated not only like an adult and a peer, but like a company member. I made friendships I still have to this day, more than thirty years later. It was a joyous experience for me.

Marge Phillips, a first-rate voice and speech teacher from the Central School of Drama in London, had been hired to work with the actors in the cast of *The Winter's Tale* and *Twelfth Night* to help them interpret the texts dramatically. It was posted on the call board that since *The Winter's Tale* had not yet started rehearsal, Marge would have an open session the following Tuesday afternoon for anyone in the company.

"You should go," Mama said.

"But I don't know Shakespeare," I said.

"That's exactly why you should go," she said. "Why not learn from the best? You're a member of the company. I'll go shopping in Stratford while you go to the class."

I was the only one who showed up for the first two workshops. Marge taught me the famous "Now entertain conjecture" speech from *Henry V* and broke it down for me, word by word and line by line. At fifteen, it was an incredible experience. She took the fear out of Shakespeare for me and taught me things I will never forget about meter, scansion, and interpreting a text.

"You write her a thankyou note and tell her how much it meant to you," Mama instructed.

I received a lovely note back saying how much she enjoyed working with me as well. After that, Marge got

IN MAMA'S DRESSING ROOM DURING THE RUN OF *OUR TOWN*. SHE USED TO SAY I LOOKED LIKE HARPO MARX IN THIS PHOTO.

busy with the cast of *The Winter's Tale* and had to focus on them. I was disappointed not to be able to continue working with her, but I understood her priorities.

In the middle of the run of *Our Town*, Mama was booked for a guest spot on *The Mary Tyler Moore Show* and had to leave for ten days. She was cast as Mary's hard-boiled, wisecracking Aunt Flo, a newspaper correspondent who has done and seen it all. She and Lou Grant, Mary's gruff boss at the local newsroom (played by Edward Asner), have an instant dislike for one another. Flo and Lou are highly competitive and never stop trying to best each other. Of course, they wind up having a tempestuous affair. Mama loved the character of Aunt Flo from the moment she read the script. A big name-dropper and bluffer, she had lines like, "So, I looked him right in the eye and said, 'Sir Winston, your painting stinks!'"

My mother adored the staff of *The Mary Tyler Moore Show*, including director Jay Sandrich, writer producer Ed Weinberger, and the talented ensemble cast.

Having been around the business for so long, she knew so much camaraderie and professionalism had to start at the top. Of all the people she enjoyed and respected on the show, there was none more than Mary Tyler Moore. Mary had been a fan of Eileen Heckart's work for years and the two of them struck up a friendship almost instantaneously. She found Mary to be warm, considerate, and possessing a strong work ethic, all qualities that made Mama want to do her best. She also knew what a powerful woman Mary was in television at the time. Mary was someone who took this in stride, never getting on an ego trip or pulling rank.

Heckart also adored Ed Asner, someone she'd known from live television and the theater but had never actually worked with until now.

The entire week was a love fest and one of the best working experiences Heckart ever had. The episode, simply called "Mary's Aunt," was very successful. Television audiences loved this tough-as-nails broad who actually had the nerve to stand up to the indomitable Lou Grant and whose wry edge was the antithesis of Mary's sweetness. Heckart received an Emmy nomination and the producers insisted on bringing the character back. She did two other episodes as Aunt Flo in subsequent seasons and received another Emmy nomination. *The Mary Tyler Moore Show* was so popular that this became one of the roles my mother was most known for in her career. Much as she loved doing the show, she considered it a blessing and a curse.

"Jesus," she said, "you bust your ass for forty years in the legitimate theater and you're remembered for three episodes of a sitcom? Where's the justice in that?"

Spending this time with Mary Tyler Moore cemented their relationship and they remained close friends for the rest of Mama's life.

Mary had several series after *The Mary Tyler Moore Show*, most of which lasted one season or less. One of them was a sitcom called *Annie McGuire*, where Heckart played a series regular as Mary's mother. The two were so genuinely fond of one another, they spent a lot of time together off the set as well. If Mary was wearing a pair of two-hundred-dollar earrings and Mama happened to mention that she admired them, Mary took them off and gave them to her. That's the kind of lady she is. I went out to Los Angeles for a visit and spent some time hanging out on the set of *Annie McGuire*. Mary went out of her way to introduce me to people, make contacts for me, and help me feel at home. If there was anyone on the set she felt it would benefit me to meet, she took the time in-between takes to be sure the introduction was made. I have always found her to be generous and enormously warmhearted.

LUKE AND ED ASNER AFTER A PERFORMANCE OF A.R. GURNEY'S *LOVE LETTERS* AT THE SACRAMENTO THEATRE COMPANY.

Ed Asner and Mama were crazy about one another. In 1996, when I was slated to direct Ed in a production of A.R. Gurney's *Love Letters* at the Sacramento Theatre Company, I was in awe of his talent and scared to be directing someone of his stature. Doing my best to overcome my apprehension, I decided to take a direct approach.

As he shook my hand, I said, "Ed, it is such a pleasure to meet you. We have the most wonderful photograph in my parents' living room of you French kissing my mother."

Ed fell on the floor laughing, then gave me a big bear hug. We spent the rest of the afternoon chatting. I still consider him a buddy and a real *mensch*. He is a great listener and a true humanitarian. As we wrapped the production of *Love Letters*, he threw his arms around me and said, "Tell Heckie she saved the best for last."

Ladies à la Mode

ROSEMARY MURPHY, ESTELLE PARSONS, AND EILEEN HECKART IN AL HIRSCHFELD'S CARICATURE FOR *LADIES AT THE ALAMO*. ©AL HIRSCHFELD/MARGO FEIDEN GALLERIES LTD., NEW YORK. WWW.ALHIRSCHFELD.COM

IN 1977, PAUL ZINDEL asked Mama to do his new play, *Ladies at the Alamo*, on Broadway. Paul was considered a very important playwright at the time, having written *The Effect of Gamma Rays on Man-in-the-Moon Marigolds* and a host of popular young-adult novels, including *The Pigman* and *My Darling, My Hamburger*. In fact, Paul was one of the most accomplished novelists in the highly lucrative young-adult genre. Even so, *Marigolds* had been his only successful play and it had not played on Broadway. His other two Broadway plays had been *And Miss Reardon Drinks a Little* which ran for a brief 108 performances and *The Secret Affairs of Mildred Wild*, which ran for a scant twenty-three. It had been four years since the last play closed. Zindel was longing for a Broadway triumph.

Because of Mama's exceptional work in *Marigolds* both in the original PBS production and onstage in Boston, Paul considered her one of his favorite actresses.

Ladies at the Alamo was a thinly veiled exposé of the Alley Theatre producers Nina Vance, Zelda Fichandler, and the other women who fought for control of one of the first regional theaters in America. Zindel had wanted Heckart to play Dede, the artistic director of the theater and the leading role. After reading the script, the actress had other designs. She told him she wanted to play the supporting role of Bella, the woman who ran the children's-theater division, starred in all the local musicals, and was the town drunk and the town lay. It was a wonderfully flashy part. There was a scene where the inebriated Bella tap danced in a silver lamé dress, dripping in turquoise jewelry while singing "Lady of Spain." Taken as she was with the character, Mama felt the play was fraught with problems and was extremely vulgar at times.

"Paul," she said, "this is a great part. But there's a lot of crap in this play and I need you to make some cuts and changes before I'll agree to do it."

Zindel needed Heckart to sign on so he could start approaching potential producers and other name actresses by being able to say, "See? Eileen Heckart has agreed to do it."

Heckart and Zindel had a close relationship, so she knew she could speak frankly. He trusted her instincts about what worked and what didn't. He came prepared to listen to the actress. He knew the script was flawed and that Heckart could help to make it work. Paul agreed to come up to Connecticut for lunch and was instructed to bring his red marking pencil. After they dined on avocados (stuffed with crabmeat) and iced tea, they retired to the solarium with their scripts. Mama was ruthless. They went through the text page by page, line by line.

At times she would say, "Now what the hell is that line supposed to mean?"

At others, she'd say, "This entire scene is a crock of shit and it has to go!"

As a Pulitzer-Prize winning playwright, Paul Zindel had never had an actress be quite so tough on his work, but he acquiesced in almost every instance. Occasionally, he turned white as she drew a thin, red line through one of his favorite passages, but he gave the actress almost everything she wanted.

When Mama recounted the afternoon to me, she said, "I was very tough on Paul today, but he was a giant through it all. He gave me almost every cut I asked for, even the ones he was clearly in love with."

With the first actress in place, Zindel was able to go back to his investors and producers and start searching for the next two. Ultimately, it was decided that the leading role of Dede would be played by Estelle Parsons, who had starred in *And Miss Reardon Drinks a Little*. The other leading role, Joanne, would played by Rosemary Murphy. Heckart had reservations about this casting right from the beginning. Parsons was a wonderful actress, but was very much an advocate of the Strasberg "method" and could be eccentric and emotionally erratic. Still, Mama knew she would do the part justice.

Heckart considered Rosemary Murphy a cold and unemotional actress, but these qualities would actually serve the role of Joanne, the controller of the theater, quite well. The director was Frank Perry, a respected film director who had done award-winning movies like *David and Lisa* and *Diary of a Mad Housewife*, but who didn't have a great deal of experience in the legitimate theater and had never directed on Broadway. Again, this was a red flag for Heckart, but Zindel assured her that he understood these women and would serve the play well.

The woman hired to stand by for both Heckart and Parsons was a respected soap-opera actress named Maree Cheatham. At this point, Maree had done nearly twenty years on daytime dramas in leading roles. A wonderful stage actress as well, she was bored with the instant acting of the soaps and eager to sink her teeth into a play again. She worked it out with the producers on both shows so that she could honor all of her contractual obligations for the soap and still stand by on the play. In years to come, Maree became a good friend to Mama. When we were both living in Los Angeles in the 1990s, she was one of my closest confidantes and like a sister to me.

Maree always exuded a good time. She was a full-figured woman with flaming red hair, a large, easy smile and an infectious, deep-throated laugh. She was the real thing, a "good ol' gal" from Lampasas, Texas who had actually interned at the Alley Theatre under Nina Vance. Maree was a great storyteller and the first on everyone's list when giving a party because she was attractive, bubbly and was always so much fun. She was perfect for the two roles and really understood these women. Still, she was more than a little intimidated to find out that she was standing by for two powerhouses in the American theater, Heckart and Parsons.

In later years, she said to me, "Honey, I was so meticulous about marking my script. I wrote Eileen's blocking in blue pencil and Estelle's in red. I had one of those big, pink erasers and the staging changed so many times that after a while, my pages got furry."

Mama immediately took to Maree and discovered early on that she had been raised Catholic. The fourth day of rehearsal was Ash Wednesday, so Mama marched up to Maree and unceremoniously asked, "So where are we going for our ashes?"

The younger actress was still professionally intimidated by Heckart.

"Beg pardon, Eileen?" she replied from behind her embroidery hoop.

"Our ashes!" Heckart repeated. "It's Ash Wednesday, for Chrissake! We've gotta go find a church on our lunch hour!"

Maree asked around, made a few calls and found that St. Malachy's a few blocks away would be giving ashes at lunchtime. Ever since Audrey Christie and *The Voice of the Turtle*, Mama has always been warm and open with her understudy, but she was particularly fond of Maree and loved her sense of humor. They were both hard-drinking, no-nonsense gals who'd been around the block a few times, so that sweetened the pot all the more.

Meanwhile, the artistic team just couldn't get *Ladies at the Alamo* to work. It was a play with funny, interesting characters but a rambling story with no real resolution and no concrete ending. The three leading ladies respected each other for their talent, but weren't exactly what you'd call friends offstage. One of the

OPENING NIGHT OF *LADIES AT THE ALAMO*—HECKART AND HER MOBSTERS

principal producers was Edgar Bronfman, Jr., the Seagrams heir who later became a major Hollywood producer. Bronfman spared no expense on *Alamo*, including a lavish opening night party at The Four Seasons.

As always, my father, brothers, and I rented tuxedos for the occasion. Mama looked very glamorous in a black velvet gown with a matching, floor-length evening coat. As we entered the Four Seasons in our ruffled tux shirts, the four Yankee men were huddled around Mama. As the flashbulbs were popping, and this photograph was snapped, one of the publicists remarked, "I didn't know Heckart traveled with her own mobsters!"

Rex Reed in the *New York Daily News* said, "Like five-alarm Texas chili, there isn't one bland ingredient in *Ladies at the Alamo*. Color it jungle red! Estelle Parsons and Eileen Heckart come out of their cages with incisors flashing, finger-nails slashing, and the whole thing ends up as the most biting, hilarious female free-for-all since *The Women* and *All About Eve*."*

While the performances of the three ladies were universally praised, the play was generally not well received. It limped along on the strength of the three stars, but closed after twenty performances.

One of the silent investors on *Ladies at the Alamo* was another outspoken gal, but this one was from Charleston, South Carolina. For the sake of anonymity,

* Courtesy of Rex Reed. Reprinted with permission.

I'll call her Natalie. Natalie was divorced from a rich, Southern lawyer. She had always been enamored of show business and loved to spend her hefty alimony checks investing in plays. Since she didn't want her husband to know how his money was being spent, she never received any associate-producer credit or billing of any kind. She had also invested in another of Mama's shows and they appreciated each other's boisterous sense of humor. You knew when Natalie entered the room. She was a tall, voluptuous woman in her mid-forties with round hips and a warm smile. She could charm anyone into doing anything, especially men.

Shortly after *Alamo* closed, Mama and Daddy invited some friends up for the annual Fourth of July weekend party. This was a small, intimate gathering. Generally, it included a few special friends of Mama's from the theater community whom she thought might like to get the hell out of Manhattan for the holiday weekend. It always included Ken Lewis, a set designer in theater and television with a big heart and a great sense of humor. Ken was a special family friend and the only person I can recall who had a unique, individual relationship with every member of the family. Ken had only been up to the house a few times at this point, but he was so easygoing and fun, I was always happy to see him. Besides that, he was an openly gay man who had once been married, so I found him worldly, sophisticated and in my burgeoning adolescence, very sexy.

Another of the usual guests was a woman named Jean Thomas. Jean was a successful agent who worked mostly in the realm of voiceovers and television commercials. She was a small woman with bobbed, black hair, a fast-talking caustic wit, and a mouth like a sailor. Jean's brashness and cynicism covered great warmth, but it took a while for her to reveal that side to you. Once her brusque, outer layers were removed, she was your friend for life. She had been Mama's friend and agent on and off over the years and so she was always included. We became the family Jean didn't have and she was extremely generous to us all.

This year, the new addition to the group was going to be Natalie. Everyone in the family thought this was a wonderful idea. Aside from the fact that she was a wonderful storyteller (an important component if you wanted to hold your own in this crowd), Natalie exuded an easy sexuality which Dad, Mark, and Philip all found very appealing. I think any one of them would have considered giving her a roll in the hay under the right circumstances. I found her to be a barrel of laughs, but I certainly wasn't interested in her that way.

Ken and Jean arrived Saturday in time for lunch but Natalie had a business meeting and couldn't get away until that evening. I went with Mama and Daddy to meet them at the train and we all had lunch at the Silvermine Tavern, a charming, Colonial inn two blocks from our house. When we returned home and were lounging by the pool, Mama recited the house rules for weekend guests, even though Jean and Ken knew them by heart.

With a cigarette dangling from her lips, she said, "Now listen, you're on your own for breakfast. There's juice in the fridge, a sweet roll in the cupboard, and I'll show you where we keep the coffee. There are cold cuts if you want to make a sandwich. I'll take care of dinner, but other than that, just help yourselves."

Since Ken and Jean were repeat guests, when Mama started her spiel, they gave each other a knowing wink. These terms were perfectly reasonable, but the hostess never stuck to them. After they'd had their morning coffee and pastry, around ten o'clock Mama would prepare Eggs Benedict, Italian sausages, and a large fruit bowl. Around two in the afternoon, just as Ken and Jean were thinking, "Let's head on down to the fridge and check out the cold cuts," they would meet Mama in the garden on her way up to the pool carrying a large tray containing cups of chilled gazpacho, homemade jalapeno corn bread, and barbecued chicken legs.

Occasionally, Jean or Ken said, "Eileen, this is wonderful, but we don't want you to work so hard. We thought you said we were on our own until dinner."

She always replied, "Well what am I gonna do? Let you starve? You're our guests for Chrissake! Eat!"

Over the years, whenever she would start in with "You're on your own for breakfast," Ken would burst into gales of laughter. She always looked at him with a "What's so funny?" expression. He called this part of her "Plain Mrs. Yankee routine."

That night, just as we were on the dining terrace in the middle of a glorious summer meal of lamb kebabs, salad with fresh lettuce and tomatoes from Nanny's garden, and sweet corn on the cob, Dad looked at his watch.

"Luke, Natalie's train gets in at 8:07. You'd better go."

I hated having to leave the wonderful meal as much as the witty repartee, but I knew this was part of my responsibility as a host. Besides, Natalie was such fun, I relished a little one-on-one time with her.

I greeted her on the train platform as she stepped off the New Canaan shuttle. She looked at me with a vague recollection (we'd only met twice before in crowded theater lobbies) and I could tell she was desperately trying to remember my name. Natalie wore a brightly colored peasant blouse, a pleated, gauzy, burgundy cotton skirt, lots of big, clunky Southwestern jewelry (I later learned she referred to these necklaces as "bosom bouncers"), and a large, floppy straw hat. Her attractive, shoulder-length, fiery red hair cascaded down from under the hat and her sapphire eyes sparkled. Her alabaster skin had a radiance about it. I saw why all the other Yankee men were so attracted to her. I tossed her bag into the back of Dad's beige Volvo sedan and we drove along the verdant, Connecticut roads as the sun was setting.

After a moment, I said, "We had just sat down to dinner, when Dad said, 'Luke, it's time to go get Natalie.'"

"Ohhh, Honey, I'm sorry to have interrupted your dinner!" she intoned in her mellifluous Southern drawl. I said this not to make her feel guilty, but so she'd know my name. I could tell it relieved her.

"No, I was happy to do it!" I said. "We'll get home just as the rest of them are having dessert and I can eat dinner with you."

"Aren't you just the sweetest thing?" she cooed. It wasn't quite the way my Aunt Agnes said it. It had a different sort of directness. I wondered for a second if she was flirting with me, but quickly dismissed the notion. For the rest of the ride, we chatted about the Broadway shows we'd recently seen, about *Ladies at the Alamo*, and I briefed her on the other weekend guests, whom she had never met. She was twenty years my senior and she was treating me like an equal. I sat up straighter in the driver's seat of the Volvo.

As we returned to the dining terrace, everyone was enjoying Mama's favorite summer dessert, peeled peaches soaked in white wine. At each place, there was a brandy snifter containing a whole, skinned peach and just enough Chardonnay to cover the fruit about three-quarters up. You sipped the wine all through the meal and then used a long, iced-tea spoon to eat the peach for dessert. It was incredibly elegant—until you had a fuzzy peach pit sitting in the bottom of your empty brandy snifter. At that point, the glasses were whisked away, usually by yours truly. I had some more kebabs with Natalie while the rest of them carefully stabbed their peaches with the long spoons. The dining terrace was ablaze with candles and kerosene torches. The air was thick with the odors of citronella, Chanel No. 5, freshly mown grass, barbecue sauce, and Johnny Walker Black. The showbiz stories were flowing as freely as the scotch and I was in heaven.

Mama told a wonderful story about the out of town tryout of *Ladies at the Alamo*. There was a bit in the script where Estelle Parsons came onstage holding what looked like a long, dark brown, leather staff, which was in fact a bull's "goober," a stretched, dried, bull's penis with the testicles used as the head of the cane. The prop man was unable to locate one in Manhattan, so Maree Cheatham had called upon one of her ranching friends in Lampasas to procure the precious artifact and ship it to New York. The climactic scene of the play called for Dede (Estelle Parsons) to threaten to blackmail Joanne (Rosemary Murphy) and, after a five-page argument, to chase her offstage brandishing the goober like a harpoon. During the entire scene, Heckart sat upstage drinking and enjoying the catfight.

Estelle loved the baseness of this scene and twirled the bull's goober like a cheerleader with a baton. Rosemary Murphy, on the other hand, was disgusted by it and cautioned Estelle not to actually touch her with the goober, but to give the appearance of doing so.

While the show was having its out-of-town tryout in Philadelphia, one night during a note session, Rosemary said to director Frank Perry, "When I cross upstage, Estelle is holding the goober out so far, she isn't leaving enough room for me cross around her without touching it."

"I don't know what the hell you're talking about," Estelle whined with a sneer. "There's plenty of room for you to get around me, Rosemary. You just need to cross further upstage."

Frank Perry wanted to avoid a schism at all costs. The second act wasn't working and the play already had enough troubles without tension between the leading ladies. The director gently asked the two women to please both be mindful of this moment and to work it out for themselves. He said he would watch the scene and try to come up with alternate blocking if necessary.

During the following evening's performance, just as Estelle began the five-page argument, Rosemary Murphy got up and walked offstage. Parsons, not knowing what else to do, raised the goober over her head and followed her. Heckart turned around and realized she was all alone onstage.

"What the hell am I going to do now?" she thought to herself. "Give the people a little Eleanor Roosevelt?" She was referring to her recent one-woman tour. Out of desperation, she said her next line.

"By God, that was fun!"

Since there hadn't been any fight scene preceding it, this line made no sense whatsoever. In her character's Texas drawl, Heckart turned tentatively towards the wings.

"Dede?" she said. "Y'all coming back?" After a long pause, Estelle returned to the stage.

"Honey," Mama recounted to the weekend guests, "I was never so relieved in my life as when I saw Estelle's green chiffon gown come floating back out there."

Still holding the goober, Estelle ad-libbed, "Gee! She was easier to get rid of than I thought!"

"That audience must have thought this was an awfully peculiar play," Mama said.

Frank Perry assembled the company after the performance and simply said, "Ladies, it's been a rough night. Let's all go home and sleep on it."

"Sleep on it?" Heckart shouted. "We're not gonna sleep on it! Rosemary, I want to know why the hell you walked off the stage in the middle of a performance!"

"Estelle hit me with the goober on purpose!" Murphy cried.

"Oh, Jesus!" Parsons started in, only to be abruptly cut off by the director.

"We are NOT going to talk about this tonight!" Perry said. "We will meet at two o'clock tomorrow afternoon in the lobby for notes. Good night."

He turned on his heel and quickly exited the theater. Heckart was livid. She thought this was one of the most cowardly acts she had ever witnessed from a director.

The next day during notes, the issue was perfunctorily addressed.

"Well," Perry said, "I trust nothing like that will ever happen again."

Heckart was outraged. She went to him privately and said, "Frank, how could you not address that? They both walked offstage in front of a full house! It was my ass up there alone onstage. And what if Estelle hadn't come back?"

Frank Perry looked at her squarely. "Eileen," he said, "I was so angry, if I had addressed it, I would have wound up firing both of them. This play has enough problems without starting from scratch with two new leading ladies. Now, I'm as sorry as you are for what happened, but can we please just move on?"

Mama told this story to the enrapt audience on the dining terrace. Everyone had a sense of horror and delight. Natalie talked about being in the audience that night and how confusing and upsetting it was.

The following evening, the weekend guests were in rare form. Before dinner, Natalie had sneaked off to the studio to smoke a joint with Philip. Jean was tossing back the Courvoisier as if it were soda pop and Ken was holding his own with the Stolichnaya. Mama and Daddy went to bed soon after dinner. After a few more cocktails, Jean and Ken quickly followed suit.

After sharing another joint with Natalie on the back patio, Philip went off to a local bar to meet some girls. So there I was, alone in my parents' living room at 1 AM with this sexy, semi-stoned Broadway investor. By now I thought her playful banter might have had an ulterior motive, though I still wasn't sure. After all, Natalie was flirty and coy with everyone. When she turned on her Southern charm, it was infectious. She had been physical with me all day, hugging me, touching my arm, taking my hand to go to the dinner table. And more than once, I felt her gaze upon me for uncomfortably long stretches. At eighteen I loved the attention, but I didn't know what to make of it or how to respond.

There was a comical moment at dinner as I was scooping the French vanilla ice cream onto slabs of Nanny's homemade apple pie. I wasn't watching what I was doing and managed to drop a large scoop right onto Natalie's hand. The table froze for about two seconds, then everyone burst out laughing. Grabbing her hand, I shouted, "It's not *Ladies at the Alamo*, it ladies à la mode!"

I took her ice cream laden fingers and shoved them into my mouth, licking them clean. Again, everyone howled, Natalie the loudest of anyone. I didn't mean it sexually—I was just getting the biggest laugh of the night. That was always an important title to hold at a Yankee family gathering.

Back in the living room, my confused adolescent mind was racing as fast as my heart was pounding. Will she be offended if I make a pass at her, I wondered, or will she be offended if I don't? When I'd come out to my parents, six months earlier, Mama had asked me to keep my options open. Was this my opportunity? We sat there on the sleigh-bed sofa, my eighteen-year-old awkwardness obvious even to the furniture. I was all elbows and knees, yet other parts were starting to stir. Why would this worldly woman have any interest in a gawky teenager like me?

You could have driven a Pinter play through the long pauses in the conversation. After one, I said, "You know, all the men in this house are just crazy about you."

"Really?" she asked, sounding surprised.

"Oh, yeah. They were all talking about it before you arrived. Dad, Mark, Philip, they all said you're one of the sexiest women they've ever seen."

"That's very sweet," she said, "but there's only one man I'm interested in at the moment."

"Yeah?" I said, "Who's that?"

"You." She looked deep into my eyes, holding my gaze.

I was so nervous and inexperienced, I didn't know what to do. At the same time, I felt a familiar twitch in the center of my Levis.

Natalie was snuggling up against me and putting her head on my shoulder. She was laughing as awkwardly as I was.

"I'm sorry, Natalie," I said. "I know I'm not making this easy for you."

"It's all right, sweetie," she said, stroking my cheek.

The next thing I knew we were French kissing on my parents' brocaded living room sofa.

Afraid of getting caught, I suggested we go someplace else. Jean and Ken were upstairs sleeping on either side of my room, so that was too dangerous. But Natalie was the only weekend guest who wasn't sleeping in the main house. She was staying across the driveway in Nanny's cottage while Nanny was away, visiting her niece in Rhode Island. We skulked out the back door and across the wet grass. There was something sacrilegious about the fact that I was about to "do it" in Nanny's bed, but that didn't stop me.

We kept the lights off and Natalie immediately got naked and crawled under the covers. Wow, I thought, I guess that's the way grownups do it. There was no time for self-consciousness, though I had enough to populate a small town.

"Now, honey," she said. "It never occurred to me to bring my diaphragm . . . and I don't suppose you have any protection . . . do you?"

I flashed a wry smile as I reached into my wallet and pulled out a foil-wrapped Trojan Philip had given me a year before.

"You never know when you might need this," he had told me.

Natalie was delighted and genuinely surprised that I was so well equipped. Moments later, we were thrashing around, quietly moaning on Nanny's Simmons Beautyrest. We seemed to go on for hours. Natalie was a very experienced lover and really made me feel good. She repeatedly told me how wonderful I was and how much she was enjoying herself. I returned the compliment, but my heart wasn't really in it. Still, I felt very powerful to be giving Natalie such pleasure. On my end, since I'd had a bit more wine, it took forever for me to climax. Under the circumstances, I wasn't really sure that I could, but I was so afraid of seeming inadequate, I wouldn't stop trying.

"This is pretty fun," I thought to myself, "but it doesn't feel as good as fooling around with a guy."

When I finally came, my entire body shuddered. I collapsed onto Natalie in a pool of our mingled perspiration, panting and giggling.

When we awoke with the sunrise, half asleep, she said, "You were just wonderful. Strong and sexy and passionate. Thank you so much."

"Thank you," I said into her disheveled red hair. "I've never had an experience quite like that. It was . . . something else!"

"So, darling," she said, "this will be our little secret, won't it?" There was a hint of nervous caution in her voice.

"Absolutely," I assured her.

"I wouldn't want you to think that I was leading you on or . . ."

"It's okay, Natalie." I said. "I don't expect anything. But thank you for clarifying."

"You're wonderful," she said, breathing a sigh of relief.

I stumbled into my clothes and glanced at my watch. It was five AM.

"I'd better get back to my room before anyone notices I'm gone," I said. "Besides, I have to go to work in a few hours and I think I'll sleep better in my own bed."

"I understand," she said, watching me get dressed. "I'll see you later."

She kissed me on the mouth one last time, fluffed her pillow and rolled over.

As I slipped back into the main house and into my own bed, I thought how envious Daddy, Mark, or Philip would be if they knew. And Mama would have a fit. Better keep this to myself for a long time.

I was working as a security guard at a warehouse to make money for the summer before attending Juilliard that fall. The job was deadly dull but it gave me time to read scripts. I hated being away from the weekend guests and all the show biz stories, but I was the low man on the totem pole at work, so I got stuck with the Fourth of July shift. I thought about Natalie most of the day, sorting through my feelings and trying to figure out if I'd really liked it or if I was merely trying to convince myself that I did.

Three days prior, I'd had my audition for the local summer-theater production of Robert Anderson's Pulitzer Prize–winner *Tea and Sympathy*. At the end of the play, the wife of the headmaster offers herself to him, with the now famous closing line, "Years from now, when you speak about this—and you will—please, be kind." Of course, now I was thinking of this in the context of Natalie and laughing to myself about it.

When I rang home at lunchtime from the warehouse, Mama told me that the director of *Tea and Sympathy* had called and wanted me to come for a callback the next day. I was ecstatic.

That night, Natalie was the one who turned in early, still exhausted from our frolicking the night before. She'd given me some surreptitious looks over the shrimp cocktail at dinner, but I didn't dare look back. I was too afraid that Mama would find out.

Later, Ken, Jean, and I sat up in the living room, sipping white wine spritzers. Even though Jean could have a sharp tongue, I'd known her all my life and under-stood that her acerbic wit covered over great vulnerability. As we laughed and joked in the living room, she fixed her gaze upon me.

"Luke," she said, "I'd like to ask you something and I hope you won't mind my mentioning this in front of Ken."

"Of course not, Jean. You're both like family. What's up?"

"You know, I'm a very light sleeper," she said. There was a sinking feeling in my stomach. "Where were you until five o'clock in the morning?"

A pregnant pause filled the air. Ken lit another cigarillo and tried not to smirk.

"You didn't say anything to Mom and Dad, did you?" I asked, gulping my wine spritzer.

"Of course not," Jean replied. "I wouldn't do that. So . . . were you with Natalie?"

There was no point in hiding anything now. I was busted, so I might as well come clean. "Well, as a matter of fact, I was," I said.

I didn't know where to look.

"Oh God," Ken chimed in, "he's not a Twinkie anymore!"

"Did you have a good time?" Jean asked. It was obvious from her tone of voice she didn't think we'd been playing Parcheesi.

"We had a great time," I said. "But how did you figure it out?"

"Oh my God," Jean said. "She was all over you at dinner last night. It was so obvious!"

"Was it really?" I asked.

"Of course," Ken said.

"And licking the ice cream off her hand wasn't exactly subtle," Jean said.

I fixed myself another spritzer.

"Do you think my parents are aware of it?" I asked.

"No, I doubt it," Jean said. "They were too busy playing host and hostess."

"Besides," Ken added, "you're still Eileen's baby and she doesn't think of you as . . . as . . ."

"As someone who would *shtup* one of her investors?" Jean suggested.

They both guffawed as I turned red.

"So . . . are you upset with me, Jean?" I asked.

"Not at all!" she replied. "In fact, I think it's wonderful!"

"You do?" I asked.

"Absolutely," she said. "Get a little experience under your belt!"

"So to speak!" Ken said, laughing again.

"Well, I'm not sure my mother would see it that way," I said.

"I think you're right about that." Jean said.

"I'm not so sure," Ken said. "She may surprise you."

"I don't want to take the chance," I said. "So *please* don't say anything, okay?"

They assured me that my secret was safe. Still, I knew for someone like Jean who loved to have the goods on people, this was a secret that would be hard to keep.

Having won the evening, Jean announced she was going to sleep. Ken and I sat and had another wine spritzer. He talked candidly about his ex-wife and about the fact that he had been married for a number of years before realizing he was gay. Several thoughts came into my head.

"Hey!" I said, "What would you think about going for a midnight skinny-dip?"

"Why not?" he replied.

We grabbed a couple of towels and quietly headed up to the pool. This acceptance as an adult and a man of the world was making me feel quite full of myself. I suggested we keep the pool lights off so we wouldn't wake anyone.

"Good idea," Ken said.

As we started to get undressed in the July moonlight, I said, "You know, last night when I was with Natalie, most of the time I was wishing I was with you instead."

I reached over and patted his bare ass.

"Now stop that!" he said, laughing self-consciously. "I'm old enough to be your father, you little shit!"

"Well," I reasoned, "Natalie's old enough to be my mother. What's the big deal?" I reached over and rubbed his ass again.

"The big deal," he said, pulling my hand away, "is that I've known since you were a kid and it ain't gonna happen! Now if you want to swim, let's swim, but if you want anything else, I'm going back to the house."

I turned and dove into the pool, my body shimmering against the water. Ken dove in as well, but stayed at the far end.

As we toweled off, I said, "Ken, I didn't mean to make you feel uncomfortable. I'm just not very experienced yet and . . ."

"I understand," he said, "and I want you to know I'm very flattered. But we're too good friends, Luke, and I am very close to your folks. Give yourself time. You'll figure it out."

I was grateful for his honesty and friendship.

The next day, I had a callback for *Tea and Sympathy* and was cast in the leading role of the boy grappling with his sexuality who is seduced by an older woman. I snagged Natalie in the hallway and told her.

"Honey, congratulations," she said

"But isn't it funny?" I said, "I mean, after you and I . . ."

"It's hysterical," she replied.

"*Please . . . be kind,*" I said, quoting the last line of the play.

"You really were wonderful," she said, looking at me intently.

"Thanks," I said, blushing. "So were you."

A few weeks later, Mama was dishing on the phone with Jean Thomas, who inadvertently let something slip about Natalie's escapades over the Fourth of July weekend.

"What are you talking about, Jean?" Mama asked

"Oh, shit," Jean said, "You weren't supposed to know."

"Know what?" Mama said. "You can't get off the hook now!"

"About Natalie . . . and Ken!" Jean said.

"*Really?*" Mama asked.

Jean figured it was safer to keep my secret and that Ken could take care of himself. Jean said that Ken and Natalie would be very distressed if they thought she knew and Mama said that as a good hostess, she would never say anything to embarrass her guests.

When she got off the phone, she turned to me and said, "You won't believe what Jean Thomas just told me about the July Fourth weekend!"

"What?" I asked, not looking her in the eye.

"She told me that Natalie and Ken had a tryst."

I laughed loudly.

"Did you know about it?" Mama asked.

"Well," I said, "let's say I had my suspicions."

"I'll be damned," she said. "I thought Ken preferred men these days!"

"Does it bother you, Mama?" I asked.

"No," she said. "I'm a little surprised, but not upset."

As time went on, I was the one who became annoyed. I appreciated the fact that Jean had shielded me, but it was *my* conquest, *my* rite of passage into manhood, and someone else was getting the credit. Mama mentioned it repeatedly over the next few months, almost as if she didn't quite believe it. I wondered if perhaps Jean had told her what really happened and she was trying to get me to confess.

"I still can't get over the fact that Ken and Natalie had a fling that weekend," she said.

One day, I couldn't take it anymore.

"Mama," I said. "Look, it wasn't Natalie and Ken. It was Natalie and me."

"Really?" she said thoughtfully. "Well, that makes more sense. I'm glad you're keeping your options open."

I was expecting shock, recriminations, even anger. And all I got was, "I'm glad you're keeping your options open." Still, there was some relief that my deep, dark secret was out in the open. She asked me a few questions about it and it was important to me to be sure she understood that all the advances had come from Natalie. She listened intently, but I couldn't really tell how she felt about it. It was unlike Mama to be so cryptic.

Now a student at Juilliard, I called Natalie and asked her if we might have dinner sometime. I wanted to cultivate her as a friend and, as a young acting student, the fact that she was a well-connected Broadway investor just might come in handy once I graduated.

"Darling," she said into the phone, "I am so happy to hear from you. Meet me at 'Café Un, Deux, Trois' Thursday at eight o' clock."

I arrived early and the maitre d' escorted me to the table. "Are you her son?" he asked.

"No," I said, "I'm . . . just a friend."

It was about four months since the infamous Fourth of July weekend. I wondered if Natalie might want to take me back to her penthouse for a repeat performance. While it would be flattering to be asked, I really wasn't interested. In fact, I thought, it might be good if I came out to her. I wondered how she'd take the news and I hoped she wouldn't be too upset.

Natalie swooped into the restaurant in a sable coat as if she owned the place. The maitre d' took her fur and escorted her to the table. When she saw me, she waltzed over and planted a big kiss on my lips. As always, her presence filled the room. As we came out of our embrace, she said, "Now wait, I've gotten lipstick all over you. Hold still."

Natalie grabbed her napkin and unfolded it with a flourish. She stuck it into her water glass and daubed my cheek as if she were stripping the varnish off an antique table. In the sixty seconds since she had entered, I had watched her transform from Dolly Levi to Mrs. Robinson to June Cleaver. It was going to be an interesting evening.

Natalie immediately ordered a very expensive bottle of Cabernet Sauvignon and we started chattering endlessly, just like in the car on the way to the house that night. We laughed easily and drank too much wine over roasted chicken and russet potatoes. As the subject rolled around to the Fourth of July, I figured I'd better tell her what had occurred with Mama.

"You *told* her?!" Natalie said.

"Well, the way she kept bringing it up," I said. "I think she already knew but was waiting for me to spill the beans. I think Jean Thomas must have told her."

"Oh my God," she said. "The next time I run into Eileen at Saks or Bonwits, she's going to rip my head off!"

"She didn't seem too upset about it, Natalie," I said.

She rolled a small potato around with her fork. "Since we're telling the truth here," she said, "I guess I'd better tell *you* something, too."

"What's that?" I said, fingering the rim of my water glass.

"You need to be careful with those condoms that have been lying around for awhile. Six weeks ago, I had a miscarriage."

I stopped with the water glass halfway to my mouth. A few seconds later and I'd have done a spit-take.

"What?" I said.

"Well, I wasn't sure I should tell you," she said, emptying the bottle of Cabernet into her glass. "But I was on the road with that new musical I'm producing and my periods were so irregular. I didn't think anything about it until I started passing tissue. I went to the doctor and he said I was miscarrying."

I shoved a breadstick into my mouth. "But . . . Natalie . . . are . . . you sure?"

"Honey, I'm certain," she said. "After my last relationship, I'd sworn off men for so long. I traced it back very carefully and it only could have been you."

I gulped down the rest of my breadstick with a large pat of butter. The reality of food was the only thing I could hold onto. I watched the waiter light a flaming cherries jubilee at the next table as I tried to process all of this. I had been seduced by a woman twenty years my senior and a friend of my mother's. I'd had my first real sex with this woman to try and figure out my gender preferences, and I'd gotten her *pregnant*! What if she hadn't miscarried? What if ten years from now a strangely familiar little blond urchin had shown up at my door? This was enough to put my shrink's kids through college. As the flames dissipated at the next table, I loosened my necktie and turned to Natalie.

"So, what do you need me to do?" I asked.

She was touched by the question. "Nothing, sugar. I have very good health insurance through my ex-husband. It's all taken care of."

As we continued to talk it out, I realized that everything really was okay. She hadn't had the child, nor had she wanted to. Her health was fine now and she was telling me as a future warning about condoms, with which I had no previous experience. She wasn't asking me to help with any doctor's bills, even if I could have. In retrospect, I realize what a caring gesture she was making.

Still, at eighteen I was proud to know that I was potent. It's one of those questions a man asks himself until he actually finds himself in the position of fatherhood. As flipped out as I was by Natalie's news, I was happy to know I wasn't shooting blanks.

I took my tie off, folded it, and stuck it into the pocket of my blue blazer. Fidgeting with a lemon rind, I said, "There's one other piece of this puzzle I still need to share with you Natalie."

"What," she said, draining her wineglass. "You mean that you're gay?"

I was shocked that she already knew.

"Um . . . well . . . yeah," I said.

"Oh honey," she said, "I know that. I knew it the night we made love."

I couldn't tell if I was light-headed from too much wine or if my emotional circuits were overloaded.

"But . . . then . . . how come . . . I mean, why me?"

She looked at me like I was a kitten in a pet store window. "Oh Luke," she said, "you were so sweet and good to me. A physical expression just seemed to be the next step for us. It just unfortunate that I didn't have my diaphragm and had to get . . . so sick afterwards."

"You know, Natalie," I said. "My mother must *never* find out about that!"

"Are you kidding?" she said. "I'm still processing the news that you told her anything at all!"

"I don't think she has a problem with it," I said.

"Oh honey, just wait," she said. "You're her fair-haired precious baby. She'll skin me alive."

Two months later, Mama invited Natalie to the Christmas party. Natalie didn't dare refuse. Still, she figured she'd better keep her head down.

I'd never seen Natalie as subdued as she was that day. Instead of the vibrant colors and clunky jewelry she always wore, she had on a pearl-colored satin blouse, black slacks, and a simple gold chain around her neck. Mama greeted Natalie at the door and threw her arms around her.

"I'm so glad you're here," Mama said. She marched Natalie into the living room. "Doesn't Natalie look beautiful?" Mama said to the assembled crowd.

"Thank you, Eileen," Natalie said, not yet sure how to take this.

"Let me get you a drink and let's get caught up," Mama said. "I want to hear everything."

I was surprised by her doting behavior and frankly, a little miffed. Being with Natalie had confused me all the more about my sexuality. And now she was being lauded for it.

After the party, I said to Mama, "Why did you go out of your way to be so nice to Natalie?"

"Well, why wouldn't I?" she said.

"After what I told you about us, I thought you might be angry with her," I said.

"You know," she replied, "in some European countries, that's just what they do."

"What?" I asked.

"They send the teenage boy off with an older woman, generally a friend of the mother's," she said. "The woman shows the young boy the ways of the world. She educates him."

"*Educates* him?!" I asked.

"That's right," she said. "I mean . . . isn't that what occurred?"

I hadn't thought about it in those terms before. I had just put it in the context of added confusion. But I saw her point. In retrospect, I think Mama knew how much I was questioning myself and she was grateful to Natalie for trying to "straighten me out."

In the years that followed, Natalie and I often laughed about that weekend. She made amends for any anxiety she caused me and acted with grace and compassion over the whole scenario. In truth, I think she was proud of having seduced me and wore it like a merit badge. I know I did. It was an important step into manhood for me and I am grateful for her compassion.

Daddy

MY PAPA, JACK YANKEE

JACK YANKEE WAS the warmest, most lovable man I have ever known. He quietly supported his family over the years and let everyone else take center stage. My father would get very lonely when Mama would be on the west coast for long periods of time. There was one time in the early sixties where she was going to be away for several weeks doing a TV movie and she made a suggestion.

"Jack," she said, "the Town Players is doing a production of *Mister Roberts*. There are so many great small parts of colonels and admirals. Why don't you go audition?"

Since my parents had met doing amateur theatricals in college, he wasn't unaccustomed to such things, so after he mulled it over a bit, he picked up a script and glanced through it.

A few days later, Mama phoned him from L.A.

"So how were the auditions?" she asked.

"They went pretty well," he said.

"So, did you get a part in *Mister Roberts*?" Mama asked.

"Well, as a matter of fact, I did," Jack replied.

"Good for you, sweetheart," she said, "Which part?"

"Mister Roberts."

"The lead?!" she asked in amazement. "You got the LEAD?"

"Yup," he said.

"Oh for God's sake," she said. "On top of everything else, now I need to give my husband acting lessons?!"

By the time Mama got back from doing her TV movie, Daddy's production was just about to open. For once, the shoe was on the other foot. Jack was the one going off to rehearsals at night and leaving her alone. As he came home from the office, ate a quick dinner and raced off the theater, he would turn to her with a broad smile and say, "Revenge . . . sweet revenge!"

It was so hard to play a leading role and hold down a full-time job, my father didn't act in another play for twelve years. He had a good time doing *Mister Roberts*, but it was a terrible strain on him.

When I was fifteen, just before I got my license, I asked him to drive me to the Wilton Playshop, where they were having auditions for an evening of original one-act plays and musical scenes. Most of the material was pretty bad, but a few of the scripts were passable, with good parts. A friend had requested that I audition for the lead in a play called *The Strong Among Us*, about a young man during World War II who becomes a freedom fighter in Poland to avenge the deaths of his father and brothers. I read well and I felt pretty sure I would get it.

I looked around the theater lobby and Daddy was nowhere to be found. I heard three of the directors bickering in the green room.

"No, I want him for *my* play."

"Well, I have to have him in mine—there's no one else who can do it!"

"But I need him for two different roles."

I wondered who the lucky actor was that everyone was fighting over.

"Maybe we should just let him decide," one of the directors said. Turning to me, she said, "Luke, where's your father?"

"My father?" I asked.

"Yes!" she said. "We all want him, so now he has to decide."

"Wait a minute," I said. "He was just driving me to the audition."

"Yes, but while you were auditioning in the other room, he read for us out here. Now we're fighting over who gets him!"

I had to laugh. Mild-mannered Jack Yankee was the most in-demand actor of the day at the Wilton Playshop. He could float on this for weeks.

Jack decided to play the ghost of my father in *The Strong Among Us* so that we could work together. And Philip wound up playing the ghost of my brother.

This particular one-act play was being produced for political reasons. The little theater was on land owned by the Wilton Congregational Curch, and the play was written by the church's minister. One of Dad's lines was "It is the reign of a silent litany for pain." The script was full of pretentious lines like that, but some of the characters were interesting and I had a pretty juicy role as the young freedom fighter. Besides, it was the only time that Dad, Philip and I appeared on the stage together, so we made it fun.

Mama was on tour with her one-woman show as Eleanor Roosevelt. One night on the phone, she said, "Well if all three of you are in it, should I fly up and see this thing on my day off?"

"No!" we all screamed into the phone. "Please don't!"

She never brought it up again.

Once the acting bug bit Daddy again, it became a wonderful pastime while Mama was on the road or in Hollywood. Over the years, he did supporting roles in community theater productions of *Carousel*, *Dear World*, *Of Thee I Sing*, *The Little Foxes*, *The Crucible*, *The Rope Dancers*, and, of course, our infamous production of *Tea and Sympathy*. He actually got pretty good. No, he wasn't going to give Jason Robards or Christopher Plummer a run for their money, but for community theater, he had a strong presence and an honest simplicity. Mama never critiqued his performances the way she did mine. She might give him a few simple notes, but left it at that. His wife knew he was acting for the sheer enjoyment of it, so she wouldn't do or say anything to hinder that.

In 1986, I directed my first full-length play the Sterling Barn Theatre in Stamford. The community theater was twenty minutes from where my parents lived, so I commuted out from Manhattan where I was living and working as a temporary legal secretary at a law firm on Wall Street. The play was a production of Jim Leonard's Depression-era drama, *The Diviners*, about a fallen preacher in Indiana whose faith is restored and then lost again after encountering a backward boy with the power to divine water. There was a lovely supporting role, a character named Basil, who was a country doctor to the kids and the cows. I couldn't find anyone else to play the role and I thought Daddy would be perfect for it, so I asked him to do it. He didn't like to do plays when Mama was home, but he reluctantly agreed. Mama convinced him it would be a good father-son bonding experience. Besides, it was an interesting part.

The first hurdle we had to overcome was what I should call him in rehearsal. Years later, I would have this same problem when directing Mama in *Driving Miss Daisy*. We decided I would call him by his character name. He had a eulogy that opened and closed the play and set the whole tone of the piece.

"Now, Basil," I said to him in rehearsal, "you're pushing that opening speech. If you rush and try to do too much with it, you're going to screw it up. Just be simple and honest and tell the story, okay?"

It took awhile for him to grasp what that meant, but ultimately, he did. Daddy hadn't played a large a role since *Mister Roberts* and it made him nervous. He was getting older and didn't know if he could remember all his lines. He was very concerned about doing a good job, largely because he didn't want to let me down. I rarely saw him without his script in his hand during this time. He even put his lines on tape and would play them on his Walkman while he was doing chores around the house.

"How's it going?" Mama asked me.

"It's kinda rough," I answered with a heavy sigh. "Will you run lines with him again this weekend?"

"All right," she'd say. "But you must be very patient with him. He's trying so hard."

"I know, and I am. But it's not always easy."

One Sunday, after a particularly bumpy rehearsal with Daddy, he was driving me back to the train station. He knew I wasn't pleased with his work that day.

After we drove in silence for a while, I said, "Now, Daddy, rehearsal is over for the weekend. Let's just forget about the play for the next few minutes. I *know* you'll have your lines for the second act down by next week. So, until the train comes, let's be dad and son, okay?"

"Okay, buddy," he said, drumming his fingers on the steering wheel.

As he put me on the train, he said, "Listen, I know you haven't been able to temp as much because of the play, so maybe this will help."

He slipped a twenty-dollar bill into my coat pocket.

"Are your bribing your director?" I said with a laugh.

"Maybe," he replied.

"Well, I accept!" I said, throwing my arms around him and kissing him on the cheek.

When I returned to Manhattan, I called my best friend Joanne Jaworowski and said, "The great thing about directing your old man is that when he blows his lines, he slips you a fast twenty!"

Up until opening night, Daddy never went onstage without his script in his back pocket. It became such a habit, I think he would have done it in performance if I hadn't reminded him. I loved this simple, lyrical play and wanted to do it justice. And, as the first full-length play I had directed, I was anxious that it come off right. The opening-night performance went extremely well. Mama and all of her local showbiz friends were in the audience to support Daddy and me. The minute he came offstage, I stopped him in the wings. I put my hand on his shoulder and leaned in very close.

"Now listen to me," I said, staring at him intently. "There were a lot of important people in the audience tonight with a lot of fancy opinions. But I have to tell you that as your director *and* as your son this is the best I have ever seen you in anything you've done onstage. Daddy, I am so proud of you."

As he continued to stare at me, I watched two small tears well up in his eyes and cascade down his cheeks. I told him that I loved him and we hugged for a long time. It was one of three times in my life I ever saw my father cry.

I had such respect and admiration for my father. He came from a generation where men weren't openly demonstrative, but he loved his family so much. Not a day goes by that I don't think about the ways he expressed his love: by tucking me in at night, bringing home freshly baked doughnuts from the store next to his office, driving me to school. For all those years, he was selling insurance, helping us with our homework, building our tree houses, doing the endless raking, weeding, and gardening. With the exception of the times he trotted the boards locally, he was always content to take a backseat to his wife and kids, to let them have the spotlight while he was in the shadows.

Jack Yankee was a wonderful businessman, partly because he was so affable and humane. It seemed appropriate that he should be handling property insurance, because he was so good in a crisis. When someone called him to report that their jewelry had been stolen or their house had been damaged in a fire, he was calm, nurturing and supportive. Jack was just the sort of person you wanted to have around in an emergency, because he remained unflappable.

One of my favorite stories of Daddy's is about a business call he received one day from a client named Bill.

"Jack," Bill said, "You're not going to believe this one, but I need to know if my insurance will cover this."

"Try me," Jack said.

It seems Bill had a red Volkswagen, parked right near Madison Square Garden. He and his wife were planning a dinner party and he had a very expensive case of wine in his trunk, which he'd purchased that morning. The circus was in town and this happened to be the street where they were exercising the animals in between shows. There was an elephant named Tiny (who was anything but) that had been trained to sit on a red stool. Seeing the red Volkswagen, Tiny immediately went over and sat on the hood of the car, crushing the trunk and smashing the case of wine. Tiny sat there patiently waiting for her reward after having done her trick.

The authorities managed to track Bill down and explain the situation to him. Inexplicably, the car was still drivable and he insisted on taking it back to his mechanic in Connecticut. As Bill was driving on the Merritt Parkway, the state police pulled him over in Westchester.

"Sir," the policeman said, "why are you driving such a damaged vehicle? Have you reported an accident?"

"Well you see, officer," Bill said, "an elephant sat on my car and . . ."

"What?" the policeman grunted. "This car reeks of booze. I wouldn't be surprised if this is a hit and run as well as driving under the influence. I'm hauling you in, buddy!"

After several hours at the station, poor Bill was able to get hold of the Manhattan police who confirmed his story.

"So do you mean to tell me," Jack said chuckling into the phone, "you want to know if your liability insurance covers *elephants?*"

I think Bill got some sort of compensation from his insurance company. Jack filed the claim as an "act of God."

While Bill's story may be an extreme example, it's the type of thing Daddy handled on a regular basis. He hardly ever talked about work or brought it home. With five mouths to feed (six if you include Nanny), he quietly did the same job for forty years so that the rest of us could be grand and extravagant.

I never fully appreciated him until after he was gone.

Juilliard, Jackie, and Joanne

ME WITH MAMA AND DADDY IN ATLANTIC CITY AFTER HER TAPING OF *THE HONEYMOONER'S REUNION*

IN THE FALL OF 1978, I moved into Manhattan and started my first year studying acting at the prestigious Juilliard School of Drama. By the end of my first semester, I was really full of myself. I had spent the past three months studying Shakespeare, Ibsen, Chekhov, Euripides, voice, speech, and movement. After all those years of just "doing plays," now I was becoming a serious actor. On my Thanksgiving break, Daddy and I drove down to Atlantic City to meet Mama. She was taping *The Honeymooner's Reunion Special* with Jackie Gleason, Art Carney, and all the regulars, playing Gleason's mother-in-law. She said, "Considering I'm three years younger than Mr. Gleason, this casting is a little peculiar . . . but never mind."

They were rehearsing the show at Resorts International Casino on the Boardwalk, and then shooting it before a live audience. This was the way Gleason had worked for years. Daddy and I were both excited about this different and adventurous Thanksgiving holiday. We were also looking forward to having some quality father and son time on the three hour car trip to Atlantic City.

I had been studying diction with Edith Skinner, a doyenne in the world of speech teachers. Edith had taught Kevin Kline, Patti LuPone, Robin Williams, and many of the best actors around. Edith told me that the proper way to pronounce my name was "Ly-ook", with what she called a "liquid U." I tried this on for awhile, and hated it. Ultimately, she conceded that the liquid U was optional after L and S, especially with a proper name. She also had me saying "syootcase" (what one uses to travel) and "tyoosdee" (the day of the week). Edith had written a book called *Speak with Distinction* and I was trying to do so at all times.

As Daddy and I were driving in heavy holiday traffic, I talked his ear off about the layers of subtlety in *Hedda Gabler*, the difference between a diphthong and an off-glide, and whether Shakespeare's sonnets were really written to the dark lady or the young boy. He listened politely.

When I started talking about my future, I said, "Well, Faaaathah, perhaps when I'm finished at Juuuuliaaahd, I'll consider going for my maaastah's degree."

He took his eyes off the road and looked at me with a cocked eyebrow.

"I guess I'm going a little overboard with the voice-and-speech thing, aren't I?" I asked. "Just a little," he said, not wanting to burst my bubble.

We arrived at the Resorts Hotel and greeted Mama. She had arranged for us to have Thanksgiving dinner the following night with the entire *Honeymooners* cast and then to see the live taping the following evening. While in Atlantic City, Mama had developed a new passion in life: slot machines. When she had visited Marlene Dietrich in Las Vegas, her philosophy was, "If I spend twenty dollars on a bad hat, then at least I've got the hat to show for it. But I would *never* throw my money away on gambling!"

Marlene had been outraged that her friend wouldn't gamble. On her last night in Vegas, Dietrich handed her a quarter and said, "For God's sake, will you be a sport and just go into the powder room and put this in the slot machine? How can anyone come to Las Vegas and not gamble, even once!"

I don't know why Mama's attitude changed, but from the time she arrived in Atlantic City through the rest of her life, she was crazy for nickel slot machines. If she was feeling really decadent, she moved up to quarters. Mama always gave herself a limit (usually fifty dollars) and played for as long as she could until it ran out. On rare occasions, she'd go for another fifty, but never more than that. "That's why I don't play quarters very often," she said. "Your money lasts longer. You can do a lot of damage at a nickel machine for fifty bucks!"

Meanwhile, she watched Jackie Gleason fritter away thousands of dollars at the gaming tables in the blink of an eye. Art Carney tended to watch from the sidelines.

The following night, we sat in the Camelot Dining Room at Resorts International for our Thanksgiving dinner. Once we were all assembled, Mama turned to Carney.

"Art," she said, "as a good Irish Catholic, would you do us the honor of saying grace?"

His eyes got very wide. After a few seconds, he stared at his plate and mumbled. You would have thought she'd asked him to recite the Gettysburg Address in Swahili. He managed to stammer out some sort of benediction which no one could understand.

When he stopped talking long enough so that we knew he was done, Mama said, "And dear Lord, may I just add that we are grateful for this food and this company and please take care of all the sick and lonely people all over the world. Amen."

Everyone looked relieved as they started passing the gravy and sweet potatoes. I sat by Jane Keane, who played Trixie, Art Carney's wife. She knew several of my teachers at Julliard, especially Marian Seldes, whom we discussed with great fondness. I was delighted that someone from television knew anything about my current world.

The following day, Dad and I strolled around Atlantic City while Mama rehearsed. Then we went to the taping. As a young student of the classics, I was appalled by what I saw. *The Honeymooners* wasn't exactly known for its subtlety. In fact, stylistically it was more akin to vaudeville than anything else. The broad gestures, mugging, shouting, and playing to the audience were antithetical to everything I was learning. My sensibilities were deeply offended.

We met Mama for supper after the taping. She was ravenous and ordered a shrimp cocktail and a chef's salad. After she told us how she felt it had gone, I turned to her and started speaking with distinction again.

"Good God, Mothah!" I said in my best rounded Juilliard tones. "How could you *do* such a piece of shit?!"

She put down her shrimp fork and looked me right in the eye.

"I know it's shit," she said, "and I know exactly what I'm doing. I am paying your tuition. So, let's not hear another word about it, shall we?"

I stopped dead in my tracks. I had chosen to think that an actress of Eileen Heckart's stature with a husband to support her only did projects of quality. But careers don't work that way. For all the wonderful, celebrated plays Mama did on Broadway, there were just as many crappy sitcoms and soap operas that came and went because one of the kids needed braces or the house needed a new roof. In the mid-sixties, she had a fancy tile floor installed in the living room. She called it her "barefoot floor." I always assumed this was because she liked to walk on it without shoes. But what it really meant was that replacing Mildred Natwick in *Barefoot in the Park* on Broadway, something she didn't want to do at first, enabled her to afford that floor. It wasn't her "barefoot floor," but her *Barefoot* floor. After that night, I never questioned why she did a role I thought was beneath her. I also stopped speaking with distinction when I wasn't in school or onstage.

By the time I left Juilliard after two years, while I had a lot of excellent acting technique under my belt, my self-confidence was shattered. Their methods were largely teaching through intimidation, the school of "we'll break you down so we can rebuild you in our image." While that works for some actors, it certainly didn't work for me. With all my wide-eyed idealism after that first semester, when I left two years later, it was one of the happiest days of my life.

⊗⊗⊗

It is no secret that my mother was a heavy smoker most of her life. Some people believed that's what made her voice so husky. Many tried to get her to quit over the years, but none ever had any luck.

In 1971, Mama did a TV version of Tad Mosel's Pulitzer Prize–winning play, *All the Way Home*, for the Hallmark Hall of Fame. The cast included Joanne Woodward, Richard Kiley, and Pat Hingle. Since these were people she had worked with in the theater and known for years, it was like old-home week for Mama. Her old friend Joanne Woodward was on a veritable campaign to get her to quit smoking. Mama was not amused.

"Heckie," Joanne suggested, "maybe if you had something else to do with your hands."

"I don't need anything else to do with my hands, Joanne." she replied. "I *have* something to do with my hands and it's called smoking!"

She lit another True Blue.

"You know," Joanne continued, "When I get bored on the set, I do needlepoint. It's not hard to do and I find it incredibly relaxing."

"I'm not good at handicrafts and they don't interest me," Heckart replied, thumbing through her script.

Joanne fished in her purse and pulled out a small, half-finished needlepoint sampler of a butterfly.

"My daughter Clea started this," Joanne said, handing the sampler to her co-star. "If Clea can do needlepoint, *you* can do needlepoint!"

The gauntlet had been thrown. Eileen Heckart never was one to refuse a challenge. The next day, she walked into Joanne's trailer, tossing the completed sampler onto Joanne's lap.

"You know what?" Eileen said. "Clea does shitty work!"

"Well, Heckie," Joanne replied. "You might give her the benefit of the doubt. She's only six."

From then on, my mother was rarely without a needlepoint canvas in her lap when she was on a movie set or backstage in her dressing room. Of course, she would have the cigarette in one hand and the embroidery needle in the other, but at least my brothers and I have many wonderful pillows, chair cushions, and wall hangings to show for it. Instead of losing one habit, she gained another.

My favorite story about my mother's smoking involves her interview for what was to be her last Broadway play, *The Cemetery Club*. In the winter of 1990, she drove into New York to have an initial meeting with the producers and director. Even at this stage of her career, she was always nervous before an interview. She was anxious to see if they would like her, if she would like them, and if indeed she would wind up doing the play. As a result, she had smoked heavily in the car. A few minutes into what was becoming a delightful meeting, her tiny clutch purse suddenly combusted, sending flames, smoke, and ashes across the producer's desk. Everyone screamed and ran for cups of water. Once the fire had been quelled, they all burst out laughing. It seems that as Mama had stepped out of the car, in her nervousness, rather than stomping it out on the sidewalk, she had tossed a lit cigarette into her purse. She was lucky the damage wasn't more extensive. Nonetheless, Heckart got the part.

The Cemetery Club was a comedy about elderly Jewish widows. It was the first time in recent years she didn't let me read the script for a new play she was going to do. She had come to rely on me to give her feedback before she made decisions on her projects. While she was being considered for the mother in Sam Shepard's *A Lie of the Mind* Off-Broadway, I happened to have visited for a weekend. She handed me a thick manuscript and said, "You have a very important job this weekend. You need to read this and tell me what the hell it's about!"

Before I left, I handed it back to her and said, "I don't know what the hell it's about either, but it's fascinating and theatrical. I think you should do it."

When the producers were unwilling to provide a car for her, the role went to Geraldine Page instead.

Not only had she not asked me to read *The Cemetery Club*, she was curiously tight-lipped about it. I think she knew I'd try to talk her out of it and she needed a project. It was a wonderful role of a flashy, Jewish matron in a tepid, sitcom-like script. She and the other actresses were universally praised, but the play was not.

Frank Rich in the *New York Times* said, "The sterling Miss Heckart has been given especially unflattering costumes . . . but such handicaps, let alone the stalled zingers in the script cannot derail this comedienne's withering sarcasm and impeccable timing."

The Cemetery Club actually went on to have a substantial life in summer stock and was even made into a film, but it closed on Broadway after only seven weeks.

The same week that Mama opened in *The Cemetery Club*, I made my Off-Broadway directorial debut with a production of Chekhov's *The Cherry Orchard* starring Penny Fuller, David Canary, and Cynthia Nixon.

In his review in the *New York Observer*, Rex Reed said, "Those damn Yankees are at it again. Connecticut's pride and joy, Mrs. Jack Yankee, better known to her legions of fans as the great Eileen Heckart, is staging a one-woman graduate course in acting in *The Cemetery Club* on Broadway. Her son, Luke Yankee, has just directed a graceful, moody, and very satisfying production of Chekhov's *The Cherry Orchard* uptown at the York Theatre on East Ninetieth Street. When they climb into their jammies after a long day of applause, I wonder if they talk about their talent."*

It was very exciting to be working in New York at the same time as my mother. It gave us an even greater level of camaraderie. We were truly working colleagues in the theater.

During the run of *The Cemetery Club*, Mama went up to the nursing home in Stratford to visit Esther on her day off. In her early nineties, Esther was pretty out of it by now and just stared out the window most of the time, lost in a kind of reverie. When Mama entered the room that day, Esther sat up in her chair as if she'd been waiting for her.

"I'm glad you're here," Esther said. "I have some very important information for you. Write these names down."

---

* Courtesy of Rex Reed. Reprinted with permission.

Mama took a pad out of her purse and wrote as her mother dictated five names to her.

"Who are these men, Mama?" she asked.

"Who are they?" Esther repeated. "Well, they were my five husbands!"

"Of course," Mama said, putting the names into perspective.

"I thought you might like to have those names after I'm gone," Esther said.

Looking down at the list, Mama said, "Rex Kirk—what did he do?"

"Who knows?" Esther replied. "But I can tell you this much—they were all gorgeous!"

Mother and daughter discussed the men for a moment, particularly Leo Herbert, Anna Eileen's father, and Van Purcell, the only one she really knew.

"Isn't that terrible?" Esther said. "I've lived ninety-two years and all I have to show for it is that I married five turds! Anna Eileen, don't you think I'm wicked to have been married so many times?"

She studied her mother's face for a moment.

"I don't know, Mama. I think it's kind of daring and wonderful!"

"Do you, really?" Esther asked.

"I do, Mama."

The two women smiled at each other. Anna Eileen thanked her mother for the names, slipped the piece of paper in her purse, kissed Esther on the forehead, and departed. A week later, Esther died peacefully in her sleep. After all the years of strife, Mama was happy that their last encounter had been such a pleasant one.

"Outing" Ellen and Stalled Sitcoms

MAMA HOLDING HER 1994 EMMY FOR THE SITCOM *LOVE & WAR.* © ACADEMY
OF TELEVISION ARTS & SCIENCES—REPRINTED WITH PERMISSION

IN THE LATE SEVENTIES, eighties, and nineties, my mother did a number of television series in recurring roles, but none of them ever lasted more than one season: *Out of the Blue* with Dixie Carter and James Brogan; *Trauma Center* with James Naughton, Lou Ferrigno, and Wendie Malick, *Partners in Crime* with Loni Anderson and Lynda Carter, *Annie McGuire* with Mary Tyler Moore, *Murder One* with Anthony LaPaglia; and *The Five Mrs. Buchanans* with Judith Ivey, Harriet Sansom Harris, and Beth Broderick. Having Eileen Heckart in a supporting role on these shows added a bit of cachet to them, but the shows themselves received disappointing ratings and all of them folded after ten or twelve episodes.

Mama never particularly liked doing television. This is surprising considering how much of it she did over the years. I think she did it for a few reasons, the chief one being monetary. She certainly didn't have to worry about finances at this point in her life. Daddy had always had a steady income, and a substantial one at that. But the sense of coming of age during the Depression haunted her. Even with her grandmother's wealth, the fear and poverty she experienced in Esther's household never left her. She worried a great deal about money.

Another reason was exposure. When Mama was offered a script she didn't particularly like, she would often say, "I'd better go do this damn thing and show my face so they know I'm still alive!" She had a powerful need to keep working. Whether it was a prestigious Broadway play or a cheesy sitcom, Eileen Heckart had to act. And now that her boys were grown, she was experiencing a bit of the empty-nest syndrome. Many times when she wasn't working, she would call Mark, Philip, or me and say, "I was lonely for you and I just wanted to talk for a minute." As happy as she and Daddy were together, her life had changed and she didn't know how to handle it. This gave her all the more reason to return to Hollywood.

Mama never liked California. She would get in and out as fast as possible. She hated the lack of seasons, the traffic, and the fact that she couldn't get away from people outside of show business, no matter how hard she tried. She found the constant sunshine insufferable. Even in February, when it was four degrees in Connecticut, she would wake up after three or four days in L.A., shake her head and exclaim, "There's that damn sun again!"

For her entire career, whenever Mama was on the road, she would go to a local stationery store and buy a cheap wall calendar. She would circle the day she arrived, the day she was leaving, and start a countdown, marking off every day with a big, black X. With all this time on the West Coast, she and Daddy even bought a condo in Toluca Lake for a while, right near Warner Brothers' Studios. Daddy would come and spend long stretches of time with her, but he got just as bored while she was at the studio as he was back in Connecticut when she wasn't there. She tried getting him a laptop, setting up lunch dates with old family friends, even adult classes at the Hollywood YMCA. Nothing gave him more than temporary relief. Jack Yankee was totally lost without Eileen.

Her first regular role on a sitcom was in *Out of the Blue*. Capitalizing on the recent success of the film *Heaven Can Wait*, starring Warren Beatty, the show starred Dixie Carter and a comic named James Brogan. Where the film had great heart, pathos, and a degree of sophistication, the series was downright silly. The plot revolved around an angel who came back to Earth to do good deeds. Heckart played the Boss Angel, who popped in for one or two scenes each week to check up on her employee. Her gimmick was that she wore a different hat every week. One time it would be a bowler, the next a fedora, a beanie, and so on.

The only saving grace for Mama was Dixie Carter. She and Dixie liked each other instantly and they remained friends for many years. When the writing on the show went from bad to worse, the producers started moving the time slot every few weeks. They even tried it on Saturday morning, which infuriated Heckart. "I did NOT sign on to do a goddamn kiddie show!" she said. The fact that James Brogan, who carried the show, was a stand-up comic with very little acting experience didn't help matters any. The producers started firing actors one by one. Ultimately, they replaced everyone except Heckart and Brogan. When Dixie Carter was let go, Mama was livid. "Who do you have to fuck to get fired from this show?" she said to the producers. That week, the wardrobe supervisor came to her. "Eileen," he said, "we thought you might like to wear this as your hat this week." It was a tall, black, pointed witch hat. Mama cracked up. She was the first to admit her behavior had been less than sterling. Two weeks later, the show was cancelled and she hopped on a plane for Connecticut as fast as possible. "One of my biggest fears," she said to me, "is that ABC will run out of summer replacements sometime and show reruns of *Out of the Blue.*"

In 1994, she did two very popular episodes of the sitcom *Love & War*, with Annie Potts and Jay Thomas, playing Thomas's flamboyant mother, a lounge singer who lives in a retirement home in Florida. Her character, Rose Stein, was constantly playing matchmaker to all the characters on the show. There was a scene where Potts (whose character had an on-again-off-again flirtation with Thomas) winds up spending the night on Thomas's sofa. When Rose shows up the next morning, she surmises they have slept together and simply says, "Oh." With a Cheshire Cat smile, Heckart's "Oooohhhhh!" stretched for about ten syllables and twice as many octaves. Once again, this was a brilliant example of the actress spinning gold out of straw. She received her second Emmy out of eight nominations over the course of her career.

Her two favorite series were *Murder One* in 1996 with Anthony La Paglia, and *Annie McGuire* with Mary Tyler Moore in 1998. *Annie McGuire* was what Mama considered "a grown-up sitcom." There was no laugh track and it was shot like a film. She played Mary Tyler Moore's mother and Mary played a local politician starting her life over with a second marriage in middle age. Mama loved the opportunity to work with Mary again. She felt this was a quality show that just couldn't find its audience. She also believed it was some of her best work on television.

She had similar feelings about *Murder One*, which was the most successful of all her series. The show ran for forty-one episodes, though Heckart was only on for one season. It was a police drama produced by Steven Bochco, the highly successful creator of *NYPD Blue*. The plot followed a detective through one case for the entire season. Heckart found the scripts to be taut, sharp, and focused. On the second year of the show, the detective, played by Anthony LaPaglia, had lunch in a restaurant with his acerbic, chain-smoking mother at the end of each episode. She loved working with Steven Bochco and was crazy about LaPaglia, who was also an accomplished stage actor, and starred in a Broadway revival of *A View From the Bridge* the following year.

In 1997, Mama did an episode of the original Ellen Degeneres sitcom, *Ellen*, playing Degeneres's no-nonsense, salty-tongued grandmother. This was shortly before the pioneering "coming out" episode, where Ellen was going to announce herself as a lesbian on national television, creating a huge stir in the entertainment industry and the culture at large. Mama was highly skeptical of this development. While she was liberal in many respects, she was very conservative regarding sexuality and did not feel it was something to be flaunted. Still, she appreciated Degeneres's talent and was eager to do the show.

As Mama was shooting a few weeks before the "coming out" episode was going to air, everyone in Hollywood was speculating about the show's future. "What would it do to the ratings? How would it play in the Heartland? Would America accept a sitcom character they had already come to know and love after she came out of the closet in their own living rooms?"

If this was all the buzz in Tinseltown, it was magnified tenfold on the *Ellen* set. Tensions were high as everyone contemplated whether or not they would still have a job next month.

Ellen Degeneres had great respect for Mama. I spent some time observing on the set and watched how Ellen looked up to her.

Over a lunch break, I heard Ellen say, "Look at that wedding band—will you look at the rocks on that hand?"

Heckart beamed at the attention from one of the younger breed who had the good sense to value her presence.

"So, how many Emmys do you have, Eileen?" Ellen asked.

"Only two," Heckart replied.

"Listen to that!" Ellen said to her director. "Only two!" Mama loved this good-natured razzing.

In one of the scenes, there was a line where Ellen said to her grandmother, "Grammy, you have such a way about you. What's the word I'm looking for? You're such a . . ."

Heckart would do one of her famous deadpan takes and say, "Bitch?"

When they were taping the show in front of a live, studio audience, when Ellen said, "Grammy, you have such a way about you. What's the word I'm looking for? You're such a . . ."

Heckart tripped over her tongue and said, "Butch?"

The studio audience roared with laughter. The director was guffawing so much, he nearly fell off his chair. Ellen turned five shades of red. Mama felt terrible about it and started backpedaling like crazy.

"Honey," she stammered, "I'm sorry, I . . . I . . . I didn't mean it, Ellen! It just slipped out. It was a mistake!"

Of course, that made it seem ten times worse. When I shared this story with Joanna Gleason, the Broadway star of *Into the Woods*, she replied, "Luke, when something just slipped out of your mother's mouth, it was as if she'd taken it to Boston for out of town tryouts for a month!"

Truer words were never spoken.

Directing the Diva

MAMA IN *DRIVING MISS DAISY* AT THE COCONUT GROVE PLAYHOUSE, DIRECTED BY ME.
PHOTO BY JAMES TILTON

WHEN I SAW THE ORIGINAL, Off-Broadway production of Alfred Uhry's *Driving Miss Daisy*, I instantly fell in love with the play. I was moved by its sincerity and the way the audience experienced the lifelong relationship between the Southern spinster and her black chauffeur who came to love one another as best friends. Dana Ivey, who originated the role of Miss Daisy, the crusty matriarch, reminded me so much of Grandma Esther, it was uncanny. As I left the theater at Playwrights Horizons in New York, I vowed to myself, "Someday I am going to direct Mama in this play."

I bought tickets for my parents for Christmas. They loved it as much as I did. Later that year, as it went on to win the Pulitzer Prize for Drama and productions started to spring up everywhere, I kept looking for an opportunity. I contacted Ed Graczyk, the artistic director of Player's Theatre Columbus. I figured if I couldn't sell this in Mama's hometown, something was seriously wrong. Ed jumped at the chance. As we got closer to production, Mama was offered a television series and had to bow out.

I was certain I would lose the directing gig as well, but I didn't. Fortunately, Ed Graczyk was committed to the play and he kept his word to me. I wound up casting an old friend of the family, an actress named Frances Helm, who had been in *Remember Me* with Mama, Bob Stack, and Marian Seldes. Frances was a very elegant cashmere-and-pearls sort of lady, the type of woman who felt naked without her earrings. She was a wonderful Miss Daisy and it was a very respectable regional theater production. But it wasn't Mama.

A few months later, I had another opportunity. Mama had great success in a production of Clifford Odets' *The Flowering Peach* at the Coconut Grove Playhouse in Miami. Arnold Mittelman, the producer, asked Mama if she'd like to come back for the 1990 season and if there were any role in particular she'd like to do.

She replied, "Well, Luke's been bellyaching to direct me in *Miss Daisy*. Would you consider that or are your audiences sick of it?"

Arnold was delighted.

The first issue we had to overcome was what I would call her. As the director, it didn't exactly seem appropriate to say, "Mama, will you please cross stage left?"

We decided I would call her Eileen in rehearsals. Even though everyone in the company was well aware of our relationship, we didn't want this to seem like a totally incestuous production.

My friends cautioned me.

"Luke," my best friend Joanne said, "are you *sure* you know what you are getting yourself into? Your mother can be pretty tough, especially on you."

"She's tough because she's demanding about her work," I said. "She's a consummate professional. Besides, having a chance to boss my mother around will be better than four years of psychotherapy."

At the read-through, as we all assembled, Arnold said a few words as producer and then gave me the floor. Miss Heckart had no interest in hearing either the director's or designer's concepts for the show. She just wanted to play the part.

Every few minutes, she would look at me anxiously and say, "Read? Shall we read now?"

She nodded her head and flashed a forced smile at me, as if to say, "Let's get on with it!"

This wasn't so much about me as it was influenced by her last experience at Coconut Grove with the famous director Robert Lewis.

"Honey," she said, "on the first day of rehearsal for *The Flowering Peach*, Bobby Lewis sat there and read the whole script to us himself, acting out all the parts just the way he wanted us to play them. Talk about an exercise in self-indulgence!"

Even though I assured her I had no intention of doing this, she was still mistrustful. Every few minutes, she looked at me like a puppy that needed to pee and said, "Read? Read?"

I would reply, "Not just yet, Eileen. We have a few other bits of business we must attend to first."

She was trying to be deferential, but clearly she was not enjoying it. We finally read through the script and I could see how marvelous she was going to be as Miss Daisy.

After lunch, when we reconvened to start blocking the play, she walked into the rehearsal studio with great intent.

"Now listen," Miss Heckart said. "We have to start by setting a few ground rules here."

"All right, Eileen," I replied.

"First of all, there's no smoking in this effing building, so we need to have a cigarette break every half hour. I want a lunch break at twelve-thirty sharp, I want fresh orange juice in the fridge in the green room . . ."

As the litany continued, I said to myself, "You've watched Daddy play this game for years. Pick your battles carefully. Capitulate on all the small points and then, when something really matters to you, you've got the ammunition to stick it to her and win!"

When she was finally done, I said, "OK, Eileen, I don't see any problem with that."

The stage managers were watching me like a hawk to see how I handled her, both as Eileen Heckart and as my mother. Thank God I had the advantage of having directed a successful production of the play before, so I understood how to make it work, where the laughs were, and the arc of each scene.

On the second day of rehearsal, I did something no director should ever do. I figured since Frances Helm was a friend of Mama's, it was fine to hold up her performance in Columbus as an example. I did it several times over the course of the day. I was underestimating my new star's ego.

"You know, Eileen," I said, twirling my pencil, "when I directed Frances in the role, during this scene, she did this wonderful bit of business with a hat pin . . ."

Heckart wiped a bit of orange-juice pulp off her lip with a paper napkin and crumpled it into a tight ball as she spoke.

"You've mentioned that several times now. In the first place, I'm not a hat-pin kind of actress. In the second place, if you think Frances was so fucking wonderful in the part, why don't you just fire me and hire her!"

"I'm sorry, Eileen," I replied, looking at the floor. "I will never mention Frances *or* the hat pin again."

"Thank you so much!" she said. "I'm taking a ten-minute break."

For the next two days, she challenged everything I asked her to do. If I wanted her to cross left, she'd rather go stage right. If I asked her to sit, she preferred to stand.

At first, I let each of those moments cut me to the quick without ever showing it. I'd wanted this experience more than anything and I had fought for three years to make it happen. Now I felt not like a director but a useless, incompetent traffic cop.

By the fourth day of rehearsal, I was at the end of my rope. As I asked her to move towards the window, she glowered at me and delivered one of her now customary remarks. "You want me to do *what*?!"

This time, I chose a new response. I felt like I was channeling my mentor, Hal Prince. Back when I was one of the production assistants on *Grind*, I was awed by the way Hal handled people, especially actors. He was charming, affable, and yet had an iron fist in a velvet glove. I had kept in touch with him and I had always considered him a guiding force in my career. If there was ever a moment to call on some of his strength, this was it.

I perched my eyeglasses on the top if my head and bellowed, "Excuse me, Miss Heckart! I am your director and I want you to at least TRY IT before you say 'No!'"

"Well, I don't know what the hell his problem is!" the actress muttered under her breath. She had seen how far she could push and I pushed back. I had drawn a line in the sand and I let the diva know when she crossed it.

Years later, I learned that evening she had called our dear family friend Ken Lewis in New York.

"How's it going down there?" Ken asked.

"It's pretty rough," she said. "I'm so afraid Luke's not going to be a good director."

"Well, Eileen," Ken asked. "Are you giving yourself a chance to find out or are you just assuming he's not any good?"

There was a pause on the other end of the phone while she considered this.

"I guess I'm assuming," she said.

"Well, that's not very fair to either one of you, is it? Give him a chance to show you what he's got. You've certainly worked with enough bad directors over the years that if he's no good, you'll adjust and make it work for yourself and the audience. But if you let him, Luke just might surprise you."

After that, our only disagreements were about where to have dinner. Maybe this was going to be better than four years of psychotherapy after all.

After the first preview performance, she called Ken again.

"Honey," she said, "thanks for what you said to me a few weeks ago. Ken, he's really good. I'm not just saying that because he's my kid. He's *really good.*"

"And isn't it nice to know that," Ken asked, "both as an actress and a mother?"

"Oh yeah," she said.

Ken told me this story about a year ago. It is more than fifteen years since I directed her in *Driving Miss Daisy* and I had no idea.

One day, a few years after the production, I said to her, "You were a brilliant Miss Daisy."

"Well," she said, "I had a good script . . . and a good cast . . . and good designers . . . and we played in a good theater."

Did it simply not occur to her to say, "and a good director" or was it intentional? Should I have added that phrase, or simply asked her? I think I was still too afraid the answer might be one I didn't want to hear. Sometimes I wondered if she was following the Victorian principle that you mustn't compliment your children or they'll get a big head. I had to resign myself to the fact that she was proud of me, even though I might never hear the words.

On opening night I sat in the audience, watching my mother get a standing ovation as Miss Daisy in the production I had directed. It was a thrill that can never be repeated. In directing my mother as Daisy Wertham, I had made a dream of mine come true. After the success of *Miss Daisy*, I directed several more shows over the years at the Coconut Grove Playhouse and Arnold Mittelman became a respected colleague.

Newspaper critic Charles Steinmetz in the *Tropical Times* said, "Miss Heckart soft-pedals Daisy's underlying kind spirit so that when it peeks through the cracks in the tough exterior, it positively glows. Under Luke Yankee's direction, *Driving Miss Daisy* meanders from episode to vignette, deliberately, steadily, not hurrying, at last arriving at its touching conclusion."

Syndicated columnist Buddy Clarke said, "Eileen Heckart is outstanding. It is a joy to watch her . . . . The staging by director Luke Yankee is superb."*

The legendary director, George Abbott, was now over one hundred years old. He and Mama had kept in touch since doing *In Any Language* with Uta Hagen more than forty years ago, but only in a superficial way. The old man tottered up to her at the opening-night party and said, "No one should ever play it but you, Heckie."

The real revelation to me was when I came back to see *Miss Daisy* at the end of the run. Mama said to me beforehand, "I'm playing some things a little differently. I hope you don't mind."

If what she had done before was good, this was extraordinary. The actress had taken my direction and made it completely her own. The choices were more interesting and the moments more fulfilled. There is a scene in the play where Hoke tells Miss Daisy about the time as a boy he witnessed the lynching of a black man. Daisy, hiding her fear, replies, "Why did you tell me that?" Mama had played it originally with petulant annoyance covering the fear. Now, she choked back the tears and looked away as she said the line in a shaky, childlike voice. It was downright chilling.

---

* Courtesy of Buddy Clarke. Reprinted with permission

Now she *was* Miss Daisy in every sense of the word. I knew I could take very little credit for it, if any. I said to myself, "This is what makes Eileen Heckart such a fine actress." Her performance was subtle and delicate and unlike any Miss Daisy I have seen before or since. Over the course of a four-week run, she had found new ways to tell the tale, to connect with the character and to make it fuller and richer than I had ever imagined possible. Sure, Eileen Heckart was tough as nails and not always easy on her director. But the result made it worth every second.

The Leader of the Band

ONE OF MY FAVORITE PHOTOS OF MY DADDY—WITH OUR DOG, MORGAN

THE SUN WAS BRIGHT THAT DAY. It was late February and unseasonably warm, even for Los Angeles. I opened all the windows and let the whiteness of the day wash over me. Large shafts of blinding light crossed my desk.

It was February 1996. I had lived in L.A. for about two years now. Mama and Daddy had also moved, selling our childhood home in New Canaan and relocating to a condo complex in Norwalk, the next town over. Daddy was relieved not to have to deal with the endless raking and weeding anymore. The move to L.A. suited me. I was getting directing work and I'd even been lucky enough to find my life partner, a considerate, loving man named Don Hill. Don was one of the most respected theater people on the West Coast, having worked as a production manager at the Los Angeles Theatre Center and the Geffen Playhouse, associate producer at the Long Beach Civic Light Opera, and was soon to become one of the chief negotiators for the West Coast division of Actor's Equity Association. There was a gentleness in him I had only seen in one other man in my life before or since.

When I called my mother to tell her about him, I said, "Mama, I've found my Jack Yankee."

"Have you really, darling? Is he that special?"

"Yes, he really is."

"Well, that's just wonderful."

There was never a doubt in my mind that Don was my life partner. He had come for Christmas and my parents had been wonderful to him, not only because they genuinely liked him, but because they saw how good he was to me. Over the years, Mama and Daddy had come to terms with my sexual orientation. I was very grateful for that.

This particular Sunday, Don had gotten up early to go to a Theatre L.A. board retreat. Afterwards, he was stage managing his final performance of *The Student Prince* for the San Gabriel Civic Light Opera. I wasn't particularly fond of the show and called it *The Stupid Prince*, but they were treating him like gold, so what did it matter?

I had this beautiful, lazy Sunday all to myself. Strangely, I didn't feel like talking to anyone. I was looking forward to a quiet, reflective "Luke" day. I had recently returned from directing a successful production of A.R. Gurney's two-character play, *Love Letters*, in Sacramento with different celebrity actors at every performance. Since the play is a collection of letters, it is often staged for a long run with different actors every week. My production had a different cast every day. Some were TV personalities who weren't good stage actors, but I'd had a ball and it was a prestigious gig. I wrote a letter I was going to send out with some reviews to other producers and theater companies, maybe even a friend or two who wanted to know what I was up to these days. I ended the letter with "I just wanted to share my joy." I wonder in retrospect if the gods saw this as hubris.

After I went to Office Depot and photocopied the letter and the reviews, I decided to take advantage of the glorious day and go for a swim at the gym. I love to think and reflect while I am gliding through a pool. Water is incredibly healing and nurturing to me. Maybe that's part of being an Aquarian.

As I swam, I thought about a session I'd had the day before with Alima, a psychic healer. She'd made many wonderful predictions about my future, but she said one thing that was vexing me.

She said, "You're about to go through a chasm, but you'll come out on the other side."

What could she have possibly meant by that? The more I thought about it, the more annoyed I became, so I decided to dismiss it.

The sunlight was waning now. Earlier, it lit up my desk in such a way that I couldn't see anything on it very clearly, including the blinking light on my answering machine. Now I saw the infared sensor flickering like a beacon. Was it blinking faster than usual? I could tell there were several messages. I wondered how I could have gotten so many calls in such a short period of time.

The first message had come early that morning, before I was even awake. I hadn't heard the phone.

"Luke, it's Mark. Give me a call at Mom's house at soon as you get this."

Why would my brother have called so early on a Sunday? There were two hang-ups, then the next message.

"It's Mama. Call home."

"Oh shit," I thought, "something is really wrong."

Mark answered the phone. "Mark, I am so sorry. I didn't see the light on my answering machine until now. What's up?

"Luke, Dad passed away today."

It felt as if my brother had shoved his foot through the phone and kicked me in the stomach with a pointy cowboy boot. I couldn't get my breath. My body felt both heavy and weightless. I looked out at the setting sun over the Hollywood sign. Daddy had been so thrilled that I had such a view. The sunlight magnified the dust on the bookcase—the one we had built together for my first New York apartment. It wasn't possible. Not Daddy. Not my dear, sweet, gentle Papa, the glue who held the family together. Out of the corner of my eye, I saw my old CD player. I'd upgraded to a new model and I'd asked him two days ago if he wanted the old one. He was delighted at the offer since he didn't have one at all. It was all boxed up and sitting at my feet. Now, it had nowhere to go.

That morning, Daddy had gone for his daily walk while Mama fixed his eggs. He put on his faded, heather-gray sweatsuit with his black, knit stocking cap and gloves. The crisp, biting chill of winter was still present in the Connecticut air. Daddy had done these morning walks for years, ever since the doctor had diagnosed him as having an irregular heartbeat. He'd had one or two minor health warnings and a few heart fibrillations, but nothing too serious.

Walking every day kept him regulated and gave him an opportunity to say hello to the neighborhood dogs. While many of them greeted him with territorial yaps, once they realized it was him, they came out with their tails wagging. He often kept Milk Bones in the pocket of his sweatpants to dole out along the way. Some of the dogs even strolled with him for a few blocks. My Papa, the Pied Piper of Norwalk.

About twenty minutes later, Mama was preparing breakfast while Charles Kuralt's *Sunday Morning* show blared in the background. She looked out of the bay window in the kitchen and saw Daddy round the bend on Foxboro Drive. As he returned towards the house at the end of the cul-de-sac, she put the eggs on the stove and popped the bread down in the toaster. Glancing back toward the driveway, she saw Daddy put his hand to his head and collapse onto the pavement, folding like a card table.

"Jack!" she screamed, running outside in her slippers. She leaned over his body, shaking him a few times, but he didn't respond. She immediately flew into the house and called Mark.

"It's Jack," she shouted. "Come quick!"

"I'll be right there," he said. "Call 911."

As she dialed 911 and explained the situation, the operator told her that someone had already called and the EMT's were on their way. She looked outside and there was a neighbor, a middle-aged, African-American gentleman who had looked out his window the moment Daddy fell. I wish I knew his name, for he was truly a guardian angel. I'll call him Robert. When Mama ran back outside, Robert had taken a pillow, placed it under Daddy's head and covered him with a blanket.

In a matter of seconds, Mark's car was barreling up the hill. Thank God he lived less than seven minutes away. When he saw Mama crouched over Daddy's body in the middle of the quiet road, he slammed on his brakes, jumped out of the car, and started pounding on Daddy's chest. Robert came over and put his jacket over Mama's shoulders and gently moved her aside.

"C'mon Dad! Come back! Come back, Dad!" Mark spoke breathlessly as he tried to perform CPR on the lifeless body. Mama was sobbing as Robert was patting her hand and rubbing her shoulders, all eyes transfixed for any sign of movement from Jack. None came.

The paramedics arrived and after a few more advanced techniques with no response, they scooped Daddy up and took him to the hospital. Mama rode in the ambulance with Mark following close behind in his beaten-up, red Camaro. The two of them were in the waiting room less than twenty minutes when the doctor on call came out, shaking his head. Daddy had been DOA—Dead On Arrival. He had passed the minute he hit the ground. The doctors diagnosed it as a massive heart attack.

As they walked quietly to the car, Mark noticed a man leading his very pregnant wife into the E.R. "She's going into labor!" the man shouted to the admitting nurse.

Mama and Mark got into his car. Mama turned to him and put a cigarette to her lips. Her hands shook as she dug in her purse for her lighter.

"I'm giving you Jack's Volvo," she said. "This car is a piece of shit!"

"Whatever you say, Ma," Mark said, handing her his lighter.

Mama and Daddy had been married for fifty-three years. Sure, he was slowing down and his hearing was going, but to be gone so soon? He was seventy-six. Wasn't he supposed to live forever? How would Mama get on without him? How would any of us?

Back in L.A., I hated my Sunday to myself. I hated the sunlight for masking the light on the answering machine, I hated Don for stage managing this stupid operetta which meant I couldn't reach him for another two hours, I hated that I lived across the country from my family, and most all, I hated Mark for telling me this terrible lie.

I shoved my front teeth into my bottom lip to stave off the tears.

"Mark, what should I do?"

"How soon can you get here?" he said.

"I'll call the airport right away. How's Mama? Can I talk to her?"

"She's too upset to come to the phone right now. She'll call in a little while."

"Oh my God, Mark. I am so sorry."

"Yeah, me too. See about the flights and get back to me. I'll stay off the phone for a few minutes."

A jumble of emotions descended upon me as I dialed American Airlines, including guilt that I hadn't gotten the message sooner and remorse that I hadn't had a chance to say goodbye to my beloved Papa. My brain was racing, trying to remember if our last conversation had been a happy one or not. Then I recalled our discussion about the CD player. He'd seemed pleased about that. At least our last communication was positive.

I booked my ticket for the following afternoon and waited for Don to phone me. He was in the midst of calling the show, but I knew he'd telephone the moment the curtain came down. It occurred to me that if I had gotten the calls from the family earlier, I would have been home alone all day. Maybe the sunlight on the answering machine was God's way of protecting me.

I pondered the lyrics of that Dan Fogelberg song about his own father's passing, "The Leader of the Band." This was my leader, the man who had always been there to take care of me, who loved me unconditionally. It took me years to understand his quietness. I related more to Mama. She was flashy, theatrical, and vociferous. She expressed her emotions easily and tended to wear her heart on her sleeve. Dad was the opposite. He was quiet, pensive and, at times, seemingly unemotional. It took me a long time to realize that his still waters ran deep. Men of his generation weren't raised to express emotions, but that certainly didn't mean he didn't have them. Until my early twenties, I often interpreted his lack of response as disinterest, so I didn't share my feelings openly with him. I had to meet him on his terms. I didn't always give him the chance he deserved.

Years after I came out, he was having lunch in L.A. with Maree Cheatham, Mama's understudy from *Ladies at the Alamo*, who was now one of my closest friends. She said, "So Jack, are you okay now about Luke's sexuality or is it still difficult for you?"

Daddy got a guilty look as he stared out into space, absentmindedly twirling the pasta on his fork. "If only I'd played more ball with him," he said.

When Maree recounted this to me, I was amused by his innocence and naiveté, thinking that my sexual orientation could have been altered by tossing a softball around the backyard. I was also moved by the fact that he felt somehow responsible. No wonder he tried so hard to get me to lock my knees and stand up straight when he was taking pictures of me in my kilt as a little boy. He felt that if he'd only been a better parent, things would have turned out differently. Even though

I'd said it frequently, at this moment, I would have given anything to have been able to tell him once more how much I loved him.

I arrived in Connecticut the next day. We were able to arrange the service for the following week. Mama asked me to deliver the eulogy. Don generously rearranged his work schedule and came to support me. He'd only met Daddy a few times, but they were very fond of one another and understood each other as men who stepped aside to let their spouses be in the spotlight. Don and I took over many of the responsibilities of planning the actual service. After all, it wasn't that different from producing a show, which was what we did for a living.

Up in the guest room, I was putting together a large photo collage of Daddy to place in the vestibule of the church, when Kelly, my seven-year-old niece, wandered in. She didn't understand why no one would play with her and why all the grown-ups looked so sad. Her mother, Patti, was Mark's wife. Patti had explained to her that her "Pop-pop" had gone to Heaven, but she had no context for death at that age. Her older sister, Tara, Mark's stepdaughter, was very nurturing with Kelly. She'd had a long talk with her baby sister as well, but didn't know if it had sunk in. Kelly kept trying to get me to stop what I was doing to play with her. Usually, she and I had a great rapport, but I wasn't in the mood to indulge her.

"Kelly," I said, as I continued arranging the photos, "I'm sorry but I cannot play with you today. It has nothing to do with you. I don't have a Daddy anymore and I'm really sad about it."

"Sometimes I think it's my fault," she said.

"What do you mean, sweetie?" I asked.

"Sometimes, when I came over, I used to wish it would be just Gram and me and not Gram and Pop-pop."

"Kelly," I said, "You mustn't blame yourself. We all wish things like that some-times. But we don't really mean it. Your Pop-pop was old and he had a weak heart. It was his time to go."

Kelly thought about what I said, but she didn't seem convinced. I know it's typical for children to blame themselves in a situation like this, to feel somehow responsible. Still, I was moved by her simple expression of grief.

On the day of the funeral, the family sat in the front row of the tiny country church at the Benedictine Grange. This was a rustic house of worship in the middle of the woods with rough-hewn wooden benches and no icons, save for a hand-carved crucifix. The only added ornamentations on the altar for the day were a picture of Daddy in a silver frame and a single, yellow rose in a bud vase beside it. Father Giuliani, the priest, was an old friend of Mama's and we loved his sermons as well as the simple surroundings. One of the elements that attracted her to the Catholic Church in the first place was the theatricality, the pomp and circumstance of the swinging incense balls, the colorful robes, the dramatic stark-ness of the nuns. Now, she eschewed all of that for something more direct.

Mama sat there waiting for the service to begin, wearing a full-length black mink coat and a large pair of dark glasses. They were the type of glasses that are worn by cataract sufferers—extremely large with wraparound pieces on the sides. They were almost the size of skiers' goggles. Mama held a rosary and the small area of her face that wasn't hidden by the large glasses seemed to have no expression whatsoever. If there was ever a stronger subliminal message of "leave me alone and don't even try to speak to me," I haven't seen it.

As the service began, Kelly wormed her way in and sat right next to Mama. Patti tried to move her, but Mama said, "It's all right, Patti. She's fine."

Still, Patti watched her youngest daughter closely for any squirming or other signs of disruption. She was a wonderful mother as well as a respectful daughter-in-law and she wasn't going to let anything disrupt this day. Philip, his girlfriend Adrienne, Tara, Mark, Don, and I filled the front pew of the church.

As I delivered the eulogy, I talked about Daddy's life, ending with directing him in *The Diviners* and how the tears sat on his cheeks when I told him how good he was on opening night. By the time I finished, I was sobbing uncontrollably and so was everyone else in the church.

After I'd sat down, while a reflective hymn was being played, Kelly grasped the enormity of it all. A look of terror crossed her tiny face. She looked up at Mama and yelled, "Gram! I want him to come back!"

"I know, darling," Mama said, wrapping her arms around the hysterical child, who was bawling into the side of her grandmother's mink coat. The moment summed up how we were all feeling.

I stayed another five days and cooked for Mama. She had little appetite, but she seemed to like my turkey meatloaf, so I made two extra and put them in the freezer for her. When I visited her four months later, I noticed they were still there.

"Mama," I asked, "how come you never ate the turkey meatloaf I made for you?"

"I don't like them. I only like my meatloaf with ground beef," she said.

"But when I made one for you after Daddy died, you said you thought it was so tasty."

"Well, what was I gonna say?" she asked. "Your father had just died."

On the last day of my stay, I stood on the landing waiting with my suitcases as the horn honked. The driver had come to take me to JFK. This was harder than anytime I had ever left before, because now Mama was going to be alone. Of course, Mark and Philip were both nearby and they'd be over regularly, but she was going to be living alone for the first time in fifty-three years—and for the rest of her life.

"I have to go," I said.

"I know you do."

"I'll call you as soon as I get home."

"That'd be nice."

I hugged her as tightly as I could. We were both trying to keep from crying again.

"I love you, Mama."

"I love you, too."

"I'll be back as soon as I can," I said.

"I know," she said. "I'll be all right."

I didn't believe her. As she stood there in the kitchen doorway watching me drive off, we stared at each other for a long time. Her posture was very straight and she looked at me with an expression I'd never seen before. Was it grief? Was it fear? I wanted to jump out of the moving car and throw my arms around her, saying, "Mama, I'll never leave you! I'll move back home so you won't be alone, ever!"

The driver started yammering well-intentioned words of condolence and I responded appropriately, but I didn't hear a word he said. I stared out of the car window at Mama as she got smaller and smaller until she disappeared. I had never seen her look so lost.

New Beginnings

MY FAVORITE PHOTO OF MAMA—TAKEN AT THE WILLIAM INGE THEATRE FESTIVAL.
NOTE THE "NO LOITERING" SIGN BEHIND HER. COURTESY OF THE WILLIAM INGE
THEATRE FESTIVAL

ONE DAY, MARK SAID TO ME on the telephone, "Luke, do you know what the
Hemlock Society is?"

"No, why?"

"Mom's been talking to them a lot and sending for all sorts of literature.
It's making me nervous. I think it has to do with assisted suicide."

After Daddy died, for a while Mama simply didn't want to go on. Her
wonderful agent at the time, David Kalodner, had become a good friend and

he offered her roles in a number of good television scripts and even a play or
two, but she turned them all down. She was so despondent, she had contacted
the Hemlock Society, an organization for terminally ill people who wish to
take their own lives. Named for Socrates' method of suicide (he had poisoned
himself by drinking hemlock), the organization provided people with information on how to end it all. They were, of course, not condoning such an act, but
merely providing resource information. They sent her numerous books and
pamphlets on how to take one's own life. I didn't waste any time confronting
her about it.

"I'd been saving my leftover prescription drugs for quite some time," she said.
"And I've read all of the Hemlock Society pamphlets very carefully. Guns in the
mouth are too messy. Besides, I don't have a steady hand. My head in the gas oven
was a thought, until I remembered I have an electric range. I seriously considered
carbon-monoxide poisoning in the car. I was going to take a handful of Percodan
and start up the Mercedes with the garage door closed, but I was afraid Mark
would find me. I couldn't dump that on him."

As she was telling me this in a matter-of-fact way, her voice had a strange
directness to it. I knew she was serious. My stomach started churning. I'd just
lost one parent three months ago and I wasn't ready to lose another. I had to act
quickly.

I contacted a friend of a friend, Cheryl Fluehr, who was the entertainment
director at Holland America Cruise Lines. I pitched the idea that I would interview Mama about her career and show video clips from her films and television
shows, followed by a question-and-answer session with the audience. We, in turn,
would get a nice stipend and a free cruise anywhere in the world. Cheryl loved the
idea. Now I just had to convince Mama.

At first, she was unresponsive. The more I told her about these exotic itineraries
and places she'd never seen, the more intrigued she became. I said what a great
opportunity it would be for us to share. Still heartbroken over the loss of Daddy,
she responded out of grief and anger.

"So, you need me to be your friggin' meal ticket, is that it?" she asked.

"If you want to look at it that way," I replied, "you go right ahead. But it would
get you out of the house, back into the real world, and keep your mind off the
goddamn Hemlock Society for a few days!"

We did three two-week trips over the next year and a half: Juneau to Tokyo,
Sydney to Hong Kong, and Bombay to Athens. We had a marvelous time and
had experiences we would never have shared otherwise. We did two lectures
per cruise and the rest of the time we were free to do as we pleased as VIP
passengers.

I'd always known that Mama didn't like interviews, but I'd never really experienced it first hand. As we waited backstage while the cruise director introduced
us, she would shake, sweat, and chain-smoke.

"God, I hate this!" she said.

"What's the problem, Mama? You know exactly what I'm going to ask. You've told these stories a hundred times. After the film clips, first you'll talk about the Oscars, then Marilyn, then Dietrich . . ."

"I'd rather be dead!" she said.

"Just be yourself, Mama."

"That's what I'm afraid of!"

This made no sense to me. She could tell these stories in her sleep. She'd told each of them a thousand times in the living room or the kitchen or some green room backstage. If she forgot anything, I could prompt her. And it wasn't exactly

MAMA AND ME IN HONG KONG ON OUR SECOND LECTURE CRUISE

like I was Mike Wallace or Barbara Walters. There would be no embarrassing questions. It was just her son—and it was all rehearsed. Still, to go out onstage without the mask of a character terrified her.

Of course, once we got in front of an audience, she was perfectly fine. The crowds loved her and her stories, and we always received a standing ovation.

Once we left the stage, I said, "See? They stood for you."

"What the hell does that mean?" she answered, lighting a cigarette. "Audiences stand for everything these days. They stood for those terrible jugglers last night. Besides, they just wanted to get to lunch sooner."

There were times over dinner or in port where she would get particularly lonely for my father. She would look out the porthole as we were sailing past some stunning island and with a wistful look in her eye, she'd say, "Jack would have loved this so!"

Once or twice she left the dining room in tears because she was so overcome with emotion. While it wasn't always easy, I gave her the space she needed to mourn. That was part of my responsibility as her son. There were times I felt like saying, "I miss him too, you know. He was my father. You're not the only one in grief mode here." But her grief was still so large, there wasn't much room for mine—at least not when we were together.

My favorite cruise ship story about Mama occurred in 1998 on formal night in the middle of the Pacific Ocean. The news about the affair between Bill Clinton and Monica Lewinsky was just hitting the airwaves. Often, due to poor satellite transmission, the news one gets on a cruise ship is sporadic at best, so not all the passengers were aware of the political scandal that had rocked everyone's world back in the States.

We were in the formal dining room on the *M.S. Rotterdam.* I was in my tux and Mama was in an elegant, teal Shantung silk suit. We sat across from Judith McNaught, the successful romance novelist who was lecturing on the ship. Judith, a very elegant woman, was dressed in a silver strapless gown. As the string quartet was playing a Bach cantata and the waiter served the soup, Judith sipped her Dubonnet.

"So tell me, Eileen," Judith said. "I haven't really been following this story. What exactly do they claim this woman has done with President Clinton?"

Taking a large bite of a breadstick, Mama said loudly, "Oh, for God's sake, Judith! She was giving him *blow jobs!*"

At that moment, I blew my vichyssoise across the table and started choking as I gasped for breath. Mama looked at me disdainfully and handed me her water.

"What?" she said. "You think your mother doesn't know what a *blow job* is?"

The two words were so incongruous in this setting, they seemed to turn the dining room into an echo chamber.

"Yes, Mother," I said, wiping the soup off my lapel. "I'm sure you do."

"Well, believe me, I know what a *blow job* is!"

At that moment, one of the blue-rinsed cruise-ship ladies at the next table turned to her husband and whispered, "Herbert, isn't that Eileen Heckart talking about blow jobs?"

Another thing kept Mama going in her later years was the William Inge Theatre Festival. This was a theater conference honoring great American playwrights in Inge's hometown of Independence, Kansas. The inventive and persistent founders of this annual event got playwrights of international stature to come to this rural town in a remote part of Kansas to honor William Inge and to be feted themselves. Because of Mama's connection with Inge, she became a fixture at the festival. It was one of the highlights of her year.

When my father died, the morning before I left to return to Los Angeles, she suggested that I go through Daddy's closet and take whatever clothes I wanted. Daddy and I were pretty much the same size and there were many elegant shirts and brightly colored sweaters Mama had bought to try and "jazz up his wardrobe" which he'd worn once, if at all. I put on a fashion show for her, trying on expensive jackets, slacks, and blazers. She was thrilled to see these clothes going to good use. After I was finished, we both sat on the bed in silence next to the large pile of clothes I was taking to California. The emptiness in the room was palpable. I was leaving in about an hour and we were both trying to avoid the inevitable goodbye.

"You know," I said, "I've been racking my brain trying to think of other ways for us to spend time together and I had a thought."

"What's that?" she said.

"Well, you always talk so excitedly about that William Inge Festival. Since it's coming up in a few months, what if I were to pay my own way and meet you out there in Kansas?"

"The hell you'll pay your own way!" she said. "We'll get you on a panel or two. They'd be damned lucky to have you. I'll write them a letter next week."

It was the first time I saw Mama sparkle since Daddy had died. However fleeting it may have been, it promised a moment of hope for the future.

We met in Kansas the following April—and for a number of years thereafter. I have been on the advisory board of the William Inge Theatre Festival ever since and I have done ten years' worth of workshops, readings, panels, and classes with some of the most renowned theater professionals in America. Over the years, I have observed local high-school and college drama teachers from Oklahoma City and Wichita rubbing elbows with Neil Simon, Bernadette Peters, and Stephen Sondheim, among others. It has become one of the highlights of my year, as it was for Mama.

A few months after the first cruise, Davis Kalodner from William Morris called.

"Now Eileen," he said, "I have an offer for you. It's a small, recurring role in a new series. It shoots in New York, one day a month. Better still, it's being produced by Steven Bochco, who is one of the hottest producers on TV. I want you to think about this one very carefully before you say 'no.'"

Nearly eight months after Daddy had died, it was *Murder One* that got her back in the saddle. Later that year, she did the film *The First Wives Club*, playing Diane Keaton's mother. The film starred Keaton, Bette Midler, and reunited her with her beloved Goldie Hawn. Even though Heckart had a relatively small supporting role, this film garnered so much attention, she received many other film offers, all of which she turned down. Mama was seventy-seven. She was in her sunset years and slowing down. She could afford to be very selective about what projects she took on. Who would have thought that one of her greatest triumphs was yet to come?

Back in the Spotlight

THE CAST OF *THE WAVERLY GALLERY.* PHOTO BY CAROL ROSEGG. REPRINTED WITH PERMISSION.

"Darling, I've been offered a *wonnnderful* part in a new play," my mother said into the phone.

"Really, Mama?" I hadn't heard her sound this excited about anything in a long time. "That's great!"

"In fact," she continued, "it may be the best part I've ever been offered."

"My God," I replied, "now *that's* saying something."

"So, it's going to be my swan song. It will be the last thing I ever do onstage."

I'd never heard her utter these words and they filled me with longing and sadness. Still, the practical side of me leapt to the fore. "Mama, are you sure you're up to eight shows a week again?"

"They've agreed that I don't have to play matinees. I couldn't anyway, this part's too hard."

The play was *The Waverly Gallery* by Kenneth Lonergan. He was a very hot writer at the time, having had great success with an Off-Broadway play called *This is Our Youth* the year before. In addition, he had just written and directed his first independent feature, a sharp and poignant film called *You Can Count On Me*, which would put its two stars, Laura Linney and Mark Ruffalo, on the map. *Waverly* was about Lonergan's grandmother as he watched her descend into the madness of Alzheimer's disease and the devastating effect it had on him and his family. It was a powerful and disturbing play. The leading role of Gladys Green was a tour de force. Written the way an Alzheimer's patient speaks, Gladys would have three pages of nonsense monologues at any given time. In the wrong hands, the role of Gladys could be an actor's worst nightmare. In the right hands, it could be a vulnerable, funny, pathetic, and heart-wrenching bit of brilliance.

They were to try out the play for a short run at the Williamstown Theatre Festival in Massachusetts and if it was successful there, they would bring it in to an Off-Broadway theater for a limited run. The rest of the cast included Josh Hamilton, Maureen Anderman, Mark Blum, and Anthony Arkin. Scott Ellis was set to direct.

When Mama started to learn the role of Gladys Green, she was fraught with terror. At eighty-one, she didn't memorize as quickly as she used to and this was the most difficult script she'd ever had in her life. Mark and Philip cued her at every opportunity. I even flew home for a week and took a stab at it. Because of work commitments in Los Angeles, I wasn't going to be able to see the Williamstown run, but I got daily reports from the diva herself. She seemed very dissatisfied with her work, much more than in the past. Perhaps it was because she knew the potential of this role and didn't feel she was meeting it under the constraints of a two-week rehearsal schedule. Still, audiences were deeply moved by her portrayal and there was lots of buzz surrounding the play for the fall theater season in New York. Chances were good it was going to have an Off-Broadway transfer.

Mama was suffering from macular degeneration at this point, which meant her vision was severely limited and getting worse all the time. She could barely see the other actors across the stage. She also had chronic emphysema, brought on by all those years of a two-to-three-pack-a-day habit. And she was performing the most difficult role of her career.

I don't know what places Mama had to delve into in order find Gladys Green, but she did it beautifully. She had witnessed many friends go through the devastating effects of Alzheimer's disease and she drew upon those experiences. She even went to a nursing home to observe some afflicted men and women, but found it too disturbing. At her advanced age, she wondered if she might still succumb to the disease herself. The thought was overwhelming to her.

Mama's doctor said, "Eileen, if you were going to get Alzheimer's, chances are we would have seen the signs long before now. I really don't think this is something you need to worry about."

This fear, combined with the difficulty of the role, had a terrible effect on her. Just before the final week in Williamstown, David Kalodner called me. He was very upset. It seems Mama had a severe attack of nerves and was leaving Williamstown within one hour. As her agent, David called to see if there was anything I could do, and if I could possibly talk her out of it. The final five performances were sold out and there were no understudies.

I immediately called her hotel room. She was hysterical.

"Mama, what's wrong?"

"I was up until one-thirty last night studying my script. I woke up this morning, and I couldn't remember a single line—not one word!"

She spoke rapidly, without breathing.

"Now, Mama," I said. "It sounds like you're having a panic attack. Why don't you just get back into bed and take the day off?"

"No!" she screamed. "I'm leaving. The car is coming for me in an hour. I've never felt like this before."

"Why don't you try to sleep it off? Maybe you'll feel better in the morning."

"No," she screamed again. "It's not like that. I'm leaving!"

Since she wouldn't listen to reason, I got angry.

"Look," I shouted, "if you do this, you are committing career suicide! It will be all over Shubert Alley in a matter of hours that Eileen Heckart can't cut it anymore! Is that the way you want to end your career?"

I'd never spoken to her like that before. I was out of ideas and out of time so my last, best hope was tough love. It backfired. She burst into tears.

"I'm scared! And I'm going home!"

"Okay, Mama," I said. "I'm sorry. Will you call me when you get home?"

"Ye . . . yes . . . ," she choked through muffled cries as she hung up the phone.

I'd really blown it. She needed support and I gave her anger. Would I ever forgive myself?

I called David Kalodner and told him it was a lost cause. He was deeply concerned for my mother. Later that afternoon, Scott Ellis called me. Scott was a buddy of mine and, as the director of *The Waverly Gallery*, he wondered if his leading lady would ever get back on the horse.

"Luke," he asked, "what's your honest opinion? Do you think she'll ever do the play again?"

"Scott," I said, "I've never heard her like that in my life. If I were a betting man, my answer would be no."

Meanwhile, Mama's longtime friends Joanne Woodward and Paul Newman were up in Williamstown for the weekend to see their beloved Heckie in this role everyone was talking about. Michael Ritchie, the artistic director, asked Woodward, a longtime supporter of the theater, if she'd be willing to carry a book and read Mama's part for the remaining performances. Woodward stepped into the role of Gladys Green with one rehearsal. The rest of the company led her about the stage, pointing to where she was supposed to move next. She had some pages of the script on the sofa, some on the kitchen table, anywhere she might need them.

Joanne said, "No wonder poor Heckie got sick! She was probably exhausted, poor thing. No actress in her right mind could learn this role in two weeks!"

Joanne also sent Mama a large basket of white orchids with a note saying, "From your loving understudy—get well soon—we love you—Joanne & Paul."

When I spoke to Mama that night, she sounded better, but still not herself.

She said, "How could you have spoken to me that way this morning when I was already feeling so terrible?"

I could tell the wound went very deep.

"I'm so sorry, Mama. I really didn't mean to hurt you. I was so scared for you and you sounded hysterical. I was trying to slap some sense into you, I guess."

"I needed love at that moment, not a slap—especially from you."

"I see that now. Can you forgive me?"

"All right. But please don't ever do that again."

I told her about my concerned phone call from Scott Ellis and asked her if she thought she'd ever go on with the play.

"Well, of course," she said. "If they'll still have me!"

I was wrong again. Not only was she willing to go on with the most demanding role of her career, she seemed eager to do so. This was turning into a day where I was making one colossal misstep after another.

That fall, *The Waverly Gallery* opened at the Promenade Theatre and Eileen Heckart received the greatest reviews of her career.

Ben Brantley in the *New York Times* called her performance "a beautifully coherent and intelligent portrayal of a woman sliding into incoherence."

Charles Isherwood in *Variety* called her performance "flawless, meticulous, truthful, and utterly unsentimental."

David Kaufman in the *New York Daily News* put it simply: "*The Waverly Gallery* features one of our greatest actresses, Eileen Heckart, giving a great performance."

My mother's performance as Gladys Green was compared to the most dazzling moments in American theatrical history: Laurette Taylor in *The Glass Menagerie*, Jason Robards in *The Iceman Cometh*, Julie Harris in *The Member of the Wedding*. And she won more awards for a single performance in a single season than any actress ever had: the Obie, the Drama Desk, the Outer Critics Circle, The Drama League, two Lucille Lortel Awards, the Alzheimer's Foundation Humanitarian of the year, and an honorary Tony. Once again, Eileen Heckart was at the top of her game. It was the pinnacle of her career at age eighty-one.

The Tony Award had eluded her over the course of her lifetime, going all the way back to *The Dark at the Top of the Stairs*. She was famous for saying, "All those plays and I've never won the damned thing? I'll probably get as old as Helen Hayes and they'll hand me one!"

Well Mama, be careful what you wish for. That is exactly what happened. I was planning a trip to Connecticut in early June 2000. She called me a few weeks before and said, "Listen, would you like to come in a week earlier and be my escort when they give me my Tony?"

"You're getting a Tony?" I said. "Finally!"

I was honored to be with her that night. As we walked the red carpet past all the paparazzi, she was treated like the elder statesman. When Isabelle Stevenson, the president of the American Theatre Wing, presented the Lifetime Achievement Tony to Mama, the entire audience at Radio City Music Hall leapt to their feet. It was the only standing ovation of the entire evening and a well-deserved one at that. I stood backstage watching it on a monitor. I welled up with tears of pride. As always, her speech was simple and eloquent:

> "My husband gave me a beautiful life. God blessed us with three sons. Kenneth Lonergan wrote a luminous play about his grandmother and that little lady sitting in the window of the Waverly Gallery brought me so many riches. And now to finally get my Tony just dots the 'i's in my own little millennium. I thank you."

The Lucille Lortel Award as Best Actress in a Play was presented to Mama by Broadway legend, Zoe Caldwell. Zoe was married to the great Broadway producer Robert Whitehead, who, in addition to having been the stage manager when Mama did *Burlesque* in summer stock with Bert Lahr in 1946, also happened to be the producer of *Finishing Touches*, the Jean Kerr play I was offered at age twelve. Zoe had won numerous awards herself several years earlier for her portrayal of Maria Callas in Terrence McNally's *Master Class*. I think her speech summed up with eloquence and her trademark theatricality how so many people felt about Mama in *The Waverly Gallery:*

> "Eileen Heckart doesn't ever 'play' anything. Eileen Heckart is some sort of strange magician—who, while seemingly bold, is subtle and intricate and you can never figure out how she does it. I always go whenever Eileen is playing and I never, ever can see how she does it. We went to the Promenade to see 'Waverly Gallery' and there was Eileen—the very focus of life while heading towards death. She made us laugh and laugh and laugh while she was gradually falling apart and she made us weep and weep and weep. And I really still have Gladys Green in my head.
>
> As she was limping offstage, I said to Robert, 'We can't possibly go back!'
> He said, 'Why not?'
> I said, 'Because Eileen's become too dilapidated.'
> He said 'Well, I'm going.'
> So we went. The door opened and sitting before her mirror was the most elegant woman in white linen trousers and white silk shirt and a glorious jacket. And I thought, 'Oh my God, she's done it again! She wasn't dilapidated—but she made me feel all the humanity. And now she's back—just being Eileen.'"*

* Courtesy of Zoe Caldwell. Reprinted with permission.

Even with very good reviews for the play and astounding ones for Mama, *The Waverly Gallery* didn't have a very long run. Once the serious New York theater community had seen it, the public at large wasn't interested in a play about a woman dying of Alzheimer's disease. Mama had a six-month contract and the play closed on May 21 after only eight weeks. The fact that people still talk about it after such a short run is a testament to my mother's astonishing performance.

When it was announced that the last performance of the play would also be Eileen Heckart's final stage performance, there wasn't a ticket to be had. As she came out for her final bow, tears streaming down her face, the audience leapt to its feet and cheered endlessly. Maureen Anderman handed her a large bouquet of roses and the audience threw flowers at her feet. The ovation seemed like it would never end. The *Waverly* cast joined the audience in cheering their leading lady. This was where Eileen Heckart had truly been a star—not on film, not on television but on the stage, playing a woman who broke your heart and made you laugh.

Mama was overcome with emotion. She was crying so much as the applause went on and on, she finally had to blow a kiss to the audience and leave the stage. I spoke to several people who were in the audience for that final Sunday matinee at the Promenade Theatre, including playwright Terrence McNally. He said he'd never experienced anything like it.

Shortly after *Waverly* closed, I went with her to see Mary Louise Parker in *Proof* at the Manhattan Theatre Club before it transferred to Broadway. Mama was so moved by Parker's touching, thoughtful performance, she said she wanted to go backstage.

"Do you know her?" I asked.

"No," she replied, "but I want to congratulate her on her work."

The backstage area at the Manhattan Theatre Club is a veritable rabbit warren of alleys and hallways. The house manager told us we should wait in the theater and someone would summon her. There was a dark hallway off to the side of the stage where the actors were coming out.

I heard an awestruck voice in the darkness say, "Oh my God, it's my favorite actress in the entire world!"

Mama turned toward the voice and opened her arms. Mary Louise Parker, with tears in her eyes, stepped out of the shadows and into my mother's waiting embrace. As they held each other, no other words needed to be uttered. It somehow felt as if the baton was being passed. And I got to witness it.

A Diva Departs

MAMA ONSTAGE AT THE PROMENADE THEATRE DURING THE RUN OF *THE WAVERLY GALLERY.* ©MOHAMMAD OZIER–*NEW YORK TIMES.* REPRINTED WITH PERMISSION.

I REMEMBER A STORY Mama told me several times when I was a teenager. It was an example of the gutsy quality of people in show business and the old adage, "the show must go on." When Rex Harrison was doing *My Fair Lady* on Broadway, he was married to a gorgeous British film actress named Kay Kendall. She was the love of his life. Every night, Kay would come to the theater and watch the end of the show from the wings and walk Rex home afterward. During the run of *My Fair Lady*, Kay Kendall was diagnosed with leukemia. It was terminal and she only had a few months to live. I remember Mama saying to me, "Honey, can you imagine how Rex must have felt as he stood onstage every night, seeing his sweetheart standing in the wings as he sang:

> *I've grown accustomed to her face.*
> *She almost makes the day begin.*
> *I've grown accustomed to the tune that*
> *She whistles night and noon.*
> *Her smiles, her frowns, her ups, her downs . . .* *

* "I've Grown Accustomed to Her Face" by Alan Jay Lerner and Frederick Loewe ©1956 (Renewed) Chappell & Co. (ASCAP). All rights reserved. Used by permission—Warner Bros. Publications, Inc., Miami, FL 33014

Mama always concluded the story with a deep groan, exclaiming, "How do people *live* through things like that?!"

I couldn't help but be reminded of this when, in the Fall of 2001, Mama was diagnosed with terminal lung cancer. I wondered if this story she'd told so often about Rex Harrison was some sort of an omen. My brothers and I weren't particularly shocked with the news after her sixty-plus years of smoking. We were just a bit surprised it hadn't caught up with her until the age of eighty-two.

Mama was aware of her diagnosis for several days before she told any of us. She had been going in for a number of tests, but as far as my brothers and I knew, she hadn't received any results. As one of my "bread-and-butter" jobs, I was producing a trade show for the Mattel Toy Company. I had produced so many of these meetings in the past two years, I'd recently purchased a second home in Palm Springs, which I laughingly referred to as "The House That Barbie Built." It was a very intense and often stressful job, but having a weekend home in a resort town more than made up for it.

I sat in my tiny, gray cubicle at Mattel headquarters in an industrial park in El Segundo, right next to the Los Angeles airport. It wasn't exactly picturesque. It was 4 PM on a Friday afternoon when I called Mama at the hospital in Connecticut to check on her. She told me she wouldn't have any test results for a couple of days. Her voice cracked with an unfamiliar vulnerability as she stumbled over her words.

She said, "I want to ask you something, but I'm afraid."

Afraid? The woman who was famous for going "Fire—ready—aim" was *afraid* to *ask* me something? Wow, I thought, this must be important.

"Mama, you can ask me anything. What is it?"

Through the receiver, I could hear her drumming her fingers on the aluminum hospital-bed railing.

"Well," she said, "do you think Don would want to call me Mom?"

A smile crossed my lips, and then a sense of warmth enveloped me, as if someone were pouring melted butter on my soul. The person who'd had such a difficult time accepting my sexuality, who didn't understand my gayness and used to think of it as something that needed to be cured like the measles, was asking if my male lover wanted to call her "Mom."

"I think Don would be very touched," I replied. "You can ask him yourself at Christmas."

"No!" she said. "You ask him. I'd be too afraid of the rejection if he said no. So, you tell him what I said and let me know."

My mother sounded so timid. I was deeply moved by her fragility. This was a quality she hardly ever revealed, except onstage. I was surprised it was coming out now, and in response to my domestic partner, of all people. I told her I loved her and that we'd speak in a day or so and to be sure and call me as soon as she had her test results.

I immediately called Don at his office at Actor's Equity Association and told him what she'd said. As I suspected, he was overwhelmed.

"Oh, my God," he said. "Did she *really* say that?"

He'd been such a fan of Eileen Heckart all his life, he sometimes felt unworthy to be related to "theatrical royalty," as he called her. Now she was embracing him as a member of her family. Don immediately dialed her room at the hospital.

"Hi Mom!" he said.

"Oooooh, that's what I wanted to hear!"

She sounded joyful and wistful all at once. She choked up as if she were about to cry.

Looking back, while she was crazy about Don, I wonder if this complete acceptance of him was a way for her to heal any old wounds from the past between the two of us. I guess I'll never know for certain.

Two days later, on Sunday morning, I woke up to a slight earthquake tremor. It wasn't strong enough to knock anything down, but it raised me from a sound sleep. Don and I turned on the news to see if this was an aftershock from a bigger California quake. The news we heard instead was that the U.S. had invaded Afghanistan that morning. I felt sick to my stomach.

I was scheduled to have brunch that afternoon with our friend, Chad. Chad is one of those West Hollywood pretty-boys who knows how attractive he is and plays it to the hilt. But when he wasn't preening and giving off an attitude of "I'm going to act really cool while I decide if you're good-looking or powerful enough for me to bother to speak to you," he could be a sweet, sincere guy. We were having lunch at a très gay restaurant in West Hollywood called the French Market Place. It's an upscale coffee shop right in the heart of the gay ghetto known as Boys Town, where all the gay men convene for dining, cruising, and gossip. I called it "The Margaret" because there were so many "girls" there.

As I was brunching with Chad at The Margaret, listening to the never-ending saga of his unfulfilled love life and how all men are pigs, my cell phone rang. I welcomed the diversion. It was my brother, Mark.

I said, "Yank! *Que pasa*, dude?"

"What are you doing?" he asked.

"It's a glorious October day and I'm having brunch with a friend outside. What's up?"

"Luke, can you talk for a second?"

He sounded very serious. Even though there were chattering queens all around me, I figured I'd better say yes.

"Sure, Mark. What's wrong?"

"Luke, Mom has lung cancer. It's terminal."

As his words rang in my ears, I felt my stomach turn over and over. I looked down at my half-eaten omelet and watched a fly crawl across one of my steak fries. Chad was looking at me with great concern one minute and trying not to listen the next. I wanted to be anywhere else in the world.

"Mark, how long does she have?" I asked.

"They're not sure yet. Probably six months. Maybe a little longer."

The cacophony of the restaurant patrons and traffic seemed to get louder. Didn't they *know* what I was talking about, for Chrissake?

"Yank, it's really noisy here. Let me call you from home in half an hour."

"Okay. Sorry to have ruined your brunch."

As if I gave a shit about that. I told Chad about the conversation and asked him to drive me home immediately. Hard as he tried, compassion was not his strong suit. He decided the best thing to do would be to take my mind off the news, so he continued yammering about the guy who'd dumped him last week. I feigned interest, but I thought I'd never get home.

Two days later, I was on a plane for Connecticut. I dropped my bags and went straight to the hospital. Maureen Anderman was walking in to see Mama at the same time. Maureen is tall, statuesque, and exudes elegance at all times. She also has one of the biggest hearts of anyone I have ever known. Maureen is a wonderful stage actress who has done roles like Lady Macbeth at Lincoln Center and starred in several Edward Albee plays on Broadway, including *Seascape* and *The Lady from Dubuque*. She played Mama's daughter in *The Waverly Gallery* and, as she was also a Connecticut neighbor, they commuted back and forth every day during the run. She had great respect for Mama and they had become very close. Maureen was originally from Birmingham, Michigan. They were both Midwestern gals and shared that sensibility. Maureen had two teenage daughters so they had many conversations about parenting.

Maureen and her husband, character actor Frank Converse, were a vital part of what I referred to as "The Connecticut Mafia"—all the great actors who lived near us in Fairfield County. In addition to Mama, there was Jason Robards, Colleen Dewhurst, the Newmans, June Havoc, Keir Dullea, Mia Dillon, and James Naughton, to name a few. Maureen was close with many of them and she had been there to support some through their final days, including Jason Robards. Now she was starting down that path with Mama.

As we met in front of the hospital, Maureen gave me a warm embrace and asked if she should leave. She knew that I had just flown in from the coast and she wanted me to have time alone with my mother. I actually found Maureen's presence a comfort. Besides, I knew Mama and I would have plenty of time alone. The part of me that was scared by this whole process was happy to see Maureen and glad to have her there for support.

As we walked into her room, Mama was sitting up in bed waiting for us. I greeted her with our favorite term of endearment.

"Hello, little person," I said, as I leaned in and kissed her on the cheek. She looked at me with her ever-present directness.

"Well," she said, "I know which train I'm on. I'm just not sure where it's going."

"How are you feeling, Mama?" I asked.

"Not too bad today," she replied. "I just can't wait to get out of this damned hospital." She was doing her best to keep the conversation bright.

"Mama, have the doctors given you any kind of prognosis?"

Her mood shifted.

"Why?" she asked. "Are you trying to get rid of me?"

I was devastated by the question, even as a joke, and I'm not certain it was one. Why would she even *think* that, let alone say it? I had to recover before I could reply.

"No, Mama. I just need to make some plans. Do you want me to move back home until . . ."

"You mean until I die?"

I hated hearing the words. How could she be so blasé about it? But the raspy tremor in her voice revealed her fear.

"No," she said. "We'd drive each other crazy.

MAUREEN ANDERMAN

I don't know how long I've got. It could be a while yet. You visit with me for a few days now, and then I'll see you again at Christmastime."

"I can come back for Thanksgiving too, if you like."

"Oh, that'd be loverly," she said, cheery once again. "Would Don come, too?"

"I'll have to check if he can get free from work. But I'll be here."

She touched my cheek, and then turned to Maureen.

"Now, listen," she said. "I have to talk to you about something very seriously."

Taking orders from the diva, Maureen sat on the edge of the bed with her hands folded and leaned in.

"I'd like you to have my mink coats if you want them."

Maureen's jaw dropped.

"Eileen! I can't believe you're talking about this *now!*"

"Why not?" Mama said. "I'm just being practical. Mark's wife and Philip's girl-friend don't dress up the way you do. They don't go to opening nights and fancy parties. A couple of my fur coats are in really good shape. I've got a gorgeous silver fox that's almost new. I want you to have them. If you don't want them, you can tell me. I promise I won't be offended."

Maureen pretended to brush a hair out of her eyes as she wiped away a tear. When she spoke, it was with humility.

"Eileen, I'd be honored to wear your furs."

"Good," Mama said. "Then it's settled. I've got a mess of fancy clothes you could probably wear, too—some Halstons and Adolfos. You come over next week when I'm out of here and we'll have a fashion show. Take the lot of 'em if you want."

"Next week?" Maureen asked. "You've still got lots of dressy occasions left in your life. You're going to get strong again and . . ."

Mama raised a hand to silence her.

"I'm telling you," Mama said. "Next week. But if you wouldn't mind, just leave me my one black, Japanese mink to get thought the winter. Then, I'll have it cleaned and you can have it later."

Maureen looked aghast.

"Eileen, I don't want to take *any* of them until you . . ."

"I know," Mama interrupted, "But why wait?" It's a chilly winter. You could get some use out of them. I just want to keep the black one. Then *you* can pay for the cleaning."

Maureen couldn't help but laugh. She looked at me as if to say, "Do you *believe* what you're hearing?!"

I stayed a few days before returning to L.A. to finish my Mattel project. As she got sicker, my brother Mark started on round-the-clock nurse duty. There was only one bedroom on the ground floor, so he slept in a recliner in the living room, a few doors down the hall from Mama. The poor guy didn't get a real night's sleep for weeks. Finally, my mother hired her friend, Judy Wade, who was an experienced health-care worker. It was a great comfort to have someone with whom Mama felt totally at ease to serve in this intimate capacity. Judy had no problem saying, "Eileen, you're being a pain in the ass!"

Of course, Mama would give it right back to her. She could still dish it out *and* take it. We got a baby monitor and put it in the upstairs guest room for Judy.

Judy was a wonderful caregiver and friend. Like Mama, she was a tough, wiry older woman with a big heart. Since she had been a nurse, Judy was able to explain Mama's various symptoms to us with great clarity. I pitied the poor hospital attendants whenever Mama had to be admitted. As an EMS worker, Judy had full hospital access. She would flash her credentials and be in their faces reading Mama's charts and supervising their every move. She drove them nuts, but Mama got the best care possible.

When I visited over Thanksgiving, Judy had gone on vacation to visit her family. Rather than having Mark return to the job of caregiver, I felt it was my turn to give my brother some relief from all he'd been doing. Mark was extraordinary during this whole ordeal. We had been speaking daily ever since that day at the Margaret. I told him I was more than a little apprehensive about taking over full-time nursing duties. He offered to return to his post in the recliner, but I insisted that he go home.

By now Mama was wearing a morphine patch for the pain and the doctors were having difficulty regulating the doses. On my first night, however, she slept straight through until morning. When she awoke, she got out of bed and asked me to fetch her jewelry boxes. I was puzzled by the request, but I knew better than to argue.

I followed her into the dining room with them. She laid out all her gold, silver, diamonds, and any pieces that were more than costume jewelry on the dining table. Then she handed me a notepad.

"Make a note," she said. "I want Teresa Wright to have my pearl earrings. And I want Mary Tyler Moore to have this gold necklace from Italy."

She was doling out her goods like a charity auction. I was of two minds. On the one hand, it made her death seem even more imminent, which saddened and angered me. I was trying to relish every moment and make her last as long as I possibly could. She was acting like her final hours were right around the corner and she was treating this like an everyday occurrence. On the other hand, it was a sign of her practicality. She didn't want to leave anything to chance and she was determined to control whatever she could right up to the end. I felt like I was going through the various stages of grief on a daily basis.

Mama wanted all the pieces of jewelry to be individually wrapped and to be distributed at her wake. I made copious notes. The gifts included her gold charm bracelet with a charm for every show. She wanted that to go to my eleven-year-old niece, Kelly (her only granddaughter by blood) on her Sweet Sixteen. I was there to see Kelly's face when she opened it, five years after her gram's death. She had special pieces of jewelry for Tara, Patti, Philip's girlfriend Adrienne, and all of her closest friends. For the men, she had autographed copies of the hardcover edition of *The Waverly Gallery*, even though her vision had deteriorated to the point where her handwriting was almost illegible. To be that caring, that forward-thinking in her final days touched me deeply. It also made me realize how much I would miss her.

I guess this behavior shouldn't have surprised me. Ever since Daddy had passed away six years earlier, every time I'd come home, she'd say, "What do you want when I'm gone? Go around the house and mark the furniture. I'm making a list for the safe-deposit box."

I was hesitant to say anything at first, until she said, "Your brother Philip has already claimed the portrait over the mantle and the antique oval table and mirror. If you want anything, you'd better speak up." I felt more comfortable since she had taken it out of the realm of morbidity and into the world of Yankee pragmatism—Eileen Heckart Yankee pragmatism.

I was at the hospital when the oncologist came in and explained her treatment options to her. He was one of those brash, young doctors in blue jeans and an open lab coat. She had agreed to radiation, but not to chemotherapy. He was really pushing her to do the chemo.

She said, "Thank you doctor. No chemo."

"Yes," he said, "but you should really consider . . ."

"Doctor," she said. "Read my lips. No fucking chemo!"

And that was the end of that.

A few weeks later, she called Maureen and said, "It's time for you to go through my clothes. Come over and we'll have a fashion show."

Maureen said, "Oh, no, Eileen, not yet . . ."

"Maureen," she said, "it's time."

"I'll be there tomorrow at noon," Maureen said.

Mama was experiencing great physical discomfort, but she put it aside for Maureen. As Mama sat there propped up on pillows, she'd say, "Now look on the left side of the closet and see if you can find a silk burgundy jacket."

Maureen would hunt around and present the garment to her friend on a hanger.

"That's an Escada," she said with a smile. "I wore it in that TV movie with Tyne Daly and the designer let me take it home. I looked great in it. Let's see how it looks on you."

Later, Maureen told me, "Every garment had a story. She lit up as she told them. It was the old Eileen before she'd gotten sick. I could tell how much it meant to her to pass on her fancy clothes. It was like she was flashing through the last ten or fifteen years of her life through her wardrobe. It wasn't a sad occasion. It was a joyous celebration of Eileen's rich, full life."

Mama also presented Maureen with an antique ivory necklace. It had belonged to Katherine Cornell, one of the great ladies of the American theater. "It was passed onto me," Mama said to her friend, "and now I'm passing in onto you."

Maureen was overcome with emotion. She mounted it in a frame which now hangs on her living-room wall.

The radiation caused Mama a great deal of pain. If she had known this would occur, I am certain she never would have agreed to it. It burned her esophagus so badly, even swallowing water was painful. The doctors over-radiated her to the point where she ultimately died not from cancer, but from malnutrition. I'm convinced this shortened her life by several months.

She said to the doctors, "I just want to make it through one last Christmas."

Her oncologist said, "Oh, you'll see Easter."

She shook her head. "I just want to make it through Christmas."

With tremendous effort, she did. To see this major force in my world reduced to a small, frail, delicate bag of bones who would choke on a glass of water was one of the most difficult experiences of my life. Daddy had gone quickly, dropping dead of a heart attack on his morning walk. I was always sorry I'd never gotten to say goodbye. Mama and I had plenty of time to share our final thoughts, but the price of seeing her suffer was far too dear. My mother's greatest fear was losing her dignity. She always said she wanted to die before that occurred. As the severity of her macular degeneration increased, she became practically blind. She was on oxygen for her emphysema and unable to bathe herself or go to the bathroom without assistance. I couldn't help feeling this was her worst nightmare coming true. Thank God she was too doped up on morphine to realize it.

Back in the early eighties, Mama had done an episode of the television series *Trapper John, M.D.*, where Hermione Gingold was doing a guest spot. Mama and the young director had lunch with Hermione one day. Miss Gingold's health was really failing at this point and she made no attempt to hide her infirmities. As they sat down to dine on the patio of an upscale Brentwood restaurant, Hermione tossed out her hearing aid, flung her wig onto the floor, and even yanked out her teeth as she spit and gummed her way through her lunch, flinging bits of food all over the table.

Afterwards, the director said to Mama, "Isn't it wonderful to reach a point where you just don't care anymore?"

"NO!" she said. "It's disgusting!"

Now she was at that same place and was too out of it to even care.

One day I entered her bedroom and heard her sighing.

"What is it, Mama?" I asked.

"It's my bottom," she said.

"What's wrong? Are you getting bedsores? Are you in pain?"

"No, it's nothing like that," she said in a faraway voice. "All my life, I always had such a silky, smooth bottom. It was one of my best features. Now it's all hard and cracked and scaly."

My heart ached for her. She had so few pleasures left in life. Who'd have guessed that one of them was her pride in her rear end? She didn't even have that anymore. As she stood in the doorway of her bedroom, framed in the afternoon glow of the December sunset, her tiny, brittle body was sheathed in a large flannel nightgown. It reminded me of a voluminous *shmatta* draped over an insignificant coat hook.

"I could put some cream on it for you," I said. "Would you like that?"

"Oh, would you?"

She sounded like a lost, little girl.

"Sure, Mama," I said.

I sat on the edge of the bed as she stood with her back to me. The bony fingers of her left hand were braced against the wall as she hoisted up her nightgown with the other. She was right—her behind was red and scaly. I reached for the Jergens on the night table and pumped an ample amount into my palm as Mama stood there wordlessly staring into space. Her gaze rested on Daddy's jean jacket. It hung there on the doorknob of his closet, right where he had left it before he died six years earlier.

I had the fleeting thought that what I was doing was somehow wrong. I shouldn't be touching my mother's ass, her husband should be here doing this—or at least a nurse. I was reminded once again of how much I missed Daddy and Nanny. Emptiness and longing hung in the air. Was this the same woman who always broke off a hug first, saying, "That's enough"? She was such a proud and intensely private person. In an earlier time, my mother would never have allowed me to do such an intimate thing. But all bets were off now.

As I rubbed the cool, pink lotion into my mother's dry, fleshy, bottom, she murmured, "Oooh, that's nice."

"I'm glad," I said, getting past my own self-consciousness. I smoothed out the red blotches and scaly spots. I thought of Daddy doing woodwork with very fine sandpaper. Just as I was becoming more nonchalant about the task at hand, I felt Mama become tense.

"I need to lie down now," she said. "Thank you, that feels much better."

"You're welcome," I said. She reached for my hand to steady herself as she crawled back into bed.

In her final days, the phone seemed to ring off the hook. Sometimes she was too out of it to speak, but usually, she accepted the call. Some people, like Doris Roberts, called once, said their goodbyes, and were done with it. A week before Doris called, while I was still in L.A., I had seen her at a Christmas party in Beverly Hills at the home of Marion Ross, the star of the television series *Happy Days* and *Brooklyn Bridge*. Doris and I always ran into each other at openings and parties and I adored her. We'd met when I was a teenager and she was doing the play, *And Miss Reardon Drinks a Little* in Florida with Mama and Linda Lavin. Doris always greeted me with a warm hug.

"Hi, honey! How's Mom?" she said.

I'd been lying to most people, but I couldn't lie to Doris. I looked her in the eye and said, "She's in the final stages of lung cancer."

Doris fell back against the buffet table as if someone had pushed her.

"Tell me everything," she said.

It was as if we were the only two people a room crowded with celebrities and festooned with holiday garlands. When I had finished telling Doris what had occurred in the past three months, I said, "Forgive me if I sound matter-of-fact about it, Doris. I assure you I'm not feeling that way."

She reached out and touched my cheek.

"Oh no, honey," she said, "I know you."

Doris called Mama the following day. They laughed and joked about old times and said goodbye. Mama said, "Now that was really classy. I feel complete with her."

Kenneth Lonergan, who had written *The Waverly Gallery*, called every day. He always asked to visit and she always refused. She would no longer see people outside the immediate family. The only exceptions were her caregiver, Judy Wade, and her close friend, Maureen Anderman. Maureen came by almost every day, bringing her cans of Ensure to try and keep weight on her and giving her all the Broadway gossip. She had strung some fabric-covered Christmas lights shaped like stars on the window at the foot of her bed. Mama stared at them for hours as she went in and out of consciousness.

Mama was in constant pain. Eating became more and more difficult for her. On a good day, she managed to force down half a container of yogurt or some vanilla pudding. Nothing tasted good to her.

"Mama," I asked, "do you have an appetite for anything at all?"

"Just one thing—Doris Bowlby's crème brulee!"

Doris Bowlby was the daughter of one of her neighbors and a gourmet cook.

"Mama," I said, "do you know how much work it takes to make crème brulée? And it's two days before Christmas. I'm sure Doris has other things on her mind right now, if she's even in town."

"You asked what I was hungry for," Mama said, sounding like a deprived child, "and that's all I want!"

I went over to Doris' mother next door and pleaded my case. Yes, it was a huge request, outrageous and absurd, but how was she going to say no? Imagine someone saying, "Pardon me, the movie star next door is dying and her last request is to eat your daughter's crème brulée!" What choice did Doris Bowlby have?

Jonathan Freeman is a wonderful character actor who had worked with Mama in *The Flowering Peach* with Eli Wallach at the Coconut Grove Playhouse in the late eighties. Best known as the voice of Jafar, the villain in Disney's *Aladdin*, Jonathan has had a very respectable career. A few months before Mama had taken ill, Jonathan called her for some career advice.

"Eileen, I am in such a quandary," he said. "I have been offered two jobs at once. One is the role of a lifetime in a new play Off-Broadway at The Manhattan Theatre Club. The other is a thankless "second banana" role in the revival of *42nd Street* on Broadway. What should I do?"

"Honey," she said. "Go for the money."

"But Eileen," he said. "The other is such a good part and . . ."

"Jonathan," she said. "Do you have much in savings?"

"Well, um . . . no," he said.

"Listen to me," she said. "How long is the run Off-Broadway? Six weeks . . . for five hundred dollars a week?"

"Something like that, yeah," he said.

"Versus a Broadway production contract—which is at least double, if not triple that amount—that could run for years? Take the Broadway show, play the second banana, then you can afford to do the great roles whenever you like!"

Jonathan took *42nd Street* and stayed with it for well over a year.

She had said she wanted no gifts that final Christmas, at least not from anyone outside the immediate family. Millicent Martin, the West End musical-comedy star, was doing a stint as Daphne's mother on the popular sitcom, *Frasier*. Millie and her husband Mark had lived in Connecticut for many years and were close friends. They had called to say they were sending a gift.

"Goddammit!" she said, "I told you no gifts!"

"OK, Heckie," Millie said, "then this isn't a gift. It's a loaner and I want it back when you're done with it."

"Well you're in luck," Mama replied. "Because that probably won't be too long."

The "loaner" was a chocolate-brown, velvet scarf. I unwrapped it for her, and draped it around Mama's neck as we sat in the living room. Her body had gotten so frail and weak, she almost disappeared into the scarf and her lavender cowl-neck sweater. All her clothes these days made me think of that line from Tennessee Williams' *Cat on a Hot Tin Roof* where terminally ill Big Daddy hunkers down into his cashmere bathrobe and says, "This is my soft birthday." This was Mama's soft Christmas.

Every time a pain would shoot though her, she'd say, "Is it time? Can I have more morphine?"

Often I had to say, "No, you still have an hour to go."

She lit another cigarette. We always had to remind her to turn off her oxygen tank before lighting up to prevent an explosion. "I know you're ready to go," I said, "but you don't have to take the whole house and the rest of us with you."

As we sat there in the living room where she'd held court in such grand style, she asked me to read her the daily Christmas cards. Sometimes she would nod off, but I kept on reading. One of the cards was a message from Jonathan Freeman, who was still doing *42nd Street* on Broadway six months after his phone call for career advice. He wrote how much that conversation had meant to him and how he had always loved and respected Mama as a professional of the highest caliber. She beamed and said, "Isn't he dear?"

Somehow, I knew this would be one of our last times together. I tried to memorize everything in the room: the dappled, winter sunlight falling across Mama's face, the Christmas tree bursting with handmade ornaments, Mama's cigarette ashes falling onto the Oriental rug as she winced in pain, her luminous spirit trying to break free. In an instant, it would all be gone.

On Christmas Eve, the family all convened for the last Christmas dinner. Mama clomped to the dinner table in her walker. She had tremendous physical discomfort and was in and out of lucidity due to the morphine. As she approached the table, she stopped.

"Who set this table?" she asked. She sounded like a district attorney cross-examining a witness.

"I did, Eileen," Don said. "Is something wrong?"

"The knives are on the wrong side!" she replied.

"Oh, I'm sorry," he said. "Let me fix it."

Before he could reach the table, she had already righted the misplaced silver. As she started sliding the dinner knives around on the table, she said, "Well, I knew it wasn't one of *my* boys. My boys *know* how to set a proper table."

Even in the throes of death, the perfect Christmas hostess emerged triumphant. That night, while the rest of the family was dining on roast beef and Yorkshire pudding, Mama's holiday feast was two cups of Doris Bowlby's crème brulée.

Don and I had splurged and gotten scalper's tickets to *The Producers* for the day after Christmas—five hundred bucks for a pair of seats. We'd never paid anywhere near that for theater tickets. In fact, with both of us being in show business, paying for theater tickets at all was a foreign concept. But we knew this holiday was going to have its challenges, so we decided to treat ourselves to the hottest tickets in town. Mama said she would spring for a pre-theater dinner at Sardi's as a Christmas gift. She told me to use her name with the maitre d' though she didn't know if it would matter anymore.

On the morning of December 27, I went in to check on Mama and tell her about the show. She was groggy from all the painkillers, but she laughed and smiled, especially as I told her about Gary Beach's hilarious performance in the "Springtime for Hitler" number—Adolf Hitler as if it were played by Liza

Minnelli. More importantly, she wanted to know if we had a good table at Sardi's. I told her it was the best table in the house. She beamed. Even as she lay dying, the Broadway diva had to know that her name could still command a good table at one of the theater district's finer restaurants.

With great difficulty, she planted her elbows and sat up in bed, facing me.

"I want you to do something for me."

"Sure," I said. "What?"

"Call your brothers and tell them it's time to come and say goodbye."

I stared at her in complete shock. I was totally unprepared for this. All the doctors had said she'd make it until April or May. Don and I were catching the 3:40 flight back to L.A. that afternoon. I thought I'd go back to the Coast, talk to her every day, come back in early February for a week or so, and then be here for an extended goodbye in the spring. But this was it.

Still numb, I reached into the back pocket of my jeans and pulled out my plane ticket, almost as if seeing it would make her change her mind. I waved it at her as I spoke, struggling to keep the words from sticking in my throat.

"Mama . . . do you want me to stay? Because if you want me to stay, you know I will."

"No, honey," she said, "I want you to go."

True to form, the actress wanted a clean exit. Don was upstairs packing for L.A. I called to him and he met me on the landing at the bottom of the stairs. He had been so loving and attentive. Don had learned by now that on this trip, when I called for him, there was no time to waste.

As I told him about my conversation with Mama, the impact of it finally hit me. I stood there and sobbed in his arms until his forest-green cable-knit sweater was wet and clammy from my tears.

He looked me in the eyes and he said, "Luke, are you sure you want to go? This is about you now. Will you be okay with not being here as she takes her last breath?"

I pondered this for a moment. "She doesn't want me to. She wants to go with dignity," I said. "Besides, I'm not sure I could take it."

I wiped my nose and called Mark and Philip. In a hurried, business-like manner, they both said they would be there within the hour.

Just then, the driver arrived to take Don and me to the airport. I'll call him Stu. He was an old high school chum of Mark's. Stu was cheaper than most of the car services around, but he was a large, clumsy man who was short on words and even shorter on emotions. What's more, he seemed so surly with Don and me, in addition to his lack of social skills, we wondered if he suffered from a bit of homophobia. As his car arrived, Don ran out to the driveway to head him off at the pass. Stu rolled down the car window as Don spoke with great intensity. He could see his breath in the dank, December air.

"Now look," Don said. "Luke is in there saying goodbye to his mother for the last time. You're going to wait. It may be ten minutes, it may be an hour, it may be longer. You are welcome to come into the house and use the bathroom and if you're cold, I'll bring you a cup of coffee, but nothing is going to rush this moment or fuck it up for Luke. Are we clear?"

The terrified driver looked at Don and nodded. "We're clear, man! We're clear," Stu said, and he rolled the car window back up.

As I entered the master bedroom, I glanced at the fancy, embroidered, star-shaped Christmas lights Maureen Anderman had strung at the foot of Mama's bed. I sat there for a while and ran my fingers along the brown, mohair afghan covering her skinny legs.

"Take me into the living room," she said, "I want to look at the Christmas tree one last time."

I lifted her pale, wizened body, fragile as a dried-out twig, into the wheelchair. Her eyesight had deteriorated so much, she couldn't see more than a few feet ahead of her. I wheeled her right up to the tree, the Douglas Fir needles practically touching her face. I knelt at her feet. We sat there in silence for a few minutes, looking at all the colored ornaments and brilliant lights. How often had we stared at the Christmas tree together? This time, she gazed at the lights with the wonder of a small child. Her mouth fell open slightly, as if she were gasping at the beauty of it all.

Finally, I said, "Well Mama, I guess it's time to say goodbye."

"Yeah, honey. I guess it is."

"Even though I'll miss you every day for the rest of my life, I want you to know that I'm going to be okay."

"Oh, I know you will, honey," she said, brushing one of my tears aside with her finger and putting it to her lips.

"So, Mama, give Daddy and Nanny a hug and a kiss for me. I'll see you in the stars."

"I'll be there," she replied.

Then I put my arms around her for the last time.

The World Says Farewell

DRAWING DONE BY KELLY YANKEE, MAMA'S ELEVEN-YEAR-OLD GRANDDAUGHTER, THE
DAY AFTER MAMA DIED

SOMEHOW, THE PUBLIC NATURE of this death hadn't fully dawned on me. The day after Mama died—New Year's Day, 2002—the news was broadcast on all the major television and radio networks and CNN. There were large obituaries in the *New York Times* and the *Los Angeles Times,* and the story was picked up by UPI in newspapers across the country. Over the next week, the tributes spread across the United States in *Time, Newsweek*, and *TV Guide.*

When I got off the plane, instead of going directly to the house with my grieving brothers, I went to the local TV station to do an interview for the evening news. How could I not have expected this? I was so busy facilitating everyone else's grief, I had no time to consider my own. While she was far from a household name, a small part of her belonged to the world. The last thing I wanted to do was share this moment with everyone, but I had no choice.

Getting home for the funeral was no picnic. Don and I had been back in L.A. for about a day-and-a-half, then went to Palm Springs to spend a quiet New Year's Eve at our weekend home, trying to relax and wait for the call from Mark saying that Mama had died. At 6 AM on New Year's Eve, it came.

"This is it," I shouted to Don as I leapt out of bed and reached for the phone.

"Luke," my brother said into the phone. "She passed."

"How long ago, Mark?"

"About an hour."

"I'll call the airlines and see what I can do. It may be tough to get a flight on New Year's Day, but I'll get there as soon as I can."

"Right," he said. "I hadn't thought about that. Well, do what you can."

During those final days, Mama had told us that she had special letters for us in her funeral file. This was a large, manila folder she kept with her personal papers which simply said "My Funeral." While the idea of ever having to open this envelope disturbed me, I knew it was Mama's attempt to be organized and in control right up to the very end. I speculated as to what might be in my personal letter—some deep, dark secret, a declaration of love and pride she didn't feel she could say until after she was gone. Maybe at last she'd tell me she was proud of me. What a lovely gift that would be.

I tore open my envelope. It read:

Dear Luke:

I know you and Don will be the "idea men" as far as the planning of my funeral is concerned. I know you'd probably like something more flashy and upscale than a simple service at The Grange, but that's all I want. You know I want someone to sing "Quiet Please." See if you can get Millie Martin. If she's not available, I know you'll choose someone suitable. You might want to open the event with the recording of me singing "My Son, the Lawyer" from "A Family Affair." It would set a cute mood. You'll give the eulogy as we discussed. Enclosed are some other passages I'd like read. See if you can get Maureen Anderman, David Kalodner and Keir Dullea to read. Maybe Tad Mosel or Paul Zindel could write something. I told Mark to be sure to pay Father Giuliani enough—I felt like we kinda stiffed him at your father's funeral. At the reception afterwards, don't use the same caterers we used at your father's wake—they were terrible! Be sure they serve the mustard-mayo. Most people like that.

Love,
Mama

Sandwich spreads? I was expecting a profound epistle, some outpouring of unexpressed feelings and I get *sandwich spreads*? Leave it to Mama to have the last word, and to be practical, even in death.

When she called Father Giuliani to administer the Last Rites (which Catholics now call the Blessing of the Sick), she still had a few days to go.

"Well, if I waited until the end," she said, "I wouldn't be able to enjoy it. Besides, Father John does so much work with the poor and running all those soup kitchens, he might have been ladling out the minestrone when I really needed him."

I could have explained to her that one wasn't necessarily supposed to enjoy the final blessing at the time of death, but what would have been the use?

The song she was referring to in her letter was a Peter Allen song, "Quiet Please, There's a Lady Onstage." He wrote this as a tribute to the great cabaret and Broadway performer, Julie Wilson. The essence of the lyric is, "Quiet please, there's a lady onstage. She may not be the latest rage, but she's always been honest in her songs, so let's give her one last celebration." It starts off as a tender ballad and winds up as a rousing cheer that gets everyone on their feet.

In the summer of 1980, Mama and I were both cast in different productions at the Williamstown Theatre Festival. Dwight Schultz (who later became one of the stars of the TV series, *The A Team*) sang this song in a cabaret one night and Mama fell in love with it. Even though it was about a singer, she always interpreted it as a song about a great artist who had fallen out of fashion. After we heard the song at Williamstown that night, she said to me, "I want that sung at my funeral." She was so enamored of the song, she even went so far as to create her own lyrics in hopes of singing it one day. I never saw them, but I remember her telling me about them.

In 1993, there was a rare Hollywood publicity photo taken of all the women still living who had ever won an Academy Award. There was Mama alongside Whoopi Goldberg, Sally Field, Celeste Holm, and fifty or sixty others, including Carole Bayer Sager, who had co-written "Quiet Please" with Peter Allen. Mama went up to Ms. Sager and told her how moved she was by the song and how much it meant to her. Without missing a beat, Ms. Sager said, "You know, we're having a tribute to Peter next month at UCLA with Bette Midler, Liza Minelli, Melissa Manchester, and an all-star cast. We'd be honored to have you sing that song."

Mama froze. The thought of actually performing with all those *real* singers was terrifying to her.

"Oh . . . um . . . thanks, honey," she replied, "but I'll be out of town that day."

"But I haven't even told you the date," Sager said.

"It's OK," Mama replied, "I'll be out of town."

I knew how important it was for her to have just the right person sing it at her service. Millicent Martin was doing *Frasier* and would be tied up on the West Coast. I asked Jonathan Freeman if there was any chance he could miss a matinee of *42nd Street* in order to do it. He desperately tried to make it work, but couldn't. Finally, I called a friend of mine, a cabaret singer named Mark Basile who had been in several Broadway shows, including *On the Twentieth Century*. He didn't have a strong connection to Mama, other than being a fan and having met her at a few functions, but I knew he would sing it beautifully. I asked him to arrive at the church early with the pianist so that I could work with him on it.

"Mark," I said, "I don't mean to be strange about this, but I know what my mother wanted, so I need to direct you."

"Luke," he said, "I completely understand. Direct me!"

The memorial service was held on a bleak January day. There was sleet and freezing rain all morning. The roads were very treacherous. Since Mama had requested that the service be held at the Benedictine Grange, that little church in the middle of the woods, traveling on unplowed roads on a wintry Connecticut day didn't make things any easier. Anyone who showed up for the service *really* wanted to be there.

When Mark, his accompanist, and I arrived for the rehearsal of "Quiet Please," guests were already showing up. People had gotten an early start because of the weather. Don was outside in his Sunday best shoveling the walks and dealing with the huge floral arrangements that were being delivered every few minutes from Broadway and Hollywood producers and old family friends. Just as I was about to begin the rehearsal, Don turned to me, brushing the damp snow from his lapels.

"Luke," he said, "Teresa Wright and Mary Tyler Moore have arrived. They're outside in the parking lot. What should I tell them?"

Without hesitation, I said, "Tell Teresa and Mary they'll have to wait in their cars until I finish this rehearsal. If anyone will understand, they will."

My therapist had said this was my time to be a little selfish. If there was ever a moment to heed her advice, this was it. As I sat there in the cold, empty church, looking at Mama's picture as the one adornment on the altar, Mark Basile began to sing:

> *Quiet please, there's a lady onstage.*
> *She may not be the latest rage,*
> *But she's singing and she means it*
> *And she deserves a little silence.*
> *Quiet please, there's a woman up there*
> *And she's been honest through her songs*
> *Long before your consciousness was raised.*
> *Now doesn't that deserve a little praise?*
> *So, put your hands together*
> *And help her along.*
> *All that's left of the singer's all that's left of the song*
> *Rise to the occasion*
> *And give her one last celebration . . .**

This was it. The moment I had dreaded all of my adult life was at hand.

I was in a church saying goodbye to Mama, having someone sing the song she had chosen twenty years earlier. I'd never felt so alone as I did in this moment.

I noticed there were a few drops of brightly colored pollen on the frame of Mama's picture where one of the floral arrangements had brushed up against it.

---

* "Quiet Please, There's A Lady On Stage" from THE BOY FROM OZ Words and music by Peter Allen & Carole Bayer Sager. Copyright © 1975 by Alley Music Corp., Trio Music Company, Irving Music, Inc., Woolnough Music Inc. and Jemava Music Corp. Copyright renewed. All rights for the United States and Canada administered by Alley Music Corp. and Trio Music Company. International copyright secured. All rights reserved. Used by permission.

I heard the soft, constant rhythm of the sleet outside, as if someone were tap dancing on the roof of the church. I imagined Mama up there in her silver lamé costume from *Ladies at the Alamo* dancing to "Lady of Spain" and laughing about how serious we were all being. I tuned back to Mark, the singer in front of me. My mother was dead. I was living the moment she had asked me to stage, the one I had hoped I'd never have to.

I was flooded with the enormity it all and I started to cry. As tears fell onto my gray wool overcoat, I said to myself, Luke, you have a task at hand. Keep the director's hat on. You have a role to play here.

It was no use. By the time Mark finished singing, my shoulders were shaking in convulsive sobs. Still aware of the duty I had to perform, I attempted to give him notes on the song.

"That's . . . great . . . Mark," I stammered, wiping my nose on the back of my sleeve. "But when you . . . get to the bridge . . . if you could take your time and really . . . mmmmodulate the phrase . . ."

I broke down again. Mark was so moved at the sight of me, he started to cry, too.

"Okay, Luke," he said, "I can do that—but please stop crying or I'm going to lose it here."

"I'm sorry," I choked. In all my years of directing, it was the first time I'd ever given notes through tears. Then again, it was the only time I would ever be directing my own mother's funeral.

In my eulogy, I talked about the full person: Miss Heckart, The Diva and Mama. I also told the story of saying goodbye to her for the last time. Somehow, I never envisioned myself as the emcee of Mama's funeral. But who else would do it? Mark was too shy when it came to speaking in public. Philip wasn't up to it. That left only me.

A few days earlier, as I started to rehearse the eulogy in front of Don, I said to him, "Honey, how am I ever going to get through this?"

He clasped my hands and looked deep into my eyes.

"You're going to go into performance mode for Heckie," he said.

A wave of calm washed over me.

"I can do that," I answered.

"I know you can, sweetheart," he said with a smile. "And that's how you're going to get through it."

Mama had wanted the guests to share funny stories from her past. Elizabeth Wilson, the great Broadway character actress, talked about understudying her in *Picnic*. Mary Tyler Moore shared about her work as Aunt Flo and about their great friendship. She also wrote an affectionate tribute which appeared in *TV Guide*. Friends of my brothers told great stories about Mrs. Yankee. Letters were read from Tad Mosel about their work together in live television and from Robert Stack about being on tour with her in *Remember Me*. Kenneth Lonergan talked about *The Waverly Gallery*. The love and the warmth in that little church almost made us forget there was no heat in the place.

Then there was the jewelry. When we got back to the house for the reception, I ran around handing out packages to all the ladies. Don had spent three days wrapping these little parcels in shiny, light blue paper, tied with white ribbon. The looks on their faces as I put a small bundle in their hands and said, "Mama wanted you to have this," ranged from shock to disbelief to abject humility. Anna Eileen loved a good party and she was going to make damned sure she was present at this one.

Mama always said she wanted her ashes scattered in front of the stage door of the Music Box Theatre, her "hit house." Lee Silver, a dear friend of my parents for most of their lives, was one of the top executives with the Shubert organization, owners of the Music Box. His wife, Joy, had worked in the box office when Mama had done summer stock in Milwaukee with Tec D'Acosta. Lee made a special arrangement with the cop on the beat in the theater district, who made sure that no one disturbed us. We scattered Mama all along the side of the Music Box Theatre. There was even enough left over for all three boys to spread some of the ashes in the flower beds at our respective homes. My roses were glorious that year.

The New York theater community wanted a memorial, but she was adamant that there wouldn't be one. She found those tributes maudlin and cold. She figured anyone who wanted to honor her that badly could get his ass up to the Benedictine Grange in the ice and snow. I presented a video tribute to her at the William Inge Theatre Festival that spring and recorded the accompanying voiceover track. Sreedar Nair, our beloved East Indian family doctor for many years, arranged a scholarship for emphysema research at Norwalk Hospital in her name. I also did a tribute at Ohio State where my brothers and I had set up the Eileen Heckart Theater Scholarship Fund to buy books and supplies for drama students in need. When I stepped off the stage after the OSU tribute, I felt a huge weight off my shoulders. Finally, the public grieving was over.

One of the clippings in the "Mom's Funeral" file was something she wanted read at her memorial. It has given me great solace since her passing. It is by Henry Scott Holland, the canon at St. Paul's Cathedral in the late 1800s.

"Death is nothing at all. It does not count. I have only slipped away into the next room. Nothing has happened. Everything remains exactly as it was. I am I and you are you, and the old life that we lived so fondly together is untouched, unchanged. Whatever we were to each other, that we are still. Call me by the old familiar name. Speak of me in the easy way which you always used. Put no difference into your tone. Wear no forced air of solemnity or sorrow. Laugh as we always laughed at the little jokes that we enjoyed together. Play, smile, think of me. Pray for me. Let my name be ever the household word that it always was. Life means all that it ever meant. It is the same as it ever was. There is absolute and unbroken continuity. What is this death but a negligible accident? Why should I be out of mind because I am out of sight? I am waiting for you, for an interval, somewhere very near,

just around the corner. All is well. Nothing is hurt; nothing is lost. One brief
moment and all will be as it was before. How we shall laugh at the trouble of
parting when we meet again!"

This piece has given me permission to talk to my mama on a regular basis, to share our silly, private jokes, to hear her laughter, her outspokenness, her pain. While I have been writing this book, I feel as though she has been over my shoulder the entire time, coaching me, guiding me, making me add or amend certain passages. It has made me feel closer to her and brought her back to me in a palpable way.

Unlike most children who have lost a parent, I have a wonderful advantage. Because of the depth of her body of work on film and television, I can see my mother again and again—at thirty, at fifty, at seventy. Many times I will be channel surfing and I will stumble upon her on television. I'll say, "Hi, Mama!" and I'll sit and enjoy something I've seen repeatedly as if I were watching it for the first time. Now that she's gone, I study these old programs more. What am I looking for? Who knows? Perhaps I'm searching for another trace of me in her, a mannerism or gesture I hadn't noticed before. I could be looking for some further insight into what she was like at various ages. Or maybe I'm just enjoying a visit with Mama.

From the time I started in show business, she said to me, "You know, I probably won't be around when you win your Oscar or your Tony—unless I'm so old they have to wheel me in. So that night after the ceremony, you go out and look for the brightest star in the sky. That will be me, smiling down on you."

Mama will always be the brightest star in the sky.

SPECIAL THANKS

THIS BOOK has been a labor of love, and many people have gone though the birthing process with me. First, there is Mark Glubke, my publisher, who has been nurturing and supportive ever since I first sent him the proposal. I never would have found him without Mari Lyn Henry and Gilbert Parker. He assigned me an incredible editor, Gary Sunshine, who has been a joy to work with. He has kept me on track, consistent, and he has been very sensitive to the important details. I couldn't have asked for anyone better. Next is my researcher, Sue Terry, who tirelessly found the rights and clearances to all of these photographs, drawings, and quotes. My partner, Don Hill, has been a rock—proofing, listening to chapters, and supporting me with such love during every step of the journey.

My brother, Mark Yankee, has been amazing—unearthing photographs, sharing stories, clearing up dates, and promoting his "Little Bro" to get Mama's stories out into the world.

When Mary Tyler Moore agreed to write the foreword within three days of receiving the request, I said to myself, now that is one classy dame! I'd always felt that, but this reinforced it.

Thanks to my writing teacher, Jack Grapes, who gave me such extraordinary feedback on chapter after chapter, and my magnificent career coach, Dean Regan, whose mantra to me became, "Stop whining and just write the fucking book!"

Thanks to my trusted readers who gave me feedback: Greg Nimer, my marketing guru, John Sgueglia (also the patient director of my one-man show and one of my dearest friends), and Charles Stroud, my "West Coast Dad." Thanks to my literary agents, Mitch Douglas and Buddy Thomas, for saying "yes," to my publicist, Harlan Böll, and to Pam Miller for guiding me in so many ways.

Lastly, my sincere gratitude to all of the people who generously let me use their photographs, drawings, and quotes and to those who have supported *Diva Dish!*, my one-man show (especially Mark Ciglar and Carrie Dobro), and to everyone who said, "You know, this would make a great book!"

I could not have done it without any of you. Thank you.

—*Luke Yankee*

ABOUT THE AUTHOR

LUKE YANKEE (yes, it's his real name) is a theater director, producer, actor, teacher, guest speaker, and writer. He served as Producing Artistic Director of the Long Beach Civic Light Opera (one of the largest musical theaters in the U.S.) and the Struthers Library Theatre, a historic landmark in northwestern Pennsylvania. He has also directed extensively Off-Broadway and at regional theaters throughout the country. Luke has assistant-directed six Broadway plays, including *The Circle* with Sir Rex Harrison, *Grind* with Ben Vereen (directed by Harold Prince), and New York City Opera's *Brigadoon* with Tony Roberts. He has also produced numerous award shows and corporate events with all-star casts around the country.

His first play, *A Place at Forest Lawn* (co-written with James Bontempo), is the recipient of the New Noises Award for playwriting and received its first full Equity production at the Arvada Center for the Performing Arts in Colorado in the Fall of 2005. He has served on the faculty of the American Academy of Dramatic Arts, Northwestern, Columbia College, and AMDA, and has guest-directed and taught workshops at universities across the country and abroad.

For the past four years, he has been touring the country with his multimedia one-man show, *Diva Dish!*, a collection of anecdotes about growing up as the son of actress Eileen Heckart, which led to the writing of this book. Luke has also performed the show on cruises around the world and as a guest speaker for corporations. He currently resides in Los Angeles and Palm Springs. For more information, go to www.lukeyankee.com.

INDEX